May 1982

Gift from the author —
who used to work for me

p. 358 – ref. by name

International Politics and Policymakers' Ideas

International Politics and Policymakers' Ideas

Amos Yoder
University of Idaho

KING'S COURT COMMUNICATIONS, INC.
BRUNSWICK, OHIO 44212

ISBN 0-89139-035-9
Library of Congress Catalog Card No. 81-80409

Printed in the United States of America

1 2 3 4 5 6 7 8 9 0 KC 9 8 7 6 5 4 3 2

To Janet
Whose affectionate moral and intellectual support
through the years has made this book possible.

Preface

I started to write this book when I had trouble finding a text for an introductory course in international politics at the University of Idaho. I could find no general texts on international politics that I thought adequately explained and analyzed ideas of policymakers. This book puts more emphasis on policymakers and their ideas than many texts on international politics, which take an impersonal and theoretical approach.

Some of the ideas for the book originated at the University of Chicago when I studied under Professor Quincy Wright, a prominent internationalist, and Professor Hans Morgenthau, a famous philosopher of power politics. Their conflicting ideas stimulated and bothered me the many years I spent as a student, diplomat, and professor analyzing foreign policy problems. I frequently used their concepts to shed light on international issues and anticipate how American and foreign officials would react.

The analysis focuses on major international problems since World War II. It is designed to give a conceptual and factual framework for understanding major international issues affecting today's students. The text has been reviewed critically by a number of professors, and the ideas have been tested in many classes. The book, therefore, reflects a critical view of international policymaking from the academic as well as a policymaker's viewpoint.

Also, there have been so many fundamental changes in the international scene of the past few years, I believe there should be a new look at international politics. The prospect of the spread of nuclear weapons, the U.S.-China detente, the Strategic Arms Limitation Agreements, the victory of North Vietnam, the energy and financial crises, and the growing economic and political power of the Arab states are examples. More and more foreign policy decisions are being limited by economic factors and some issues, such as international monetary and trade reform and the role of multinational corporations, are of fundamental importance to international affairs. Many texts on international politics are either out of date on such economic issues or skim over them.

It is hard to get a frank policymaker's view of international issues. Government officials often tell the truth and nothing but the truth, but they rarely tell the whole truth. In other words, governments rarely give both sides of a question, and they either do not release or they minimize details that would be damaging to their policies. I hope to provide some new insights into the foreign policy process not only by explaining ideas of policymakers but also by giving information on more than one side of an issue.

When I take issue with the conventional wisdom, I admit it. Analysis of international relations requires an open mind, and experts and laymen alike are influenced by powerful images in their minds that have been fixed by the government, news media, and other factors. Some of these common images, I maintain, are seriously distorted. Justice Oliver W. Holmes once said that an effective catchword can prevent serious analysis of a problem for many years. I would agree and add that a powerful image can have the same effect. For this reason I avoid where possible using loaded or ambiguous words. For example, I use "social democratic" instead of Marxist, which to some readers means Communist. One of the big advantages of a democratic system is that it invites debate and provides a framework to attack images and to question the slogans of a powerful government.

In this text I have tried to meet the standards suggested by James Rosenau and others in a *World Politics* article analyzing the contents of texts in the field. He proposes that such a text "should, even as it presents a comprehensive picture of world politics, take note of alternative approaches and explanations, be explicit about the concepts on which the analysis is founded, be precise about the links between causes and effects, be sensitive to the need for evidence in support of assertions made about the motives, dynamics and ramifications of the actions and interactions examined, and be permeated by phrases that convey the probabilistic, tentative, and qualified nature of the interpretations and conclusions that it offers."[1] My text reflects uncertainties of international politics, and I try to indicate where there are major controversies over interpretations.

A few political scientists would question an extensive use of historical facts in an introductory analysis of international affairs. They would hope to throw light on international politics by proposing theories supported by a case study or two. However, even political theorists by definition should analyze a set of facts before suggesting their ideal relations to one another. International politics, as indicated throughout the text, is infinitely more complicated than many of the phenomena of natural science. Policymakers with different ideas act on each international crisis, which is affected by a unique set of factors. A case study or two would not be adequate to support hypotheses where so many variables are involved.

The book is shorter than many texts on international politics. Partly this is due to its limited time frame. The book does not cover developments as far back as the Congress of Vienna of 1815 or the Thirty Years War of the early 1600s, as some texts, but analyzes the nuclear era since World War II. Almost all students already have some knowledge of the history of this era. Also, it has the policymaker's selective approach of focusing on international problems and analyzing the historical and factual background most important to understanding them. It is not a chronicle of international affairs since World War II, since many events do not have a major impact on critical international problems.

The book discusses major ideas of policymakers which influence international issues and provides the background for understanding them. The moderate length of the book permits professors to use supplementary material of theoretical and historical nature to fill in as desired. I like to use memoirs and primary source materials, but others may prefer an additional text or selected readings and interpretative materials.

Many policymakers try to use direct, easy-to-read language, because they are in the business of explaining and gaining support for policies. Their product is more saleable if it is easy to read, because superiors and other policymakers do not have the time to linger and reflect on erudite phrasing. I try to use easy-to-read language in this text relying on a common dictionary (*Webster's New Collegiate Dictionary*) for definitions, and thus the language is similar to that used in the news media and by most policymakers. Some texts develop their own definitions and terms, but I believe commonly used language makes it easier to communicate. The simple language may cause some to think there is little analysis in the book. I would argue, however, there is little or no relation between elaborate language and a high quality of analysis. I believe the dictionary is adequate for expressing complicated ideas. The easily understood terms of policymakers have a strong influence on the political process and I use them throughout the text. Also, at the urging of the editor, I have added examples and anecdotes to make points and enliven the text.

Where possible I attempt to evaluate the major ideas of key policymakers. However, to describe the philosophies of the leaders and policymaking factions competing in decisions for all the events covered in this text would take many volumes. For convenience and ease of reading, therefore, I often refer to a country making a decision although the decisionmaker was an individual or a group of individuals. My reference to the country as an entity is meant to mean that the action was taken by responsible authorities, who are usually the head of state, foreign secretary, or foreign office officials.

In my analysis of international policies I focus on the substantive views of key policymakers or a group of policymakers, such as the Department of Defense. I do not usually evaluate the bureaucratic process by which these policymakers get policies approved and implemented. There are excellent analyses of bureaucratic tactics, but this would divert attention from my major concern with substance of issues and with the major ideas of policymakers; moreover, a detailed analysis would take up too much space. For example, W.L. Kohl in *World Politics* of October 1975, makes a penetrating analysis of Secretary Kissinger's tactics on key issues such as Soviet-U.S. relations and the SALT agreement, and how he achieved backing for his policies. That article takes up more pages than my entire chapter on United States foreign policy. My approach notes that Kissinger was a dominant policymaker in the Nixon and Ford Administrations, evaluates his substantive views, and provides a general analysis of key policies.

I try to avoid a cynical or a moralizing approach to foreign policies, even to the United States policy in Vietnam. While the Vietnam policy may have been disastrous, it is easy to confuse analysis by impugning motives of leaders who have acted in what they saw as the interest of their country. Too often the news commentators and others assume leaders take action to stay in power. This easy assumption, I believe, often seriously distorts an analysis of international politics by causing analysts to overlook other factors. Moreover, after an event, policymakers, political scientists, politicians, and other observers can too easily remember cases when their instincts were right and overlook the times they were wrong and did not propose constructive alternatives.

To help give students more perspective on the difficulties of predicting how an international situation will develop and of suggesting courses of action, I suggest using some current supplementary material. This could include *Great Decisions* by the Foreign Policy Association, newspapers such as the *New York Times,* Washington, D.C. newspapers, and TODAY: *The Journal of Political News and Analysis,* and air editions of the London *Economist.* By following through on a developing world crisis, and there usually is one, students can test their judgment on real situations. I am convinced that using real information is much more instructive than playing games with contrived foreign policy problems.

I would like to thank colleagues who have discussed and debated issues in this book, even before it was conceived. I also appreciate the challenges and comments of professors and students, even though I could not name them all. I appreciate the support by the Department of Political Science, including that of secretaries who typed the many drafts, and by the University of Idaho. Despite this assistance I am sure there are weaknesses and oversights in the text. I would welcome further written comments and particularly constructive criticisms. I will try to acknowledge such comments in a subsequent edition, if it goes to another edition.

---

[1]James Rosenau, Gary Gartin, Edwin P. McClain, Dona Stinziano, Richard Stoddard and Dean Swanson, "Of Syllabi, Texts, Students and Scholarship in International Relations: Some Data and Interpretations on the State of a Burgeoning Field," *World Politics,* January 1977, pp. 264-340.

Contents

PART ONE
Introduction

In this section I describe the book's framework for analyzing important issues of international politics. The most relevant action has taken place since World War II, but I briefly outline previous historical events that set the stage for post war diplomacy. My approach is like that of policymakers who analyze ideas and objective factors which influence those who make critical decisions. I also discuss other frameworks of analysis, including those of certain behavioralists who have thrown light on current issues.

1

Evolution of the International System

The crucial problem facing policymakers in today's international systems is to build a basis for peace and prevent nuclear war. In recent years, as the world has grown more interdependent, the international system has been burdened with more immediate problems such as limited supplies of energy and food, trade restrictions, financial strains, and problems in economic development. We will examine how policymakers have dealt with these other problems, but the issues of war and peace dominate international politics.

Since earliest history, mankind's tribes, city states, and states have fought each other. In the past 200 years the large nation states, cemented by common traditions and languages, have dominated the world scene. Wars among nation states have become larger and more terrible as they involved whole populations giving allegiance to these states, providing manpower for conscription into their armies, and making more terrible weapons of destruction. Most of the old monarchies did not have the legal power of conscription, but relied on smaller mercenary armies. Today, defense and war are the major concerns of the leaders and the entire populations of modern nation states; although international cooperation is increasing, it receives only a small fraction of the attention and funding that is given to the military.

The Emergence of the Nation-State System

Our early traces and records of history show that conflict and war have always plagued mankind. Tribes and the city states of the earliest known civilization of Ur waged wars in Mesopotamia more than 5,000 years ago, in the general area known today as Iraq. One of the earliest known treaties, which settled a boundary dispute between two states, dates from that era. Succeeding dynasties of Ur were able to establish by war a temporary empire of all the city states in the area of the Tigris and Euphrates Rivers. About the same time, Egyptian kingdoms were founded, and their hieroglyphics also tell of war among themselves and neighboring tribes.

A Semitic tribe from Ur under the leadership of Abraham migrated about 2,000 B.C. to the area now controlled by Israel. The chapters of the Old Testament are full of accounts of wars of the tribes of this area. Some of the paintings of Egypt show its subjugation of the descendants of Abraham, perhaps the tribe of Moses.

The claim established by Abraham's descendants in Palestine was a political basis for the Jews' determination to establish the state of Israel in 1948. Their claim and those of rival tribes have been the cause of warfare and conflict in the Middle East since the end of World War I. The current claim of groups of Palestinian Arabs for a separate state on the West Bank area, now under Israel's control, is the most difficult problem for negotiating a Middle East peace settlement.

The history of wars between states began in the Middle East. Hopefully, history does not end with a war that arises from the conflicts of that area.

Historians and political scientists traditionally give little attention to the Middle East prophets who have called for peace. The originator of the Christian religion, who lived in Palestine 2,000 years ago, received only a few indirect references in the Roman histories of the time. Despite Jesus Christ's basic message of peace, groups have warred under his name, and only this aberration gets much attention from the historians. News media still feature war and conflict in the name of "Christians" of Lebanon and Ireland.

The city states of Italy in the Thirteenth Century formalized practices of receiving ambassadors, registering treaties, keeping diplomatic archives, and reporting by diplomatic dispatches. The famous philosopher Niccolo Machiavelli engaged in diplomatic intrigues there, and his accounts of diplomacy and wars among the small states of that area are full of trickery and deceit. His writings have made his name mean "cunning, duplicity, and bad faith," and this still taints attitudes toward diplomacy.

After the Thirty Years War ended in 1648, European rulers redrew the map of Europe and established the outlines of many of today's important countries of Europe. Germany was a major exception. It was broken up into about 300 small states and principalities which remained weak for about 200 years. In 1648 new boundaries for dynasties were established by the Peace of Westphalia without involving the patriotic emotions of masses of the people. Since that time nationalism and allegiance of peoples to nations have grown, until this idea has become a basic element of today's nation state system. In part, the ideas of nationalism have arisen out of economic development and improved communications which have brought people closer to the capitals of their states. The American and French revolutions helped accelerate the growth of nationalism. Public participation in the revolutions, the spread of the ideals of democratic government, and growth of education and literacy have intensified patriotic feelings of the masses. Multinational dynasties have been fractured by nationalism, and people have demanded and fought for the right to form nation states cemented by common languages and culture.

In the latter part of the Nineteenth Century Bismarck forged a new German state out of loose confederations of small states left by the Peace of Westphalia. He used the military strength of Prussia to promote German nationalism and waged wars on Denmark, Austria, and France to form a new German nation. This powerful new nation in the center of Europe has dominated continental European politics since that date. The name of Bismarck is closely associated with realpolitik — practical politics and reliance on armed strength to achieve aims of policy.

In 1914 the German Kaiser's support to the Austro-Hungarian empire to suppress Serbian nationalism and hold together the empire's conflicting nationalities helped trigger World War I. Demands of the German and Russian military to maintain their mobilization schedules and commitments to alliances, which were important elements of the European nation state system of that era, helped bring about the worst war in history. World War I and its settlement set the stage for the next World War.

After World War I, Hitler fanned the fires of German nationalism by exploiting Germans' resentment of a harsh peace and the loss of German territories under the Treaty of Versailles. His appeal to nationalism and to redressing wrongs of the Versailles treaty plus his virulent anti-Communism helped delay a building of a defensive coalition. By the time major European powers began to cooperate to oppose him, he had achieved domination of Europe. He had perverted the ideals of German nationalism to support imperialistic ideas of a German master race destined to rule Europe, and later the world. Japanese imperialism, based on Japanese nationalism and resentment of Western colonialism, exploded in Eastern Asia about the same time as Hitler's European war. History shows that the U.S. refusal to supply oil for the Japanese conquests in China was the immediate cause of the Japanese decision to attack Pearl Harbor. The fact that the Japanese were closely allied to Hitler's Germany helped Hitler decide to declare war on the United States, which gave further momentum to the chain of events that brought most of the world into World War II.

The League of Nations Covenant had been placed in the first chapters of the Treaty of Versailles of 1918 with a major aim of maintaining the peace established by that Treaty. Despite the ardent support of President Wilson, the United States Senate had refused to permit the United

States to join the League. In the 1930s the League proved
to be no match for the aggression of Japan, Germany, and
Italy. Japan and Germany withdrew in 1933 when the
League made a half-hearted attempt to oppose their plans
for conquest. Italy withdrew in 1937 after the League's
attempt to impose an embargo to stop Italian aggression
in Ethiopia was undermined by French and British
diplomacy. Hitler, encouraged by the failure of the
Western powers to stand up to aggression, took over
Austria and Czechoslovakia. German aggression was
finally challenged by Britain and France, and when
Germany attacked Poland, World War II officially began.
Meanwhile, the 62 League members had been reduced to
49, and in June, 1940, M. Avenol, the Secretary General,
dismissed the employees of the League of Nations
Secretariat and resigned.

World War II led to drastic changes in the composition
of the organization of the international system. Our
analysis starts with the close of that terrible war, which
was ended in the nuclear devastation of Hiroshima and
Nagasaki.

The Superpower System —
Bipolar Diplomacy

At the end of World War II the United States was the
only nation which possessed nuclear weapons. The glow
of wartime cooperation between the Soviet Union and the
West quickly vanished as the Soviet Union consolidated
control of Eastern Europe and supported a revolution in a
corner of Iran. Russia did not achieve "superpower"
status, however, until after September 23, 1949, when
President Truman reported Russia had exploded its first
nuclear bomb. Russia, with this weapon and its large
conventional forces, and the United States, with more
advanced nuclear weapons and delivery systems, were
recognized as the world's two superpowers.

During this period Britain and the United States took
steps toward letting Germany manage its own recovery,
thus ending Russian hopes for four power control of what
it saw as a German threat. Russia responded with the

Berlin blockade, and in 1950 encouraged its North Korean satellite to attack South Korea.[1] Since that era, international politics has centered on the Cold War led by the two superpowers. In this atmosphere the NATO alliance of Western Europe led by the United States and its counter, the Warsaw Pact, have flourished. We will analyze the superpower diplomacy in Europe, which has centered around these opposing alliances and the problems of Germany.

China, which is destined to be a superpower, entered into the major leagues in 1950 when Chinese "volunteers" helped save North Korea from complete collapse as a result of the offensive under General MacArthur in the Korean War. During this period China was closely allied with Russia, but this alliance split dramatically at the end of the 1950s and the Soviets and Chinese have been at odds ever since. Since then international politics in Asia have revolved around the Sino-Soviet Split and the complicated three-way power politics among China, Russia, and the United States.

The Middle East has been a principal area of conflict since World War II with Israeli and Arab nationalists waging four wars with countless acts of terrorism and retaliation in between. Oil has been in the background with the threat of superpower intervention in strategic areas. In recent years petroleum politics by the Arab states and Islamic nationalisms have added further explosives to that powderkeg. Part Three of the text analyzes the complicated superpower diplomacy in the Mideast, as well as in Europe and Asia, concentrating on wars and violence in these areas. Although superpower politics has dominated the world area, the U.N. has also played an important role.

The U.N. System And An Interdependent World

The nuclear age opened in August, 1945, with the explosion of one bomb that destroyed most of Hiroshima and may have killed over 100,000 Japanese civilians. Scientists realized then that more terrible weapons would be developed. Some of the weapons in the U.S. arsenal now targeted against the Soviet Union are over 100 times as powerful as the one that destroyed Hiroshima. The Soviet Union has tested warheads 3,000 times that powerful. The United States has purposely developed multiple warheads which are more destructive than a single warhead with the same power. Thousands of warheads could be launched within minutes of an outbreak of a major war between Russia and the United States, and each one could destroy most of a large city. The fallout from such an attack could kill people over 100 miles downwind from such a blast. Some scientists say an all out nuclear war could fatally contaminate the northern atmosphere or possibly that of the entire world. Thus, the fate of the civilized world is tied together in a ghastly interdependence, and the power to launch a holocaust rests in the hands of a few leaders.

Many nations have expressed their concern about the nuclear arms race in speeches in the U.N. Many resolutions and a number of agreements for limiting nuclear arms have been approved. Experts commissioned by the U.N. have pointed out the terrible effects of using even "tactical" nuclear weapons as well as the high economic and social costs of arms expenditures.

Yet peacemaking involves much more than the few steps that have been taken to limit weapons of mass destruction. It also involves establishing machinery for settling disputes and for ending conflicts. At the close of World War II 50 nations met in San Francisco to conclude a charter of a world organization dedicated primarily to ending war. The designers of the U.N. Charter tried to avoid weaknesses of the League of Nations Covenant by providing for an international force to maintain the peace. This fitted in with the ideas of President Roosevelt, Prime Minister Churchill, and Marshal Stalin, leaders of the wartime coalition against the Axis powers. However, the major powers could not agree on arrangements for organization and command of such a force, so these provisions of the U.N. Charter have not been implemented. The United Nations, therefore, became more of a forum for negotiation than a body with power to enforce peace. We will analyze in Part Five how the United Nations with limited power has assisted in settling disputes in an international system dominated by the superpowers and the conflicts of sovereign nation states.

The economic interdependence of the world was not as evident to the stronger powers after World War II as it has been in the decade of the 1970s. The '70s opened with a worldwide monetary crisis characterized by a skyrocketing price of gold and extreme financial pressures on some of the major European powers. By 1972 there was a major food crisis as Soviet purchases helped drive up the price of grain to two and three times the previous level. Shortly after that the 1973 war in the Mideast brought about an oil cutback led by Saudi Arabia, which caused shortages throughout the industrial world, particularly in the oil-hungry United States. Simultaneously, a strengthened organization of oil producing nations drove the price of petroleum to about five times its historic level. This gave to these oil producing nations in one year an additional $85 billion of revenue, most of which they could not spend but only invest or use for aid programs. Their tremendous new financial power, added to their control of a major world energy source, has dramatized world economic interdependence almost to the same extent that nuclear weapons have demonstrated military interdependence. How the United Nations System, which encompasses the Superpower System and the new economic power centers of the multipolar system, has risen to this challenge is analyzed in Part Five.

New Power Centers — A Multipolar System

Since the 1960s thinking on nuclear strategy has been dominated by the policy of Mutual Assured Destruction (MAD). In plain English this means that the superpower leaders recognize defense against nuclear rockets is not practical. They, therefore, agreed in SALT I not to construct more than two anti-missile (ABM) defensive weapons systems. Subsequently, they agreed to limit their ABM systems to one. The United States has even deactivated that last one at Grand Forks, North Dakota, because ABM weapons are not capable of shooting down a multi-missile attack.

This MAD policy of no feasible defense against the terrible potentials of nuclear weapons has discouraged their use. The United States never seriously considered using nuclear weapons in the Vietnam War. Its close ally, South Vietnam, eventually suffered a defeat as the United States withdrew in frustration over its inability to muster political and material support to win a conventional war. The standoff on nuclear weapons is permitting other power centers to arise. It is not possible to measure precisely their relative power, but other centers of power, in addition to China, which is destined to be a superpower, include some of the wealthy oil states, OPEC, the European Community, and Japan. Their power is based on economic strength.

The Third World of developing nations has also become more assertive, particularly in international bodies. These countries are backed by the oil producing states, and they maintain a tight U.N. caucus on economic questions, which has important implications for the international system and makes them a force to be reckoned with.

Finally, a group of non-state entities are exercising an important influence in international affairs. The European Community, OPEC, and the multinational corporations are the best known. There are numerous poles of power in this new interacting system, which makes it a "multipolar" system. The potential of these new power centers — states and non-state actors — and their relative influence as a new interacting economic system are analyzed in Part Four.

The Roots of War

Leaders in their philosophical moments often call for mankind to sublimate its warlike impulses in economic and other forms of competition. Other leaders blame economic factors as the cause of wars. While much of international politics focuses on the problems of war, mankind's conflicts seem to have basic human elements that transcend societal organization of tribes, states, or nations. A nation's policymakers must continue to try to cope with these elemental drives for war, which can perhaps be better explained by philosophers or psychologists.

While we can note some of the psychological and moral dimensions of the problem, it is not possible in a text on international politics to examine the vast literature on root causes of war.[2]

Reinhold Niebuhr, a famous theologian who foresaw the disaster of World War II, has given a persuasive psychological and moral explanation of the human drive for war as follows. He states that every group, just as every individual, has expansive desires which are rooted in the instinct of survival. These desires have expanded beyond simple attempts to survive. The "will-to-live" has become a "will-to-power." Moreover, the "economy of nature" has provided that means of defense may be quickly changed into means of aggression. Therefore, there is no possibility of drawing a sharp line between a group's will-to-live and a will-to-power. Man strives to enhance his own and his collective power, and the resulting conflicts of groups are conflicts between survival instincts.

Moreover, Niebuhr states that people are willing tools of imperial ambitions of their group or leaders. They often get satisfaction out of the power and aggrandisement of their nation. Also, people's love of their countryside and familiar scenes of their youth are transmitted into a patriotism, so that in a crisis people have given a blank check to their nations' leaders in the use of power. As members of a group, people lose their identity in the nation and they permit or encourage a much greater violence at a national level than when it is confined to a personal level.[3] This helps to explain the emotional basis, both for the arms races and willingness to go to war under the banners of nationalisms, that is a prominent feature of the international system.

Although human nature is basically the same and many leaders and their peoples still support policies that can lead to war, other features of the nation state system have changed drastically since World War II. Before that war, there were approximately 70 states. Britain, France, Belgium, the Netherlands, and other countries controlled great world empires. Today colonies have virtually vanished, and the number of states have more than doubled. The disruptions caused by World War II enabled many colonial people to assert their demands for national self-determination and nationhood in line with the nationalistic ideals of Western democracies which controlled them. Particularly in Asia and Africa the map was changed. Japan, in the Asian theater of World War II, took over former colonies of France, the Netherlands, and Britain, as well as the Philippines Commonwealth, which had virtually achieved independence. After the war the colonial peoples who had united in cooperation or in conflict with Japan asserted their right to independence, forming new nations of Burma, Ceylon, Indonesia, Malaysia, Singapore, Laos, Cambodia, Vietnam, Korea, Taiwan, India, Pakistan, and Bangladesh. African colonies followed suit, and today there are about 150 sovereign states in the United Nations.

All the new states carry on conventional diplomatic relations. They have a vote in the United Nations General Assembly just as the larger states, and their leaders participate in chairing meetings, passing resolutions, and other games of United Nations diplomacy. They have established diplomatic posts throughout the world, and they enjoy diplomatic privileges and carry on foreign relations like the established states.

Unfortunately, some of the new states war among themselves just as their elders did. Most of the conflicts are based on nationalistic emotions reinforced by ethnic, linguistic, and religious differences, but these wars also involve other controversial ideas and ideologies, including Communism. The examination of these conflicting ideas and ideologies as they affect the international system and superpower politics will be the major focus of this book.

Summary

The central problem of international politics is war, which has cursed societies since the beginning of history.

Some writers suggest war is rooted in human nature and the struggle for survival. Others suggest those who report history have distorted the picture by featuring war rather than peaceful activities. With the emergence of nation states calling on the allegiance of entire populations and with the development of nuclear weapons, a war could destroy civilization itself. Although war is the principal problem, we will also analyze other issues.

In the last century and in this century German nationalism has caused major wars. Conflicting nationalist ideologies of the Middle East have been at the center of other conflicts and threaten world stability today. Other ideologies, and particularly that of Communism, have helped cause major conflicts of our era.

Since World War II international politics has revolved around the competition of the two superpowers, and almost all crises are seen as affecting their position. The United Nations System, which was designed to overcome the weaknesses of the League of Nations, has attempted to contain the threat of nuclear war. The U.N. is also challenged by problems arising from growing economic interdependence of nation states. In this process the Third World of developing nations, backed by oil producing states, has become more assertive. Meanwhile, the economic power of some of the new oil producing nations, as well as that of certain non-state entities, has created a world economic interdependence comparable to that caused by the terrible potential of nuclear weapons.

FOOTNOTES

1. See Chapter 9, page 3.

2. The following are worthy of particular note for their insights and information on the causes of war: Bernard Brodie, *War and Politics* (New York: Macmillan, 1973).

Kenneth N. Waltz, *Man, the State and War* (New York: Columbia University Press, 1959). Discusses theories of war.

Quincy Wright, *A Study of War* (Chicago: University of Chicago Press, 1941). This massive study foreshadows behavioralist studies of the post World War II era.

Sidney Fay, *The Origins of the World War* (New York: Macmillan, 1929) and,

Liugi Albertini, *The Origins of World War I, 1871-1914.* These books have detailed accounts of the actions of policymakers leading to World War I.

16   International Politics and Policymakers' Ideas

Barbara Tuchman, *The Guns of August* (New York: Macmillan, 1962). Very readable account about events leading to World War I.

William Shirer, *The Rise and Fall of the Third Reich* (Greenwich, Conn.: Fawcett, 1960); Winston Churchill, *The Gathering Storm* (Boston: Houghton Mifflin Company, 1948); Herbert Feis, *The Road to Pearl Harbor* (Princeton: Princeton University Press, 1950). Perspective on actions of policymakers.

The best books on the Vietnam war are: George Herring, *America's Longest War* (New York: John Wiley, 1981); David Halberstam, *The Best and the Brightest; The New York Times, The Pentagon Papers;* Peter A. Poole, *The United States and Indochina from FDR to Nixon;* Leslie H. Gelb, *The Irony of Vietnam* (Washington, D.C.: The Brookings Institution, 1979); Paul M. Kattenburg, *The Vietnam Trauma in American Foreign Policy 1945-75* (New Brunswick, N.J.: *Transaction,* 1980).

A number of political scientists have attempted statistical analyses of war based on data in *Cross-Polity Time-Series Data,* Assembled by Arthur S. Banks; *The Wages of War, 1816-1965: A Statistical Handbook,* by J. David Singer and Melvin Small; *World Handbook of Political and Social Indicators,* by Charles Lewis Taylor and others; and *Managing Interstate Conflict, 1945-1974: Data with Synopses,* by Robert Lyle Butterworth.

3. Reinhold Niebuhr, *Moral Man and Immoral Society* (New York: Charles Scribner Sons, 1952), pp. 18-19, 92.

2

Approaches to Analyses

The basic challenge for an analyst of international politics is to set up a framework for making sense out of a vast array of reports on international events and foreign policies. Although it may be a truism to say that ideas of policymakers are fundamental units for analysis, this statement should be stressed at the beginning of building an analytical framework. Foreign policies consist of policymakers' ideas supported by governments in the international arena. Those who make and implement specific policies use and promote ideas about the national interest; ideologies such as nationalism, communism, social democracy, and liberal democracy; and foreign policy strategies. They are also influenced by these ideas.

States do not make policy, although our language often implies this. Human beings, particularly in governments, are the ones who think, speak, and act with policy ideas. Reporters and other participants in the process also use their ideas in analyzing foreign policies. In this way, ideas achieve a reality and momentum in international affairs. International politics is politics among policymakers and not *Politics Among Nations*.[1] If we are to understand foreign policy, we should examine crisis areas of foreign policy, analyze the basic concepts lying behind ideas of policymakers, and see how they are implemented.

Policymakers' Approaches

This type of approach is natural for policymakers trying to understand policies of foreign governments. Their first questions are who made the policy and what did they have in mind. Moreover, officials keep up with the speeches and announced policies of their superiors in their own governments, and particularly the ideas of their president or foreign minister, in order to represent them effectively. They then keep score on how the ideas are put into practice. This is the political process by which institutions tend to reflect the policies of their leaders. This is also the approach of this text.

In the next two chapters we will sort out approaches of officials by defining national goals that have wide acceptance, describing ideologies, and categorizing foreign policy strategies. Table 2-1 provides a framework for this policymaking analysis focusing on major approaches of key policymakers since World War II. This is the period that has had the greatest impact on ideas of present world leaders; and their ideas, for the most part, can be fitted into the categories of Table 2-1. For example, a policymaker could accept all the elements of national interest under category 1, accept the values of a nationalist and a liberal democrat under category 2, and work within the strategy of power politics of category 3. United States policymakers often take such an approach. The terms and concepts of this table are used throughout the text.

Many of the ideas about foreign policy are simple or taken for granted which give them great public appeal and power. Policymakers use the concept of national interest to support their policies, and they present policies within the framework of accepted ideologies of

**Table 2-1   Major Ideas and Objective Factors
Affecting Foreign Policies**

A.   Ideas of Foreign Policy (Chapters 2 & 3)

---

1.   National Interest Goals
   Peace
   Protection
   Prosperity
   Power

2.   Ideological Approaches
   NATIONALIST
   Communist
   Liberal Democrat and Social Democrat
   Religious
   Colonialism and Other

3.   Foreign Policy Strategies and Attitudes
   Power Politics
      Balance of Power
      World Policeman
      Imperialism   Pragmatism
      Collective Security
      U.N. Peacemaking   Moralism
      Neutralism
      Self Reliance
      Bureaucratic

B.   Objective Factors (Chapters 4 & 5)

---

1.   Geography
2.   Population   Economic Strength
3.   Raw Materials   Military Strength

---

democracy, nationalism, and others. They support or attack slogans such as detente and Cold War, trying to get influential groups on their side. The above types of ideas are the currency of international politics and logical tools of analysis.

The above approach assumes policymakers are not acting under secret instructions from mysterious networks like the military industrial complex or multinational firms, but that officials usually act and speak in line with their own policy ideas. Policymakers obviously are subject to political pressures from many sources including the above groups, and such leaders may "play poker" or "sell out" and conceal their true motives. In the process of carrying out policy, however, their ideas usually surface and become subject to analysis. Even lobbyists find they can be most effective if they express themselves in conventional terms of national interest, power politics, and accepted ideologies.

Some critics suggest the foreign policy process is controlled by an elite working behind the scenes which is influenced by economic motives. This criticism is particularly easy for those using the Marxist dictionary and narrow concepts of Marxism. In that dictionary private trade and investment are "imperialistic," government policies are controlled by capitalist circles, and smaller countries participating in trade and investment with the Western industrial countries are under control of "neo-colonialism." One of the favorite approaches of the Communists on the left and the John Birchers on the right is guilt by association. Both groups give as evidence of the existence of a policymaking elite in the United States the fact that some leading officials of the Carter Administration were members of the Trilateral Commission or Council on Foreign Relations. These organizations, which are made up mostly of businessmen interested in promoting better relations among the United States, Western Europe, and Japan, are criticized for supporting measures to make it easier to trade and invest abroad. The accusation is true, but one of the fallacies of arguing this proves they constitute an elite in control of policy, is that a great majority of American people support similar ideas of promoting American trade and investment abroad. It would be strange if American business leaders who grew up in the U.S. system did not support such economic ideas and the values of liberal democracy. At the same time there have been enough examples of exploitation through foreign investment and business bribery scandals to lend credibility to Marxist criticisms of the business organizations.

The above organizations do not have the machinery or leverage to dictate to government leaders on controversial issues. The organizations are influential pressure groups of the family of thousands of pressure groups which try to influence policies of legislatures and executive branches of many governments. They get their influence largely by publicizing and promoting foreign policy ideas of national interest, ideologies, and foreign policy strategies. In most countries this causes the ideas to surface and makes them subject to analysis.[2]

Analysts of policy should evaluate not only ideas but also actions and how actions square with words. Foreign policy philosophies not resulting in actions affecting policymaking would be empty rhetoric and of doubtful use in analysis or prediction. The media are sensitive to reporting when leaders do not keep promises since this makes "news," and the media, therefore, are a good source for policy analysis and criticism.

The above approach of looking at ideas gets us out of the box of assuming that policymakers act rationally to achieve the "national interest" or to support narrow economic interests. If policymakers were rational and had the best interests of their people at heart, the world would be able to avoid wars. Ideas and ideologies, when used to determine policy, naturally result in conflicting views, and often officials in the same agencies or with similar backgrounds will disagree violently. The winner is usually the one who sells a policy most effectively and not necessarily the one with the most correct or rational policy. Thus, policymakers do not have to act rationally or conform to certain rules of behavior. Even though they come from the same background or belong to the same organizations (and for that reason could be tagged as part of an elite), they can and do disagree on policies because of differing basic philosophies of international events.

We should be skeptical, however, about accepting ideologies of foreign policy as the only guide to understanding and action. Sometimes leaders say one thing and do another. Moreover, people yearn for easy answers, for scapegoats, or for leaders with an ideology to tell them how to act. Some political groups and observers attempt to explain American foreign policy in ideological terms as a process of supporting corrupt regimes in order to provide markets for the military industrial complex. The real world of human leaders and political forces is much more complex than that, and, as we will see, many objective and even moral factors play important parts in decisions of United States policymakers. There are also irrational factors. Professor Hans Morgenthau in his *Politics Among Nations* explains international politics as a struggle for power among nations. In the preface to the fifth edition of his book, however, Morgenthau cautions about the use of theories and calls for a study of the irrational factors of international politics.

Other factors complicate the prediction of international events even if an analyst can evaluate the goals, ideologies, and strategies supported by world leaders. There are over 150 different countries and many differing political systems in the world, as well as many officials within each country who influence policies. Many leaders conceal their real views even from their own supporters. Often world leaders are buffeted by economic crises, domestic political crises, or unexpected challenges from other countries. Such leaders are like a helmsman of a small boat in a gale. Often world leaders are forced to go in directions they do not want to take and consider themselves lucky just to get back to land, much less to arrive at the port or goal they wished to achieve. It is hard for others to determine what course they really wanted to take.

Even in times of little tension a policymaker may pick up the morning paper and read about a coup, a death, a surprise attack against a friendly country, or a domestic political crisis that changes the international outlook. A surprise attack in the Sinai, the movement of missiles into Cuba, the death of a leader like Stalin, or a domestic crisis such as Watergate can disrupt the foreign policy of a major power.

International politics, therefore, resists attempts at prediction[3] from simple theories based on an assumption of rationality, or from models, or from statistical techniques. The policymaking elements of just one country, the United States, are almost infinitely complex, with government officials, Congressmen, reporters, and other powerful leaders using ideas to influence decisions. The pattern changes from administration to administration. If you multiply this by about 150 countries, including their interactions in the United Nations, and complicate it with unpredictable close votes, by acts of violence, and by other events that defy prediction, you can understand why analysts cannot predict the future in international politics by statistical or experimental techniques borrowed from the physical sciences.

Instead we will look at the substance of important foreign policy ideas and try to understand and explain the patterns of thought that led to certain policies. After the event and after leaders emerge from the pack, it is usually possible to analyze their statements and the ideas they were promoting, and by inference what ideas influenced them. We will sort out and classify approaches of key officials by describing their ideologies, their avowed national goals, and their foreign policy strategies. Many of these ideas have been influenced by history, and they express them in terms of analogies to previous historical events. By looking at the historical record in the second part of the text, we will check the actions of policymakers to confirm if they were consistent with their guiding ideas. If not, we will try to see what factors intervened.

Traditional political analysts use other units of analysis than ideas. An approach, still in vogue, is to consider power and national interest as basic units of analysis. Hans Morgenthau, still one of the most influential textbook authors in the field, suggests that the key to understanding is to assume that statesmen choose policies most suited to adding to a nation's power, which they can use to advance the national interests of a state. These national interests include security, material gains, prestige, and other related goals which can be advanced by a nation's power. The major problem with the national interest approach to analysis is that both advocates and opponents of a policy will often invoke the words "national interest" to support their policies, and who can say who is right.

Policymakers and the media, in sifting through international events, generally recognize three major world systems — the U.N. System, the Superpower System, and the Third World of the remaining states which are relatively underdeveloped. I add the non-state actors and key developed states which are not superpowers to the Third World System and label it the Multipolar System of States and Non-State Power Centers. This system of many poles of power is based on economic interactions. The system also interacts a great deal with the economy of the United States, and to a much lesser extent, with Russia, the other superpower. The three systems achieve an importance in international politics in part to the extent they are recognized in the media and other circles as three systems. (See Figure 8-1.) These simple organizational concepts help us to sort out and evaluate the many ideas and actions affecting international politics.

After sorting out major ideologies and strategies in Chapters 3 and 4, we will look at the objective factors of international politics — geography, population, raw materials, and economic and military strength. We will note generally how they affect ideas and limit actions of leaders. Next we will look at the organization of foreign policy and how the governmental policy process affect the outcome of policy ideas. Most political scientists would describe this as an analysis of the "bureaucratic" process, but I try to avoid this term which is loaded and implies delay, red tape, and waste. At the end of Chapter 7 we take another look at the policymakers' points of view and how they affect policies.

Finally, in the last half of the text we will apply the policymakers' terms and concepts to (1) superpower diplomacy since World War II in Europe, Asia, and the Middle East; (2) to economic and political actions of nations and non-state actors not dominated by the superpowers, and (3) to the United Nations System.

In this last half of the text the analytical approach is similar to that used by policymakers. In a conventional position paper an official will identify the foreign policy problem, lay out the important historical and other data, and then draw conclusions, including making recommendations and proposing policy options. This analytical approach is similar to the basic scientific method of natural sciences which includes formulating a problem, collecting and analyzing the data, and drawing conclusions. In Chapters 8 to 14, therefore, we define key issues of international politics and present the background of the problems not with the aim of presenting diplomatic history but of highlighting the key facts affecting patterns of thought and action.

The policymaking approach to analysis of this book attempts to find political patterns by finding the ideas

that have influenced foreign policy. Since critical
decisions rise to the top and in many countries are
explained to parliaments and the public by national
leaders, it is possible to find the rationale for important
decisions. Exactly what individual or groups initiated the
ideas, and how may never be known for sure, for many of
the critical decisions are made in closed governments
where leaders and their opponents do not have access to
the media or to publishers to present their views.
Khrushchev's memoirs are almost unique in presenting
an inside view of important decisions of a Communist
government, but even these valuable books cannot be
checked against the memoirs and frank accounts of other
Communist participants in the decisions, because such
accounts probably do not exist.

   In the United States, which is responsible for many
crucial decisions in international politics, analysis is
easier because most important participants fill the media
with their statements and then later write their memoirs.
In the United States, however, presidents or secretaries of
state change about every four years or so, and each
administration has a different pattern of decision
making. Although the events themselves are unique,
certain basic ideas carry on from one administration to
another and give a degree of consistency to foreign policy
and a basis for generalizations.

   The final section of the book attempts to look into the
future of the last two decades of this century. No one can
predict the future with precision, but we may be able to see
trends. Using the policymaking framework of analysis we
will analyze ideas of foreign policy that have persisted
and that have given momentum to policies. We will also
look at objective elements of national power and how they
are likely to change in the next two decades. With this
foundation we will then make an optimistic and
pessimistic assessment, weighing ideas and material
elements which could swing the balance one way or
another toward war or peace. International politics
(politics among policymakers) involves many ideas and
unpredictable events, but that is what makes it so
fascinating.

Behavioral Approaches

As outlined above, the policymakers' approach to international politics is to examine ideas of leaders and the objective factors affecting their policies. Many political scientists also are using new ideas and concepts in their approaches to international politics. These explorers are often grouped into the behavioral school of analysis. There is no agreed definition of the boundaries of the behavioral and traditional schools, and there is much overlapping. For example, political scientists in both schools frequently use behavioralist concepts and terms such as "system," "games," and "image." Policymakers have also found such concepts useful, and frequently use them loosely in their discourse. Policymakers tend to think in traditional terms, however, and their philosophies and policies in the foreign arena can be described with traditional concepts.

Most of the journal articles and books on international affairs are by authors who use traditional concepts. They tend to take for granted that policymakers accept values such as liberal democracy, socialism, or communism, and they use standard concepts such as balance of power and collective security in their foreign policy analyses. Behavioralists, however, have pointed out that many of these terms have no precise definitions, and they have proposed new concepts and vocabularies.

Behavioralists often analyze a series of international events to draw broad generalizations, while traditionalists generally focus on a single issue or crisis. Unlike the behavioralists, the traditionalists usually do not attempt to find new theories about the conduct of international affairs. The traditionalists writing in journals like *Foreign Affairs, Foreign Policy,* and *Orbis* often have had extensive policy as well as academic experience. They criticize, draw conclusions, and give advice on specific policy areas such as Korea, SALT, and European integration. They seldom, however, try to derive broad policy conclusions for other areas of policy.

Behavioralists, in general, believe they are at the beginning of the search for theories of international behavior. They often call their theories "pre-theories" or "middle range theories." They are interested in strategies of bargaining, the causes of internal and external violence, how and why policymakers act in crises, and similar issues. Many of them use computers and vast amounts of data to try to find patterns of international behavior and to develop theories about why events are associated. Most of their articles are not addressed to current policy issues, and, therefore, are largely ignored by policymakers. Some of the behavioralist concepts, however, are useful in analyzing current international problems. Those that I think are most relevant to policymaking are singled out for discussion in this chapter. Every political scientist would have a different list of favorites, but many would recognize these schools of thought as important.

A simple definition of a behavioralist is one who analyzes human action and seeks generalizations on people's behavior in society. In a general way all political scientists come within this definition, but the behavioralists attempt a rigorous application of the scientific method to international politics. They develop and test generalizations, often using masses of data. The purists among them avoid using traditional definitions, making clear that they do not take certain values and political systems for granted. Many apply the same framework of analysis of political activities to different political systems such as the Communist and democratic systems. Often they use ideas and language of other disciplines in their analyses. Those who use large masses of data and computers to discover patterns of behavior are easily recognized as behavioralists.[4]

The behavioralists rarely publish journal articles on current policy problems. Many of their articles are patient and detailed explorations and defenses of relatively simple hypotheses covering a historical perspective. For example, a major article in the *American Political Science Review* of September, 1975, concluded that there is some support for hypotheses that (1) in a stable balance of power system alliances will occur randomly with respect to time; (2) the time interval between alliances will be randomly distributed; and (3) a decline in alliance formation precedes events such as general war. This has little interest for policymakers since there have been few major changes in the world alliance system in the last 20 years. Policymakers are interested in relatively short range political developments, even those occurring from day to day.

Moreover, most policymakers are of the age group which went to universities before behavioralism came into vogue, so their background originated in the traditional school. The press of work and their lifestyles do not permit these policymakers to question and debate the values of their societies. They could not effectively represent their governments if they did this openly. They often incorporate traditional values in their speeches and writing, and both friends and foes study these to determine the goals of a particular policymaker. Also, the traditional diplomats, contrary to the popular impression, accept values of other societies, and do not try to change them. Usually, they attempt to avoid ideological debates and use instead the language and ideas of power politics or pragmatic foreign policy strategies to achieve their goals.

It is not possible in one chapter to survey the views and approaches of important behavioralist writers. At least two excellent texts are available on the international affairs area.[5] Nevertheless, it is possible to describe certain approaches that are used in policymaking and that help bring order to the vast amount of foreign affairs data that we must consider. The following behavioralist approaches which are useful in providing insights into policymaking problems are discussed below: (1) Systems Analysis; (2) Different Levels of Analysis; (3) Images and Stereotypes; (4) Mathematical Analysis; and (5) Game Theory and Bargaining Theory.

Systems Analysis. A useful tool in bringing order to the vast array of information on international events is the concept of a system. A system is a group of regularly interacting items forming a unified whole such as (1) a group of interacting bodies under the influence of related forces such as the gravitational system; (2) a form of social, economic, or political organization such as the capitalist system; and (3) a group of body organs that provide one or more vital functions such as the digestive system. Under these definitions a political system can be tightly or loosely organized. The U.N. System, for example, includes interacting organizations under the general influence of the U.N. General Assembly and the 150 governments of the U.N. System. This system is tied together by formal agreements on common administrative practices between the Specialized Agencies and the U.N. Economic and Social Council, and by the attendance of the same representatives at various meetings.

We also use the widely recognized concept of the Superpower System in this text. The United States and the Soviet Union, which lead the two major world alliances, interact on almost all key issues of international politics in their diplomacy and within the U.N. framework. In Part Three we analyze the ideas and economic and political forces that cause this interaction. There are many reasons for the interactions, but the ghastly interdependence caused by the threat of nuclear war is the overriding one.

The third major concept of a system used in the text is the multipolar system of state and non-state actors. A similar system, the "Third World," with roughly similar boundaries is recognized by the media and in most analyses of international affairs. I have broadened the concept to include major countries not dominated by the Superpowers and the non-state actors such as the Organization of Petroleum Exporting Countries (OPEC), the European Community (EC), and multinational corporations (MNCs). Economic forces tie this system together, and its numerous poles of power are based on economic forces. OPEC and Saudi Arabia are new centers of power in this system, and almost all countries are dependent on their oil and influenced by their tremendous financial power. This economic power is also being translated into political power.

This latter system is the most loosely organized of the three and has the most indefinite boundaries. For example, it has many economic interactions with the United States, one of two power centers of the Superpower System, but the United States no longer dominates the world economic system, and the multipolar system can be regarded as a separate system.

Since the dramatic space flights and pictures of earth from outer space, it has been easier to regard the whole world as a political or ecological system. The aim of this

Figure 2-1 Easton's Systems Analysis Model

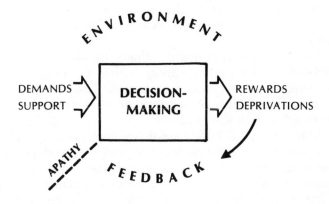

text and other texts on international politics is to provide a frame of theory for politics in the world system and its subsystems.

Political scientists have carried systems analysis much farther than using it as a framework for hanging data. Systems theory was developed before behavioralism became fashionable in political science, and it has had a great impact upon academicians, especially since the computer has come of age. System theorists who number themselves among the social scientists have been heavily influenced by the biological and physical sciences and use their language and concepts.

Whether such theorists rely upon a biological model or a computer model, they would probably agree that a system (including the international system of nation-states, a government, or a foreign ministry) has the following characteristics:

a) *Inputs* — David Easton, one of the main proponents of systems theory, defines inputs to a political system as the demands made upon it.[6] Herbert Spiro maintains that the issues placed before the system are inputs.[7]

b) *Processing* — The system processes the demands or issues placed before it.

c) *Outputs* — The system resolves the demand or issue or comes up with a decision.

d) *Feedback* — As the system is operating it continually receives feedback from its external environment, and it interprets that feedback by using some sort of coding process to discard information which is not useful and retain that which is meaningful.

e) *Memory* — The system retains information for use at some later date.

Systems analysts define the variables going into decisions and trace the activity within a political system to bring about a decision or output. Their writings are often accompanied by charts to show the flow of action and feedback in the system.

Although academicians believe that system analysis provides a powerful tool for evaluation, policymakers generally do not use its diagrams and elaborate theoretical analysis. A major exception to this is the use of systems analysis by administrators of aid and military programs such as those responsible for contracting weapons, carrying out construction projects, and implementing other government programs that flow out of decisions of policymakers. They commonly use flow charts based on the idea of a system to show progress in their programs. Another major exception to this is the policymakers' use of the systems concepts for the international economic system. Economists traditionally took a systems approach to economic problems long before systems analysis was developed. Since high level policymakers have been increasingly involved in international economic problems, they, too, depend upon economic systems analysis. Nevertheless, so many political factors are involved in top level economic decisions that policymakers rarely, if ever, base decisions on options presented in a formal systems analysis.

Professor Morgenthau in his *Politics Among Nations* also saw the nations of the world comprising a system. Although not a systems analyst as such, his evaluation of the international scene pictured nations competing in a gigantic game of pursuing their national interest, trying to increase their power, and allying with one another to keep one nation from upsetting the balance of power. He saw it almost as an organic, self-monitoring process.

Harold and Margaret Sprout see the world as a psychological milieu for the policymaker where a policy will have an effect. They propose an ecological perspective in which policymakers recognize a change in one part of the system can disrupt other parts of the system.[8]

Other academicians have analyzed international politics on the basis of the theoretical permutations of activities in a bipolar system, a loose bipolar system, and a multipolar system. They then pursue theoretical discussions of which systems are more stable. Some say that a bipolar system is more stable. Others say that if there were only two powers, they would compete and focus on their differences and thus tend to develop frictions that could tend to lead to instability. In a multipolar world, on the other hand, some theorize that there are so many distractions that nations are not able to pay as much attention to each other and cultivate hostility among themselves. Such concepts are of very limited interest to the policymaker who is interested in factors affecting actions of a particular country, such as the views of leaders, the status of their armed forces, the status of their economy, and their political or international support.

Richard Sterling and George Modelski, using language of system theorists, come to the conclusion that statesmen should begin to think in terms of international interest and a world society. They admit, however, that in order for a reasonably stable international system to develop, statesmen must use normal diplomatic methods of managing power and force in world affairs. This, too, fits in with Morgenthau's thesis of using diplomacy with the ultimate aim of achieving a peaceful world order. Sterling and Modelski are hopeful the effects of rising interdependence of nation-states will aid in the process of creating a stable international system.[9]

Some policymakers, pressed in a theoretical discussion, will state that they realize that in the present era it may not be possible to establish a new international order or organization that has the power to enforce peace, but they hope governments by prudent use of power will eventually achieve a world community or an orderly world system where war is not used to settle disputes. Policymakers often call for this type of international system in their U.N. speeches, but in their day to day business they work with military budgets, agreements, alliances, and other instruments of international power to achieve stability, leaving the formal building of an ideal international system to a later date.

Levels of Analysis. We could also examine international politics from different levels starting at the bottom with the policymaker, going up the ladder through the government organization, the state, regions, and finally, up to the whole world with its system and subsystems of international politics. Another way of presenting this problem is to ask what should be the units of analysis — the individual actor or decision maker, the state, intergovernmental organizations, or world systems and subsystems of political activity? J. David Singer, one of the first to present the levels of analysis problem, has stressed that looking at the same problem from different levels provides one with different insights and opportunities to evaluate issues.[10]

Graham Allison, in his *Essence of Decision,*[11] has made a revealing analysis of decisions during the Cuban missile crisis from three levels using different "conceptual models": (1) the nation state as a "rational actor"; (2) organizations having certain patterns of behavior; and (3) the top leaders playing bureaucratic games. He was addressing both policymakers and political scientists in this study, and he has provided useful insights for both sets of readers.

He admits that a traditional approach to the Cuban missile crisis would cover insights provided from his three levels of analysis, but nevertheless some of his conclusions stand out more clearly as a result of his systematic approach. For example, in looking at the missile crisis from the organizational approach, he explains Russian actions to bring in thousands of military personnel to Cuba, which made concealment very difficult, as a normal bureaucratic operation by Soviet military organizations in setting up missile sites. He concludes it was not some Machiavellian attempt to give a signal to the United States. From the top leadership level of analysis Allison points out how President Kennedy was under serious pressures to take forceful action, since he had previously assured Congress the Russians were not going to place offensive missiles in Cuba. Using the nation-state model, he pointed out how the Russian move, if successful, would have given it a much greater missile capability and helped it catch up in missiles by allowing Russia to target medium range missiles against the United States, in addition to their relatively small number of long range missiles.

Allison also provides interesting insight into the value of analytical studies. He notes that President Kennedy during the Cuban Missile Crisis was influenced by Barbara Tuchman's *The Guns of August* account of how World War I developed and how dangerous it could be to miscalculate the other side. In musing about this Kennedy was especially careful not to force the Russians into a corner from which they could not retreat.[12]

Policymakers and traditional analysts also look at international developments from different angles, but they do not self-consciously specify levels like Allison did. Policymakers recognize when the policy of a state or government agency is fairly solid. For example, they often use the shorthand of saying that a "country" or organization takes a certain action or has a policy. For example, they might say that Syria's policy is to confront Israel on the Golan Heights issue, or the Pentagon takes a stiff bargaining line on SALT issues. Policymakers, however, resist taking for granted the point of view of a state or a government agency, because policymakers watch factions within organizations and support those who are sympathetic. Regarding an organization or a state as an entity is useful as long as foreign policy is on a steady course. However, in times of changes and crisis, which are the major concerns of policymakers, they want to know which leaders and groups are proposing policy options and what chance there is for a change in course.

For example, for years many observers took for granted the desire of Egyptians and their leaders to get back their territory from Israel by confrontation and force. They would say "Egyptian" policy was not formally to recognize the existence of Israel but to maintain a united Arab front against Israel. More perceptive analysts would have taken more seriously the hints of leaders for negotiations and the desire of the Egyptian people and elements of their leadership for negotiation.[13] They might have tried to head off the 1973 war, and they would not have been taken off balance by President Sadat's subsequent visit to Jerusalem in 1978 and by his other peace initiatives.

Thus, while policymakers are most concerned with individuals, including leaders of political groups, many of the academic community are more interested in higher level theories about relationships among states, regional groups, political groups, agencies, and systems. This helps to explain one difficulty in communication between many behavioral political scientists and policymakers.

Images. An image as defined in the dictionary includes the following concepts: (1) "a mental picture of something not actually present" (2) "a mental conception held in common by members of a group and symbolic of an orientation" and (3) "a popular conception (as of a person, institution, or nation) projected especially through the mass media." Professors have developed the use of these concepts in political science and other disciplines and they commonly use "image" to cover all three meanings. The word and ideas of images have also been widely incorporated into the language of policymakers and politicians.

Kenneth Boulding has elaborated on how images affect foreign policy. He notes that humans in learning select information on the basis of a particular mental frame of reference or image. This image can cause the changing of the information into something different from the information itself. The resulting human behavior is a response not to the factual situation but to a knowledge structure of the individual and how this distorts the information.

He believes that symbolic images of nations have developed to the point that it is almost pathological. He states national relationships are seen as an image of personalities in conflict instead of a stable network of societies which are cooperating. He believes removal of the conflict images would have a tremendous effect on international behavior by eliminating a major cause of war.[14]

Boulding states that it would be fallacious to think of images as being cleverly imposed on the masses by the powerful. If anything he believes the reverse is true; particularly in the case of old nations the image is transmitted through the family and long-established traditions. Karl Deutsch and Richard Merritt once analyzed the ability of people to change their popular images of other nations on international problems. They concluded that "almost nothing in the world seems to be able to shift the images of 40 percent of the population in most countries, even within one or two decades. Combinations of events that shift the images and attitudes even of the remaining 50 or 60 percent of the population are extremely rare."[15]

Robert Jervis in his *Perceptions and Misperceptions of International Politics* discusses the way in which false images of another state can lead to an arms race. In what he calls the "spiral model," he states that the drive for security promotes false images — what one state sees as additions to its security, the other will see as encirclement. Leaders assume the worst and the quest for security soon becomes an arms race.[16] Once a hostile image develops even discrepant information can be misinterpreted to fit that image. In some cases such misunderstandings can be self-fulfilling and lead to confrontation or war.

President Kennedy's management of the Cuban missile crisis is often cited as an example of how to avoid misunderstandings. He was in contact by personal letters to Khrushchev during the critical period of that crisis. He was careful to make the U.S. position clear, give time to Khrushchev to make a prudent decision, and not force him into a corner. Ole Holsti and others have praised this performance and stress the dangers of misperceptions in American-Soviet relations.[17] Jervis suggests that trying to see the opponent's point of view is a way to lessen the dangers in such crisis situations.[18]

False images are a fundamental problem of international politics.[19] Many wars have been started because the aggressor or victim underestimated an opponent or initiated policies whose results were not foreseen. If policymakers, the news media, and other analysts could approach problems with open minds and come to conclusions based on facts not distorted by prejudices, as an ideal political scientist should, we would be close to the millenium where war could be abolished.

Although images and stereotypes hinder an understanding of international affairs, relatively little research has been done on current images and stereotypes the West has of Asian nations and much less of how people in these nations view the West. One of the West's common images of Asia that hinders an understanding of its problems is that it is a continent where people scratch out a living at the subsistence level and where masses constantly are on the verge of starvation due to the rapidly growing population. Another image is that Asian countries are mostly corrupt military governments supported by the military industrial complex of the United States whose leaders are primarily interested in preserving markets for their exports and military equipment. Communist propaganda and socialist ideology reinforce this image.

Responsible policymakers have not accepted such a distorted view of Asia. Those who have lived or worked in countries such as Japan, Malaysia, Thailand, Hong Kong, the Republic of China, Korea, and Singapore know that many of the government leaders of these countries are able, and have helped bring about rapid economic development. They have seen modern agricultural and industrial techniques applied in these countries and are aware of their potential in other countries. They know many of these countries have been able to relieve pressures on food supplies as they developed and improved their standards of living.

Sometimes images can be basically correct or, in other words, an image may represent a useful idea in international affairs. The image that finally emerged of the Nazi government as evil with the aim of dominating Europe, Russia, and possibly the world, was essentially correct. This latter image was slow in developing in the United States because Hitler spread the image of Germany establishing a "new order" in Europe. This image was reinforced by claims the Nazi system was the "wave of the future" and a product of a "managerial revolution" where managers and engineers would bring order and prosperity to the world. Propaganda about Nazi Germany during the Great Depression of the 1930s showed an image of efficiency and cleanliness with people busy at work. It took years for a more accurate image to emerge.

The purpose of this section is not to attempt to prove that one series of current images of Asia or of other areas is correct or incorrect. The purpose is merely to point out that an understanding of international policymaking and of international issues is clouded by powerful and often false images that are deeply embedded in the minds of observers. Those trying to understand international politics should try to keep an open mind. Although an image or political principle may be useful for understanding one government or an area of a country, this does not mean that the image is true for all groups in a country or for another country.

A moral issue is also involved. A moralist would not judge people of a nation on the basis of an image arising from a government or its leaders who have taken an offensive action, particularly when that government is authoritarian. A moralist would have as much regard for Asians as Americans, and Africans as much as Europeans, despite the actions of a particular government at a particular time in history.

A common approach of policymakers and diplomats is first to understand the point of view from the other side before proposing a reasonable compromise. This is also a basic approach of this book which can help in counteracting some of the deeply etched images that many people have of other nations and their problems.

Mathematical Analysis. Image analysis and the related field of psychological analyses of policymakers and of political groups are at a low, personal level of analysis. Most of the mathematical analyses by political scientists are at a much higher level with states as units of analysis. The great expansion of mathematical analysis after World War II reflected the access both to the computer, which can bring order to millions of bits of data, and to improved statistics based in large part on raw data collected by U.N. organizations which have developed and improved the comparability of national data.

Basic handbooks of political statistics designed to provide variables for the development of international theories include the *Cross-Polity Time-Series* Data by Arthur S. Banks, *The Wages of War, 1816-1965: A Statistical Handbook* by J. David Singer and Melvin Small, and the *World Handbook of Political and Social Indicators* by Charles Lewis Taylor and others. The authors of these works have checked and analyzed data to improve their comparability among nations. Moreover, the data from these handbooks and from many other serious studies are classified and filed in computer banks with the International Relations Archive by the Inter-University Consortium for Political Research at Ann Arbor, Michigan.

Political scientists with access to computers and to these data can readily make complicated statistical comparisons and correlations. The ease with which such data can be used can obscure the basic unreliability of the data, which depend on the accuracy and extent of reporting. This varies widely depending on the type of society involved. Also, much of the data is distorted by the governments reporting it, particularly in the field of development indicators.[20]

Scholars of the mathematical school of analysis have devoted a great deal of effort to showing statistical correlations of economic and political data with national policies. For example, some analysts have made elaborate correlations between economic development indicators such as GNP or energy consumption, democracy, size, and population increase with delegates' votes on various issues in the United Nations. Jack Vincent in an elaborate study found relatively low correlations of .5 to .7 between these types of factors and U.N. votes. It should be noted that statistical correlations of this magnitude explain only .25 percent (.5 x .5) to .49 percent (.7 x .7) of the variance between factors. Political scientists commonly call these correlation figures "predictors" although they show relationships of certain factors to the final votes only *after* the vote is taken. Some of these correlations may be useful as "explainers." Seldom, if ever, however, do such studies attempt to predict future votes in advance and then evaluate predictions against a final vote or outcome.[21]

The usefulness of such a mathematical analysis of voting in the U.N. is questionable since policymakers have predicted important votes in advance with much higher levels of accuracy equivalent to correlations of over 95 percent on critical votes without using computers and without correlating economic and political indexes. They do this on the simple basis of assuming that delegates of certain groups of nations such as the Soviet Bloc, the Middle East Arab countries, the Africans, and

Professor Amos Yoder

Correlations Are Not Causes

Policymakers can also get caught in the trap of assuming that correlation coefficients show casual relations. I had an argument with an American government econometrician evaluating the Thai economy who came up with a 97 percent correlation between the Thai economic expansion after 1965 and U.S. military spending in the Thai economy. Knowing that the Thai economy for years had been heavily influenced by agricultural production, I took issue with him by saying his correlation did not prove a causal relationship. Finally, to prove my point, I took two United States series at random from the *World Almanac,* one of which was the number of bets placed annually on horse racing in New York. I ran that series through the computer with his formulae and his cooperation and came up with a similarly high 98 percent correlation of these irrelevant factors with Thailand's economic expansion.

The problem with his analysis was in the mathematical formula being used. In this formula almost any series showing a rising trend over a period of five or six years would result automatically in at least a 97 percent correlation with Thai economic growth, which was also rising. Many economic series show rising trends, including United States horse racing bets, but that does not mean one series of events influenced the other.

the Latin Americans caucus together and tend to vote alike. Past votes of other countries that vote independently from their caucuses are then assessed carefully, and with such a conventional technique predictions can come within a few votes of being correct.

This points to a major problem of using mathematical correlations. Elementary texts on correlations warn that correlations themselves do not show which factors *cause* changes in votes or in other dependent variables being assessed. Determining causes requires political, historical, and other forms of analysis, only some of which can be put into mathematical terms. The Vincent study mentioned above continued with other forms of elaborate correlations including factor analysis and canonical correlation, but like most mathematical studies it spent probably less than 10 percent of its efforts evaluating the key question of whether the correlation coefficients actually showed a causal relationship between a factor being analyzed and the U.N. vote.

Sportswriters and sportscasters who spend their lives reporting on baseball games and compiling elaborate statistics often fail to predict contests where the teams are reasonably matched. Political scientists and policymakers should not expect to predict events in international politics by correlating factors that are infinitely more complicated and remote than batting averages and similar statistics. There is no agreed handbook of rules and no reliable current statistics on many key variables in international affairs, and the leaders of the countries involved are continually changing and trying to conceal their strategies. For these and other reasons mathematical correlations in the field of international politics, as yet, have not demonstrated predictive value for the policymaker.[22]

One very important qualification should be noted. Statistical analysis and prediction are the bread and butter of most economists including international economists. Thus, economic policymakers necessarily rely on masses of data and statistical analysis in making economic policy decisions. (See discussion above under systems analysis.)

Moreover, it should be stressed that mathematics and computers are used in the most critical area of foreign policy — that of nuclear policy. Generally, such use is made within the framework of game theory and bargaining as described below.

Game Theory and Bargaining. Game theory articles appear often in journals used by behavioralists. Moreover, policymakers have adopted game theory concepts in one of the most critical areas of foreign policy — that of nuclear weapons policy.

Game theorists usually assume that the participant in a game will play to win and, in doing so, will make the most rational choices possible. If, as in chess, one side wins and one loses, or there is a draw, it is called a zero sum game. If there are more than two players, the game theorists refer to it as an N-person game.

Non-zero sum games introduce the possibility that all players may win or all may lose, or some may win and some may lose with no necessary balance. TV giveaway games to advertise a product are an example of non-zero sum games. Some game theorists contend international relations is like an N-person, non-zero sum game.

Many game theorists work out options in matrices to demonstrate solutions to problems in politics and international affairs. Such gaming exercises usually assume players make rational choices, at least that are rational in the eyes of the game designer and within the confines of the game. Sometimes the gamesters will set up a hypothetical international crisis and ask students or another test group to make choices. They will then try to draw conclusions about international affairs with the gross assumption that policymakers from various countries would tend to make the same types of choices that the test group did.[23]

The most important application of gaming to international relations is in war gaming of nuclear policy. War games for centuries have been used by the military for training. They usually would involve field exercises against a simulated enemy. In the age of rockets and nuclear weapons, experts used computers and high level mathematics to get data on accuracy of missiles, explosive power, damage, and casualties. Gamesters can sum up many assumptions and calculations in a simple matrix, like the following, for a non-zero sum game and policy evaluation.

**Table 2-2   War Game — Millions of Deaths From
A Theoretical Nuclear Attack**

	(1) No Warning	(2) 30 Min. Warning	(3) 24 Hour Warning
Soviets attack U.S. cities (A)	10 (100)	25 (90)	30 (40)
U.S. attacks U.S.S.R. cities (B)	20 (120)	60 (80)	100 (10)

Note: Opponents' deaths are in parenthesis.
      Many more options than three can be designed.

In the above game the obvious strategy for the Soviet Union would be A-1, a surprise attack against the United States with no warning, since this would cost the Soviets "only" 10 million casualties and would impose a tremendous loss on the United States. Gamesters have pointed out that a 10 million loss for the Soviets is less than they suffered in World War II. In such a game computer calculations would provide the statistical support that in such an attack the Soviet Union would be able to destroy most of the U.S. land-based missiles as well as many bombers and submarines in port. The conclusion is obvious that the Soviet Union would be tempted to launch a surprise attack and that the United States should strengthen its offense and defense to deter such an attack.

For example, General Graham, former Director of the Defense Intelligence Agency, in a debate with Admiral Gene La Rocque asserted that the Soviets "were now at the point where they could limit their casualties to 10 million people in the event of a nuclear attack. We, on the other hand, had no defense. We would lose 110 million to their 10 million and that would be a win for the Soviets."[24] He obviously had made calculations similar to the above. Professor R.J. Rummel, a foremost advocate of applying computers to politics and international affairs, gives in detail the many assumptions involved in this type of calculation. In an *Orbis* article and in other articles he arrived at the alarming conclusion that by 1980 the Soviets would have been able to launch a surprise attack against our cities killing 100 million Americans with a Soviet loss of 10 million. What was more possible, according to Professor Rummel, was that they could have launched an attack against our offensive rockets retaining enough missiles to threaten to kill 90 million more Americans, thus forcing us to surrender without retaliating against their attack.[25]

Many observers are impressed with these games and their complex computer calculations. They overlook, however, the assumptions, many of them fallacious, used to build up a simple matrix. For example, in his testimony before a U.S. Senate Committee, Secretary of Defense Schlesinger presented many complicated calculations on the capabilities of Soviet and American nuclear weapons, and at one point stated that a Soviets in making an attack limited to certain U.S. military targets such as ICBMs would cause relatively few U.S. civilian casualties, hundreds of thousands, he said, and he explained that hundreds of thousands must be regarded as "relatively few in number." In the context of his testimony he supported planning for limited use of nuclear weapons.

Sidney D. Drell and Frank von Hippel in an article in *Scientific American* gave a detailed technical account of how Secretary Schlesinger's estimates of casualties were challenged and changed drastically in subsequent calculations. The Department of Defense admitted later that under new calculations a Soviet strike against each of the United States' ICBM silos would cause 5.6 million deaths, including those from radioactive fallout in the dust of the explosions. A heavier strike to destroy 80 percent of the ICBM silos would cause 18 million deaths, and still leave a capability for the United States to make a massive response.[26] This means original estimates of U.S. casualties from a limited Soviet attack were changed by a factor of over 2,000 percent, because they had not included estimates of fallout.

The speed of prevailing winds, alone, carrying fallout could affect results by 300 percent or more. Assumptions about how the civilian population takes cover can affect results by a much higher percent. Some of the alarmists reporting the Soviets were far ahead of the United States in civil defense based their data on an assumption the Soviet city population would walk out into the country and dig a rudimentary shelter to protect themselves from the initial blast and radiation, without stating how they would survive 30 days in such a shelter from the fallout or from the Russian winter.[27] Applying such large margins of error to the game matrix shown in the above table could change the calculations drastically and show the attacking country in effect committing suicide with an attack on the victim. This is probably a truer picture of reality. In short, only a madman would base a decision for an attack on such iffy calculations. Nevertheless, it is frightening to see the respect that is given to such data, particularly when they are the product of complicated graphs, formulas, and computer runs.

There is even a more fundamental fallacy of the above type of game. The matrix with its confining assumptions does not show the best "saddlepoint" or solution for policy, which is no attack at all. In such an event the losses would be zero on each side, which is obviously better than the minimum loss of 10 million people for the Soviets. Moreover, such a game matrix does not take into account the tremendous benefits from expanded trade as well as savings in the heavy burden of defense costs that would come from a prolonged period of peace. Policymakers who are working for arms control agreements make this latter type of non-gaming calculation.

Thomas Schelling, a Harvard economist and game theorist, has worked out a less formal gaming approach for a type of non-zero sum game in which participants are not engaged in negotiations. This type of situation he believes is relevant to bargaining problems of conflicts and war. He calls attention to "reference points" or policy options where two sides can obviously reach a tacit agreement on limiting actions. For example he believes poison gas was not used in World War II because this was the obvious reference point other than both sides using it. In other words, it would be too hard to draw a line on using gas only on military personnel, having only defending forces use gas, using gas only with prior warning, etc. Thus the contestants settled on no use, which is simple and unambiguous.[28]

In Appendix A of his *The Strategy of Conflict,* Schelling applies this reference point argument to the use of nuclear weapons. He admits that with the development of small-yield nuclear weapons there is little technical difference between the small nuclear weapons and large *conventional* weapons in the conduct of a limited war. However, he stresses that psychic, perceptual, and symbolic distinctions are important in establishing tacit reference points. He argues "What makes atomic weapons different is a powerful tradition that they *are* different." Because of the continuous gradation in sizes there is no natural break if nuclear weapons are used, so, the obvious solution is non-use. Moreover, he states, the principal inhibitions on the use of atomic weapons may disappear with their first use, and we should be concerned with the terrible results of escalating use in a future conflict.

A political scientist trying to apply Schelling's theory might decide that nuclear weapons have not been used since World War II for similar logical reasons that poison gas was not used since World War I. However, when one enters the real world with such a theory, one runs into difficulties. For instance, the United States' policy for defense of Europe is based on the use of tactical nuclear weapons, and there are over 7,000 tactical nuclear weapons in Europe. Also, former U.S. Secretary of Defense Schlesinger indicated that the United States would consider the use of nuclear weapons if there is another attack by North Korea on South Korea. (See below.) It would appear that military planners are not impressed with Schelling's arguments.

This leads to the theories of coercive diplomacy and deterrence which assert that serious and convincing preparations for war will deter the other side from an attack. Alexander George, David Hall, and William Simons have listed the conditions which favor the use of deterrence. They caution on taking the theoretical principles too seriously, however, and warn that coercion should be used only on behalf of the most important national interests with only modest demands on the other side.[29]

It is very dangerous to regard international politics as a game and particularly as a rational game. Herman Kahn's book, *Thinking About the Unthinkable,* recognizes the dangers of analyzing options about conducting a nuclear war.[30] In other words, both experts and policymakers could get carried away in basing decisions on theoretical gaming options for international crises, forgetting that there is one essential difference between a game and the deadly serious business of international politics. Teams can make mistakes or even lose a few games and still be champions. However, if leaders of a country make just one mistake in a serious crisis, that decision could lead to a nuclear war which could be disaster for the United States as well as the rest of the world.

It is frightening to read about the extent to which a gaming approach to nuclear war has gone. For example, in the hearings before the Committee on Foreign Relations of the United States Senate held on March 4, 1974, Secretary of Defense Schlesinger defended the new policy of improving the accuracy of nuclear weapons in such a way that the United States would have the option of attacking selected targets in the Soviet Union in the event of aggression against Western Europe.[31] Secretary Schlesinger said under such circumstances the United States could go after the Soviet's oil production capacity to cripple their ability to wage war against Western Europe.[32] In response to a question from Senator Fulbright, Secretary Schlesinger thought that the Soviets might well retaliate with nuclear weapons but he added that if we were to maintain continued communications with the Soviet leaders, the leaders would be "rational and prudent." And he added, "I hope I am not being too optimistic." The statement appears both optimistic and naive. Russian military leaders have planned for total war,[33] not limited war, and leaders are rarely rational and prudent when their country is attacked.

In his visit to South Korea in September, 1975, Secretary Schlesinger hinted at the use of nuclear weapons in the case of an attack by North Korea against South Korea. What such a statement does not allow for is the irrationality, confusion, and misinterpretation of actions that often occur in a crisis which involves a reckless ally, such as North Korea, which can take independent action. Both the U.S. and the Soviet Union have many accurate nuclear weapons and have considered the superficially rational strategies of using weapons in a first strike to wipe out as many as possible of the opponent's weapons. In a confused crisis situation such as the use of nuclear weapons in Korea, the military or top leaders of a country could jump to the conclusion that a general nuclear war may be imminent and that they should launch a nuclear strike to destroy as many of the enemy's offensive weapons as possible before they could be used. This may be good gaming strategy but disastrous foreign policy. Restraint is needed to give time to negotiate when an ally takes reckless action.

In a crisis when top leaders are together reading incoming messages, making decisions on movements of troops, alerting nuclear forces, and trying to evaluate what the enemy is doing, the exercise has many elements of a game. Before the outbreak of World War I the European leaders did not realize how the system of alliances and schedules of mobilization could get out of control, and World War I was triggered in confusion and errors. Irving Janis, in analyzing the dangers of "group think," has pointed out the dangers of men participating in a small group making decisions in a crisis. One of the major dangers, he points out, is the strong team spirit which develops and persuades a person to go along with a decision that involves resorting to a war where many will be killed. He believes that similar forces were probably at work in regard to Pearl Harbor, the Bay of Pigs in Cuba in 1961, and other crises where people, who normally could express disapproval of an action, felt compelled by the group spirit to join with the rest in supporting a crisis decision.[34]

Human beings make errors in judgment, tend to be seduced or corrupted by power, and are subject to pressures of joining the crowd. If they keep in mind they are not playing a game but making decisions that could kill millions, the chances for a peaceful solution are much better.

Policymakers have picked up and used some of the new concepts and language of the behavioralists, and particularly in the field of nuclear strategy there is extensive use of mathematical and games techniques. The process has gone too far, however, with some military officers and policymakers using these ideas to support their strategies without heeding reservations of academics who have warned about misuse of these techniques.

We will start the process of analyzing international policies by examining the major ideas that influence policymakers. Their success in implementing policies depends on the political support they can mobilize for their ideas. We will later look at the material resources, including military strength, used in backing their policies.

Summary

Individual policymakers, rather than something called a nation, establish foreign policies by selling their ideas to government leaders. Reporters and others repeat these ideas which through their use achieve a momentum in international affairs. These ideas, therefore, can be used as basic units of analysis. An analyst then can sort out these ideas such as nationalism, Communism, democracy, and other concepts of international politics, and determine how actions square with words. In this book we will see how such ideas have been applied within three world systems — the U.N. System, the Superpower System, and the Multipolar System of States and Non-state actors.

Many political scientists use behavioralist approaches, some of which are useful in analyzing current policy issues. These approaches include regarding political activities as taking place within "systems," analyzing actions at different "levels" of government, evaluating the effect of "images" on policy, using mathematics to analyze political data, and using game and bargaining theories to evaluate political events. These behavioralist approaches can give insight into important issues, but policymakers in their day-to-day activities are more interested in information focused on a particular foreign policy problem, such as the intent of policymakers and the degree of political and material support for their ideas. An exception to this is the wide use of games theories in nuclear strategy. Such games theories can be dangerous if reservations about their use are not heeded.

FOOTNOTES

1. Hans J. Morgenthau, *Politics Among Nations* (New York: Alfred A. Knopf, 1976).

2. Cecil V. Crabb, Jr., *Policy-Makers and Critics* (New York: Praeger, 1976), pp. 289-293.

3. "Prediction" as used in this text means to foretell future events. I do not use the term, as some political scientists do, for the process of explaining by statistical methods patterns of past events.

4. See David Easton, "Introduction: The Current Meaning of 'Behavioralism' in Political Science" (Philadelphia: A Symposium Sponsored by the American Academy of Political and Social Science on the "Limits of Behavioralism in Political Science," 1962) for a basic definition of the behavioralist school.

5. See James E. Dougherty/Robert L. Pfaltzgraff, Jr., *Contending Theories of International Relations* (Philadelphia: J.B. Lippincott Co., 1980), and Patrick M. Morgan, *Theories and Approaches to International Politics* (Palo Alto, Calif.: Page-Ficklin Publications, 1975).

6. David Easton, *A Framework for Political Analysis* (Englewood Cliffs, New Jersey: Prentice Hall, 1965), pp. 248-249.

7. Herbert J. Spiro, *World Politics: The Liberal System* (Homewood, Illinois: Dorsey Press, 1966), p. 51.

8. Harold and Margaret Sprout, *An Ecological Paradigm for the Study of International Politics* (Princeton: Center for International Studies, 1968), Research Monograph No. 30.

9. Richard Sterling, *Macropolitics* (New York: Alfred A. Knopf, 1974), and George Modelski, *Principles of World Politics* (Glencoe: Free Press of Glencoe, 1972). For a good discussion of these theories and others, see Patrick Morgan, *Theories and Approaches to International Politics* (Palo Alto, Calif.: Page-Ficklin Publication, 1975).

10. See Klaus Knorr and Sidney Verba (editors), *The International System* (Princeton University Press, 1961), article by J. David Singer, "The Level-of-Analysis Problem in International Relations," pp. 77-92.

11. Graham T. Allison, *Essence of Decision* (Boston: Little, Brown and Company, 1971).

12. *Ibid.,* p. 174.

13. Edward R.F. Sheehan, "Step by Step in the Middle East," *Foreign Policy,* Spring, 1976, pp. 3-70.

14. Kenneth Boulding, *The Image* (Ann Arbor: University of Michigan Press, 1973), pp. 110-114.

15. Karl Deutsch and Richard Marrett, "Effects of Events on National and International Images," in Herbert Kelman (ed.), *International Behavior* (Holt, Rinehart, and Winston, 1965), pp. 54-55 and 132-187. See Donald Puchala, *International Politics Today* (Dodd Mead, 1971), pp. 54-55; William Buchanan and Hadley Cantril, *How Nations See Each Other* (University of Illinois Press, 1953); Patrick M. Morgan, *Theories and Approaches to International Politics* (Palo Alto, Calif.: Ficklin Publications, 1975), pp. 94-104; James E. Dougherty and Robert

52   International Politics and Policymakers' Ideas

Pfaltzgraff, Jr., *Contending Theories of International Relations* (Philadelphia: J.B. Lippincott Co., 1971), pp. 104-106 and 221-232.

16. Robert Jervis, *Perception and Misperception in International Politics* (Princeton: Princeton University Press, 1976), pp. 117-137.

17. Ole Holsti, Richard Brady, and Robert North, "The Management of International Crises: Affect and Action in American-Soviet Relations," in Dean Pruitt and Richard Snyder (eds.), *Theory and Research on the Causes of War* (Prentice Hall, 1969), pp. 62-79.

18. Robert Jervis, *op. cit.,* Chapter Three.

19. John G. Stoessinger, *Nations in Darkness: China, Russia, and America* (New York: Random House, 1980).

20. See Ted Robert Gurr, "The Neo-Alexandrians: A Review Essay on Data Handbooks in Political Science," *American Political Science Review,* March, 1974, pp. 243-252.

21. Jack E. Vincent, "Predicting Voting Patterns in the General Assembly," *American Political Science Review,* June, 1971, pp. 471-495. Two correlations in the Vincent study were as high as .8 but these involved factors that described whether a country was a member of the Soviet Bloc (allied with the U.S.S.R.), or Western Bloc (allied with the United States), and thus are not a political or economic index like the others being analyzed.

22. Many correlations of multiple factors in international affairs are based on some form of multiple regression assuming that the functions are straight line and not curvilinear. This is necessary because multiple regressions with curvilinear functions have so many permutations that they would exceed the capability of a computer.

23. Karl W. Deutsch, *The Analysis of International Relations* (Englewood Cliffs, N.J.: Prentice Hall, 1968).

24. "AIM Report," (Washington, D.C.: Accuracy in Media, Inc., December, 1976), p. 5.

25. R.J. Rummel, "Will the Soviets Soon Have a First-Strike Capability?," *Orbis,* Fall, 1976, pp. 579-594.

26. "U.S.-U.S.S.R. Strategic Policies," Hearing Before the Subcommittee on Arms Control, International Law and Organization Subcommittee of the Committee on Foreign Relations, United States Senate, March 4, 1976 (Washington, D.C.: U.S. Government Printing Office, 1974); and Sidney D. Drell and Frank von Hippel, "Limited Nuclear War," *Scientific American,* November, 1976, pp. 27-34.

27. Peter J. Ognibene, "Walk and Dig — That's Soviet Civil Defense," *Washington Post,* July 6, 1977, Editorial Page.

28. Thomas C. Schelling, *The Strategy of Conflict* (London: Oxford University Press, 1966), p. 74.

29. Alexander George, David Hall, and William Simons, *The Limits of Coercive Diplomacy* (Little, Brown, 1971). For a thorough discussion of deterrence theory see Patrick Morgan, *Deterrence, A Conceptual Analysis* (Beverly Hills, Calif.: Sage Publications, 1977).

30. Herman Kahn, *Thinking About the Unthinkable* (Horizon Press, 1962), and *On Thermonuclear War* (Princeton University Press, 1960).

31. United States Senate Committee on Foreign Relations, Hearings before the Subcommittee on Arms Control, International Law, and Organization, "U.S.-U.S.S.R. Strategic Policies" (Washington: U.S. Government Printing Office, 1974), top secret hearing held on March 4, 1974: Sanitized and made public on April 4, 1974.

32. A year and a half later Senator Symington took issue with this argument indicating the death toll in a limited nuclear war with the Soviet Union could be immensely greater than earlier Defense Department estimates. *Washington Post,* September 17, 1975, p. 5.

33. Joseph D. Douglass, Jr., Amoretta M. Hoebber, *Soviet Strategy for Nuclear War* (Stanford: Hoover Institution Press, 1979), pp. 1-8.

34. Irving Janis, *Victims of Group Think* (New York: Houghton Mifflin, 1972).

PART TWO
Policymaking Factors

Policymakers compete in international politics by selling ideologies and strategies to political groups and leaders. Their ideas are processed in government structures and by the news media before winning policies emerge. How the ideas are implemented depends largely on how leaders mobilize public support and economic and military power to support their policies. In this section we examine the important ideas and objective factors of international politics and how the above process affects the viewpoint of policymakers.

3

The Power of Ideologies

Ideologies are the most powerful political ideas, and the most powerful ideologies are those of various nationalisms. Activists use nationalist ideologies to create nations, and men will march off to death under their banners. Nationalism as an idea is capitalized in Table 2-1 to indicate its overriding importance in international politics. Followers of ideologies such as those of Communism, liberal democracy, and social democracy usually subordinate them to the ideology of a nationalism.

he National Interest and Nationalism

The ideas of national interest are commonly used by leaders of established states to sanctify the goals they define for their countries. Policymakers as officials of a government take the nation state for granted. Normally they take an oath of allegiance to a state, and therefore are pledged to promote its national interest or goals. This means nationalism in the dictionary sense of "promotion of a nation's culture and interests as opposed to those of other nations or supranational groups" is an inherent part of policymaking.

Many observers believe that the national interest is something concrete that can be defined and analyzed like the objective factors of international politics. They overlook the fact that policymakers and analysts often honestly disagree on what is in the national interest, and that there is no authority to say who is right. Nevertheless, because of its appeal, few, if any, political leaders would dare to question the concept.

Professor Hans Morgenthau's *Politics Among Nations* states that international politics is governed by objective laws. The main signpost, he states, is that statesmen strive to realize goals by striving for power. "International politics, like all politics is a struggle for power." Power is defined as anything that maintains control of man over man, whether it be social, psychological, doctrinal, or religious. He suggests that political realists and policymakers first ask how a policy affects the power of nations, and then choose the policies most suited to adding to their nations' power.

Morgenthau states that statesmen must define the objectives of foreign policy in terms of the national interest and support these objectives with adequate power. Thus, he combines the idea of national interest with that of power politics. One major problem with looking at national interest or national goals and a striving for power as a guide to understanding and predicting international policies is that policymakers often do not act in a rational way, and he admits that this needs further investigation. Another problem he recognizes is that ideologies often confuse policymakers about what is in a nation's best interest.[1]

When we analyze international politics from a policymaking point of view, we see policymakers selling ideas of national interest, ideologies, and strategies of foreign policy. These ideas obtain a hold on the minds of officials and people of a country and achieve a momentum of their own. A logical first step in political analysis is to categorize ideas that become enshrined with the goals or national interest of a country.

Most leaders today would publicly define their country's general goals in approximately the same way. These elements of national interest could be listed under four "Ps" — peace, protection, prosperity, and power. Most leaders assert peace and protection (or defense) are at the top of their lists, and would say their aim is to achieve the prosperity and well-being of their citizens. Few would admit that power is an overriding aim of their country, but actually this, too, is an important goal. Leaders in stressing the importance of a category of national interest often will label it as a vital interest. At the least the term evokes self-righteousness; at the most it is used to justify aggression.[2]

Some leaders, called "revolutionaries" on the world scene, have had unsatisfied nationalist goals and have wished to upset a government that stands in the way of such goals. Examples are the drive of North Vietnam's leaders to conquer South Vietnam and the attempt of North Korea in 1950 to conquer South Korea. Groups with such revolutionary aims usually claim their goals are limited to national goals and that their ultimate aims for the "nation" are the four Ps — peace, protection, prosperity, and power.

A historical or political study of international affairs in the era before World War II would devote a great deal of study to nationalisms as they created the basis for the nation-state system, were diverted by leaders into the totalitarianism that caused World War II, and broke up colonial empires.[3] After World War II nationalists finished up the process of breaking up the great world empires and created about 90 new states, more than doubling the number of states that existed before World War II. These new states in most cases have not remained in orbit around their former colonial masters but have begun to coalesce in a new multipolar system. They use

Australian Nationalism

Marshall Green, one of my former bosses in the State Department, tells the following story. In 1973 after the Australian Minister of Trade denounced the United States as an aggressor in Vietnam, Ambassador Green commented to the Australian press that however unfortunate things had turned out in Vietnam, to accuse the U.S. of being the aggressor was an opinion he thought very few Americans or Australians shared and that he found it quite unwarranted. The statement produced headlines in Australia and some columnists even called for his dismissal.

As a result, several months later when a relatively obscure Australian publicly attacked Ambassador Green as America's leading hatchet man sent out to topple the Australian Labor Party from power, Ambassador Green kept silent despite calls from the press to comment. Finally the Labor Party's Prime Minister responded by calling the Parliamentarian a "miserable, cowardly creature to attack a foreign diplomat who could not respond." The Prime Minister then went on to praise what Ambassador Green had done for Australian-American relations.

Ambassador Green concludes that this bears out his view that nationalism is the strongest force in international diplomacy and that in any debate between an Australian and an American there was a nationalist tendency for them to side with the Australian even if "most Australians did not agree with the Minister in question." He added this also demonstrates it is best for diplomats not to speak bluntly and to let others speak out when they can do the job more effectively.[4]

the United Nations System to help achieve their aims.

Policymakers take the nation-state system for granted and work with the political forces of nationalisms like they work with other powerful ideologies. They see various nationalisms as the most important ideologies of international politics, embracing or competing with other ideologies.

Nationalism is a constant concern of diplomats. Diplomats, who are forced to deal with nationalistic leaders and news media of other countries, quickly learn how a criticism or challenge to national pride can cause an international incident and complicate negotiations. This is a major reason officials try to maintain secrecy in negotiations, which by definition require compromises. Suspicion of foreigners usually is so strong that demagogues and opposition politicians could easily exploit concessions by labeling them harmful to the "national interest" or national security. Officials must defend many international agreements before legislatures, and many of these agreements might never be concluded if officials had to defend each concession along the way against nationalist criticism.

Nationalism has been at the center of wars and turmoil that have occurred since World War II. Following is a summary of the part that nationalist pressures played after World War II in three critical areas of international politics — Germany, the Middle East, and East Asia.

Germany. The fear of a revival of a virulent German nationalism has dominated European politics during most of the period since World War II. Leaders of the Western occupation powers (United States, England, and France) feared that their decisions to split Germany and permit Russia to annex or turn over to Poland about 25 percent of Germany's prewar territory could set the stage for World War III. The Western leaders were acutely aware of Hitler's success in exploiting German resentment of the loss of territory under the Versailles Treaty and creating a German nation that led the world into World War II.

The Russians inadvertently laid the basis for the Western nations to develop close cooperation with Western Germany after the war. I entered Germany with the U.S. Strategic Bombing Survey while the war was still being fought. My image of that era is one of immense destruction with Germans on the move, mostly fleeing from the invading Russian troops. Stories abounded of Russians looting and raping in the months after the end of the war. Subsequently, the Russians uprooted industrial machinery as reparations and detached about 25 percent of German territories, forcing additional Germans to flee to the West. Altogether by the time the Berlin Wall was created in 1961, 13 million Germans had fled to Western Germany.

Chancellor Adenauer's goal was to keep Germany from being permanently held down by the Potsdam Agreement, in which the four occupation powers had set low ceilings on the German war-making potential. His strategy was to cooperate with the Western occupying powers as the only realistic way to get them to grant Germany sovereignty in stages. Adenauer later used their desire to strengthen the Western Alliance with German soldiers against the Russian threat as a lever for their granting full sovereignty to Germany in 1955.

Chancellor Adenauer banked the fires of German nationalism under generous political arrangements of the Western powers. Not only did they let Germans manage their own affairs at an early date, but the United States provided Germany with billions of dollars of aid under the framework of the Marshall Plan. During the period 1950 to 1952 France welcomed Germany as an equal in the European Coal and Steel Community, which held forth the promise of uniting Europe economically and eventually politically. This permitted the German people to sublimate their longing for restoring the prewar borders of Germany by looking west to the European Community.

An element of Adenauer's strategy was also to gain strength and support from Western allies in order later to bargain with the Soviet Union and Eastern Europe for restoring German unity. A widespread fear of unsatisfied German nationalism helped him in this strategy of gaining support from the West.

This strategy prepared the way for Willy Brandt's "settlement" of the "German problem" through reconciliation with the Soviets. Aided by Germany's economic power and prestige, Chancellor Brandt concluded treaties that formalized the boundaries imposed on Germany after World War II. The treaties recognized two German states, but the way is still open for peaceful unification of the two Germanys, since the treaties refer to two states but "one nation." There was more of a concession to the desire for German unity than these words, however. In 1975 after a treaty was signed, 8 million West Berliners visited East Germany, a 300 percent increase in four years. Meanwhile, the Soviet Union permitted 10,000 Germans to emigrate and reunify with their families in the Federal Republic of Germany.[5] Figures such as these help explain the great support in the Federal Republic for *Ostpolitik,* a pragmatic German version of detente. The *Ostpolitik* ideology has proven to be an antidote or tranquillizer for extreme West German nationalism and revisionism. On the other hand, it has stimulated all-German nationalism in the East.[6]

The Middle East. At the center of the Middle East maelstrom is a conflict of ideologies — those of Jewish and Arab nationalisms. The foundation for Arab nationalism was formed with the expansion of the Moslem faith (Islam) and Arabic language under the Prophet Muhammed in a broad area extending from the Middle East along the north coast of Africa. Many peoples of the conquered area acquired Arabic as their language, and the people assimilated the Arab stock. The Arab language and culture are decisive elements that help leaders of Jordan, Lebanon, Syria, Iraq, Egypt, Libya, Morocco, Algeria and Saudi Arabia, and smaller Arab countries develop an anti-Zionist foreign policy.

Arab nationalism was set back as the Ottoman Turks conquered part of the Arab empire, but Arab nationalism emerged with renewed strength after the defeat of the Ottoman Empire in World War I. During World War I the British — in a series of negotiations with the Arab religious and political leader, Sharif Hussain — made a series of pledges in the McMahon correspondence supporting independent Arab nations in areas of the Ottoman Empire. There were reservations about certain "districts" in the general area of Palestine. (Palestine approximates the present area controlled by Israel.) Also during the War the British Government made a commitment to the Jews in the Balfour Declaration which stated the British Government would "view with favor" the establishment of "a national home for the Jewish people" in Palestine. Foreign Secretary Balfour's letter became a source of bitter controversy. The Jews viewed it as a pledge to support Jewish settlement in Palestine, their Biblical homeland, looking toward eventual creation of a Jewish state. Arabs claimed the Declaration was inconsistent with British pledges in the McMahon correspondence and other World War I commitments to the Arabs.[7]

As part of the World War I Versailles settlement the Allied Supreme Council approved a British mandate of Palestine that would report to the League of Nations. During the 1920s and particularly in the 1930s large numbers of Jews immigrated into Palestine buying land and developing farms and businesses. The British administration under pressure from Arabs within Palestine limited Jewish immigration. By 1942 the British estimated about 30 percent of Palestine's population was Jewish, about 60 percent Moslem, with Christians and other elements making up the remainder.[8]

In Hitler's Germany six million Jews were killed in Nazi concentration camps, and there was a tremendous desire among many surviving Jews to leave Europe. Many emigrated to Palestine, their Biblical homeland, with the aim of establishing their own state, where they would be free from persecution. Many were kept out of Palestine in 1946 and 1947 by the British, who were still trying to limit immigration because of unrest and Arab pressures. The British Government finally gave up the effort to control conflicting nationalisms in Palestine and announced it would turn over the area to the United Nations as of May, 1948. Civil strife in Palestine intensified after this announcement.

The United Nations had inherited mandate problems from the League of Nations, and it formed a committee for the Palestine problem. The Committee recommended with a majority vote the partition of Palestine into Jewish and Arab states; this was approved by over a 2/3 vote in the U.N. General Assembly. The plan satisfied the Jews, but the Arabs violently objected because they considered Palestine their land. When the British withdrew on May 12, 1948, the State of Israel was proclaimed. On that same day at President Truman's order the United States recognized the new state. (During my tour of duty in Tel Aviv on the 10th anniversary of that event, Israeli friends told me of the gratitude of the Jews for Truman's act and said half seriously that in Israel, Truman was second only to Moses in esteem.)

On May 13, 1948, armies of the neighboring Arab nations attacked. The Jews had prepared for the attack and somehow managed to mobilize equipment and the forces to defend themselves. The United Nations Security Council launched a mediation effort, and a truce was achieved in 1949. The State of Israel was consolidated behind the armistice lines to control both the Jewish and much of the Arab portions of the original U.N. partition plan.

Three wars followed in 1956, 1967, and 1973, based on conflicting national claims of the Jews and the Arabs. During the 1967 war the Israelis occupied the West Bank of the Jordan with about 800,000 Palestinian Arabs, and areas of Egypt and of Syria. In the following years the Palestinian Liberation Organization came to the fore as the nationalist spokesman for the Palestinian Arabs. It is an alliance of Arab groups, including terrorist groups operating in non-Arab countries. Its basic charter does not recognize the right of the Israeli nation to exist.

It is difficult to evaluate the PLO strength. It seemed to have lost ground when Palestinian groups failed to unseat Jordan's King Hussein by force in 1970. In 1976 the PLO was forced by Syrian troops to end an insurrection in Lebanon and accept a 15,000 man peacekeeping force of Arab nations. Nevertheless, the PLO has widespread support in its campaign to regain Arab land. In 1974, U.N. bodies recognized its right to act as a spokesman for the Arab Palestinians, short of a voting right. At the beginning of 1979, Yasar Arafat, its leader, rallied Arab nations to break off relations with Egypt because of its approval of the Camp David agreements for a peace settlement with Israel. (See Chapter 9.) The PLO based its appeal on national and religious factors and effectively blocked moves of Israel to make peace with Arab states other than Egypt.

To sum up, a combination of historical and religious factors brought Arab and Israeli nationalisms into confrontation. The Jews consider Israel as the Biblical homeland and a refuge from the terrible persecution they had suffered under Hitler. Israel insisted as a condition of negotiation over the Sinai, the West Bank, and the Golan Heights — lands acquired in the 1967 Six Day War — that the Arab states recognize Israel as a nation and end their state of belligerency against Israel. Minimum demands of many Arab leaders included restoration of the pre-1967 boundaries of Israel, establishing a Palestinian state on the West Bank, and restoration of Palestinian land and property in Israel. Tensions and distrust from previous wars have hindered negotiations.

China. Forces of nationalism have also been at the center of Asian wars and disputes. The Korean and Vietnam wars were brought about by an alliance of nationalist and Communist ideologies — these are discussed in Chapter 9. The conflicts between China and Taiwan since 1949 resulted from the claim of each government to control both areas as one China.

Japan had taken over Taiwan from China in 1905. At the end of World War II Taiwan had been returned to Chinese control by the Allied Powers, which noted that a final settlement awaited a peace treaty. Initially there was friction between the government imposed by the mainland Chinese and the Taiwanese. At one point thousands of Taiwanese were killed in civil strife, but the harsh rule was then ameliorated. In 1949 about one million mainlanders fled to Taiwan from the Communist revolution and set up the Government of the Republic of China to rule nine million Taiwanese, most of whom spoke the Amoy Chinese dialect and could read Chinese. Within a few years the mainlanders in control of Taiwan saw their chances for taking back the mainland fade, and an accommodation developed with the Taiwanese.

The major problem of nationalism is that the Peoples' Republic of China (Communist) and the Republic of China (Taiwan) both claim to represent the Government of China. These claims brought the two regimes and the United States, which supported Taiwan, close to a shooting war in 1954 and 1958 in a conflict over control of islands close to the mainland still held by troops of the government on Taiwan. (See Box.)

A breakthrough occurred in 1972 with President

Two Chinas?

The intensity of nationalist feelings of rival leaders of Taiwan and mainland China is the most difficult element for non-Chinese to understand in the dispute between the Republic of China (Taiwan) and the Peoples' Republic of China (Communist). Neither regime will recognize the other and both insist there is only one China for both areas. If one Chinese government is recognized by another state, the other Chinese government will break off relations with that state. Neither regime has belonged to an international organization in which the other is a member. On the U.N. membership issue, which came to a head in the early 1970s, neither the Peoples' Republic of China nor Taiwan would accept a proposed compromise in which the Peoples' Republic would take over the Chinese seat on the U.N. Security Council and both Taiwan and the PRC would be members of the U.N. General Assembly. Nevertheless, well meaning peacemakers and experts have persisted through the years in proposing a "two Chinas" solution for their dispute, assuming time would heal the breach.

During my tour on the China Desk of the State Department and later I often tried to explain how intense Chinese nationalism prevented a two China solution. In recent years I have had some success by drawing a parallel with the intensity of American nationalistic feelings generated over the Panama Canal Treaty issue, which opposed giving up control over the Panama Canal Zone. The issue was heatedly debated for many years before President Carter put the treaty before the Senate for ratification. Few observers gave him much chance of success at first. After the Senate by a margin of only two votes gave its approval to turn back the Zone to Panama, the nationalistic issue lingered in presidential and congressional politics and echoed into the 1980 campaigns. Yet the Panama Canal Zone was never even American territory. The 1901 Treaty with Panama gave the United States control over the Panama Canal Zone as if the U.S. were sovereign, which was not the same as full sovereignty.

Nixon's visit to mainland China with a joint communique pledging to work toward "normalization" of relations between the Peoples' Republic of China and the United States. That process was consummated on January 1, 1979, when the United States and China officially recognized each other by upgrading their missions to embassies. The U.S. gave notice of breaking the mutual defense "treaty" with the government of Taiwan although it arranged for unofficial economic and cultural relations. Over 20 governments continued to recognize the Taiwan government as the government of China, but the U.S. was the last of the great powers to end that relationship.

Time may solve this problem, which is based on the stubborn nationalistic attitudes of the two regimes. The Chinese Communist government appeared to be patient, and in 1979 was proposing to resume mail, travel, and trade contacts.[9] The people of Taiwan would strongly resist an invasion, and the United States would, if necessary, probably intervene to assist them with instruments of diplomacy and power politics.

Japan. The friendly relations between the United States and Japan after World War II are based on the restoration by the U.S. of Japanese sovereignty. The U.S. occupation after World War II was committed to permit the Japanese to retain their emperor, and it permitted Japanese government bodies after a purge and reorganization to continue administration of Japan. I was attached to the occupation forces after World War II, and many examples of cooperation between the Japanese and the occupying forces stand out in my mind. These include invitations to Japanese homes for dinner, a soldier filling up a jeep to take Japanese children for a ride, Japanese and Americans singing "The Messiah" together for the first Christmas, and an American soldier driving a Japanese lady in a kimono around the Olympic stadium track in a horse and buggy during a U.S. military show three months after the occupation began. This type of reconciliation was particularly impressive since the center of Tokyo had been devastated and about 100,000 people killed in a U.S. "fire bomb" raid on Tokyo early in that year. Some of these images of the occupation are recorded on my home movies I took as an American soldier.

This conciliatory U.S. occupation policy was based not just on generosity but also on a pragmatic concern about the potential of a resentful Japanese nationalism. By 1947 the Japanese were granted constitutional government. Under the constitution the Japanese renounced creating military forces, which has been interpreted to mean forces more than a minimum required to maintain local security. In return the United States assumed a treaty responsibility to defend Japan.

In 1951 the peace treaty, which was signed by Japan and 48 other states, formally granted sovereignty to Japan. The U.S.-Japanese Mutual Defense Treaty, which accompanied this peace treaty, generated socialist and left-wing opposition, particularly to provisions permitting American troops to remain on bases in Japan. After about two decades of controversy about this, the issue of Japanese national pride was neutralized in the reaffirmation of the Treaty in June, 1970, which provided for its staying in force indefinitely but permitted termination on one year's notice. The winding down of the Vietnam War also improved the atmosphere in Japan. Finally, the bothersome issue of Okinawa was settled. After World War II the United States had retained control over Okinawa, which had been captured after much bloodshed. In November, 1969, President Nixon authorized negotiations to return these islands to Japan. The negotiations were successfully completed in 1972. I remember reading and hearing reports of discussions between the Pentagon and the State Department on this issue, which were more heated than those with Japan. The Pentagon was very reluctant to give up Okinawa, one of their most strategic bases in the Far East. Many officers recalled the American lives lost in taking that area during World War II. The State Department won in getting permission to return Okinawa to Japanese control, but the U.S. military were allowed to retain many of their military installations on Okinawa after the islands were returned to Japan. Returning Okinawa to Japanese sovereignty mollified many Japanese nationalists.

The harmonious Japanese relations with the U.S. contrast with Japan's cool relations with the Soviet

Union, which opposed the 1951 peace treaty with Japan and which still retains islands of the Kuriles just north of Japan. In prewar days they were occupied by only about 15,500 Japanese fishermen, but the Soviet refusal to return these islands after World War II is a major irritant preventing the final signing of a Soviet peace treaty with Japan. Observers speculate the Soviet Union does not want to give back the territories for fear of stimulating other nationalist pressures to return areas in Eastern Europe, which it took over after World War II, and to return areas the Tsars took from China.

Other Facets of Nationalism. Nationalism is also a major force where no territorial or sovereignty issues are involved. Leaders can quickly mobilize national pride to support a forceful move against another nation to right a "wrong," particularly when the other nation is weaker. In the Mayaguez incident of 1975, when Cambodian forces captured a U.S. merchant ship in their territorial waters with 39 sailors, the U.S. Congress and news media supported a strong U.S. military intervention to free sailors, even though a few weeks earlier congressional pressure had forced the United States to end military aid to Vietnam and make a complete withdrawal of U.S. elements from that area.[10] President Carter's attempt to rescue 50 American hostages from the center of Teheran in April, 1980, with a small strike force, received widespread approval in the media and by public opinion, even though the attempt aborted and seemed ill-advised to some critics.

Economic nationalism is also a powerful force. Tariff and trade negotiations are complicated by the fear of labor groups that allowing more imports will cause a loss of jobs by the importing nation. The oil embargo of 1973-1974 by Arab states sparked the expensive "Project Independence" in the United States to end dependence on "foreign" energy supplies. How to reduce U.S. dependence on foreign energy supplies became the major government problem during the rest of the decade. National pride as well as a desire to strengthen the U.S. hand in power politics supported the program.

In almost all phases of international policymaking nationalism is a primary force to be reckoned with.

Communism

The Communist ideology with about one-third on the world's population under its banner is the second most powerful ideology in the world. Its influence has been expanded through linking up with nationalisms of new states and their anti-colonial ideas as well as by allying with anti-racist and other powerful ideas. Moreover, many non-Communist policymakers throughout the world, particularly in developing countries, are influenced by Marxist elements of the Communist ideology. Most of the world, therefore, responds to at least some of the ideological appeals of the Communists.

The basic elements of the Communist ideology are easily explained, which accounts for much of their appeal. There are a few Communist and Marxist theologians who have waded through and who can cite from the massive texts of Lenin and Marx, just as a few Christians have intensively studied the Bible. However, most of the Communists' appeal arises from their slogans and propaganda based on a few basic ideas of the doctrines.

The Communists argue as follows. They say that history involves a continual class struggle. For example, the middle class and commercial class undermined the power of the nobles and guild masters. Similarly, the theory holds, the laboring class is undermining the power of the capitalist or bourgeois class which dominates governments and their politics. According to Marx because laborers receive minimal wages, they cannot buy the total production of the capitalist system, so the capitalists, and particularly the banking interests, are forced to find markets abroad; they invest surplus profits and capital there. Lenin wrote that this would result in a struggle by the developed capitalist countries for colonial markets and also for cheap raw materials. Thus, they say, the Nineteenth Century was a history of imperialist wars for colonies. In the Twentieth Century, the Communists hold, a new form of colonialism, "neocolonialism," arose in which the capitalists maintain control of countries through investment and trade. They are said to control local industry by using the "national or local bourgeoisie."

The Communists hold that the solution to the world's

problems is for the working class (the proletariat) to abolish capitalism and create a world community of Communist nations. This, they say, would remove "contradictions" in societies, and there would be no more wars.

Lenin's major contribution to Communist theory was that the Communists should not wait for historical forces to bring about the overthrow of the capitalist system. His view was that an elite, disciplined group should seize control of the governmental apparatus and bring about the Communist revolution.

There are a number of historical facts that undermine the above theories. The great movement to take over colonies (colonialism) came before capitalism was developed and was stimulated primarily by trade profits. Moreover, the Soviet Union, the original leader of world Communism, established a colonial type of control over Eastern Europe by keeping troops in a number of East European countries and exploiting them economically in the years following World War II. Russia still keeps most countries of Eastern Europe under political and economic control. On the other hand, in many capitalist countries labor (the proletariat) has been able to organize in unions and in political parties to achieve benefits from society, while in Communist countries labor unions are subservient to the government, which is controlled by the one-party Communist system. (The Polish trade union movement in early 1981 was struggling to remove these controls. See Chapter 8.) Labor in many capitalist societies has the leverage for obtaining a larger share of output than Communist labor, and in some countries labor union leaders are among the most ardent opponents of Communism and strong supporters of the enterprise system.

The call for revolution by Communist ideology created the split that prevented formation of alliances to block Hitler's early aggression and that later led to the Cold War. Western democracies with their belief in peaceful change through political action cannot establish a trusting relationship with Communist regimes, which have announced an aim of overthrowing them. The United States and other Western countries can establish detente with Communist countries despite their revolutionary aims, but this detente can become strained or broken if Communist countries openly support revolutionary movements with arms and manpower. For example, China opposes the hegemonism of the Soviet Union and has not openly supported revolutions in recent years. Nevertheless, China in its normalization agreement with the United States in 1972 stated frankly: "Countries want independence, nations want liberation, and the people want revolution — this has become the irresistable trend of history." As indicated in Chapter 9 this permitted development of a closer relationship that resulted in the U.S. making limited sales of arms to China. On the other hand there was almost no U.S. reaction in 1978 when a Communist government took over Afghanistan, since there was no obvious Soviet intervention. At the end of 1979, however, when Soviet troops invaded and replaced a relatively independent Communist leader with a puppet, there was a strong world reaction led by the United States that included severe trade restrictions and boycotting the Olympic games in Moscow.

President Reagan stressed the incompatibility of democracy and communism in his first months in office. He blamed Russia for the support by its Cuban satellite for the revolution in El Salvador. President Reagan as an ardent anti-Communist also saw a Soviet threat of direct military action as well as revolutionary activity against strategic areas. Thus in 1981 the Cold War intensified as the U.S. began a rapid rearmament program to match what it saw as a Communist threat in many areas of the world. Initially the U.S. maintained correct relations with China and even continued limited sales of arms, but relations with China were several degrees cooler than they had been under the Carter Administration.

The basic elements of the Communist theory have a great appeal to the developing world, much of which has a long history of colonial control and exploitation. Policymakers of former colonial powers are often at an ideological disadvantage when they try to promote or protect business interests in a former colony that has achieved independence. They are attacked by Communists and leaders of the new states. Many current debates between the developing world and the Western powers over economic and raw materials issues are laced with ideological rhetoric about neo-colonialism, exploitation of raw materials, and similarly loaded ideas.

The aggressive or revolutionary elements of Communist theory when joined with nationalism are a formidable force. The Vietnam War, the longest war in which the United States has been involved, started in a Communist-nationalist revolt against French colonialism.

As the United States became deeply involved in the Vietnam War in the early 1960s, it encouraged the French withdrawal and used the slogan of self-determination for South Vietnam. The Communists, however, accused the United States of replacing the French colonial masters over the Diem Government. United States' efforts to help South Vietnam fight the Communist-nationalist expansion from the North were defeated in 1975 after a long and bitter war. U.S. forces were forced to withdraw and South Vietnam was absorbed in the North. Factors such as geography, the personal leadership of Ho Chi Minh, and U.S. war weariness were also involved, but the strength and appeal of the ideals of Communism and nationalism must be understood if we are to understand the Communist victory in Vietnam in that war.[11]

The basic differences between the ideologies of Communism and democracy have fueled the Cold War. As we will see below, however, there are certain common elements of Communist theories with social democratic theories which add confusion to the international scene. This can give casual observers of European and Third World politics an exaggerated view of the appeal of Communist doctrine.

Democracy — Liberal Democrats and Social Democrats

Democracy, which is a dominant ideology of United States and Western European policymakers, is based on the belief that supreme power should be exercised by the people through a system of representation involving free elections. In this process political and civil liberties should be protected, particularly the rights of an opposition party to organize.

Figure 3-1   Definitions of Governments and Economies

Communism (capitalized) — a totalitarian form of government under which one party controls political life and the state-owned means of production. The word "communism" (not capitalized) refers to a social organization in which goods are held in common or to the classless society where the state has withered away as envisaged by Communists as the end result of Communism (with a capital C).

Democratic — relating to a government in which supreme power is vested in the people and exercised by them directly or indirectly through a system of representation involving periodically held free elections.

Authoritarian — relating to concentrating political power in a leader or elite not constitutionally responsible to the people.

Totalitarian — relating to a political regime in which the individual is subordinated to the state which strictly controls all aspects of life including the economy.

Market — an area of economic activity in which buyers and sellers come together and the forces of supply and demand affect prices.

Socialist — relating to a social organization based on governmental ownership and control of the means of production and distribution of goods.

The above concepts of government and the economy could be graphed on continuums as on page 75:

The social democrats, like the liberal democrats, insist on free elections, individual freedoms, and freedom of an opposition party in a competitive political process. The liberal democrats differ by not incorporating into their ideology socialism, or public ownership, and socialist theories about imperialism. Liberal democratic spokesmen often advocate private enterprise in industry and agriculture. They may also support a wide range of government social services. There is no clear line, in practice, between liberal democratic and social democratic governments. For example, liberal democratic governments may have government ownership of major transportation and communication facilities and of public utilities. (See Box.)

In the foreign policy area the democracies usually have provisions for the legislature approving important

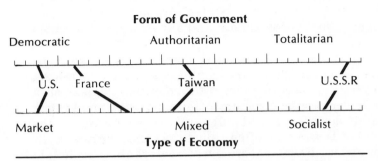

Form of Government

Democratic   Authoritarian   Totalitarian

U.S.   France   Taiwan   U.S.S.R

Market   Mixed   Socialist
Type of Economy

Note: Figure 3-1 is designed to clear up problems of definition and help in communication. Its concepts are commonly used in the U.S. media. Communists, for example, use other definitions and call their form of government socialist, which confuses the issue by hiding the fact their *political* system is controlled by a one-party "dictatorship of the proletariat," which does not allow an opposition to organize and which controls most aspects of life through its control of government. In *economic* terms the Communist governments are socialist since they also own and control economic enterprises.

The above lines measuring each nation's form of government and type of economy are illustrative only. Each political scientist would draw lines to different points on the scales, but the average would be close to the above. Other schemes are used, but the above is easily understood since it is based on the dictionary.

treaties or foreign agreements. Under the United States system formal treaties require a two-thirds vote by the Senate. The advantage of this larger than majority vote is that strong bipartisan support helps provide continuity in basic elements of foreign policy after elections and a new administration.

Under most democratic systems the legislature has an important voice in foreign policy through the power of the purse. This is true particularly in countries with large foreign aid and foreign military programs such as the United States. In the smaller democracies without such programs the focus of foreign policy is usually with the head of state, his foreign minister, and a relatively few policymakers, but basic treaties are submitted to the legislatures for their approval.

Two of the most successful applications of the

democratic ideology to international politics have been the occupation policies of the United States after World War II. The United States promoted democratic constitutions for Germany and Japan while it occupied them.

The German and Japanese democracies in the 1970s were still based on these constitutions and were firmly set in their course with no important domestic challenges to their democratic structures. Germany called its system social democracy, while Japan was dominated by the Liberal Democrats, often called the conservatives. Both countries have experienced remarkable economic expansions, and their currencies in the late 1970s were in a much stronger position than the dollar, so that the United States, their former benefactor, was able to obtain substantial loans from them to bolster the international position of the dollar. The political relationship of the United States with these two former enemies was close and friendly.

The social democrats accept many Marxist elements of Communist theory, but they do not accept the need to use force to end capitalism and establish state control of the means of production. The aim of many social democrats is to achieve state ownership and control of the means of production through winning elections. This means that an opposition party would be free to organize and promote a program. The British Labor Party does not look to Marx, but to British socialists such as Beatrice and Sydney Webb, other Fabian Society socialists, and to Harold Laski as socialist theorists. The German social democrats tend to look at Marx and to German socialists such as Kautsky as their inspiration. Many of today's social democrats, influenced by the non-Marxist theories of John Maynard Keynes, believe that government and military spending and exports stimulate the economy. They believe, moreover, the leaders of the United States and other countries supported militarism and aggressive policies in South Korea and South Vietnam for economic motives.

The ideologies of the Communists and social democrats and sometimes the Keynesians reinforce each other. On important political issues, however, Communists and social democrats are often fierce competitors, because both groups seek support of the laboring class. The social democrats fear if the Communists take over, they would suppress all opposition including that of the social democrats. The Communists know that in order to take power they must take political support away from the social democrats.

The classic clash between Communists and socialists was in the early thirties in Germany, when their political and physical battles prevented their joining to oppose Hitler. In recent years fierce civil strife in Portugal in 1975 occurred when Communists and social democrats each competed for support of workers and the military.

Since 1975 there has been a blurring of positions of the Communists and social democrats as certain West European Communist parties have supported democratic rights. In the preparation for the 1976 Berlin meeting of Communist parties called by the Soviets, the French and Italian Communist parties issued a "Eurocommunism" manifesto. At the meeting the Italian Communist leader, Berlinguer, openly criticized the 1968 Soviet invasion of Czechoslovakia. Other speakers attacked Soviet treatment of dissidents and abuse of prisoners in labor camps.[12] In March, 1977, leaders of the Spanish, French, and Italian Communist parties agreed on the "Declaration of Madrid," which supported universal suffrage, political plurality, and individual freedom. Some observers point to the past history of Communist movements which have asserted these democratic rights until they gained power, and warn that they then established a "dictatorship of the proletariat" without conventional democratic rights. They point to how Fidel Castro soon after his revolution arrested his pro-democratic supporters and began ardently supporting the Soviet Communist line.

With the new Eurocommunism tactics or basic change in philosophy, the Communist parties of France at first made marked gains in the polls. In the March, 1978, parliamentary elections in France the socialist and Communist parties came close to defeating the conservative parties. In the wake of the defeat, however, the socialists and Communists began quarreling and ended their cooperation.

The blurring of the differences between the Communist

and socialist ideologies are fascinating to political analysts. Some say the Eurocommunists' support for democratic rights is a temporary tactic like Communists have used before in Eastern Europe and elsewhere, and that they would reassert their control through the dictatorship of the proletariat if they controlled the governmental levers of power. Henry Kissinger after leaving office featured this charge in his first major TV program in January, 1978. Others point to their attack on abuses of the Communist system in Russia and Soviet distress about these attacks as evidence of Eurocommunists' sincerity.[13]

On the other side of the social democratic spectrum, the social democrats of Germany are not far from a liberal democratic position on economic issues, since they have stopped pressing for extending government ownership of the means of production. In return, German workers have achieved a major voice in business decisions of enterprises. Chancellor Helmut Schmidt, a Social Democrat, contrasted the German success with this "codetermination" system with the problems of the state owned coal mines under a socialist government of Britain, which had experienced serious strikes.[14]

Officials of the German social democratic governments do not speak in doctrinal terms on international issues. They realize that their government represents all of West Germany, and about half of the voters support the Christian Democrats and Free Democrats, who are more oriented towards private ownership and the market economy. The social democratic leaders support the present somewhat mixed economic system of Western Germany and friendship with the United States. In practice this results in close association with the United States on many foreign economic issues. Thus, the foreign policy speeches of the social democratic officials do not reflect the anticapitalist rhetoric and views that many other social democratic speeches and policies do.[15]

The biggest inroads of social democratic theory have been made in the Third World of developing nations. Leaders of these nations have taken control of their governments, often by military coups. In the process of extending their power and influence, they have extended the sphere of state control of the economy and put friends and supporters in control of state owned industries and businesses. These new leaders often use social democratic theories as tools to justify their control, even though their governments are authoritarian and not democratic. They attack the past history of colonialism to support their case that industries should not be turned back to the private sector and domination by former colonial business interests. In Asia, this pattern has appeared in Indonesia, India, Pakistan, Burma, and Ceylon. Many of the authoritarian Black governments of Africa also subscribe to the social democratic theory that capitalism leads to exploitation.

On the other hand, there are a number of countries such as the avowed socialist government of Singapore, which welcome private investment. Leaders of such countries realize that private firms have the technology, funds, and selling organizations necessary to create efficient business enterprises. The governments of developing countries, and even of developed countries, do not have the expertise to produce a vast array of products that can compete with production of private firms.

The social democratic ideology in practice, therefore, on one end of the spectrum blends in with the Communist ideology and on the other end with the enterprise philosophy of the liberal democratic states.

Religious Ideologies

Religious ideologies have had a major impact on the international scene since World War II by reinforcing nationalisms. At the end of the 1970s a nationalist-religious ideology emerged in Iran which brought down the Shah's powerful government, challenged a superpower, and threatened to undermine the economies of the major industrial nations of the world. Ayatollah Khomeini, a Shiite Muslim leader, from his refuge in Paris agitated the Iranian mullahs and street crowds into open rebellion, forcing the Shah to flee the country. The Ayatollah entered Iran in triumph with millions demonstrating in the streets. Within a few months he had established a strict Islamic, authoritarian government with him at the head.

In the fall of 1979 when the Shah entered the United States temporarily for treatment of cancer, militant supporters of the Ayatollah stormed the American Embassy and captured over 50 diplomatic hostages, insisting as a condition for their release that the United States return the Shah for trial in Iran. The captors continued to insist on the Shah's return even after he left the United States and settled in Egypt.

Ayatollah Khomeini, the acknowledged leader of the captors, and his Revolutionary Council propagated a blend of conservative Islam, extreme nationalism calling for cutting ties with Western nations, and socialism or government ownership of leading parts of the economy. He expressed his belief the world was dominated by perhaps 50,000 government leaders who exploit the masses, and that the masses should either force their governments to end this exploitation or destroy them. He continued during 1980 to challenge and defy the United States on the hostage issue even after it gained support of unanimous decisions of the U.N. Security Council, the World Court, and the U.N. General Assembly.

The depth of passions in Iran was demonstrated by militants of the Islam faith who paraded in long white shirts symbolizing their willingness to die for Khomeini and his principles. The Shiite faith is based on a tradition of martyrdom beginning with the assassination of Ali, Mohammed's cousin and son-in-law who had been picked by the Shiites to succeed Mohammed. The Islamic suspicion of corrupt modern influences supported Iranian socialists' suspicion of large industrial firms and products from capitalist states. Khomeini's influence extended in Middle East countries with most of the world's oil resources.

Only extreme economic and political pressures finally forced the Iranian Government to negotiate return of the hostages. These included loss of territory from the Iran-Iraq War that began in 1980, the loss of oil export revenues, the freezing of many billions of dollars by the United States, and disapproval of the world's diplomatic community of Iran's action on the hostages. As President Reagan took the oath of office, the Iranian Government finally released the hostages in return for U.S. unblocking funds Iran needed to continue the war.

Religion has also joined with nationalism in other areas of the world to form powerful and dynamic ideologies. As has been noted, Jewish nationalism is strongly entwined with the Jewish faith, which led to the establishment of Israel. The conflict of Jewish and Arab nationalisms, both reinforced by religion, has been at the center of the Middle East wars since World War II. Irish-Catholic nationalism has kept Northern Ireland in a turmoil since World War I. As the 1980s began there was no relief in sight for Britain in its efforts to suppress that rebellion. The nationalist-religious conflicts of "Christian" and Muslim movements kept Lebanon in a turmoil into the 1980s.

Recognizing that nationalisms joined with certain religions and Communism in various areas of the world have elements in common helps in analyzing international politics.[16] These movements draw support from other countries, they can promote terrorism, and they inspire a revolutionary fanaticism. Also, these religious movements, just as the Communist movements, often split into opposing factions. For example, some devout Islamic groups support a political conservatism tied to traditional forms of social relationships such as in Egypt, Saudi Arabia, and Jordan. Other Islamic groups have embraced a radical socialism that challenges the world order, such as Iran, Syria, and Libya. The Soviet authorities are concerned that their Moslem minorities want to embrace an Islam community that extends beyond the Soviet Union.[17]

To understand, therefore, the actions and goals of religious zealots, we must examine and understand other ideologies, such as nationalism and socialism, which have been grafted to religious roots. We must also examine various foreign policy strategies, which are covered in the next chapter.

Colonialism and Other Ideologies

There are many other ideologies and beliefs that have influenced foreign policy. In the 100 years before World War II, support of colonialism was a major factor in foreign affairs. Leaders of major powers believed that acquiring and retaining a colonial empire was important for national power. During this era Britain, France, Belgium, and the Netherlands as major colonial powers consolidated their empires, and before the Great Depression of the 1930s they prospered. Before World War II the Axis powers, Germany, Italy, and Japan — who considered themselves the "have nots" in colonies, territory, and resources — tried to expand their empires in Europe, Asia, and Africa and in the process triggered World War II. For a while their success in avoiding a challenge from the "haves" was due in part to the bad conscience of groups in the colonial powers who thought the Axis had a case for acquiring more territory and resources.

World War II sounded the death knell for colonialism. Most colonial people, particularly in Asia, achieved new responsibilities under the Japanese during the disruptions caused by the war. In the years after the war there was a tremendous move toward independence among the former colonies. Often the process involved wars and internal conflicts. The ideology of colonialism became unpopular and was submerged by what one might call an ideology of anti-colonialism, in many areas reinforced by new nationalisms and by Communist and socialist ideologies. These ideologies blamed the low levels of political and economic development entirely on the former colonial masters.

A common denominator of the anti-colonialism was the resentment of colonial people of being treated as inferiors. Most of the leaders of the Third World countries who achieved independence after World War II can remember with bitterness some of the colonial experiences. Their difficulties in getting a good education and responsible jobs in government and business contrasted with the high standards of living of the colonial masters, who more often than not had many servants from the local populace. The fact that after World War II and after independence representatives of foreign business firms in the former colonies still could afford servants and a much higher standard of living than many of the politically conscious local people, added credibility to the Communist and socialist doctrines that foreign business firms were establishing a new method of exploitation called neo-colonialism. Arguments that foreign business brings modern production and managerial techniques to backward countries and hires and trains local people in modern methods were not very persuasive against such obvious examples of relative wealth of foreigners.

Thus, anti-colonialism and a fundamental suspicion of close business ties with industrial nations is a strong image among leaders and policymakers of the Third World. It provides a basic advantage to socialist and Communist ideology in world politics.

As noted above, many leaders and policymakers of Third World countries in their economic policies welcome private investment and foreign firms, but this economic pragmatism often does not affect their political rhetoric and their political tendencies to side against rich and powerful countries who were formerly colonial masters. The legacy of bitterness from the colonial era thus affects actions of policymakers of the Third World even though they might prefer democracy and capitalism rather than socialism and authoritarian government.

The Communists keep the Western industrial powers off balance by propaganda directed against their colonial history and particularly against its racist elements. The power of anti-racist ideologies in foreign affairs when joined with anti-colonialism should not be underestimated. The fact that over 95 percent of the colonial areas existing after World War II have become independent has little effect on the deep opposition to remaining colonial regimes, particularly in South Africa. The new states formed out of African empires have united in the U.N. with other developing countries to condemn apartheid, a racist ideology of white supremacy, in the Republic of South Africa and succeeded in blocking its government from attending sessions of the U.N. They also succeeded with British support in mounting economic sanctions against the British colony of Rhodesia (Zimbabwe) and an arms embargo against the Republic of South Africa for apartheid policies. The pressures helped Foreign Secretary Carrington negotiate a new Black-dominated government for Zimbabwe in 1980.[18]

Racist ideas and even ideologies, apart from the above, are still prevalent in other areas. There is a strong anti-

Chinese feeling in some areas of Southeast Asia such as Burma, Indonesia, and the Philippines, where strong Chinese influence in business is resented. There is still some dislike of the Japanese in Asia because of their oppressive policies in the World War II era and before. To some degree there is a racist anti-European and anti-American feeling in former colonies of the Far East.

Other unique racial, religious, or cultural ideologies may affect foreign policy issues among certain countries. Diplomats try to avoid complicating negotiations with ideological heat, realizing the potential dangers of certain ideas when exploited by unscrupulous leaders. We will now look at the foreign policy strategies of policymakers, which usually are not tied tightly to any particular ideology we have been examining.

Summary

Various nationalisms are the most powerful ideologies in international politics. The fact that leaders on both sides of international issues appeal to the "national interest" is one illustration of the strength of national feelings. Professor Morgenthau's framework for analyzing international affairs is based on an assertion that leaders naturally select policies that achieve the most power for their nations.

German nationalism was at the root of the two world wars of this century, and a concern about its revival helps explain the East-West contests centering on Germany since World War II. German nationalism has now been diverted into the building of the European Community.

The 1980s opened with the unsolved nationalistic dispute between Jews and Arabs over the control of the West Bank. This poisoned political relations throughout the Middle East. In East Asia the unsettled issue of how and when Taiwan was to be united with the mainland was alleviated after the death of Chairman Mao, when a more patient leadership took over control. The new leaders, however, did not renounce a right to use force against Taiwan to reunify it with the mainland.

Communism is another powerful ideology that is

revolutionary in nature. It often joins with nationalism in appealing to leaders of new nations who blame former colonial and capitalist powers for their troubles. In the West, doctrinal differences between Communists and Social Democrats have become blurred by Eurocommunists, who try to straddle social democracy and Communism. Religious ideologies also have contributed to conflicts in the world arena. At the close of the 1970s Khomeini's Islamic supporters overthrew the Shah of Iran and threatened other oil powers in the region. Blends of nationalism with Communism and certain religions, or conflicts among them, can generate a revolutionary radicalism. Although many diplomats try to avoid ideological debates, conflicting ideologies lie at the roots of superpower and many other conflicts on the world scene.

FOOTNOTES

1. Morgenthau, *op. cit.*, pp. 9-11 and 88-99.

2. Bernard Brodie, *War and Politics* (New York: The Macmillan Company, 1973), pp. 343-345.

3. Quincy Wright, *A Study of War* (Chicago: University of Chicago Press, 1942), Volume II, pp. 998-1011; Leon P. Baradat, *Political Ideologies — Their Origins and Impact* (Englewood Cliffs, N.J.: Prentice Hall, 1979), pp. 30-47.

4. See Marshall Green, "Reminiscences: Diplomatic Lessons Learned the Hard Way," *Foreign Service Journal,* February 1977, p. 15.

5. London *Economist,* August 28, 1976, p. 43.

6. Melvin Croan, "New Country, Old Nationality," *Foreign Policy,* Winter 1979-1980, pp. 142-160.

7. See George Antonius, *The Arab Awakening* (Beirut: Khayt's College Book Cooperative, 1955). S.A. Morrison, *Middle East Tensions* (New York: Harper and Brothers Publishers, 1954).

8. ESCO Foundation for Palestine, *A Study of Jewish, Arab, and British Policies* (New Haven: Yale University Press, 1947), pp. 302, 497.

9. Frank Ching, "A Most Envied Province," *Foreign Policy,* Fall 1979, pp. 122-146.

10. Richard G. Head, Frisco W. Short, and Robert C. McFarlane, *Crisis Resolution: Presidential Decision Making in the Mayaguez and Korean Confrontations,* (Boulder, Colorado: Westview Press, 1978).

11. Rand Corporation researchers who carried out extensive interrogations of North Vietnamese insurgents stress how powerful the anti-colonial themes were in enlisting support in the South for the Communist cause. See for example the following Rand (Santa Monica)

reports: John C. Donnell, "Viet Cong Recruitment: Why and How Men Join," RM-5486-1-ISA/ARPA, December, 1967; W.P. Davison and J.J. Zasloff, "A Profile of Viet Cong Cadres," RM-4983-1-ISA/ARPA, June, 1966; Frank Denton, "Volunteers for the Viet Cong," RM-5647-ISA/ARPA, September, 1968; Stephen T. Hosmer, Konrad Kellen, Brian M. Jenkins, "The Fall of South Vietnam: Statements by Vietnamese Military and Civilian Leaders," R-2208-OSD(HIST), December, 1978; and J.S. Zasloff, "Origins of the Insurgency," RM-5163/2-ISA/ARPA, May, 1968.

12. *Washington Post*, July 1, 1976, p. 1.

13. Roy Godson, Stephen Haseler, *Eurocommunism* (New York: St. Martin's Press, 1978; Rudolf L. Tokes, *Eurocommunism and Detente* (New York: New York University Press, 1978); Wolfgang Leonhard, *Eurocommunism — Challenge for East and West* (New York: Holt, Rinehart, and Winston, 1978); R. Neal Tannahill, *The Communist Parties of Western Europe* (Westport, Conn.: Greenwood Press, 1978).

14. See London *Economist*, September 4, 1976, pp. 82-87.

15. Werner J. Feld (ed.), *The Foreign Policies of West European Socialist Parties* (New York: Praeger Publishers, 1978).

16. Although many political scientists classify Communism as a religion, I use the traditional definition of religion which incorporates belief in a Supreme Being and thus excludes Communism.

17. Helene Carrere d'Encausse, *Decline of an Empire* (New York: Newsweek Books, 1979).

18. David Ottaway, "Africa: U.S. Policy Eclipse," *Foreign Affairs*, 1979, pp. 637-658.

4

Foreign Policy Strategies

Foreign policy strategies are general guides for action that policymakers use to achieve their goals in international politics. It would be impossible to trace the origin of some strategies like power politics and its associated idea of balance of power. These strategies appear to be a part of human nature and probably originated under different names with mankind's first societies. Policymakers often use a generally accepted foreign policy strategy to help sell a foreign policy. For example, presidents commonly support increased budget requests for the military with the need to maintain a "balance of power" in Europe or with different words, to maintain a "credible deterrent" against an attack. Dr. Henry Kissinger uses terms like "equilibrium" or structure for peace and order, which are based on the concept of a balance of power.[1] Following is a discussion of major foreign policy strategies which have influenced policymakers since World War II.

ʼower Politics

Government leaders and analysts traditionally have used concepts of power politics in approaching international issues. Such leaders assess the power of the countries concerned to determine what elements of power could be used to achieve their goals. These power brokers generally deny the relevance of morals or international law elements in the international arena because they would say there is no international community to enforce standards of conduct.

As used in this text, the term power politics is limited to such a nationalist oriented strategy as distinguished from an internationalist's approach, who would recognize limits imposed by international law or by an international body such as one of the U.N. organs. There is no necessary association between the strategy of power politics and most of the ideologies of the previous chapter. However, ardent nationalists and also Communists naturally would put their ideologies above others and use the strategy of power politics. They seldom would recognize international law and other constraints, except perhaps for tactical reasons.

Power as the "possession of control, authority, or influence over others" by definition is a central element of all politics. The dictionary defines politics as the "art or science concerned with guiding or influencing government policy" and thus implies the use of power. Hans Morgenthau, as indicated in the previous chapter, bases his analysis of international politics on the propositions that all politics is a struggle for power, and that power can be defined as anything that maintains the control of man over man. Even internationalists such as Presidents Harry Truman have used elements of power in their policies, and for this reason Professor Morgenthau and others assume all nations base their policies on power politics. I will maintain, however, that other strategies also have strongly influenced decisions of policymakers.

At first glance the elements of international power seem to be self-evident. In international affairs military strength is often equated with power, particularly in the pre-World War II era. It was relatively easy then to assess the size of national armies and the quality of their equipment. Many still believe that nations with the most military power, conventional and nuclear, can have the most influence on international issues. Others would say economic elements also are important.

There are many indexes available of military and economic power to help in such a simplistic assessment. The problem is that powerful nations have been frustrated and stymied by nations which are much weaker by such conventional measures. North Vietnam's defeat of U.S. and South Vietnamese forces, and Egyptian President Sadat's expulsion of thousands of Soviet advisors in the early 1970s are examples of successes by comparatively weak nations. What has happened is that the reluctance of nuclear powers to start an atomic conflict has brought economic and psychological elements of power to a position of greater importance.

The analyst of international politics then can shift the focus to such factors as the degree of support for certain ideologies, and to the importance of certain foreign policy strategies, as well as objective factors which can be used to implement policies. This, of course, is the basic approach of this text which is largely concerned with the application of these elements to international power politics. The text also focuses, however, on the influence of international organizations and internationalist and other policies which are not encompassed by the Morgenthau definition of power politics.

Power politics since World War II has been dominated by two types. The first is a balance of power strategy which implies a defensive use of power by nations to maintain an equilibrium to discourage aggression. The other, which I designate as the world policeman strategy, implies a more active policy of using a country's power to dominate an area of the world, to deter or repel aggression there, and to maintain a dominant position.

Before World War II Germany and Japan used power politics in a third type of strategy, an imperialistic strategy, to bring vast areas of the world under their direct control. Many observers accuse Russia also of imperialism in Eastern Europe after World War II. At the end of 1979 when Russia moved over 100,000 troops into Afghanistan to help a Marxist leader under Russian influence take over control, these charges of imperialism were renewed by Western observers. Also Vietnam was accused of imperialism in its invasion of Cambodia during 1979.

The policies of power politics could be pictured on the following continuum with one type of policy merging into the other:

Power Politics

Defensive	Offensive	
Balance of Power	World Policeman Hegemonism	Imperialism

└─┴─┘

The Communist aggressors normally tried to defend themselves against charges of imperialism by accusing the United States and others of trying to subvert the countries which are being assisted (attacked) by the Communists.

Not being bound by Communists' concepts and their dictionary helps non-Communists see how Russia through troops and the threat of military intervention has continued to dominate Eastern Europe in an imperialistic type of policy. The Eastern European Bloc almost always votes with the Soviet Union in the U.N. and backs its foreign policy moves. Their economies are also tied closely to Russia's through trade and other arrangements. Nevertheless, few Third World representatives, because of persuasiveness of Soviet propaganda, accuse the Russians of imperialism. The Chinese Communists, however, have found a word for it — hegemonism — and they apply this to Russia, Vietnam, and also by implication to the United States.

Apart from the invasion of Afghanistan and Cambodia, the terms "balance of power" and "world policeman" generally described power politics of most of the 1960s and 1970s, and leaders who might have had imperialistic ambitions were contained.

Balance of Power. Many believe the balance of power is inherent in the nation-state system. Thus, countries form alliances naturally to prevent an aggressive power or another alliance from gaining a superior position where it could take over other countries and increase its power even more. Professor Hans Morgenthau in his *Politics Among Nations* states:

> The balance of power and policies aimed at its preservation are not only inevitable, but an essential stabilizing factor in a society of sovereign nations.

He sees the process as similar to that in nature in which, if one element threatens to destroy other parts of a system, other parts of the system mobilize or react in a way that protects it from destruction.[2]

The term balance of power has been used in Europe for several centuries to describe a strategy of diplomacy. The principle is older than the term, and the recorded history of wars has been one of alliances and counter alliances to keep a balance of power. It is a well-known principle of political life that people tend to take advantage of those who do not have the power to defend their interests. Unions are formed to give workers bargaining power against the employer. An opposition party is needed to protect against the excessive power of one-party rule. Courts and legislatures are needed to protect the individual from the power of the executive. Similarly, alliances are needed to protect weaker nations from a stronger nation or another alliance.

The minimum aim of the balance of power strategy is protection — the same aim as collective security. A collective security policy, however, depends on cooperation of states in decisions of a world organization to protect every member. The balance of power policy may involve formal alliances or commitments by individual nations. The alliances, such as NATO, may involve a joint military command.

The United States considers a balance of power strategy for Western Europe under NATO as fundamental to U.S. foreign policy. Sometimes the concept is expressed in the idea of maintaining a credible deterrent to Soviet aggression in Europe. Major United States efforts to establish a balance of power in Europe after World War II started with aid programs including the Marshall Plan of 1948. The target of the Marshall Plan was "hunger, poverty, desperation, and chaos" in Europe and revival of a working world economy, which depended on Europe. Policymakers selling the program appealed to generosity and other motives, but support also came from a desire to block the extension of Soviet power in Europe. Dean Acheson, Under Secretary of State in 1948, explains this motive as follows in his *Present at the Creation:*

> I have probably made as many speeches and answered as many questions about the Marshall Plan as any man alive, except possibly Paul Hoffman, and what citizens and the representatives in Congress alike always wanted to learn in the last analysis was how Marshall aid operated to block the extension of Soviet power and the acceptance of Communist economic and political organization and alignment.[3]

The Marshall Plan was followed by the North Atlantic Alliance (NATO), which was strongly supported by both Democratic and Republican members of the Senate and in fact was initiated by Senator Vandenburg's Resolution calling for association with collective arrangements for defense. (See Chapter 8.) The President and his policymakers were concerned about the pressures of the Soviet Union demonstrated by the Berlin Blockade and the takeover of Czechoslovakia in 1948. They feared the Soviets would move into the "vacuum in central and eastern Europe where German power had once prevailed."[4]

The Senate approved the Treaty decisively by a vote of 82 to 13 in July 1949. In 1950 Secretary Acheson entered into secret conversations in NATO to include West German participation in defense, which Truman considered as necessary to make NATO effective.[5] This policy of maintaining an economic and military balance of power in Europe against the threat of Russia has continued to be the cornerstone of U.S. foreign policy.

Russian leaders also saw maintaining a balance of power in Europe as a major foreign policy objective. The Treaty of Friendship, Cooperation, and Mutual Assistance (The Warsaw Pact) with the Eastern European satellites was signed on May 14, 1955, as their counter to the NATO Treaty and in particular to the admission of West Germany as a full fledged member to NATO on May 5, 1955. Many of the Warsaw Pact provisions are patterned after NATO. Khrushchev reports in his memoirs the balance of power motive for the Warsaw Pact:

It was perfectly clear to everyone that until our former allies, who had organized NATO, agreed to a peace treaty, our troops would have to remain in the German Democratic Republic. After all, the West had a fairly sizable force stationed in West Germany, and we had to preserve the balance of power.[6]

After the 1950s the United States drifted away from supporting the idea of collective security under the U.N. and relied almost exclusively on power politics to support those countries it considered important to its own security and well being. In the 1970s after the bitter Vietnam War it further restricted the number of countries to which it made priority commitments. This balance of power policy restricting major U.S. commitments to only its most important allies could be called *selective security* in contrast to the collective security policy under the U.N. framework.

A theoretical argument for selective security can be made that neither Western Europe or the United States has the power or political will for a collective security policy to prevent or repel attacks on all the 155 countries of the world and that, therefore, the U.S. should make commitments only to countries where it is in its "vital interest." Nevertheless, it is hard to define in precise economic or political terms where one draws the line. Why should the United States support Berlin, which has become of less psychological importance in recent years and whose economic importance is relatively small, compared to important countries of the Far East or the Middle East? Should Yugoslavia, a Communist country of no great strategic value but major psychological importance, be supported from an outside attack? Why should the United States under selective security support Israel, which has a minimal economic importance, compared to that of the Arab opponents with the tremendous oil reserves that are vital to both Western Europe and important for the United States? In other words, selective security, with the image of weighing material and political elements on a scale to obtain a balance, in itself is not a useful strategy to define the rationale for U.S. foreign policy.

If the proponents of selective security are ever faced with an aggressor such as Hitler who would want to pick off countries one by one, these advocates would find it very difficult to rationalize defending certain European countries, particularly if the threat of nuclear war were involved. If such proponents argued for keeping as a deterrent only those commitments to Western Europe and Japan under the U.S. alliance system, they would find it difficult to show why commitments under the NATO Treaty and the non-treaty commitment with Israel are more binding than formal commitments under collective defense agreements with countries in the Far East (Philippines, Australia, New Zealand, Korea, and Thailand), and Latin America, and in fact, under the overall collective security commitment of the United States to nations of the U.N. Charter.

World Policeman. In the Vietnam War the United States took more and more of a leading role until it found itself obtaining only nominal help from its other allies. I categorize this policy as that of a world policeman in Southeast Asia. President Johnson and his advisors were greatly influenced by the origin of World War II. He became convinced that only by the United States stopping aggression in South Vietnam, which was supplied by Russia and China, could the security of the United States be maintained.[7]

The U.S. allies did not see the situation in this light and sat back while the United States assumed the burden of protecting South Vietnam. United States civilian and military leaders at that time thought the United States with its vastly superior power could force North Vietnam to withdraw to its own borders and to forego trying to take over the South by force. The U.S. military, still unhappy about the difficulties of working with other nations in Korea to oppose the North Korean aggression in 1950, thought it would be easier with the United States' superior forces to bring the war to a quick end without the political struggle it would have taken to get other countries to help repel aggression. The reasons for the failure of the Vietnam policy are complicated and, as we have already noted, involved ideological factors, but the U.S. policy there illustrates the essentially unilateral policy categorized as that of a "world policeman."

President Jimmy Carter in the first years of his Administration beginning with his inaugural speech emphasized internationalist aims such as limiting nuclear arms, reducing the military budget, and extending the areas of cooperation with Russia. However, by the third and fourth year of his first term his views had been seasoned by images of superpower rivalry, and he was drifting into power politics. Even before the Afghanistan crisis he called for an increased military budget, preparations for establishing a new family of tactical missiles in Europe, and the initiation of the tremendously expensive MX nuclear weapons. The factors that went into the Soviet decision to invade Afghanistan in December, 1979, are not known. Some observers, including the Soviets, suggested the above power moves by the United States played a part. Even if the U.S. policies were not a factor and it was a simple case of Russian Communist aggression to take advantage of a target of opportunity, a Russian reluctance to back down in the superpower game of power politics probably played a part in the Russian decision not to withdraw all of its troops from Afghanistan.

The change in Carter's policies toward a world policeman role in the Mideast coincided with the apparent increase in the influence of Zbigniew Brzezinski, the hardline adviser on national security matters. Secretary of State Vance, who seemed more oriented toward an internationalist position, resigned in the spring of 1980 in protest over a world policeman type of decision to use a small military force to invade Teheran to take back the American hostages. This was probably only one of the elements in Vance's decision as evidenced in his first major speech after his resignation which was given at Harvard's commencement. The speech emphasizes fundamental elements of the internationalists' point of view, as described in the next section, which was in contrast to that of the power brokers. (See box.)

Although power politics concepts have been the most commonly used tools of policymakers and analysts, there are serious problems in their use. There is an implication in the balance of power and world policeman ideas that as long as the basic balance of power is not upset, it is legitimate for countries to act against weaker countries. Some observers implied during the Vietnam War that Vietnam or China should be permitted to subvert or dominate weaker countries of Southeast Asia if this would not basically affect the world balance of power between the United States, China, Western Europe, Japan, and the Soviet Union. How then would one draw the line between this and the type of piecemeal aggression that led to World War II?

Also, not only do the elements of power keep changing but they are not addible. One cannot add nuclear weapons, GNP, and geographical position to get an index of power that can be used to determine if a balance exists. The United States, the most powerful nuclear and economic power in the world, attempted to save the government of South Vietnam from attack from the North, but was defeated by a much weaker power as calculated in conventional balance of power terms. The fact that major elements are not really addible, even to achieve commonly agreed subtotals of major weapons systems, contributes to different interpretations of a balance and the insecurity that leads to arms races.

Moreover, other political and even moral attitudes do affect foreign policies. The United States dominated Japan after World War II. A balance of power analyst in looking back at history might conclude that the United States gave Japan a peace treaty restoring its sovereignty so it could be a factor in a balance of power against the Peoples' Republic of China. However, such an analyst would have a hard time explaining why the United States' occupation under General MacArthur insisted on a provision in the Japanese constitution that Japan would not create armed forces, and why the United States continues to press Japan to forego manufacture of nuclear weapons. Japan's position is very weak in comparison with Chinese military manpower and nuclear weapons, and the U.S. policy to keep Japan militarily weak cannot be explained in traditional balance of power terms.

Although balance of power and world policeman concepts by themselves do not provide an adequate guide for policy decision and understanding international politics, they do assist in analysis. Policymakers in presenting intelligence reports and budget requests to other officials or to legislatures often make national balance sheets of military, economic, and other elements of power. In designing policies, policymakers are forced to estimate the strength of opponents and allies and work

Cyrus Vance's Valedictory

Excerpts from a speech by Cyrus Vance at Harvard's Commencement in June, 1980, soon after his resignation as Secretary of State,[8] probably reflect differences that developed between him and Zbigniew Brzezinski, the President's national security adviser.

It seems to me that much of the current dissatisfaction with the world and our role in it rests on certain fallacies ... The first fallacy is that a single strategy — a master plan — will yield the answers to each and every foreign policy decision we face. Whatever value that approach may have had in a bipolar world, it now serves us badly ... Given the complexity of the world to which we have fallen heir, the effect of a single strategy is to blur this complexity and to divide nations everywhere into friends and enemies.

A second widely accepted fallacy is the fear of negotiation, the worry that somehow we will always come out second-best in any bargain.

A third myth is that there is an incompatibility between ... human rights and the pursuit of interests. Certainly the pursuit of human rights must be managed in a practical way. ... We know from our own national experience that the drive for human freedom has tremendous force and vitality. .... In a profound sense then, our ideals and our interests coincide.

Further is the dangerous fallacy of the military solutions to nonmilitary problems. It arises in particularly acute form at time of frustration, when the processes of negotiation are seen as slow-moving and tedious. American military power is essential to maintaining the global military balance. Our defense forces must be modernized — and they will be. But increased military power is a basis, not a substitute, for diplomacy. . . . .

Finally, there is the pervasive fallacy that America could have the power to order the world just the way we want it to be. It assumes, for example, that we could dominate the Soviet Union — that we could prevent it from being a superpower — if we chose to do so. This obsolete idea has more to do with nostalgia than with present-day reality.

with elements of national power. To achieve security or a military equilibrium policymakers naturally try to prevent another country from organizing an alliance and taking control of an area that threatens the economic or military position of their country or that of a close ally. This leads to power politics. It also leads to tensions and conflicts. Just as it is impossible to draw the line between offensive and defensive weapons, it is impossible to draw a line between a defensive balance of power and a more offensive world policeman type of power politics. Thus, superpower conflicts and rivalries continue to threaten today's world just as war has always cursed society.

Internationalism

The internationalists aim to promote cooperation among nations under the U.N. or a similar world organization. One of their favorite words is "interdependence," which implies the nations of the world to survive must work together for peace and economic well being. Two major categories of their anti-war strategies are "collective security" and "U.N. peacemaking." Both of these philosophies imply action under a world organization, usually the U.N., rather than through power politics and alliances among nations.

Since these strategies are ideas in the minds of policymakers, who are human, there are no pure models of behavior to observe. For example, internationalist leaders know the limitations of the U.N. because of the veto and the need to coordinate policies of many states, and they often use power politics to achieve goals when the U.N. machinery is not adequate. A small minority, including the World Federalists, are holding out for a world organization stronger than the U.N., but they have little influence among policymakers, so their views are not analyzed below.

Following is a description of two major categories of internationalist strategies:

Collective Security. The slogan and idea of collective security was popular among policymakers in the decade after World War II. Many of them blamed that war on the weakness of the League of Nations and its failure to support its ideal of collective security. The League failed to impose sanctions against Japan when it took over Manchuria and continued invading China during the 1930s. The League did levy economic sanctions against Italy, but two foreign ministers — Hoare of England and Laval of France — undermined the League's effort by a secret agreement, later revealed to the press, to grant some of Mussolini's demands for territory in Ethiopia. The League completely failed to cope with Hitler's brutal campaign to subjugate Europe by picking off countries one by one. Therefore, the ideal of collective security in a stronger world organization was foremost in the minds of those designing the Charter of the United Nations.

President Truman was determined not to repeat the failure of the League to live up to its ideals of collective security, and he proudly states in his memoirs that his first decision as president was to confirm the San Francisco Conference would be held to adopt a U.N. Charter as President Roosevelt had directed. Truman adds, "It was of supreme importance that we build an organization to keep the future peace of the world." President Truman took a personal interest in the Charter negotiations, briefing the delegates, talking by phone with congressional delegates during the Conference, and discussing the conference each day with Secretary of State Stettinius who headed the U.S. delegation.[9]

President Truman was responsible for the Marshall Plan, NATO, the revival of Germany, and many other policies relating to power politics and balance of power ideas, but his administration also supported an active policy in the United Nations. A few months after the ratification of the U.N. Charter the United States raised a major fuss in the Security Council on Russia's failure to keep its promise to withdraw from Northern Iran after the War. In 1947 the U.N., under Truman, led the move to get the U.N. Security Council and General Assembly to set up a committee to investigate the Communist insurgency in Greece, which was supported by its Communist neighbors. The U.N. General Assembly with United States support was the major policy body in the Palestine question and in the establishment of the State of Israel in 1948. (See Chapter 9.)

When the Korean War broke out, Truman's first decision was to ask for an emergency session of the U.N. Security Council. Truman states in his memoirs that in the first policy meeting he chaired with top officials of the State Department and the Defense Department, "There was no suggestion from anyone that either the United Nations or the United States could back away from it. This was the test of all the talk of the last five years of collective security."[10] At this meeting he instructed the military chiefs to prepare orders to use American units if the U.N. should call for action against North Korea. As noted in Chapter 12 the United Nations recommended that members provide assistance to South Korea through a unified command under the command of the United States, which was authorized to fly the U.N. flag.

Korean War

The Korean War broke out shortly after I joined the Department of State. I remember discussing this with some of my young colleagues at the time, who were uncertain of what the United States would do and should do about the North Korean attack. They questioned whether it was in our national interest to defend a small country from such an attack, and in fact whether we were able to. They wondered if this was a feint to distract us from Europe where our major interests were. I tended to take a simple "collective security" view toward the conflict and assumed that President Truman had meant what he said in previous policy statements about our commitments under the U.N. I was, therefore, not the least bit surprised at his actions to repel the aggression under the U.N. flag.

The point of the above is to illustrate that President Truman took the ideas of collective security seriously, and that many of his policies can be understood if one keeps this in mind. It is interesting to note that on U.N. policymaking matters President Truman was the responsible policymaker and decision maker. Dean Acheson, his Secretary of State, was quite critical of the U.N. regarding it as "legacy of the Nineteenth Century."[11] Nevertheless, Acheson followed orders in areas of U.N. policy.

A major problem with the collective security concept arose in the 1960s when the "collective" part of the slogan became lost as the United States took the lead in military action in Vietnam, with relatively minor parts played by other major allies — Australia, New Zealand, Thailand, and Korea. Even much of the effort of these latter countries was financed by the United States. The "Vietnamization" policy was started late in the war to let South Vietnam learn to use the advanced equipment introduced by the United States and to take on the major share of defense against the North Vietnamese invasion. Nevertheless, the fact that "collective" security was erroneously applied to what was almost a bilateral U.S.-South Vietnamese effort not under the U.N., and the fact that the United States and South Vietnam suffered a military and diplomatic defeat, have tarnished the concept of collective security to such an extent that it is rarely used as a slogan now in the United States.

Professors have attacked the ideals of collective security on a theoretical basis pointing out that sovereign countries are very reluctant to go to war to protect other countries' interests, and, therefore, the ideals of collective security as embodied in the United Nations Charter are unlikely ever to be achieved. The extreme ideal of collective security would require the world organization to have enough military support or power to defeat aggression by any individual country. Since the world is composed of sovereign states, no major state is likely in the foreseeable future to turn over its control of military power and sovereignty to a world organization.

U.N. Peacemaking. The U.N. peacemaking strategy, which evolved in later years, is based on the idea of the U.N. exerting moral and diplomatic pressures against an

Author on diplomatic mission in Israel in 1958.

Israel's Realpolitik

After the Suez Canal incident, from 1957 to 1959, I was assigned to the American Embassy in Tel Aviv, Israel. I lived in a neighborhood of Israeli officers including Aric Sharon, one of Israeli's foremost generals, later Minister of Defense. I had many personal discussions with Israeli friends about the Eisenhower-Dulles policy to oppose Britain, France, and Israel and support Nasser in the Suez Canal crisis. I tried without success to explain the rationale for Dulles' policy by saying that the United States in line with the U.N. Charter opposed aggression against a country, even when that aggression was committed by allies. I pleaded with the Israelis to say they could understand the position even without agreeing to it. I never had any success whatsoever with Israelis in even getting them to say they could "understand" the argument. I could, of course, "understand" their opposition to U.S. pressure on them to withdraw from the Sinai since they were surrounded by hostile Arab states and they were threatened by terrorist attacks.

aggressor and forming lightly armed "peacekeeping" forces rather than regular military units. This is in line with Chapters V to VIII of the U.N. Charter which authorize the Security Council to use a wide range of measures ranging from conciliation to the use of armed forces to restore the peace.

President Eisenhower and Secretary of State Dulles used the peacemaking strategy effectively in the Suez Canal crisis, which began in the summer of 1956 when President Nasser of Egypt nationalized the Suez Canal. In September, France secretly initiated with Israel and Britain plans to regain control of the Canal by force. French leaders resented President Nasser's backing of the Arab insurrection in Algiers, and they were apprehensive about his control over this key waterway.

From the beginning Eisenhower and Dulles were furious at the Israeli, British, and French aggression which violated the U.N. Charter. They immediately drafted a strong speech opposing the action and demanding a withdrawal of the forces. By November 2 the General Assembly, by an overwhelming vote, supported the U.S. resolution urging a cease fire and withdrawal of all foreign forces from the area.[12]

On November 4 a Canadian resolution was approved requesting the U.N. Secretary General to make plans within 48 hours for an Emergency Force to separate the combatants. On November 5 the Assembly established the U.N. Command.

Prime Minister Eden faced with the U.N. resolutions charging Britain with aggression, the strong opposition of the United States, uproar in the opposition Labor Party, the prospects of no oil through the blocked Suez Canal, and a need for U.S. assistance terminated the venture and later resigned.

Since 1970, the General Assembly and Security Council also played a peacemaking role in putting pressure on India to withdraw its troops after attacking East Pakistan, which later became Bangladesh. U.N. organizations helped resettle 10 million refugees who fled in terror to India by facilitating their return to Bangladesh after the war. The U.N. has also played a similar role in Middle East peacekeeping after 1973 by providing approximately 7,000 troops to help keep the truce between Israel, Egypt, and Syria. Moreover, it played a similar role plus that of a mediator in the difficult Cyprus conflict of 1974 which threatened to develop into a war between Greece and Turkey. (See Chapter 12.)

The above "peacemaking" efforts do not come about by the U.N.'s using superior force against the aggressor as envisaged in the U.N. Charter but rather by a complicated series of discussions, negotiations, and provision of lightly armed forces to maintain a truce. This is a slow political process that takes weeks of debate. Those who would support the U.N. efforts point out it has been relatively successful, particularly in comparison with the costly U.S. power politics of the Vietnam War, which ended in defeat.

Neutralism

Neutrality implies staying out of wars, and international law has many provisions covering the "rights" of neutrals, although these rights have often been disregarded. The traditional country of "neutrality" is Switzerland, which has stayed neutral in the wars of this century. It is so neutral in its foreign policy that it has refused to join the United Nations or participate in peacekeeping efforts. It does play an active role in subsidiary bodies of the U.N., however, such as the Economic Commission for Europe, which is concerned mainly with trade issues. Geneva, Switzerland is the location of the U.N.'s major headquarters outside New York, and the U.N. Palais de Nations there hosts more U.N. meetings than New York. Switzerland and other neutrals such as Sweden and Finland are more conservative in economic policy than the "non-aligned," who are discussed later.

Leading policymakers of most developing countries of the world consider their policies as non-aligned, which is not quite the same as neutral. Originally they called their policies non-aligned in the sense that the countries who were members of the movement were not members of major military alliances of the United States or the Soviet Union. Cuba as a leader of the non-aligned and also a close ally of Russia has violated this precept and weakened the posture of the non-aligned movement, bringing some members close to an open split.

The main function of the organization of the non-aligned is to coordinate positions for U.N. meetings. The non-aligned countries with their anti-colonialist images and socialist orientation often flavor their resolutions with Marxist dogma and language. They usually support U.N. resolutions calling for an end to a conflict, and thus frequently are on the U.S. side of such resolutions. They also support resolutions for limiting nuclear weapons. Politically they might be called activist neutrals.

Self-Reliance

The classic period in recent history of self-reliance (usually called isolationism) for the United States was the period of the 1920s and 1930s, which followed the disillusionment of World War I. Many factors contributed to a desire for self-reliance, including the terrible losses of World War I, the economic and political disruption that followed, and the Great Depression of the 1930s. It was not a policy of complete self-reliance since the United States, of course, continued to maintain diplomatic relations with other countries and continued to carry on a large volume of foreign trade despite its high tariff barriers. However, until the last part of the 1930s the United States, in line with its "neutrality" legislation, tried to stay out of conflicts by not trading with an aggressor or its victims.

After World War II certain Communist powers and those with a strict socialist philosophy emphasized a policy of self-reliance. For example, after the Soviets abruptly withdrew their technicians from China in 1960 as a result of a political dispute over nuclear weapons, China's Mao Tse-tung advocated a policy of self-reliance. It had the lowest proportion of foreign trade of any major country in the world. Taiwan with a population of only 13 million had a higher volume of trade. Burma, a strict socialist state controlled by the military, is another example of a nation with minimal outside contacts.

The Communist regime of Cambodia in 1975 broke contacts with the modern world by evacuating its cities and sending its people to the countryside to try to scratch out a living. Fragmentary accounts indicate its leaders' efforts to completely purge its social and economic life of vestiges of capitalism and foreign influence resulted in hundreds of thousands of deaths, or by some accounts millions of deaths. The policy of self-reliance is powerfully supported by the Marxist ideology, which appeals to many of the developing countries. They are apprehensive about extensive trade with the developed world and investment from foreign countries because they fear it is a form of "neo-colonialism." The Communist countries continually stimulate such fears with their propaganda.

Nevertheless, the crisis which brought about the skyrocketing oil and food prices in 1973 and financial strains throughout the world has drawn countries together in the International Monetary Fund, the International Bank, and in other U.N. and international organizations to work out solutions together. There has been criticism and heat in debates that have taken place, but in the special session of the U.N. held in the fall of 1975 to discuss these problems, a consensus was reached by all groups on "general principles" for attacking world economic problems. A policy of self-reliance today has relatively few adherents in either a practical or rhetorical sense.

Pragmatism and Moralism

The pragmatist in international affairs examines the facts and tries to achieve a practical solution to a problem. The pragmatist will attempt to avoid, or rise above, ideological issues which can snarl up a negotiation. Policymakers can take a pragmatic, or a moralistic approach to a problem, along with different diplomatic strategies such as power politics, internationalism, or neutralism. (See Table 2-1.) The pragmatists adopt and support policies which work rather than those that fit their preconceived frameworks of ideas.

Hans Morgenthau concluded his classic text, *Politics Among Nations,* with eight fundamental rules of diplomacy. He designed these principles for diplomats who believe in power politics, as described above, but diplomats basing their actions on the following eight rules would be practicing a pragmatic approach to diplomacy:

1. Diplomacy must be divested of a crusading spirit.
2. The objectives of foreign policy must be defined in terms of the national interest and must be supported with adequate power.

3. Diplomacy must look at the political scene from the point of view of other nations.
4. Nations must be willing to compromise on issues that are not vital to them.
5. Give up the shadow or worthless rights for the substance of real advantage.
6. Never put yourself in a position from which you cannot retreat without losing face and from which you cannot advance without great risks.
7. Never allow a weak ally to make decisions for you.
8. The armed forces are an instrument of foreign policy, not its master.

Morgenthau in rule 2 defines the national interest in terms of national power. However, a pragmatist might recognize peace, prosperity, and protection as adequate national goals without trying to increase power for its own sake.[13]

The policy of *detente (relaxation of tension)* is one example of a pragmatic policy. The United States and the Soviet Union, which are major ideological rivals and balance of power rivals in Europe and the Mideast, have submerged these and other rivalries to reach agreement on the partial limitation of nuclear arms. (See Chapter 13.) Another example of a pragmatic policy is one in which leaders of developing countries such as Singapore, who use socialist rhetoric in their speeches, as a practical matter encourage private firms from the developed nations to provide the technology, know-how, and marketing organizations needed for development. In practice, many socialist-oriented leaders provide strong incentives for private foreign concerns to invest in their countries.

Moralists hold that principles of honor and virtue should prevail in international relations as well as in personal relations. They hope that some day acceptance of codes of international law or rules of conduct will prevent international wars and violence. It is hard to know when leaders are sincere, but moral arguments can have a healthy restraining effect on those who believe that power, military might, and even war are the major instruments that must be used in solving international problems. Robert Kennedy's book, *Thirteen Days,* gives one such dramatic example of the use of moral arguments against invading Cuba during the top level debates on policy during the Cuban Missile Crisis.[14] These arguments may have helped avoid an attack on Cuba and nuclear war.

Many observers take a cynical view of moral elements of diplomacy because of the long history of wars and broken promises. However, diplomats realize that on a level of personal dealing with foreign officials it is important to maintain honor and credit. If a diplomat ever lies and is caught, that diplomat's word will not again be trusted. The successful diplomat will avoid lying and usually will level with other diplomats. If cornered he or she may avoid giving direct answers to questions that could elicit damaging information or offend another country.

Policymakers in a democracy should keep the public well informed, but they also wish to keep policy differences which could damage relations with other countries from being played up by the news media. This causes a dilemma. Diplomatic gobbledygook often is the solution to this problem. Ambiguous diplomatic language can avoid embarrassing a foreign country and permit a country and its diplomats to save face. Such evasive language is usually understood by other diplomats. For example, a communique stating the "conversations were carried out with frankness" means probably that there was an argument and no agreement was reached on certain important issues. Hodding Carter III, the State Department's spokesman under Vance, when pressed with an embarrassing question once threw a rubber fish at a reporter to distract him.

Moralistic arguments came to the fore in recent years particularly in relation to Vietnam and United States activities in Asia. Moralists decried the immorality of warfare and used moralistic arguments for ending material aid to South Vietnam. Some moralists assert the United States should not support or deal with countries unless they are liberal democracies like our own. They do not look into the detailed implications of such a statement which would result in U.S. support and diplomatic relations with only a relatively few countries, mostly in Europe.

The moralists' arguments can be used in conjunction

with the self-reliance and neutralist arguments to support a policy of non-involvement in international disputes and issues. At this point arguments can become *moralizing*, which is different from *moralistic*.

The problem with the moralizer is that he tends to set standards that his or her own country could not meet. International politics and international economics are concerned with human beings, and no human being and particularly no organization is perfect. There is some corruption in every form of government and in all types of human institutions including those of the moralizer's country. A major problem of politics, including international politics, is to set up workable systems that minimize chances of corruption.

War is a scourge of mankind and anathema to the real moralist. Most policymakers and professors would say, however, that a policy of pacifism and non-involvement is not the solution to the world's ills and, in fact, encourages the strong to take advantage of the weak. The great moral dilemma of international politics is when and how to use force to try to achieve peace.

President Wilson's name is usually associated with moralism in international politics. His avowed aim in trying to keep the United States out of World War I was to use the moral strength of the United States to help in negotiating a peace. Colonel House, his principle foreign policy advisor on League matters, stated a major aim of the League of Nations was "the installation of a moral standard such as that maintained among individuals of honor." This would mean that the use of force by nations would have the same stigma attached to it as the use of force by individuals.[15]

Critics of leaders who profess moralism in international politics are afraid United States leaders might start on a moral crusade to impose their values on other nations. They note that leaders often call on the help and support of the Almighty in their wars. Other critics, callused by the Vietnam War and Watergate, suspect a President of posturing when he attempts to apply moral standards to foreign policy issues. Advocates of a power politics approach note that moral standards have little relevance on the international scene because there is no agreed system of values or international legal and administrative framework to use in enforcing a respect for human rights on sovereign governments.

Nevertheless, President Carter has espoused human rights and has made an issue of them. In his speech on May 22, 1977, at Notre Dame, Indiana, he stated that "This does not mean we can conduct our foreign policy by rigid moral maxims since we live in an imperfect and confused world." He added, however, that it would be a mistake to undervalue the power of words and ideas, since in a sense "words are action." Few would argue with him that ideas and ideologies can have a powerful influence on the world scene.

During the first year of President Carter's Administration human rights were a major focus of press comment. Academic critics asserted he did not apply the same strict standards to allies as he did to rivals or weaker nations.[16] Human rights were emphasized in his speech before the United Nations on March 17, 1977, which was well received by the delegates. He stated that he recognized ideals of human rights have not always been attained in the United States, but he stressed the abiding commitment of the American people to these ideals. He pledged to sign the U.N. covenants on economic, social, and cultural rights, and the covenant on civil and political rights, and supported their ratification by Congress. He made a similar pledge for the U.N. Genocide Convention and the treaty on racial discrimination. These treaties and covenants, which were approved by the General Assembly, were designed to give more meaning to human rights provisions of the U.N. Charter and Universal Declaration on Human Rights by establishing formal and legal obligations on the part of the ratifying states. The two covenants include recognized liberal democratic and social democratic rights such as 1) freedom from government violation of the integrity of the person, 2) fulfillment of vital needs as food, shelter, and health care, and 3) enjoyment of civil and political liberties.

An American observer committed to the principles of liberal democracy might wonder why these agreements had not been ratified earlier by Congress. Previous administrations had not signed or pressed for their ratification, because critics had asserted they would give too much authority to an international body to intervene

The Aims of President Carter's Human Rights Policies

(Excerpts from President Carter's Address at the Commencement
Exercises, University of Notre Dame)

May 22, 1977

I believe we can have a foreign policy that is democratic, that is based on fundamental values, and that uses power and influence which we have for humane purposes. We can also have a foreign policy that the American people both support and, for a change, know about and understand.

I have a quiet confidence in our own political system. Because we know that democracy works, we can reject the arguments of those rulers who deny human rights to their people. We are confident that democracy's example will be compelling, . . .

Democracy's great recent successes — in India, Portugal, Spain, Greece — show that our confidence in this system is not misplaced. Being confident of our own future, we are now free of that inordinate fear of communism which once led us to embrace any dictator who joined us in that fear.

First, we have reaffirmed America's commitment to human rights as a fundamental tenet of our foreign policy . . . This does not mean that we can conduct our foreign policy by rigid moral maxims. We live in a world that is imperfect and which will always be imperfect — a world that is complex and confused, and which will always be complex and confused. I understand fully the limits of moral suasion. We have no illusion that changes will come easily or soon. But I also believe that it is a mistake to undervalue the power of words and of the ideas that words embody . . .

In the life of the human spirit, words are action, much more so than many of us may realize who live in countries where freedom of expression is taken for granted. The leaders of totalitarian nations understand this very well. The proof is that words are precisely the action for which dissidents in those countries are being persecuted . . .

No other country is as well qualified as we to set an example. We have our own shortcomings and faults, and we should strive constantly and with courage to make sure that we are legitimately proud of what we have.

Second, we have moved deliberately to reinforce the bonds among our democracies . . . You may be interested in knowing at this NATO meeting, for the first time in more than 25 years, all members are democracies . . .

Our policy is rooted in our moral values, which never change. Our policy is reinforced by our material wealth and by our military power. Our policy is designed to serve mankind. And it is a policy that I hope will make you proud to be Americans.

in domestic affairs, that the principles were not enforceable, and that they might be used by foreign critics of the United States. President Carter in the Notre Dame speech, however, countered such critics by saying that for the United States to ignore the worldwide trend to protect the individual from the power of the state would be to lose influence and moral authority abroad. He referred to democracy's "recent successes" in India, Portugal, Spain, and Greece. Two weeks earlier, moreover, he had emphasized before the North Atlantic Council that NATO derived added strength from the fact that all 15 of the member countries are democracies. Moreover, in terms of realpolitik the human rights campaign helped put Communist Parties of Europe on the defensive. The campaign widened their differences with Moscow leaders, who were criticized both by Eurocommunists and representatives of Western nations. In this sense Carter's moralistic policies were pragmatic.

One of the most persuasive arguments for the primacy of power politics over moralism in the world arena was made by Morgenthau in his *Scientific Man versus Power Politics* as follows:

> We have no choice between power and the common good. To act successfully, that is, according to the rules of the political art, is political wisdom. To know with despair that the political act is inevitably evil, and to act nevertheless, is moral courage. To choose among several expedient actions the least evil one is moral judgment. In the combination of political wisdom, moral courage, and moral judgment, man reconciles his political nature with his moral destiny. That this conciliation is nothing more than a modus vivendi, uneasy, precarious, and even paradoxical can disappoint only those who prefer to gloss over and to distort the tragic contradictions of human existence with the soothing logic of a specious concord.

This quotation made a deep impression on Henry Kissinger when he was a student at Harvard.[17] Kissinger later did not hesitate to use military force and the threat of force to try to achieve a balance of power (equilibrium) in the Vietnam conflict and peace negotiations, and in the Middle East peace negotiations. He saw this use of force achieving the greater good, a world that was safer and more stable. The internationalist and moralist would say, however, that under the U.N. Charter force is only justified in self-defense, and as a last resort, not when it is "expedient." Power brokers, the moralist would say, are easily corrupted by power, and it is too easy for them to select "evil" acts to carry out what they think are in their nations' interest.

Human rights have much deeper roots than those cultivated by the Carter Administration. Many laws, particularly in the aid sphere, embody these rights. Consequently, perhaps the most controversial nomination of the Reagan Administration was Ernest Lefever, who ran into considerable congressional opposition when he was nominated for assistant secretary of state for human affairs. In the strict power politics tradition of Hans Morgenthau, who wrote the introduction to Lefever's book, *Ethics and United States Foreign Policy,* Lefever opposed Carter's emphasis on human rights in foreign policy. This offended many senators, and after lengthy Senate hearings and an adverse committee vote Lefever withdrew his nomination in frustration over Senate opposition. President Carter, himself, as indicated above, had indicated that a human rights policy must be seasoned with pragmatism since we live in an imperfect world. President Reagan and Secretary of State Haig, on the other hand, also indicated their support for principles of human rights although not wishing to make them a keystone of foreign policy.

The point is that the reactions of presidents and U.S. policymakers reflect a combination of philosophies and that their views vary at different times and under different political conditions. Also, different policymakers, agencies, and others compete to set the course of foreign policy. Sometimes they form alliances. Balance of power policymakers might seek support by using ideas of internationalists or world policemen. Self-reliance advocates might enlist the support of pacifists and moralists. Presidents with a moralistic inclination may be influenced by the political system and their responsibilities to be pragmatic and use instruments of power politics in foreign affairs.[18]

We have examined ideas of national goals, major ideologies, and foreign policy strategies to help understand the actions of policymakers. These concepts will be used as a framework of analysis throughout the book. They do not provide an infallible guide in analyzing specific international problems, since policymakers can always adopt new ideas and concepts and even be irrational. The concepts, however, do provide threads, which when they can be unraveled, permit us to make sense out of actions of policymakers in the international arena.

Summary

Since history began strategies of power politics have been used in relations among societies. Since World War II reporters and other observers have commonly pictured world crises as involving rivalry between the two superpowers. The prevalence of this not only has created a basis for the superpower system but has also reinforced the tendencies of leaders of the superpowers to use strategies of power politics and encouraged them toward the world policeman type of power politics. Advocates of the use of power tend not to recognize standards of international law and morality as binding. Their usual rationale is that there is no world society to enforce such standards, and that such standards are impractical. However, principles of power politics are not as clear a guide to analysis and action as some of the power brokers allege. It is difficult to measure many elements of power. Moreover, in specific cases, such as Vietnam, immeasurable elements such as ideological elements have dominated the outcome. This indicates we must go beyond conventional power elements of military and economic strength to understand international politics.

Internationalists aim to achieve peace and other aims of foreign policy under the United Nations and similar organizations. They rally under the slogans of collective security and interdependence, and they also advocate recognition of the importance of moral factors and international law. The internationalists' peacemaking, however, is not as impressive or as newsworthy as the drama of power politics, and to get perspective we later will compare actions as well as words under these banners. Neutralism, non-alignment, and self-reliance are other alternative strategies used by leaders of states, but the strategies do not seem to be practical options in an interdependent world.

116   International Politics and Policymakers' Ideas

All the above policies can be tempered with pragmatism and moralism to varying degrees. President Carter's human rights policies are probably the most direct expression of a moralistic policy, but there are also practical angles to his policy. The policies of President Carter and of other leaders often reflected a mix of the above strategies plus ideological elements. Separating the ingredients helps to make sense out of their actions.

FOOTNOTES

1. Henry Kissinger, *White House Years* (Boston: Little, Brown, 1979), pp. 65-70; John G. Stoessinger, *Crusaders and Pragmatists* (New York: W.W. Norton, 1979), pp. 203-246.

2. Morgenthau, *op. cit.*, p. 125.

3. Dean Acheson, *Present at the Creation* (New York: W.W. Norton & Company, 1969), p. 233.

4. Harry S. Truman, *Memoirs by Harry S. Truman* (Garden City, N.Y.: Doubleday and Company, 1956), Volume II, p. 248.

5. *Ibid.*, Chapter 17.

6. Nikita Khrushchev, *Khrushchev Remembers, The Last Testament* (New York: Bantam Books, 1974), Volume II, p. 250.

7. *Pentagon Papers, op. cit.*, Chapter 3; and Paul M. Kattenburg, *The Vietnam Trauma in American Foreign Policy, 1945-1975* (New Brunswick, Transaction Books, 1980), p. 98.

8. *Newsweek*, June 16, 1980, p. 28.

9. Harry S. Truman, *Memoirs by Harry S. Truman* (Garden City, N.Y.: Doubleday and Company, Inc., 1955), Volume I, Chapter 18.

10. *Ibid.*, p. 334.

11. Dean Acheson, *Present at the Creation* (New York: W.W. Norton & Company, 1959), p. 38.

12. Eisenhower, Dwight D., *Mandate for Change: 1953-1956* (Garden City, N.Y.: Doubleday, 1963; and *Waging Peace: 1956-1961* (Garden City, N.Y.: Doubleday, 1965); Townsend Hoopes, *The Devil and John Foster Dulles* (Boston: Little, Brown, 1973); Robert Bowie, *Suez 1956* (New York: Oxford University Press, 1974), pp. 29-58.

13. Morgenthau, *op. cit.*, pp. 538-546.

14. (New York: New American Library, 1969), Introduction and page 49. Later, however, Robert Kennedy supervised extensive CIA probes against Cuba. Arthur M. Schlesinger, Jr., *Robert Kennedy and His Times* (New York: Ballantine Books, 1978), Chapter 23.

15. Charles Seymour, *The Intimate Papers of Colonel House* (Cambridge: Houghton Mifflin Company, 1928), Volume 4, Chapter 1.

16. John G. Stoessinger, *Crusaders and Pragmatists* (New York: W.W. Norton, 1979), pp. 278-285; Brodie, *op. cit.*, pp. 368-374.

17. *Ibid.*, pp. 208-213.

18. James Chace, "Is a Foreign Policy Consensus Possible?" *Foreign Affairs,* Fall, 1978, pp. 1-16.

5

Geographic, Population, and Raw Material Elements of National Strength

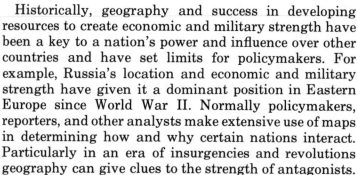

Historically, geography and success in developing resources to create economic and military strength have been a key to a nation's power and influence over other countries and have set limits for policymakers. For example, Russia's location and economic and military strength have given it a dominant position in Eastern Europe since World War II. Normally policymakers, reporters, and other analysts make extensive use of maps in determining how and why certain nations interact. Particularly in an era of insurgencies and revolutions geography can give clues to the strength of antagonists.

Economic and military strength can be exerted at a distance, but this may result in problem areas for lines of communication. The Suez Canal and Panama Canal are obvious examples of highly strategic areas which have been in the center of controversies.

When officials use their country's economic and military strength openly or skillfully to support foreign policy ideas, historians have called this "realpolitik." War is the most brutal instrument of realpolitik, while other forms range from support of insurgencies to economic aid programs.

Until the 1970s the Western industrial nations and Russia seemed to hold most of the realpolitik cards. We noted in the previous chapter, however, how North Vietnam with a relatively small population and resources defeated South Vietnam and the United States, due in large part to the power of ideas and ideologies. That war indicated a need for a fresh look at the relative importance of the so-called objective factors of international politics — geography, resources, and population — including their derivatives — economic and military strength. These are called "objective" factors since they are relatively easy to measure compared to the elusive but important political factors such as ideas and ideologies.

The victory of North Vietnam was made possible by the balance of terror or nuclear standoff, which acted to prevent U.S. consideration of the use of nuclear weapons in the war. In addition, other trends converged in the 1970s to shift attention to other types of power. The most important change was the shift in economic leverage to the oil producing countries. These countries joined together in the Organization of Petroleum Exporting Countries (OPEC) to raise the price of oil about ten-fold by the end of the decade, and they maintained adequate controls over production to keep prices up despite efforts of the industrial countries to substitute alternate sources of energy. The huge cost of U.S. oil imports weakened the dollar, which for years had been the basis of international transactions.

Associated with this crisis was the annual shift of tens of billions of dollars of oil income to the OPEC oil producers and then back again to investments in world financial centers. This has meant that oil producers, if they chose to do so, could use these funds to undermine or strengthen the economy of any country in the world. Saudi Arabia, particularly, gained power and influence by using subsidies and investments. As economic problems have come to the forefront, new centers of international power have arisen in the Mideast, in Japan, and in the European Community, including Germany with its huge foreign exchange reserves.

Also during the 1970s the voices of the developing countries, the have nots, have become more powerful and more strident in demanding better prices for their raw materials and more support from the "haves" of the world. They have been backed by the oil producers of the Mideast and other areas and have been inspired by OPEC's success in hiking oil prices.

A challenge for the analyst of international politics is to assess the amount of leverage in the hands of the oil producers and in the new centers of economic power. How effectively these states and non-state actors cooperate and use their power depends largely on their ideologies and ideas, but it also depends on the strength of their geographic position, their resources, the size and quality of their population, and the economic and military elements backing their position. Much depends on the chance character of leadership, but objective factors can shape and affect underlying attitudes toward international politics. The next two chapters will assess how these objective factors have affected political power.

Geography Sets the Stage

Most analysts of international politics take it for granted that geography sets the stage for international politics. Policymakers, professors, and reporters usually have a map well in mind in explaining the fundamentals of a country's position. We will review geographic factors as they affect world politics in areas of major international concern.

Europe. The geography of Europe has had a major influence on international issues. England, with its easy access to the sea, developed a dependence on foreign commerce and a colonial empire before World War I. Ocean commerce was both a cause and a result of the industrial revolution, which made England the leading world power before World War I.

Because of the protection of the English Channel, England in previous centuries could take a relatively detached view of power politics on the Continent, and it would intervene only when the balance of power on the Continent was seriously threatened by France or another power. In the Twentieth Century, England's concern over Germany's threat to the balance of power in Europe brought England into World Wars I and II.

The United States, separated from Europe by the Atlantic Ocean, was even more detached from Continental politics and entered World War II only as a result of Japan's attack on Pearl Harbor. United States leaders, however, had felt physically threatened by Hitler's drive to dominate the Eurasian heartland, and they provided England economic and military equipment to resist Hitler. In both World Wars I and II, Germany's submarine campaign tried to block U.S. efforts to maintain supply routes to England and helped draw the United States into the war. Thus, geography and lines of communication are basic to understanding England's and the United States' involvement in these wars.

Now there is an entirely different perspective on geography and possible war in Europe. Countries like the United States, which used to be isolated, are less than a half hour away from destruction in the event of a major nuclear war. Space and time have been telescoped, so that policymakers no longer have these cushions, which used to be an aid to diplomacy and a deterrent to war. Although United States troops are on the front line in Germany as a deterrent to East European forces of the Warsaw Pact, the Atlantic "moat" would provide little protection to the United States in the event of an all-out war.

Nevertheless, French policymakers look at the globe and many of them doubt the United States would escalate to all-out war and risk nuclear destruction of its cities to save the European continent from a conventional military invasion. Thus, the French developed their own nuclear deterrent, withdrew from the NATO command, and demanded that the NATO headquarters move to another country.

In the past 100 years Germany has been at the center of the European stage geographically and politically. The Federal Republic of Germany is situated in the heart of Europe in an area about the size of Oregon. Oregon has only 2.7 million people, but the Federal Republic with 62 million people has the largest population in Western Europe. With its key location Germany historically has either been a major threat to Europe or a possible invasion route during a war. In this century the international politics of Europe have centered on the military implications of this German position.

Map 1   Europe

—·—· German boundary before World War II
•••••• Berlin Air Corridor

As a result of World War II Germany lost eastern territory to Poland, while Poland lost eastern territories to the Soviet Union. Germany was split — East Germany lost the Silesian coal fields but West Germany still kept the Ruhr coal fields and industrial heart of Western Europe. East Germany, due to its highly skilled population, is still an important industrial country; West Germany with a population three and a half times larger and with the industrial Ruhr is a foremost economic world power. (See Map 1.)

Berlin, the former capital of all of Germany, is in the center of East Germany. Berlin is divided and occupied by the four allied powers of World War II (the United States, the United Kingdom, France, and the Soviet Union) with access routes by highways, railroad, and air through East Germany guaranteed by a series of formal agreements.

After World War II many German cities were a shambles as a result of the fighting and bombing. Major areas in eastern Germany were occupied and then absorbed by Poland, Czechoslovakia, and the Soviet Union, and about 10 million German refugees fled to Western Germany in the years after the war. Initially they were an economic liability and a potential political threat to European stability, because many of these refugees wanted to see Germany united and their lands returned. This is the geographic basis for the nationalistic ideology that worried policymakers after World War II. The West German government, however, helped the refugees settle and become attached to their new homes. By 1950 West Germany had begun a rapid economic expansion that not only absorbed the great increase in population, but also allowed West Germany, which became the Federal Republic of Germany, again to become a major world power in the center of Europe.

Just as the plains of Western Europe permitted Germany to invade France, the plains of Poland and western Russia permitted German invasions of Russia in both World War I and II. This geographic fact dominates Russian foreign policy and is the rationale for its creating an Eastern European buffer area against a possible German threat. Russia suffered tremendous casualties from World War I and World War II, and it is determined not to let down its guard again. Communist ideology reinforces European geography and history as a basis for policy, since that ideology holds capitalism by its very nature is aggressive.

The location of Western European coal and iron ore resources has encouraged another major development in international politics that is fundamentally altering the world balance of power. The center of Europe's industry has been built over the coking coal of the Ruhr, which has attracted and joined with the iron ore of northeastern France. Before World War II the iron and steel resources of Western Europe were controlled by the international steel cartel, Entente Internationale de L'Aciers (EIA), which included steel producers of Germany, France, Belgium, Luxemburg, and the Saar. After World War II it was replaced by governmental controls, first under the International Authority for the Ruhr and later by the European Coal and Steel Community. The formation of this Community represented a breakthrough in French relations with Germany and for all of Western Europe. Before 1950 France had been confronting Germany. After 1950, by accepting Germany as an equal authority in the European Coal and Steel Community and later the European Economic Community (EEC), the French created a new and powerful entity on the world scene. The EEC now speaks with as much economic authority as the United States of America.

Asia. The geography of Asia is not as well known to most observers as that of Europe. China's outlook on the world has been shaped by its geography. About two thirds of China is mountains or desert, which discourages settlement and transportation routes. Almost all the land suitable for cultivation is in the east. China's major industrial area, Manchuria, is also in the east connected to the world with ocean lines of communication. With this eastward orientation China's economic and political activities have focused more toward Japan and East Asia than toward India or Southeast Asia.

Taiwan's position 100 miles from the coast of mainland China gives it a strong defensive position and enables its refugee government to maintain a claim to be the legitimate government of China without much of a military threat from the mainland. Troops of the nationalist government of Taiwan dug in on two groups of

Map 2   Southeast Asia

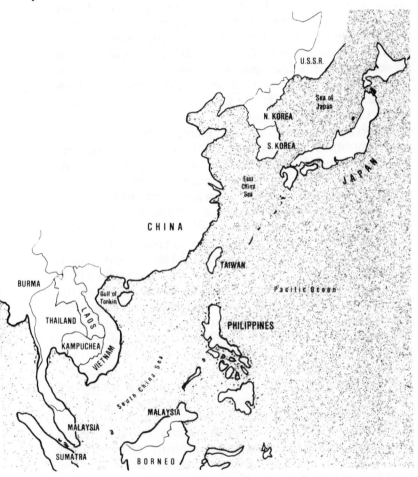

heavily fortified islands a few miles from the coast after they were forced off the mainland in 1949. This was the focus of two major international crises in 1954 and 1958 when Communist China bombarded these islands. In the early 1960s when I was a political-military official on the China Desk of the State Department, I advocated trying to get the Republic of China's troops to withdraw before there was another crisis. I had no success in persuading superiors because of their belief the highly nationalistic ROC Government would not withdraw without extreme pressure that the U.S. probably would not be willing to exert, and also because of their natural inertia and desire to "let sleeping dogs lie." In fact, there has been no major crisis there since that date.

Geography is also of critical importance in understanding insurgencies and wars in Asia. For example, South Vietnam found it impossible to defend its long border of mountains and jungles. North Vietnamese forces developed secret highways and supply lines through Laos and Cambodia, built up stocks of munitions, and launched attacks from these sanctuaries. South Vietnam could maintain a relatively good defense of its narrow boundary with North Vietnam, but particularly in the "parrot's beak" of Cambodia, only 70 miles from Saigon, South Vietnam found itself highly vulnerable to North Vietnamese attacks launched from Cambodian sanctuaries. Up until the last months, the Communist forces relied on jungle cover and guerilla tactics, as well as on political weariness of their opponents, and the U.S. and South Vietnamese conventional military strength was largely ineffective against this strategy. The *coup de grace* was administered by regular forces of North Vietnam.

The fact that Cambodia itself could not control the traffic through the jungles and mountains of its territory was largely responsible for its territory being attacked and drawn into the war. Moreover, Thailand, an ally of the United States, is geographically located so that northeast Thailand is hundreds of miles closer to Hanoi than most areas of South Vietnam. Thus, the United States sought and obtained permission to build air bases in northeast Thailand during the war for launching bombing attacks against North Vietnam and its supply lines; this also involved Thailand indirectly in the war.

One could contrast the geographic vulnerability of South Vietnam with the good defensive position of South Korea during the Korean War. North Korea is also committed to forceable unification of Korea, but South Korea's geography is such that its boundary is relatively short and well fortified. It can also defend against probes from the sea from North Korea. In order for North Korean forces to gain access to South Korea, they made long, expensive tunnels under the fortified border. These were readily discovered. South Korea with a stronger geographic position and with the aid of United States and U.N. forces won its war in the 1950s, and it has been in a much stronger position to resist attack than South Vietnam.

There are areas in Latin America and in Africa where borders are as hard to control as those in Southeast Asia. However, these borders have not been, for the most part, an arena for warfare. In other words, it is clear that geography is a key element in conflicts, but unfavorable geography does not, in itself, cause the growth of guerilla movements and war.

Middle East. An understanding of the geography of the area is essential if we are to understand the Arab-Israel conflict and the truces that have been arranged. Map 3 shows the state of Israel with the shaded sections indicating the territory occupied following the 1967 war with Egypt and Syria. During that war Israel captured the strategic Golan Heights area in the north and retained it after bitter fighting in the 1973 war. The 1974 settlement in Golan involved Israel's withdrawal from some of the Syrian territory it had taken over and the establishment of a 1,250 man U.N. force in a buffer zone under Syrian administration. Complicated arrangements were made for limiting arms on each side of the Egyptian and Syrian buffer zones.

Map 3 also shows the controversial "West Bank" area which Israel captured during the 1967 war and which creates the basis for continued conflict with the Arabs. Israeli authorities believe they must control this area since it would be much easier to defend a line at the Jordan River on the east than the former long border extending to within a few miles of all the populated areas of Israel.

Map 3   Middle East

Israeli-occupied territory after 1967 War

Hostile Arab guerilla groups operating from the West Bank could easily cause havoc in many areas of Israel. The former borders are only a few miles from all major military air fields of Israel and from Israeli cities, which could be easily reached by mortars. Although moderate Israeli elements realize that a peace settlement would probably involve turning over political control of the West Bank to Jordan or to another governmental authority, they want to be assured that such an authority will not permit or encourage guerilla or terrorist raids. The West Bank contains about 850,000 people of Arab background, and the Arab states undoubtedly would not make a peace-settlement with Israel unless Israel returned at least political control of this territory to Arab Palestinians.

Before the 1967 war, Jerusalem, the capital of Israel, was split down the middle with Israel controlling the western half. In the eastern half was the Wailing Wall, a Jewish shrine, which is all that remains of Solomon's temple. Jerusalem also includes holy places for the Moslem and Christian religions. All this adds to the difficulty of satisfying various religious and political groups in a final settlement.

At the end of 1978 and the beginning of 1979 there was a break in the stalemate when President Carter persuaded President Sadat of Egypt and Prime Minister Begin of Israel to approve a peace agreement providing for withdrawal of Israel from the Sinai. This infuriated many elements in the rest of the Arab world, since the withdrawal would take military pressure off of Israel's southern border while Israel still held the West Bank, Gaza, and areas claimed by Syria. The other Arab states following the leadership of the Palestine Liberation Organization (PLO) broke off relations with Egypt early in 1979, even though final implementation of its peace settlement with Israel depended on Egypt's approving arrangements for restoring self-government to the West Bank. (See Chapter 9.) In 1980 Israel turned back most of the Sinai to Egypt in accordance with the Camp David agreements.

Israel has fought four bitter wars since 1948, and it treasures highly the present buffer zones of the Sinai desert and the Golan Heights as well as the West Bank. It also supports Christian forces in southern Lebanon, which act as a buffer. On the other hand, Arab elements insist on regaining the West Bank and Gaza, including extremist groups which do not recognize the right of Israel to exist as a state. A final settlement of these issues will involve long negotiations over lines on the map involving in some instances a few meters of strategic positions.

Population — The Members of the Cast

If geography sets the stage, population factors determine who is in the middle of the action. The quality and quantity of a population largely determine how countries develop their assets and what governments are strong enough to become involved in the major issues of international politics. There is no racial implication in this, but the quality of a population covers its education, training, and values that are prevalent in the society. These values can change rapidly when society is disrupted, while stable societies can resist change and modernization. Two of the most striking examples of the importance of population factors are the dramatic recovery after World War II of two defeated Axis Powers — Germany and Japan.

After the war German cities were a shambles and millions of Germans were on the move through the destruction fleeing from the Russian forces or returning to their homes or what might have been left of their homes after the bombing and shelling. Transport and communications were disrupted and many large factories were severely damaged and out of operation. Restoration of prewar economic arteries was prevented by the split between East and West Germany and by occupation zone boundaries. Money had little value and the German people were able to survive only through food and other aid from the United States.

Japan was in a similar state with its flimsy cities burnt out by the American fire bombing, its empire lost, half its merchant fleet sunk, and its industrial base largely destroyed. Moreover, Japan did not have the huge coal reserves of the Ruhr. Japan's only major resource was its people. After the war I surveyed the damage in both Germany and Japan as a member of the U.S. Strategic

Bombing Survey. I was convinced from the terrible destruction it would take them 50 years to recover. Yet both Japan with its lack of natural resources and Germany, split down the middle and burdened with refugees, within five years were well on the way to recovery that would quickly bring them again to the forefront of major world powers. The industriousness and technical ability of Germany was and is world renown. Japan had a similar reputation in Asia. The occupying powers quickly turned over the responsibility for economic policy and for managing their own affairs to the defeated enemies. Initially Germans and Japanese devoted their energies to rebuilding and reorganizing their economic and political life.

It is not possible to measure precisely and weigh the qualities of technical training, industriousness, and discipline of the labor force and the ability of management, but these countries had little more than this to start with after the war, and by a process of elimination the population factor must be assigned a leading role in their dramatic recovery.

China and India, despite relatively low educational levels and low GNP, have been able to find enough scientists and technicians in their huge populations to focus on developing a nuclear potential and great power status. Thus, countries with a large population to a limited extent can compensate with strong governmental policies for a weakness in education.

Morale and managerial ability of a population can offset a major disadvantage in size. Israel is an outstanding example of this. With only 3.3 million highly educated and motivated people it has been able to defend itself and even expand its territory against neighboring Egypt and Syria, which have a combined population of over 45 million people. True, Israel has received strong financial support from Jewish communities abroad, from reparation and restitution payments from Germany, and from loans and grants from the United States. Nevertheless, even obtaining these funds reflected the ability of the Israeli government and people to mobilize outside support.

Thus, in evaluating the effect of the population factor on a nation's strength we much look beyond size and education to discover elements that bring certain nations such as Germany, Japan, and Israel to the center of the action on the international scene.[1]

Raw Materials

Before World War II coal and iron were considered the basis of a country's industrial strength and international power. Oil was considered important, but most of the great powers had their own supplies or control over foreign supplies. The Axis powers were a major exception. Germany believed itself vulnerable to a shutting off of oil supplies in the event of war and developed a major program of synthetic oil production. Japan before 1941 accumulated over a year's supply of petroleum products to support its military moves in Asia, but still believed it necessary to lash out at the United States at Pearl Harbor and take over Indonesian oil because the United States through its financial controls in 1941 had cut back U.S. supplies of oil to Japan.

Since World War II energy supplies and petroleum in particular have become a major concern of the world. The two superpowers, the United States and the Soviet Union, are relatively well off compared to other major countries. Many other countries are not so fortunate. With the great increase in the cost of imported petroleum, their rank among the world powers and the potential of their realpolitik in many cases will depend on their domestic oil supplies.

Oil leverage was used bluntly and forcefully during the 1973 Arab-Israeli war and its aftermath. The following incident from Prime Minister Golda Meir's memoirs illustrates the importance of oil. Mrs. Meir was enraged over the failure of Germany, England, and other countries with "socialist" governments in Europe to permit U.S. planes to refuel on their way to resupply Israel during the brief 1973 Arab-Israeli war. After the war she called a leadership meeting of the Socialist International in which heads of socialist parties, those in government and those in opposition attend. Mrs. Meir opened the meeting by explaining the perilous situation Israel had faced during the war, and she asked why not a single socialist country in Europe was prepared to come to the aid of the only democratic nation in the Middle East. She continued:

> On what grounds did you make your decisions not to let those planes refuel? Believe me, I am the last person to belittle the fact that we are only one tiny Jewish state and that there are over 20 Arab states with vast territories, endless oil, and billions of dollars. But what I want to know from you today is whether these things are decisive factors in socialist thinking, too?
>
> When I got through, the chairman asked if anybody wanted to speak. But nobody did. Then someone behind me — I didn't want to turn my head and look at him because I didn't want to embarrass him — said very clearly, 'Of course, they can't talk. Their throats are choked with oil.' And although there was a discussion, there wasn't really anymore to say. It had all been said by that man whose face I never saw.[2]

Western Europe and Japan depended on Arab countries for most of their oil supplies, and cutting off this oil would have strangled them economically. This, of course, accounts for their refusal to permit U.S. planes to use their landing fields to supply Israel during that war, which infuriated Prime Minister Golda Meir.

After the United States weathered the 1973-1974 oil embargo, the secondary oil shock wave hit, which was the economic impact of shifting about $85 billion of purchasing power in one year to the oil producers. We will trace the international economic impacts of the huge shifts in funds on international finance in Chapters 10 and 14, but the major political threat is another oil embargo of the United States and possibly Western Europe. This threat hangs over the Mideast issue like a dark cloud of an impending storm. Another political effect of the shifts in funds has been to permit Saudi Arabia to subsidize and influence other Mideast countries. This is discussed in Chapter 10.

Petroleum resources are in the process of creating starring roles for a number of other countries and helping in the revival of a former star — Great Britain. It seems highly doubtful that reserves of any of the other raw materials will duplicate this feat. At the beginning of 1975, when faced by a coal strike, the British economy reached a new low, but since then there has been a marked strengthening of its position, due mostly to the new North Sea oil fields off its coast. Britain expected to be able to obtain all of its petroleum needs from the North

Table 5-1   Population of OPEC Countries and Expected Duration of Oil Reserves, 1976[3]

	Population (Millions)	Crude Oil Exports ($ billion)	Life of Reserves at Present Export Rate — Years
Saudi Arabia	9	28	33
Iran	33	22	30
Nigeria	65	9.9	24
Iraq	11.2	8.7	44
Libya	2.5	8.4	33
United Arab Emirates	.7	8.2	52
Kuwait	1.0	7.3	107
Venezuela	12	5.7	18
Indonesia	133	5.4	17
Algeria	17	4.1	17
Qatar	.1	2.1	36
Gabon	.5	.7	26
Ecuador	7	.6	26
Mexico*	50	5	50-200

*Estimated, 1980.
Note: Mexico figures are from *Spokesman Review* (Spokane, WA), January 7, 1979, p. A-12. Mexico is not a member of OPEC.

Sea by the end of 1980 and have some left over for export. The improvement in its psychological position has been almost as marked as in its economic position. Commentators in 1975 were questioning whether British democratic system could survive. With its transfusion of petroleum the British economy began generating balance of payments surpluses, and its officials began speaking forth with more self-confidence.

Other countries destined to play starring roles in their areas of the world can be found by examining the following table which shows population, oil production, and the number of years oil reserves will last at present rates of production. (See Table 5-1.)

Iran, with its large population, strategic location athwart oil tanker routes, huge oil production, and dominant military strength in the Persian Gulf by 1979 had become a major power.[4] Nigeria has the population and petroleum resources to become a major African power. Significantly, the first three countries of Table 5-1 — Saudi Arabia, Iran, and Nigeria plus Venezuela, lower on the list — were on the list of the countries visited by President Carter in his first extended trip abroad. Mexico with its recent oil discoveries has also received major attention from the United States, and its reserves may match those of Saudi Arabia.

Indonesia's huge population and large oil exports will some day give it great power status in Southeast Asia. Before the transfusions of oil revenue, however, it was politically and economically close to falling apart, so it may take some years before its economy strengthens and its leaders make their influence fully felt in that part of the world.

Other oil powers on the list may be destined for much greater influence in world affairs, but with their small populations it seems doubtful they will become major world powers.

The above is a brief and conventional survey of how geography, population, and resources provide bases for economic and military strength and for foreign policies. Some political scientists use these factors and others to show mathematical correlations with policies of nations. This is discussed in more detail at the end of Chapter 2. My thesis, however, is that such factors provide limits for policy, and that analysis should be directed at how such resources are controlled and developed, and then on how policymakers use economic and military strength for realpolitik. Geography, resources, and population alone do not make great powers. It takes many years for nations to develop real power from potential power unless they are blessed with tremendous reserves of oil or other wealth or unless they have unusual leadership and organizational abilities.

We will now look at countries which have transformed resources into economic and military power and how they use this strength.

Summary

Geography, raw material, and population factors are a basis for national power, and they have helped determine foreign policies. Until the 1970s, coal, iron, and industries based on them were the key elements for great power status. In recent years petroleum and energy have come to center stage.

Germany with its industrial resources, strategic location, and energetic population has been in the middle of European power politics for the last 100 years. Similarly in Asia, China has been at the center of action by virtue of its location, size, resources, and its hard-working population. Russia, which straddles the Eurasian continent, has been forced to react with both these major powers.

Geography of border areas has played an important part in wars: e.g., Vietnam and Korea. In the Middle East, also, a series of wars have been fought over strategic areas. The disposition of the West Bank area, whose geography could threaten Israel, has stymied negotiations there for many years. The huge oil reserves in the Middle East have further complicated the situation by attracting superpower rivalry.

Geographic factors are not permanent. The most critical change for the U.S. since World War II is that nuclear weapons and rockets have shrunk the world. U.S. foreign policy no longer has the geographic buffers it had before World War II.

FOOTNOTES

1. Population growth problems and development are discussed in Chapter 14.

2. Golda Meir, *My Life* (New York: G.P. Putman's Sons, 1975), pp. 446-447.

3. *Economist* (London), July 9, 1977, pp. 86-87.

4. See Chapter 10.

CHAPTER
6
Economic and Military Power

A nation's power potential is not measured by natural resources but by how it converts resources into economic and military strength. This includes financial power, which is an element that came to the fore during the international financial crises of the 1970s. To the despair of arms control advocates, however, military products are still the most important elements of national power, and military spending continues to expand, amounting to over $460 billion for the world in 1979.

Arms control experts wring their hands at the dangers to civilization posed by mounting stocks of nuclear weapons, the superpowers' overkill capacity, and the tremendous burdens of military budgets. Military spending far exceeds other international programs, and it is matched only by education as an element of national budgets. The two superpowers alone account for about one-half of the world's military spending. Communists blame the capitalist system for the arms race, but Western analysts point out the Communist nations devote a higher percent of their resources to arms than do the capitalist nations. (See Figures 6-1 and 6-2.)

Figure 6-1 World Military Expenditures

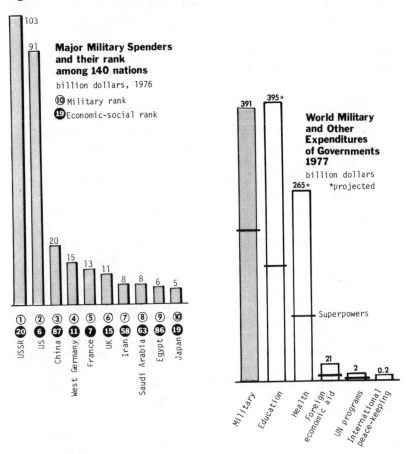

We begin our political analysis of economic and military power by describing measures of economic production and the balance of payments commonly used to measure national power. Many personal judgments go into the indexes, and although analysts can often agree on the basic data, they can come out with different assessments of the strength of countries being compared. For this reason we should look closely at techniques of making these indexes and problems of interpreting them.

Economic Strength

The most common comprehensive measure of economic strength is gross national product (GNP). This measure of total output *on a per capita basis* indicates the standard of living, the potential for producing military items, the ability to support an aid program, and by implication the technological level and potential for becoming a nuclear power.[1]

In the 1970s with the nuclear standoff and with financial pressures threatening the dollar and other currencies, foreign exchange reserves have also become an important index of national power or weakness. As of 1980, the international monetary authorities had managed to stave off an international financial crisis, but it was evident that they would depend on continued loans and investments from reserves of the newly rich oil exporters. Historians blame the collapse of the international monetary system in the early 1930s for helping bring about the world depression and Hitler's rise to power, so many analysts believe barometers of the international monetary system, such as the balance of payments, could help predict storms ahead in international politics.

Gross National Product (GNP). GNP figures are commonly used as indicators of economic and even political development. Levels of employment and the fairness of distribution of national income also make good measures of economic and political progress, but good international indexes of such factors are not available. Since GNP is widely used, it is important to understand some of the fundamental problems of its measurement.

Gross national product is the value of the total output of an economy. GNP is estimated by totaling the "value added" contributed in each stage of the production process. The added value of output can be estimated even if products are not sold. For example, for a small subsistence farm in a developing country, which does not sell any of its products on a local market, economists calculate added value as the value of housing, food, clothing, and other items that are produced and used on the farm, even though they are not sold. This figure is usually estimated through a sample survey or a census. If that small farming unit should in addition sell $20 of food products to a local restaurant, this would add $20 to the farm's added value. If the local restaurant should charge $30 for the meals prepared from the farm products, the "value added" of the local restaurant is only $10. The total added value arising from the farm sale of those particular food products and the sales of the restaurant would be $30, not $50, to avoid double counting.

Estimating elements of GNP for the manufacturing process is more complicated. This involves buying raw materials and components from many firms, but the principle is the same. As a raw material is processed to the final product, only the value added is counted at each step. Thus, double counting is avoided. For example, many developing countries assemble automobiles, but economists subtract the value of *imported* components from the automobile price to determine the value added in the developing country.

The accuracy of GNP statistics varies depending on whether the economy is that of a developed Western country, a poor country with a primitive statistical system, or a Communist nation. The previously described farming example illustrates one of the problems in estimating the GNP of a developing country. Developing countries do not have resources to develop comprehensive statistical offices. If a large part of their GNP comes from a subsistence economy, the yearly figures for GNP may be based on an old census corrected for rough estimates of current agricultural production. Even for those few developing countries where statistics are fairly good, the weather and the annual variation of crop yields can make a great difference in the overall GNP figures; thus one should be careful in using such statistics for comparisons of growth.

For the Western countries which have literally millions of bits of data from computers, tax returns, surveys, and other instruments for evaluating GNP, the figures are fairly good.

Comparisons of GNP and growth rates in the Western countries with those of the controlled economies of the Communist nations are more difficult. The Communists use a different concept for measuring output, that of "net material product." This concept does not count certain types of services in the total output. Also, in comparisons there are problems of defining added value and preventing double counting, of using comparable prices, and in determining an appropriate exchange rate to convert the value of the output to a common currency. Many economists have serious reservations about the comparability of the data. Others tend to accept at face value the accuracy of the growth rates of the "net material product" of the Communist countries. With few exceptions, Communist figures of growth rates have been consistently higher than those of the gross national products of the market oriented economies. What is not widely recognized by policymakers and professors is that there are significant elements of exaggeration which have been built into the figures of the controlled Communist economies.[2] (See Box.)

The United Nations for many years has been improving the quality of world GNP statistics by sending statistical advisors to the developing countries. The U.N. has also published a book that reconciles the concepts of gross national product with the net material product (NMP) of the Communist economies.[6] Thus, the figures were improved during the 1970s, and for these years it is possible to make more meaningful comparisons of economic growth rates of the developed countries with those of the developing countries. Also, in the 1970s comparisons with the Eastern European countries are more meaningful. However, until the Soviet Union and the other Communist states permit open and detailed criticism and evaluation of their figures, and until they publish them in much more detail, their NMP figures should be used with reservations.

Comparisons of growth rates among the developing countries of the Far East, for the most part, are fairly useful. These statistics for many years have been used by the Economic and Social Commission of Asia and the Pacific (ESCAP), formerly known as ECAFE. Nevertheless, ESCAP will not make a serious challenge of the data from one of its members, and thus the data are not as reliable as those of Western countries. African statistics are beginning to be improved, and in many countries useful series begin only in the 1970s.

Despite the limitations, GNP statistics are of

Communist GNP Data

Many economists accept Communist economic statistics at face value or discount them only to a minor extent. I am part of a minority who has serious reservations about such data, particularly for earlier years. In the early 1960s when I was on the China desk of the State Department, I was engaged in running debate with CIA experts and the State Department's research experts over the accuracy of the statistics for the Great Leap Forward, a major production drive of that era. The experts used the Chinese data with minor adjustments to come up with GNP growth rates of over 20 percent. I based my lower estimates in part on those of the Department of Agriculture's agricultural attache in Hong Kong who showed very minor growth in Chinese crop output during this period. I also used studies of private analysts. One of them found a quote from Communist China's head statistician who said, "Our statistical reports must reflect the great victory of the Party's general line and the progress of all the works guided by the Party. They certainly should not be a mere display of objective facts.[3]

It took several years for the CIA and State Department research experts to get enough data to reduce their estimates substantially. They found it too much of a temptation to use published figures, and they found it hard to believe the Chinese authorities would have two sets of economic data. Moreover, they did not want to underestimate a competitor.

In later years I did a study of Soviet output data, and found exaggerations in Soviet statistics.[4] In a private discussion I had with East European economists they admitted such exaggerations in East European and Soviet data. I, therefore, continue to have reservations about Communist growth statistics and tend to accept the lower end of ranges of estimates made by outside analysts.[5]

fundamental importance in evaluating the power of a country, and political scientists often use them in establishing relationships with political indexes.

Trade and the Balance of Payments. Trade figures are indexes of economic strength as well as indicators of relationships among nations. Economies which buy and sell a great deal on the world market must meet world competition, and usually are strong compared to the heavily protected economies. Some of the fastest growing economies in the world have high levels of international trade; Canada, Germany, the Republic of China, Hong Kong, Singapore, Thailand, and Israel are examples. Countries with extensive trade ties tend to have friendly international relations with each other. For example, the United States and the developed countries of Western Europe have high GNPs and high levels of trade, and they also have close relationships in international affairs. On the other hand, trade controls can be used as a weapon. The United States during the 1950s and 1960s was a leader in organizing an embargo on shipments of strategic goods to China, Russia, and other Communist countries, and until 1972 maintained an almost complete embargo on trade with the Peoples' Republic of China. This helped maintain a Cold War relationship.

Prior to 1960, the Soviet Union and China were developing close trade and economic connections. This relationship was fractured in 1960 when Russia withdrew its technicians over a political dispute and drastically reduced its trade with China. Thus, Communist nations also use trade as an instrument and weapon of foreign policy.

Low levels of trade of Communist nations are due in large part to their suspicious ideologies. They normally take little advantage of what economists call comparative advantage, or trading goods they can produce best for advanced technology and goods from other countries.

Balance of payments terms used to describe trading relationships are essential for an understanding of the world's economic and political problems. To understand the various meanings of the balance of payments we could imagine Americans trading with Canada having all their payments going through one checking account. American imports or purchases of goods from Canada would cause

negative trade balances. These would be offset by pluses
for sales of goods to Canadians. If at the end of the year
the Americans sold more than they bought from Canada,
the United States would have an export surplus or
"positive" commodity trade balance.

The same concept is used for services (invisibles). This
means that Americans might buy (or import) services
such as airline tickets in Canada, spend a lot of money for
tourism there, or give money to private Canadian
charities. This spending would build up the negative side
of the ledger for the United States, and such payments
might be so large that the United States at the end of the
year would end up with a "deficit on goods and services,"
although the United States might have a surplus on the
export account for trade in goods alone.

The third major classification of transactions going
through the fictitious banking account would be loans or
capital transactions. Thus, if Americans decided to invest
in a factory in Canada, they might send factory
machinery to put in a Canadian plant. This loan of
machinery would cause a "deficit" on the U.S. capital
account, balanced by increased U.S. exports in the trade
account. The Canadians would have a plus, or increased
debt on their capital account balanced by increased
imports and an increased deficit on their trade account
from the same capital transaction. Developing countries
are strengthened by import surpluses of equipment for
investment in their country, if it is a good investment, and
by "pluses" on their capital account which represent
increased borrowing.

The most important figure is the bottom line or overall
balance of payments surplus or deficit. After all the above
transactions are added up — the trade, the services, and
the capital transactions — there is a surplus or deficit. If
there is a deficit, this means a country has imported too
many goods and services and has not exported enough or
received enough loans, investments, or gifts to cover the
deficit. Such a country is then forced to pay the balance in
its foreign exchange reserves or to borrow reserves from
the International Monetary Fund, which is the world's
central bank. The country then has a balance of payments
deficit.

If a country has exported more goods and services than

it has imported, and if a country has not lent out all its resulting surplus, it has a surplus balance of payments position reflected in a surplus or increased holdings of gold or foreign exchange reserves.

These tools are useful in evaluating some of the key issues of economics and ideologies.

Capitalism and Communism — Doctrine and Reality

One of the fundamental tenets of Communist and Marxist ideology is that the capitalist nations by their very nature promote war to obtain profits and to take over control of raw material supplies in developing countries. Their ideology holds that capitalism is the major cause of war, and that world peace and prosperity could be achieved in a commonwealth of Communist nations.

The theory is persuasive to many. Some social democrats also argue that the armaments industry and the military-industrial complex have helped drive the United States and other nations into war. They note that arms exports of the United States have grown to be the second largest export, and that many nations, including authoritarian countries controlled or strongly backed by the military, obtain arms supplies from the United States. By 1980 the U.S. was exporting over $15 billion annually in military items, much of which was financed by government loans and grants.

Communist propaganda asserts the high military budget of the United States and large exports of military goods reflect capitalists' control of the political and economic system, which thrives on war. One cannot deny that the profit motive and the desire of military authorities to maintain a military production capacity plays an important part in military exports. However, if we examine military power data more closely, the easy answers of the Communist and social democrat ideologies break down. The Soviet Union's military strength by most observers is deemed to be roughly equivalent of that of the United States even though the GNP of the United States is probably 50 to 80 percent higher. China has one of the lower per capita GNPs in Asia, which reflects its standard of living, but it has developed advanced nuclear weapons and delivery systems. North Korea built up its military capacity at the expense of consumer goods, and would have easily taken over South Korea which had almost twice the population, if the United States and other nations had not rushed to its aid in 1950. North Vietnam developed a formidable military machine which overran South Vietnam, despite massive direct and indirect help from the United States. In other words the Communist economies use economic controls for building military strength and power rather than consumer goods and raising the standard of living. The Japanese market-oriented economy has less than one percent of its GNP going to military production, and it is the only large Asian country which has achieved a European standard of living.

Communist governments with their ability to organize and direct the whole society to create military power usually surpass the strength of opponents even when they have higher GNPs. Their controls enable them to man and equip large armies. This political and economic fact is essential to understanding international relations in the current world, and it is often overlooked because of the extensive Communist propaganda that asserts Western societies are oriented toward war. The Communist propaganda is still using the momentum generated from the pre-World War II era, in which the German and Japanese fascist type societies developed high levels of military production — the Communists assert these were essentially capitalist societies. Liberal democrats would say they were totalitarian societies in which the government took over control from businessmen and market forces.

There is another fundamental ideological conflict at the center of many international problems. The Communists and the social democrats claim that government ownership of enterprises, or socialism, is much better suited for a young developing country which wants to speed up development. They also assert their systems offer a chance to provide a job for all and more equitable distribution of income. Their theories are persuasive, and many representatives of developing nations reflect these ideas in their speeches and in their caucuses in the United Nations and other organizations. This assertion puts pressures on Communist and authoritarian governments to present statistics in the best possible light and to resist the type of analysis and questioning of data that is permitted in open political systems.

The Communists also blame the capitalist countries for the revolutionary upheavals in the developing world. When revolutionary elements wage wars against governments allied with Western industrial countries, the Communists call them wars of national liberation. Communists, for example, allege the Vietnam War was initiated by U.S. imperialism and opposed by the forces of national liberation. The Communists and sometimes the social democrats pictured political opponents and governments of market-oriented countries such as the Republic of Korea, Taiwan, Thailand, Saudi Arabia, and the Philippines as right wing military dictatorships that are puppets of the U.S. and Western imperialist or capitalist powers. These charges become less extreme as one proceeds along a continuum from Communist critics into social democratic critics. The above political charges of the extreme left are predictable, and any war, even involving open aggression such as the Korean War of 1950, is pictured in the above standard Communist terms.

The above ideological controversies on the international scene are often reflected in internal politics of many states. In the United States, particularly during the Vietnam War, many American critics asserted the military industrial complex was behind the war. They claimed the U.S. participation in that war was based on economic and business motives, ignoring the many complicated and confused ideas which influenced United States leaders. (See Chapter 9.)

When we examine the real world of international investments and economic development, however, a different economic picture emerges. Many of the most dynamic and rapidly expanding economies are market-oriented and make extensive use of private investments from abroad. Examples in Asia of such countries are Singapore (nominally a socialist government), Malaysia, Taiwan, South Korea, Hong Kong, and Thailand. They emphasize consumer items and none concentrate on military power so they would overshadow their neighbors like the Communist countries in their area do. The Communist countries of Asia, and not the others, have stressed military production and have been the supporters and initiators of revolutionary movements and wars.

Thus, in evaluating the economic power of various countries and how this affects international relations, GNP indexes are only a beginning for analysis. Depending on the issues involved policymakers might have to contend with powerful ideological myths about economic and political developments. To check the validity of doctrine we should look at the actual economic and military outputs of systems, rather than what ideologies claim should be the reality.

Political Implications of the Economic Crises of the Seventies

Economists are still trying to puzzle out implications of the energy crisis of the 1970s, but most agree it demonstrated that international cooperation is essential. Changes in economic and political power are emerging that could affect the future political stability of the world system. This depends not only on whether some of the newly rich oil producers will impose an oil embargo, but also on how they will handle the massive economic power arising from their growing foreign exchange reserves.

During the 1950s and 1960s overall indexes of world trade prices were relatively stable, but from 1972 to 1974 world trade prices, led by oil, increased about 70 percent in dollar terms. Many economists expected a depression and other serious disruptions of the world economy. However, the international economic system was flexible enough to permit oil countries to invest extra funds in world financial centers, which could use them to ease the adjustments. The International Monetary Fund also channeled funds back to oil importing countries which were hardest hit. However, the burdens of debt still threaten the international system.

Germany and Japan were pillars of strength in the

crisis with strong balance of payments positions, while the United States after 1976 ran tremendous balance of payments deficits. One of the major problems with the United States is that after World War II dollars had been the basic currency used in world monetary transactions. Many countries counted their dollars like gold reserves. As a result, investments from abroad were attracted to the United States. With the weakening of the dollar after the oil crisis, investments in America were less attractive. Some feared foreign investors would withdraw their dollar investments which could cause panic, like a run on the bank. This did not occur in large part because Saudi Arabia and other oil producers invested over $100 billion of their earnings in the U.S., and the world financial markets worked out cooperative arrangements for excess funds.[7]

With the ending of the Vietnam War and with the persisting energy crisis, issues such as the actions of OPEC on oil prices, the weakening of the dollar, inflation, and related economic problems took over the economic headlines. Energy supplies and economic problems rivaled traditional military issues as areas of concern for policymakers.

Elements of Military Strength

Prior to the nuclear age the military strength of nations was relatively easy to assess. The size and quality of armed forces were indicators of national strength along with a nation's potential to call up reserves and support a war effort. This in turn required a strong industrial base to produce military items and a large population for recruits.

Now there are nuclear weapons with such awesome power that they can devastate civilization, and leaders would use them only as a last resort, if at all. In fact, the United States has fought two major wars in Korea and Vietnam without using them. Nevertheless, crucial political decisions are made by Congress about nuclear weapons production, deployment, and control so it is essential for the political analysts and the public to be informed about the potential of these weapons and implications of their use. Some nuclear experts express their knowledge in extremely complex terms and formulae, but it may be that the overwhelming truth of the situation is so terrible and simple that any layman can understand it: that is, there is no defense against these weapons.[8]

Political scientists analyze military strategy as basic to an understanding of international politics. The fundamentals of the arms race are also of interest because of the tremendous burden it places on governments. Defense expenditures are the largest element of most government budgets. Moreover, the U.S. Defense Department's drain on manpower is more than all other government agencies together. Education expenditures are a close second to defense, but one-third of the world's population is in school, and governments spend only about $230 a year on each child compared to about $15,000 for each soldier. Analysts assert military expenditures add considerably to inflation, and in the United States this spending preempts 40 percent of the government's research and development funds, funds which could have been invested in technology or in human beings.[9]

Although nuclear forces are by far the most dangerous and potentially destructive, most of the military budgets stress conventional forces, which are relatively expensive. With the nuclear stalemate these conventional forces are also the most useful for national power, as illustrated in the attempts of the United States to build up its conventional strength in the Persian Gulf during the Iranian-Afghanistan crisis of 1979-1980.

Nuclear Arsenals. The growing stockpiles of nuclear weapons have greatly complicated national power calculations. The weapon that virtually destroyed Hiroshima was the equivalent of about 17 kilotons or 17,000 tons of TNT. By the 1950s both Russia and the United States had developed standard thermonuclear weapons 100 times as powerful, and the Soviet Union had tested a weapon about 3,000 times as powerful as the atom bomb that virtually destroyed the city of Hiroshima.

For a while many experts and ordinary people assumed it would be unthinkable to use nuclear weapons in a future war. These convictions have given rise to a number of nuclear arms limitation agreements and to the SALT negotiations between Russia and the United States, which are treated in detail in Chapter 13. Despite these views and these agreements scientists have been commissioned to develop more accurate and powerful warheads and missiles with multiple nuclear warheads. Experts then have come up with computer calculations to show how the United States or Russia in a surprise attack might wipe out most of the land based rockets of the other side. This caused more alarm, and the arms race has continued with more warheads and more accurate delivery systems. The announced aim of these efforts has been to deter or frighten the other side from starting a war. The result has been to multiply nuclear warheads in the hands of the superpowers and maintain the distance between them and the other nuclear powers, although any one of them could cause nuclear havoc.

Nuclear weapons, even of the second class nuclear powers, are so terribly destructive that they cannot be used for realpolitik like conventional weapons. A nation threatening another country with nuclear weapons risks encouraging the latter to try in a surprise attack to wipe out as many as possible of the nuclear weapons of the nation making the original threat. The weapons of the second class nuclear powers, therefore, have not been used in the way that conventional military strength has often been used to achieve goals in the game of power politics. Nuclear weapons of the second class powers are silent deterrents.

These silent deterrents are cheap. Britain built its nuclear weapons quickly after its scientists had helped the United States build the bomb that forced Japan into surrender. Britain's nuclear punch in the 1970s consisted primarily of four nuclear submarines, each with 16 Polaris missiles purchased from the United States and armed with British nuclear warheads. It was a bargain, costing the 1976 budget about $130 million annually out of a total government budget of about $8 billion. In addition, Britain has nuclear weapons for its bomber force, which to Russia is a threat to be reckoned with although the bombers are getting old. Of course, in a nuclear war Britain with its concentrated island population would be no match for the Soviet Union with its large land mass and far superior striking force. Britain, therefore, relies on its alliance with the United States.[10]

French "grandeur" or power was the major motive for its development of nuclear weapons. In 1959 President de Gaulle spoke out for establishing "a striking force" that could be deployed anywhere in the world. He insisted that France must make the nuclear weapons for this force or purchase them without strings so they would be under French control. His speech implied obtaining intercontinental ballistic missiles.

De Gaulle pressed forward with the strike force after being rebuffed in obtaining nuclear assistance from the U.S. in order to achieve French grandeur and independence, which were at the heart of his policy. Moreover, de Gaulle and French policymakers have indicated they did not trust the U.S. control of the nuclear trigger, since they feared in a showdown the United States would not sacrifice its people and cities in defense of France. Other French policymakers were afraid of United States belligerence. Having its own nuclear striking force gives France an option of staying out of a nuclear war involving the Soviet Union and the United States.

Although France has a formidable nuclear striking force, it would be difficult to show how that has profitted its foreign policy. French withdrawal from its overseas colonies has been as dramatic as that of Britain's. Any influence that France exerts with those colonies today, in assisting them from attacks from neighboring countries as it did for Chad in the spring of 1978 and Zaire in 1977, is from its conventional military strength.

China has been engaged in bitter disputes with the Soviet Union since 1960. One of the major causes of the split with its former ally was the Soviet's failure to provide China with a sample nuclear weapon. At times the dispute has involved nuclear threats against each other, and China's nuclear program is primarily designed with the Soviet threat in mind. The Chinese repeatedly have claimed, however, they would not be the first to use nuclear weapons, and they have not even used them to threaten the rival Taiwan government that claims to represent China, despite the fact that Taiwan controls heavily fortified islands only a few miles from the Chinese coast. The Chinese tested their first thermonuclear weapons at a time when the Soviets reportedly were considering a preemptive strike to destroy the Chinese nuclear capability. (See Chapter 9.) China reportedly is developing an intercontinental missile with a range of 3,500 miles which would reach Moscow, but the range does not extend beyond Alaska. Although the Chinese nuclear force does not approach the strength of that of the Soviet Union, the weapons would create havoc in the Soviet Union in an all-out war. The Chinese have the most active program of building deep air raid shelters of any country in the world.

Israel reportedly also has a small nuclear weapons capability.[11] This may be a major factor in strengthening its position in the Middle East. It wisely has not made a threat to use such weapons, perhaps because this would goad its wealthy Arab neighbors into a program of developing nuclear weapons. Israel, with its very small size and concentrated population in three major cities, would be extremely vulnerable to a nuclear attack. Israel, therefore, relies on its conventional weapons, and with the help of the United States maintains probably the highest conventional military capability in the world in comparison to population or Gross National Product.

Thus, even among the second class nuclear powers nuclear weapons are so awesome in their potential that there is a nuclear standoff with their potential enemies. Their value is as a silent deterrent rather than a card that can be played for positive gains in the game of power politics. These powers put relatively little money or effort into developing sophisticated nuclear missiles, and have relied on a relatively cheap deterrent. The contrast between their expenditures and that of the superpowers is demonstrated in Figure 1.

Tactical Forces. The familiar conventional military elements — armies, tanks, aircraft, and navies — are still highly regarded as instruments of power politics. After 1950 Germany's[12] military potential helped gain its independence and a major position in the NATO alliance. A German general commands the NATO forces of Central Europe, and German divisions provide more than half the ground troops of the alliance.

Nevertheless, there is no doubt that German leaders today see peace as an overriding objective of foreign policy. If during a war only a small part of the 7,000 tactical nuclear weapons in Germany under U.S. control were fired, Germany would be a wasteland. A unanimous report to the United Nations by 12 experts from 12 countries, released on October 23, 1967, by U.N. Secretary General U Thant, pointed out that a tactical nuclear war, involving 500 to 1,000 strikes against purely military targets in Germany, would result in the death of 1,500,000 civilians plus the exposure of many millions more to lethal or very serious radiation. If the attack included targets such as air fields, supply depots, and armament factories, the effects would be the same as a strategic nuclear war which would completely devastate West Germany.

Despite the importance of a strong economic productive base and large populations for building conventional military strength, morale and quality of efforts still count for a great deal. We have noted in the previous chapter how the population of Israel's neighbors outnumbers that of Israel by a factor of about 15 to one. Nevertheless, the unfavorable balance against Israel, indicated by the population figures, is redressed when one analyzes the size and capabilities of the military forces. Israel within 48 hours can mobilize its people to provide an effective fighting force of about 400,000 men and women. Arab nations with a much greater population do not mobilize to such an extent, and Egyptian, Syrian, and Jordanian forces number only about 580,000. Moreover, as long as the Egyptian army of about 322,000 is at peace with Israel under the Camp David agreements, Israel's position is relatively secure. This explains Arab fury against Egypt for signing the separate peace with Israel. (See Table 6-1.)

In the Mideast there is a perception of a balance of power in military terms since there has been no open war since 1973. The balance is precarious, and perceptions can easily change in the highly inflammable atmosphere. Israel's nuclear weapons are still an ace in the hole, a silent deterrent, but groups in Israel and among their neighbors would probably support conventional war with all its risks if there were serious provocations. We will analyze this dangerous situation in Chapter 9.

Table 6-1   Middle East — Military Manpower and Population — 1975

	Military Manpower	Population
Israel	156,000*	3,400,000
Egypt	322,000	37,500,000
Syria	177,000	7,400,000
Jordan	80,000	2,700,000
Iraq	135,000	11,000,000
Saudi Arabia	47,000	8,900,000
Lebanon	15,000	3,200,000

*About 400,000 can be mobilized in 72 hours.
Source: The International Institute for Strategic Studies, *The Military Balance 1975-1976* (London: 1975).

Arms Exports and New World Power Centers

Much of the newly created oil wealth is being converted into military power, particularly in the Middle East. Since the new arms buildups in this area that began in 1974 the conflicts have been contained. Many observers including U.S. congressional critics fear that the rulers of the area may use arms in future quarrels over its vast wealth, or use the arms in a new war against Israel. U.S. government spokesmen, on the other hand, describe their policy as trying to maintain a balance of power in the area and to keep some control over the arms through training and spare parts, which they could not do if the arms were supplied from other sources. They add that wars arise out of conflicting claims and ideologies and not from arms shipments in themselves.

Iran has made the most dramatic arms decisions. In August, 1976, Iranian and U.S. officials announced that Iran would purchase $10 billion in arms from the United States in the coming years. On August 27, Secretary of State Kissinger explained that this deal would include sales of the advanced technology items including F-16 fighters at a cost of about $3.4 billion. For a few years it was the dominant military power in the Persian Gulf. In 1979 the new revolutionary government cancelled these U.S. arms contracts, severed its military ties with the

United States, and substantially dissipated its military power.

Saudi Arabia, Iran's neighbor, is the other huge purchaser of arms and related services from the United States. It has the financial resources to build a huge army, but with a population of only 8 million it does not have the manpower base for a great power. Most of its military "imports" of over $1 billion annually from the U.S. include services and material for construction projects such as ports, roads, and airfields, and not military equipment as such. Saudi Arabia's influence and power lie principally in its diplomacy and economic power. (See Chapter 10.)

The strength of two of the major non-Communist powers in Asia, South Korea, and Taiwan, have been built on U.S. military assistance and arms shipments. As a result of the Korean War the United States provided massive economic and military assistance to the Republic of Korea. In 1977 the United States deemed South Korea's position powerful enough to permit the United States to begin limited withdrawal of its ground forces stationed near the heavily fortified border between North and South Korea, but in 1979, the U.S. reversed this decision because of continued threats from the North.

United States military and economic assistance to Taiwan, which began after 1950, permitted it to become a powerful nation in a defensive sense. Even after breaking official relations with Taiwan, the United States continued to supply it with military items on a commercial basis.

The United States, which supplies about half of the world's arms trade, has had difficult policy decisions to make on implications of its massive arms sales. The U.S. forced more realism into arms purchases by the developing countries by drastically reducing the ratio of arms supplied under military assistance. However, the wealth of the oil rich countries and their perceptions of threats from Israel, Russia, and their other neighbors has kept sales high. Iran's extravagance helped bring about a revolution. There is fear among experts that other countries of the Middle East, such as Saudi Arabia, could suffer a similar fate. In May, 1981, the Reagan Administration ended restraints on sales of arms to friendly countries. It also pressed its European allies to install more tactical nuclear missiles. The supply of arms and spare parts gave the U.S. some control over large purchasers. It was, in short, another network involving the U.S. in the affairs of the world and forcing it to act like a superpower.[13]

Several patterns are evident from the above review of military power. In the Communist orbit Vietnam is the major new planet with military strength which has emerged in recent years. After the Vietnam war many observers assumed that North Vietnam would be a major power in Southeast Asia, although under the shadow of its neighbor, China. It had accumulated a vast arsenal of modern weapons from the war, principally from the Soviet Union and to a lesser extent China, but also from the billions of dollars of U.S. military equipment left in the wake of the collapse of South Vietnamese resistance. North Vietnam's military prestige was high since it had defeated the South, which had for years been supplied and supported by the most powerful military power in the world — the United States. North Vietnam's powerful forces helped Cambodian insurgents overthrow the repressive Pol Pot Communist government early in 1979, but it is too early to say whether it will continue to use its power and prestige to attack or subvert other nations of Southeast Asia.

In the non-Communist orbits, three of the major powers — Israel, Taiwan, and South Korea — have survived because of military aid from the United States. All three of them have been engaged in a conflict with enemies who claim their governments are illegitimate and are pledged to take them over. The United States has been deeply involved in power politics to support these allies. With the possible exception of Israel, much more than territorial adjustments would be required for peace.

Saudi Arabia, Libya, and other oil states have reinforced their position through the outright purchase of arms. Their oil revenues are tremendous, and in the course of the coming years their military as well as economic power will accumulate.

President Carter, in his 1976 election campaign and during his Administration, indicated an intention to reduce arms shipments. Yet he was faced with serious dilemmas in the game of power politics. Saudi Arabia, a major oil supplier, a friend, and a moderate force in the area, wants U.S. arms and trade. Most of the arms program for Saudi Arabia is going for construction projects. Israel relies on U.S. arms for survival. Thus, a president would find it difficult to change those patterns of military supplies.

President Sadat also pressed hard for military supplies from the United States. He expelled military advisors of Russia, which then cut off his supplies of weapons. United States officials would be extremely reluctant to turn down his request and alienate a leader who concluded the first Arab peace treaty with Israel and who is threatened by Libya.

On the other hand, the Shah of Iran overreached himself in attempting to make Iran the dominant military power in the Persian Gulf area. He used Iran's vast wealth to purchase large quantities of the most modern arms from the United States, which was glad to have an ally in the world's oil center. In the rapid modernization and power-building process, however, the Shah alienated powerful Moslem elements of Iran's population, and a popular revolution overthrew his government early in 1979. Many observers assigned most of the blame to the Shah's overemphasis on national power, prestige, and military strength.

There is no longer a simple equation — international power = military strength — since political and economic factors unique to each area complicate the equation. Saudi Arabia has accumulated wealth that can probably give them more influence than their arms superiority vis-a-vis immediate neighbors. The silent nuclear deterrent of Israel and the nuclear standoff among the other nuclear powers may be creating a situation where economic power and political leadership can achieve more than brute military strength. Iran's government overemphasized military power and was overthrown. It may be a harbinger that the 1977 "man of the year" was Anwar Sadat, president of a country with a weak military machine, who won the award on the basis of a media blitz covering his peace initiative and trip to Jerusalem. Moreover, Jimmy Carter, president of the world's most powerful country, in his first extended visits abroad visited Nigeria, Iran, Saudi Arabia, and Venezuela, all of them major oil suppliers of the United States. It would be a relief to the world if contests for influence were waged with economic and political power rather than military strength.

However, the above trends did not appreciably cut into military spending. Military budgets continued to mount, particularly among the oil producers and the other Third World countries. Arms expenditures have acquired a tremendous momentum in the United States and in the Soviet Union. We will now give a closer analysis to the way in which military and economic policies are generated by the policymaking process and later used in superpower diplomacy.

Summary

A nation's power is measured by how it develops and uses its economic and military resources. With the nuclear standoff economic factors are increasing in importance. The most comprehensive and widely used measure of economic strength is GNP, which is an estimate of the total value of output of goods and services. The balance of payments, which measures the results of international trade and related transactions, is another critical measure particularly in the 1970s when the skyrocketing oil prices caused international financial disorder. Despite these economic strains, the international system managed to channel excess funds as loans and investments back to the industrial nations who are major oil importers.

A basic economic tenet of Communist and Marxist ideologies is that capitalist nations promote rearmament and war to obtain profits for the ruling capitalist class. However, even low income Communist nations devote relatively more resources to military purposes than their non-Communist neighbors. Moreover, the Communist powers are more belligerent in supporting revolutionary movements than their neighbors. The Communists also assert their system is best suited for rapid economic development. Their claims are open to serious question, and successful record of development have been registered by countries relying primarily on the market system.

Nuclear weapons have greatly complicated calculations of relative military power in part because nations fear to unsheath them. Despite the tremendous destructive capacity of present nuclear weapons, however, governments continue to develop more powerful weapons and increase military spending. Even weapons of second class nuclear powers are so destructive they are not used for threats in realpolitik. Thus, conventional weapons and trade in them have regained relative importance in international politics, particularly in the Mideast.

FOOTNOTES

1. GNP per capita by itself is not a good measure of "economic development," but it is probably the best single index available. Other indexes such as the level of education and the distribution of income, health, and housing would give a more complete picture. Such data comparing economic and social development, however, are not as relevant to an international politics course as GNP data, which reflect national power, a focus of this book.

2. Hedrick Smith, *The Russians* (Quadrangle/The New York Times Book Company, 1976), Chapter IX; and series of articles by Kevin Close, *Washington Post,* June 7 to June 12, 1980.

3. See Amos Yoder, "Communist China's Economic Growth in Perspective," *The American Journal of Economics and Sociology,* July 1961, pp. 377-390.

4. Amos Yoder, "Obstacles to Soviet Economic Growth," *Orbis,* Winter, 1966, pp. 1013-1024.

5. See U.S. Congress, Joint Economic Committee, *Soviet Economy in a Time of Change,* A Compendium of Papers, October 10, 1979. I would accept the estimates of Herbert Block's "Soviet Economic Performance in a Global Context," who through the years has carefully evaluated the many studies of economic performance of Russia and other countries.

6. See United Nations, *A System of National Accounts* (New York: Department of Economic and Social Affairs, 1968), The United Nations Publications, Sales Number: E. 69. XVII, 3.

7. See address by IMF Managing Director H. Johannes Witteveen on "Financial Stability in the World Economy," *IMF Survey,* February 20, 1978.

8. U.S. Congress, Office of Technology Assessment, *The Effects of Nuclear War* (Washington, D.C.: U.S. Government Printing Office, May 1979).

9. Ruth Leger Sivard, *World Military and Social Expenditures* (Leesburgh, Va.: WMSE Publications, 1979), pp. 10-11.

10. The International Institute for Strategic Studies, *The Military Balance* (London: 1976-1977).

11. In the fall of 1975 unofficial reports originating in the United States about this capability were supported by CIA in testimony to Congress and in briefings to the press. Thus, Israel's highly skilled and motivated population has in a military sense overcome a serious population imbalance. The International Institute for Strategic Studies, *Strategic Survey 1975* (London: IISS, 1976); and *The Military Balance* (IISS, 1976).

12. Germany or West Germany is used as "shorthand" for the Federal Republic of Germany, and East Germany for the German Democratic Republic.

13. For an excellent discussion of the composition of U.S arms sales overseas and their implications, see Philip J. Farley, Stephen S. Kaplan, and William H. Lewis, *Arms Across the Sea* (Washington, D.C.: The Brookings Institution, 1978); and Laurel A. Mayer, "U.S. Arms Transfers Data Sources and Dilemmas," *International Studies Notes of the International Studies Association,* Summer, 1980.

7

The Policymaking Process

Government structures are used to convert policymakers' ideas into foreign policies and actions. These structures permit officials and political groups to influence policy but set limits for their actions. Even a powerful official like the President of the United States must sell senators, the Pentagon, the media, and the general public on a major policy such as SALT. The end results depend more on the substance of policy ideas and how well they are sold, than on the government structure itself. For example, both Communist and democratic governments have supported the Cold War as well as detente.

There are no universal models of this policymaking process, and each of the world's 150 plus governments has its own system. Certain generalizations are possible, in part because a certain type of system may lend itself to influence by a certain type of political group. Also, similar political groups in different countries often have ideas in common. For example, the military *tends* to take a relatively hard line on military issues, while career diplomats tend to be more willing to negotiate. Civilian leadership, however, can be more aggressive then the military, as illustrated by the aggressive and reckless policies of Hitler, which were ineffectively opposed by some top military leaders. In analyzing an issue in depth it would be necessary to look closely at the governmental process of each country involved to determine which leaders and groups exercise influence as well as at current ideas affecting policy.

It is not possible in a brief introductory text on international politics to analyze the many policy processes for the critical issues of this world. This would require naming all the key policymakers, analyzing their ideologies and foreign policy ideas, and evaluating how material, political, and historical factors affected their decisions. Then it would be important to look at the governmental process and the tactics they used to get ideas implemented. The purpose of this text is to demonstrate that the above are the important elements in analysis and to sketch in broad outline how these factors affected critical foreign policy issues. The government's policymaking process is where these factors converge and the winning policies emerge.

Stated this way the importance of the government process seems self-evident. However, in the United States the problem of analysis is confused by different meanings of the word bureaucracy, which is often used to describe the government structure. The word bureaucracy to some authors means simply an administrative policymaking group, but to others it also means a system of government administration marked by red tape and a proliferation of agencies. Many observers recognize only the latter definition. They assume the government process delays decisions and hinders new, imaginative policies which could solve international problems. In examining the effect of the governmental process on policies, I try to avoid the use of this loaded and ambiguous word bureaucracy in order to add clarity to analysis of the process of putting policies into effect.

First we will look at positions in the government of key policymakers and at their agencies. Although low level officials can take important actions to avoid crises, they do not make the headlines or history books. In a crisis, decisions usually rise to the top. We will, therefore, focus mostly on top officials who make decisions affecting war and peace. We will also look at groups outside the executive branches which often influence the policy process including the legislature, the media, and the academic community.

Most of the following analysis is focused on the U.S. policymaking system, because it is best known and because the U.S. has played the major role in foreign policy since World War II. Although it is not possible to analyze the policymaking processes of the other 150 plus governments which impact on foreign policy, I do draw on examples from other countries and suggest generalizations that often apply to other governments. It would be a mistake, however, to assume that generalizations applying to the U.S. policy process can automatically be applied to other systems. As already pointed out, grave mistakes are often made by assuming that another government will act in a "reasonable" way from our particular point of view. The major focus of this book, therefore, is on the conflicting ideas of policymakers rather than on the policymaking process that puts these ideas into effect.

The Government Framework

Heads of Government. The president or prime minister usually plays the major role in controversial and critical policy decisions. Even though new heads of government may know little about foreign affairs, they must take a guiding role and responsibility since their actions, or failure to act, could bring disaster on their country. Secretary of State Kissinger in 1974 helped President Ford, who had a minimum of foreign policy experience, to get immersed quickly in foreign affairs. Dr. Kissinger put trips to Russia, Japan, China, and Europe on his agenda soon after President Ford assumed office and arranged for talks with world leaders and ambassadors. One of the early decisions of President Ford was to approve the framework for a new Strategic Arms Limitation Agreement (SALT) at Vladivostok, Russia, on one of the most technical and controversial issues that a president faces.

The major reason for this quick immersion in foreign affairs is that in a democracy the head of government must obtain parliamentary support for major foreign policy decisions, which often require funds and legal authority for agreements. This involves mobilizing public opinion in support of a policy. Even heads of police states seek support from ruling cliques which support them and are careful not to take a foreign policy action which could be exploited by possible rivals. Such leaders of states often monopolize the news media to build up public support for their policies.

The importance of the head of government in foreign affairs is recognized without question in many countries. Chancellor Adenauer and later Chancellor Willy Brandt dominated Germany's foreign policy when they were in power, and Khrushchev made dramatic changes of course in Russia's policies after Stalin died.

In the United States the National Security Council machinery is often used by the President to tie together the views of military, diplomatic, intelligence, and other organizations which make foreign policy. President Kennedy, President Nixon, and Henry Kissinger as the President's adviser on national security matters used this organization to control the government apparatus and exercise the authority of the President in crisis situations or in foreign policy matters of fundamental importance. This was true even when the NSC was used only to provide small advisory committees to carry out studies and provide advice for the President.

Leaders of most countries have no broad foreign programs to administer and great alliances to manage, so power politics to them are less important than in the United States. Nevertheless, such leaders often have sensitive foreign policy problems with their neighbors. Leaders who wish to reinforce domestic support will also be keenly aware of the publicity that accompanies an activist role in foreign policy including the glamour of red carpet treatment abroad and the coverage of the news media. President Sadat of Egypt spent the weekend at Camp David with President Carter in February, 1978, to generate more support for the Sadat peace initiative with Israel. Today some foreign leaders, particularly in the developing world, may get publicity and gain political points in the opposite way by critical speeches addressed at great powers such as the United States. Thus, the head of government becomes the natural focus of attention and authority of foreign policymaking.

Foreign Offices. The Secretary of State and the Department of State, or in other countries the foreign ministers and foreign offices, are responsible for the day-to-day operations in foreign affairs and generally for coordinating the work of other government organizations abroad. As long as issues do not involve a crisis or domestic political issues, foreign office policymakers can take care of problems with other governments with little interference from top echelons, but on critical issues policymakers get higher officials involved including possibly their heads of government. If there is military action, the foreign office probably will not control policy. Its lower level officials, however, should keep their superiors informed of military action so that top foreign office officials can intervene with the head of state with a policy proposal if necessary.

Career diplomats, particularly of the older generation, have resisted the personal participation of heads of state or top leaders in diplomacy. The diplomats believe that with their years of experience they are more qualified to negotiate complicated issues. Charles Thayer in his book, *The Diplomat,* lists at length the disadvantages of leaders taking part in important conferences, such as their brief time to absorb the facts, the danger of causing normal diplomatic channels to atrophy, as well as lack of background on the issues. Former Ambassador J. Robert Schaetzel has written several articles criticizing the practice of heads of state meeting to make important decisions.[1] Harold Nicolson, who has written classic books on British diplomacy,[2] writes that nothing could be more fatal than the habit of personal contact between statesmen of the world.[3] He even states that repeated personal visits on the part of the foreign secretary of one country to the foreign secretary of the other should not be encouraged since it could lead to misunderstanding and create confusion.

Secretary of State Byrnes made the error of not keeping President Truman fully informed of his actions at the Moscow Conference of 1945 and was scolded by President

Truman on January 3, 1946, after returning from the Conference. Truman said he would not tolerate repetition of such conduct, and then read him a letter to reemphasize the point.[4] Since that time U.S. Secretaries of State have kept their Presidents well-informed.

Many other observers of foreign affairs criticize the inertia of diplomats and poke fun at "Foggy Bottom," the location of the State Department. Professor Henry Kissinger before he joined the Nixon Administration criticized the foreign affairs bureaucracy in his book, *American Foreign Policy.* He pointed out how staffs of modern executives influence policy and how the executive is reluctant to overrule them and get them out of a rut. As a result of the "nonaggression pacts" between U.S. foreign affairs bureaucracies, he asserted, policy papers frequently came out representing a lowest common denominator rather than an imaginative policy proposal. Doctor Kissinger, when he became Secretary of State, attacked this problem by personal negotiations with heads of state and foreign ministers. He expected the State Department officials to follow along and pick up the pieces. After his four years as Secretary of State, Secretary Kissinger had high praise for the career service, although he insisted that it required "strong leadership."[5] This was his way of saying the career service had done a good job of cleaning up the debris left by his initiatives.

Before evaluating the Kissinger style of diplomacy of meeting with top leaders to settle problems we should take a closer look at the other parts of the foreign policy machinery.

The foreign secretary or secretary of state is almost always a political appointee, but normally the top advisors are career officers. The annual replenishment of about 200 U.S. career foreign service officers is selected in a written and oral examination given throughout the United States to over 10,000 applicants.[6] They come from many universities, and they have been heavily influenced there by prevalent currents of thought and particularly the power politics approach to international affairs. They eventually acquire considerable responsibility for planning and implementing foreign policies, but to be effective policymakers they must carry out policies within the broad guidelines set by the President and the

Secretary of State. They must, moreover, clear their policies with key American agencies and officials, who often have differing views. They have a real impact as policymakers, particularly in avoiding crises, but their contributions are seldom reported outside the government.

The career services of many foreign offices usually are not chosen by normal civil service rules, but they are carefully selected by tests and interviews. In most countries they are expected to have an education oriented toward foreign politics, to have studied abroad, and often to know at least one other language, such as English, fluently. In the United States Foreign Service the practice now is to train an officer intensively in a foreign language after he enters the Foreign Service.

The State Department and other foreign offices are organized along geographic lines. There is a desk for every important country in the State Department. These desks are the funnels and coordinating points for sending instructions to Ambassadors abroad. (See Figure 7-1.) In the State Department important policy messages will usually have many clearances representing other policy desks and agencies with an economic, military, or other interest in the message. The U.S. Government, to avoid confusion and criticism, should speak with one voice, and the clearance process is the only way for it to achieve this aim. This causes delays and sometimes a reluctance to start a new policy initiative because of the many roadblocks along the way.

Bureaucratic inertia is a defect of the foreign policymaking systems and also a vice of business, university, and other systems. Some policymakers have a narrow view of their jobs. The aim of these officials is to protect their own positions or offices without worrying about broad questions of ideology and national interest. They are glad to see other offices take on controversial issues, and they themselves would probably not start a bandwagon rolling, although they would be glad to jump on after it was well under way. The Communist foreign policy machinery seems to produce more than an average number of "apparatchiki." Russia's diplomatic policymakers are notoriously hemmed in by instructions from Moscow. They make long, dull speeches in many

Figure 7-1 Key Elements of the United States Foreign Policy System

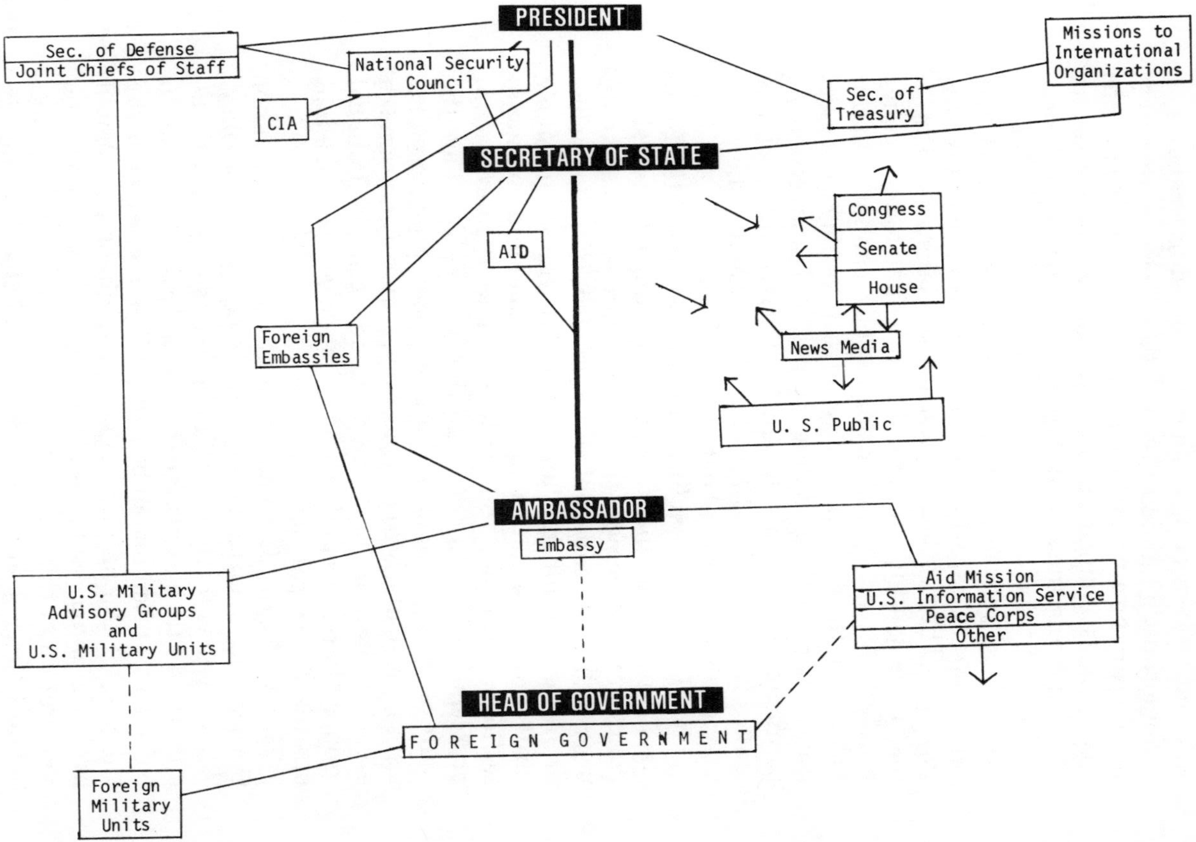

international meetings and get involved in wrangles on unimportant administrative matters. For example, year after year the Russian Ambassador in meetings of the Economic Commission for Europe would press for standardizing the size and type of paper used in reports.

United States diplomatic personnel are a competitive group. They are forced to change jobs and supervisors every few years, which keeps them from sinking into routine. They seldom become specialists within a discipline, but they are forced to face up to foreign policy problems in many dimensions. They cannot wait for years until the game is over to suggest the plays, but must make them in the middle of political and economic confusion and tight deadlines. Such an atmosphere makes it difficult for these officials to find a niche where they can worry only about keeping a job.

The "Foggy Bottom" bureaucratic image of the State Department and other foreign offices hinders analysis of policy making. Some of the criticism arises from a human urge to find a scapegoat for a problem. Foreign policy problems are difficult, and some of them are insoluble until time has a chance to erode political and emotional feelings. Although the world has many international problems, this does not mean that the problems are the fault of the diplomats working on them. Foreign policy issues, particularly in a democracy, require compromises among domestic and international groups. Political groups often force diplomats to change course and adopt unsatisfactory policies.

The Military. The military is the most influential of the organizations that compete in making foreign policy. When there is a crisis, the diplomats usually turn to the military for their assistance or advice. Crisis diplomacy to be effective often has to be backed by force, which is the business of the military. Also, crisis diplomacy should avoid the unnecessary use of force, which also requires the cooperation of the military.

The huge resources in command of the Pentagon in themselves provide a major challenge to the Department of State's management of foreign affairs. The Defense budget for 1980 was almost $150 billion. The 450,000 military and 100,000 civilian personnel overseas under the Defense Department carry on extensive relations with foreign nations. In 1975 Department of Defense personnel were stationed in about 320 major facilities abroad. Almost all of these installations required international agreements and arrangements for their operation as well as daily contacts with foreign officials. An important task of the diplomats is to keep trace of such military activities and to keep their superiors informed.

The Defense Department has its own channels of communications with its facilities abroad. In a crisis, often involving such facilities, the Defense Department policymakers are responsible through channels of command to the President and not to the Secretary of State. Often the diplomats are poorly informed. The Secretary of State or his officials may have to approach Defense with "hat in hand" to ask for military briefings or for transportation or military assistance in emergencies. This is true also in requests for help in a natural disaster, although the military is often willing to help. Diplomats are not in a position to issue orders to Defense but must get its agreement or presidential authority for use of military facilities.

The most critical areas of foreign policy are nuclear policy and military policies. The military has designed conventional and nuclear weapons, deployed them, and created the strategy for their use. Civilians are in a weak position to dispute the words of generals and experts on the capability or strategy involved in the use of military equipment. However, nuclear policy and military policy are intertwined with foreign policy so that two of the most active functional offices in the Department of State are the political-military office and the special agency attached to the Department of State for disarmament policy. Nevertheless, the Department of Defense is reluctant to give the Department of State access to nuclear secrets, to computer games on strategic problems, and to intelligence on foreign powers, and it resists guidance on nuclear policy. During my two year assignment to the Air Force under the State Department-Pentagon exchange program, I toured a number of military installations including the National Command Center. I was shocked on that tour when I discovered several top civilian officials on arms control matters, who were also on the tour, were not aware of the basic instructions under which the military commanders operated in a nuclear emergency. This military passion for independence and secrecy occurs also in the Soviet Union and Communist China, and little is known of their secret nuclear politics.

Secretary of State Kissinger's major success in controlling the Strategic Arms Limitation Talks (SALT) was accomplished only because as the "President's Advisor on National Security" he was able from the White House to carry through an extensive evaluation of nuclear weapons. In such a position Kissinger could use the President's authority to request Defense Department and State Department cooperation in providing information on nuclear weapons and strategy.[7]

In the smaller countries, and particularly in many developing countries, the local military also have a very powerful role because they are the ones with the guns, and often they are the power behind the leaders. There are relatively few governments with a tradition of civilian control of the military, and the common pattern for such countries is for the leader to be either a military type or one who is backed by the top military leaders. Even a person who has come up through military ranks, when he becomes a president or prime minister, tends to lose contact with the troops, and he must always be alert to the ambitions of a colonel or a general who may try to use his units to take over power through a coup. This type of a president or prime minister will be sensitive to the views of the military in making foreign policy and will try to avoid policies that will stir up resentment in the ranks. Moreover, the head of the government will often try to obtain modern equipment for his military forces and develop friendly and close relationships with powerful countries ready to supply equipment and training.

This pattern of military influence holds true in large part in the Communist countries. Although Communist leaders are well aware of the importance of the Communist Party controlling the military and often have a network of Party members throughout the military, in a crisis the men with the guns can control a Communist country just as they can control other countries. In China, where admittedly the information is hazy, it is probably significant that the Minister of National Defense, Yeh Chien-ying, was a member of the Politburo while the

Minister of Foreign Affairs was one step down and only a member of the Central Committee. After the Cultural Revolution at the end of the 1960s, the military exercised far reaching controls over all levels of government and were later detached only after a purge and the probable "execution" of Lin Piao, the Minister of Defense.

Thus, in many types of societies, the military plays a critical role in foreign policy. Although the liberal democratic as well as Communist ideologies would give the military a subsidiary role, when a major crisis develops policymakers and influential groups in a society often look to the military for advice and support. It takes a strong head of state to take issue with military leaders and to control a foreign crisis by diplomacy and negotiations.

Embassies and Missions. Countries are represented by embassies and other missions abroad usually headed by ambassadors, and their staffs play a key role in developing foreign policies and reporting to the foreign offices. The importance of a mission is often reflected in the buildings and size of the staff. Capitals such as Washington, D.C. are honeycombed with the embassies of over 100 countries as well as offices of international missions. Officials of these foreign missions obtain information and discuss and negotiate problems with host country officials. The missions include representatives of different agencies of the home country. Nominally these officials are under the ambassador who reports to the Foreign Office, but often they have their separate channels of communication and authority to their parent agencies.

United States ambassadors supervise the U.S. government personnel in their countries including military attaches and advisory units. (See Figure 3.) Military units engaged in combat activities such as those of the Vietnam War were in the military chain of command, but they took direction on relations with host states from the American ambassador. The ambassadors' authority over officials of other agencies has been confirmed in personal letters by Presidents Kennedy, Nixon, and Carter.[8] When I was assigned to Thailand during the Vietnam War as an embassy official I visited a number of U.S. Air Force units to determine how their spending was affecting the Thai economy. I was amused when officers in these units referred to the soft-spoken Ambassador Graham Martin with awe and would usually quickly volunteer they understood his major policy line that they were on "Thai" bases and not "American" bases.

Some ambassadors representing other major countries have less authority. Soviet ambassadors have control of only one line of communication to their home office. Other channels include the KGB intelligence organization, the commercial channel, the political channel, the military attaches, and in important missions, a high level party person who reports directly to the Central Committee of the Party.[9] The Russian foreign minister himself may be outside the mainstream of action and communications on a critical issue, particularly in areas such as the Middle East and Africa where military or paramilitary operations are under way.

Ambassadors and their staffs report to capitals under the Ambassador's name and make recommendations for action. The capitals are in the position of power, and medium grade officials write many of the instructions from capitals to embassies abroad. On important issues the ambassador's views may be made forcefully, and senior officials will respond from the capitals. On critical issues the ambassadors may draft messages to show they are written personally by them.

During the Vietnam War the personal messages written by Ambassador Graham Martin, who was assigned to Vietnam in the final stages of the war, and by Ambassador William Sullivan, then assigned to Laos, were avidly read by foreign service officers because of their frank and strong language. Distribution was often strictly limited to the State Department and White House, and their messages contrasted with the more widely distributed and watered-down policy messages.

There is a contest between the missions and the capitals, which often suspect their embassies are too sympathetic with host country officials. Ambassadors and their staffs see problems as involving foreign officials, many of whom are friends, representing real people with problems. Their State Department or foreign office counterparts in the home country may be thousands of miles away, cut off from personal contacts with the country concerned and interested mainly in calming legislative fears of getting involved with foreign countries and spending too much money. The home office also has to consider other countries and might wish to avoid getting too involved with one country that might have a suspicious neighbor which would expect similar attention and concessions. Home office-embassy relations represent a classic problem of political science of how to reconcile views of the center with those of the periphery, and to keep lines of communication and authority from getting clogged.

The United States and other countries also have diplomatic missions (not embassies) to international organizations, principally to U.N. bodies. The U.S. Mission to the U.N. in New York is located in a tall modern building across the street from the U.N. building. The other major center for United Nations activities is the Palais de Nations in Geneva. The U.N. and its associated Specialized Agencies in 1973 hosted 114 conferences and meetings there, which U.S. delegations attended. Headquarters for many of the U.N. Specialized Agencies are spread around Geneva along with numerous foreign missions to the United Nations.

Treasury and Other Agencies. Treasuries also play a key role in foreign affairs, particularly since the soaring cost of oil imports has strained the balances of payments of oil importing countries and threatened to disrupt the world monetary order. International finance is complicated, and heads of state are forced to rely on treasury experts for decisions that affect the ability of their countries to survive. Much depends on confidence, and undue political interference could undermine the system. For example, it is essential to maintain confidence in the International Monetary Fund and its management of Special Drawing Rights (SDRs), which in the past decade have become a major backing of world monetary transactions. In essence the SDRs are paper gold based on international confidence just as confidence in the Federal Reserve System backs U.S. currency. This need to maintain confidence is one reason Treasury officials tend to have a conservative outlook. Treasury officials and more liberal diplomatic officials often differ on issues such as the distribution of international assets to developing countries.

The United States Treasury Department jealously guards from outside interference its policymaking instructions to the International Bank and the International Monetary Fund, and it sends its own representatives to negotiate important international financial issues. It also has Treasury attaches in a few key posts in the world. In clearing messages of instruction for U.N. conferences I usually had the most trouble with the Treasury, which was the most conservative agency on economic issues. Only a strong Secretary of State with the confidence of the President can overrule the Secretary of the Treasury on an issue involving international financial policy. In Great Britain the Chancellor of the Exchequer is usually second only to the Prime Minister in power and influence.

Another very important agency in the government hierarchies of foreign policy is the Department of Commerce. Particularly in negotiations on trade policy and tariffs, the commercial policymakers play a strong role. The pattern is normally for U.S. Department of Commerce officials to have a less liberal trade policy than State Department officials, with conflicts settled in interdepartmental meetings. In countries such as Germany and Japan representatives of the foreign trade agency commonly play a relatively independent role from the foreign office on trade issues.

I once asked a Japanese official why the Japanese delegations were often the largest ones at important economic conferences. He told me with some amusement that many economic officials came to the conference because they did not trust the foreign office on economic issues.

Commerce officials usually work closely with private industries and are subject to protectionist pressures. In the United States the importance of trade negotiations was recognized by the President's appointment of a Special Representative for Trade Negotiations directly responsible to the President with a staff to coordinate the many export and import interests affected by trade negotiations. However, as a price for Congress approving the "Tokyo Round" of tariff concessions, the President agreed to transfer responsibility for trade policy to the Secretary of Commerce and Trade in 1979.

The aid agency, which in the United States is called the Agency for International Development (AID), reconciles demands to use funds for long term economic development abroad with demands to support immediate foreign policy interests of the donor country. The AID, which is responsible for presenting an aid budget to Congress, plays the key role in deciding how much money to allocate to various countries and purposes, with the State Department normally trying to get more allocated for foreign policy goals. For example, the Secretary of State may request large economic grants or loans to Egypt in connection with the Mideast truce agreement to offset military aid to Israel, although most AID officials would prefer to channel aid to the poorer countries such as those in Africa.

In the United States and a few other countries the intelligence organizations have played an important role in certain areas. During the Cuban Missile Crisis of 1962 President Kennedy was able to obtain intelligence that Russia was not on a nuclear alert, which was reassuring and helpful in assessing Soviet intentions. After the abortive CIA "Bay of Pigs" attack against Cuba in 1961 and the ensuing reform of intelligence operations, many observers thought the major mission of the CIA was limited to collecting intelligence. Even a good friend of mine, who was a high ranking official in the organization, thought 90 percent of their effort depended on collecting and analyzing non-secret material. Since 1974, however, former CIA officials have charged that the major emphasis of the CIA continued to be covert intervention in other countries. Victor Marchetti's book, *The CIA and the Cult of Intelligence,* indicates most of its budget went for such operations, and that this fact was concealed even within the Agency.[10] He states the Director of the CIA spent most of his time and effort directing paramilitary and interventionist activities. This included management of a guerrilla war in Laos (an operation widely publicized as a CIA activity before the Marchetti book), repressive activities in Vietnam, and association with the U.S. Company, IT&T, in intervening in Chile. A Senate committee under Senator Frank Church investigated and confirmed many of these charges. President Carter reorganized CIA pledging to end abuses associated with interventionist activity and to give Congress more control." President Reagan with congressional support reversed the policy by "unleashing" CIA.[11]

One other part of the CIA's work is worthy of mention, and this is its satellite intelligence. It helped finance and develop satellites that can pinpoint missile sites and tests. These "national means of verification" have made possible negotiation of the SALT agreements.

Another major intelligence organization in international politics is the Committee of State Security (KGB) of the Soviet Union. This is an extremely powerful organization in Russia — three of the 17 members of the Politburo in 1973 spent a significant part of their professional life in the KGB. An investigation of its operations by John Barron[12] asserts that officers of the KGB and its military subsidiary, the GPU, ordinarily occupy a majority of Soviet embassy posts and as much as 80 percent in some Third World countries. In addition it enlists some of the regular Soviet diplomatic staff to work with it. Its major operations abroad include espionage, spreading false and damaging information, and promoting demonstrations and revolutionary movements against Western policies. One of the most dramatic examples of its interference was its alleged influence over top officials of the Egyptian government under Nasser. After Nasser died, some of these officials reportedly plotted to overthrow President Sadat, who foiled the coup and then requested all Russian advisors to leave Egypt.[13] The KGB may well have dominated Soviet Middle East policy.

The CIA operations of the United States are controlled only at the top level under the National Security Council, and there is relatively little liaison with policymakers of the Department of State. Similarly, the KGB seems to be controlled in the Soviet Union at top levels. Although it is part of foreign missions, it is not subject to control of the foreign ministry.

Legislatures. Depending on the country and the issue, legislatures can play a zero role or the leading role in foreign policy. In authoritarian governments and in totalitarian governments legislatures at most play a ceremonial or a propagandistic role. In democracies in a crisis situation, when a country's territory or people are threatened, there is a strong tendency for the legislature to back strong initiatives of a president. When concessions are involved, legislatures frequently object and accuse the negotiators of weakness.

During the 1960s the role of the U.S. legislature waned and then recovered strongly during the 1970s. By the late 1970s many controversial issues were left in the hands of the Senate — the Panama Canal Treaty, which affected the course of Latin American policy; the SALT treaty which was the basis for our nuclear defense policy; aid to Egypt, Israel, and Saudi Arabia, which set the stage for Mideast peace and affected Arab energy supplies; and the Defense Budget which influences our world posture. This contrasts with the quick approval in 1964 of the Tonkin Gulf Resolution by 414 to two in the House and 88 to two in the Senate, which authorized the President to help defend South Vietnam with armed force as he deemed necessary — a blank check.

The Vietnam War was responsible for the growing assertiveness of the Congress in foreign policy during the 1970s. The growing Congressional opposition to the War culminated in the War Powers Resolution (Public Law 93-148, November 7, 1973) which limits the powers of the President to introduce United States armed forces into hostilities unless there is: (1) a declaration of war by the Congress; (2) specific statutory authorization; or (3) a national emergency created by an attack upon the United States or its armed forces. How this will work in practice is not clear since there is a question whether or not the Resolution is constitutional.

Congress chose in May, 1975, not to use this resolution to challenge the President when he used armed forces against Cambodian forces to rescue American civilians on the Mayaguez, a ship which had been captured close to one of the Cambodian islands. Within 24 hours he decided to mount an attack against a Cambodian island and ship to free its crew. In the process of mobilizing forces for the attack, and in the attack itself, 39 U.S. Marines lost their lives. Nevertheless, Congress did not challenge this use of force, even though his action was not authorized under the Resolution. The incident demonstrated the power of the President quickly to swing public opinion, congressional leaders, and the news media to back him when the United States citizens are under attack or being abused.

The most important instrument of U.S. congressional control is the power of the purse, and the President is dependent on appropriations for military and economic aid and for the military budget, both of which provide leverage in foreign policy. The requirement that treaties be approved by two-thirds of the Senate is also an important device for democratic control. The President submits major treaties to the Senate to establish fundamental directions of policy, such as the NATO defense pact or a SALT agreement. The two-thirds vote ensures when there is a change of administration that treaties will be taken seriously and will not be renegotiated.

Congressmen have a different viewpoint than that of Executive Branch officials. The business of these elected officials is to get the relevant facts and authorize or not authorize legislation necessary to implement foreign policies. The Executive Branch is on the defensive and must maintain good relations with Congress if it is to succeed. By the time policymakers and other interested persons have provided congressional committees with answers to questions and requested data, there often are volumes of printed material on foreign policy issues. This process provides some of the best and most revealing information to researchers and the media, while helping set the course of policy in the public's mind.

The Media and Their Impact

The news media have a major impact on international relations. Two of the most prominent policymakers of the 1970s owed much of their success to the skillful use of the media. Henry Kissinger was known to reporters as the best source of information on sensitive foreign policy issues. He carefully kept details of negotiations on SALT, the Mideast crises, and Vietnam negotiations under his control. Reporters wanting inside information would have to attend his informative backgrounders. At the time, I found transcripts of these conferences much more informative than standard State Department policy messages which were also circulated to officials for their information. After Kissinger became Secretary of State, a retinue of reporters would accompany him on his diplomatic trips, and he was readily accessible to answer their questions. The source designated in the media as a high government official on such trips was usually Kissinger. He kept the President well informed, but President Nixon or President Ford were no match for Kissinger's frank analysis, his wit, and detailed knowledge of critical issues.

President Sadat launched a media blitz with the aid of CBS and other reporters late in 1977 in his surprise visit to Jerusalem, and a few weeks later won *Time's* "man of the year" designation with little dissent. The TV coverage of his welcome at Lod Airport in Israel was a thrilling spectacle. Sadat probably knew, at least intuitively, that without backing from the Arab States, his constituents would have to be his own people and the world audience of the news media. Before the Sadat publicity blitz the PLO had gained prestige and power, based mostly on fear and violence, from its extensive coverage in the media. A few moderate Arab states, and particularly Saudi Arabia, also had considerable economic power based on oil and financial resources. Sadat, without oil or violence to back him, overwhelmed them all with his visit and his interviews with the media. Many reporters recognize that they can be used and are used by officials in the above manner. Reporters are in the business of reporting news, however, and they would not turn down good stories just because the stories would benefit officials by supporting their policies.[14]

This ability to be used is balanced by the tendency of reporters to be critical and even cynical about motives that might lie behind actions. Rarely, except in obituaries, do reporters indicate a leader's action was statesmanlike and taken for the good of a country or mankind. They usually cite self-serving motives to explain an action. For example, within a few days of Sadat's peace initiative to visit Israel the media were pointing to Egypt's weak military posture and faltering economy as a reason for the initiative. If he had taken an opposite hardline and threatened conflict, the media undoubtedly would have attributed Sadat's policy to a desire to detract attention from domestic problems through foreign adventure.

Reporters read each other's output which lends itself to waves of criticism developing on public figures as reporters feed on the others' reports. Although the media lives on criticism, U.S. reporters are very sensitive to critical remarks reacting as if they were a threat to the First Amendment of the Constitution. Libel laws afford little protection to public figures, and there is no important institution to criticize the press to discourage its excesses.[15]

Reporters are in the center of action for foreign news. Much of the political information coming into foreign offices is from news media or in telegrams reporting stories that originated in news reports. Diplomatic staffs check out the details and provide interpretation of such stories. Policymakers of the U.S. Department of State pride themselves on having read the morning cables and the news accounts or editorials in their fields of interest.

The watchroom of the U.S. Department of State, for example, has news tickers from the Associated Press, United Press International, United Press, Reuters, as well as the U.S. Government Foreign Broadcast Information Service (FBIS) which provides an extensive news ticker type of service on radio and occasionally newspaper items from abroad. During the Cuban Missile Crisis, for example, since I was not within the very small circle of decision makers, the only way I could keep up with developments was by watching the unclassified news tickers. These news reports reported mobilization of troops in Florida, as well as announcements and press releases of the United States, reports from the Soviet Union, and actions in the United Nations and the Organization of American States.

Many reporters cover the White House, the State Department, the Pentagon, and Congress. TV teams and radio announcers report on interviews with leading officials. These reports are read, transcribed, and summarized for key policymakers.

Today's reporters do much more than ferret out information for the public and incidentally for officials. The most successful reporters include interpretation in their stories. The influential newspapers, the *New York Times* and the *Washington Post,* have large staffs at home and abroad reporting on political and social factors that lie behind the major news stories, and few of their foreign stories rely entirely on the large news services.

The columnists, editorial writers, and news commentators exert wide influence. They often seem to direct much of their editorializing to policymakers, openly suggesting certain policies are wise or foolish, or selecting information in such a way that certain policy alternatives seem the best to take.

With the exception of a few East Coast newspapers the U.S. press in the years after the Vietnam War probably gave less attention to foreign news than it did in the isolationist 1930s.[16] However, by the end of 1979 and in 1980 with the crises and conflicts centering on Iran and Afghanistan there was a dramatic increase of news media coverage of this area. Citizens of the United States at that time probably felt more involved in world crises than they did in the 1930s because of daily TV exposure, whose intensity far exceeded that of the printed word.

The pluses and minuses of such close exposure to foreign news are difficult to weigh. TV as a medium lends itself to propaganda; it is easy to show the emotional and dramatic scenes and difficult to promote reasoned debate and consideration of issues in depth. As authoritarian governments which control this news medium are able to reach more and more people, it could become a dangerous weapon to support reckless or harmful policies. TV in the democracies like the United States at least is governed by the market. Newscasters do not take an obvious partisan view of political issues or they will lose viewers and sponsors; moreover the legislatures can hold them to the line of giving fair treatment to political parties. In countries like Britain public TV is required by law and custom to be nonpartisan.

TV has a great potential for helping understanding in international affairs by crossing national boundaries, and the growing use of satellite transmission for news and special events is tying the world closer together. Such transmissions as yet do not reach into the Communist countries to an important extent. The technology exists but not the permission to use it. One of the most controversial issues before the U.N. and the U.N. Educational Scientific and Cultural Organization (UNESCO) is agreeing on rules to govern satellite transmission of TV programs across national boundaries. The Communist and authoritarian countries generally oppose such transmissions. This is part in fear of the effects they might have on their restricted political systems, and in part apprehension about their inferiority in communications technology vis-a-vis the advanced capitalist nations.

Operation of the Foreign Policy "System"

The executive branch, the Congress, and the media all interact in the foreign policy process. The president, or head of the government, tries to form a coherent system of foreign policy using his immediate staff and the foreign office or State Department as a lead organization. Depending on the country involved, the leader may have separate systems operated by the diplomats, the military, the intelligence agencies, the treasury, and other organizations. The State Department or foreign office tries to carry out a coherent foreign policy, even though it may not control or even be able to keep informed of the operations of agencies of its own country.

To make a coherent and non-controversial policy is almost impossible, because there are formidable amounts of communications that go back and forth between the public, government agencies, and between diplomatic establishments that provide inputs and feedbacks into the system. Political groups are alert to exploit openings and try to redress grievances. Herbert Marcuse, the famous left wing professor and a former State Department official, once told me the way to stop war would be to abolish printing presses and similar machines. If this were possible, diplomacy and war would cease, but of course so would most other types of useful and harmful activities of society.

Analysts of the behavioral school have made "content analyses" of communications trying to show how a foreign policy "system" works, which involves analyses of hundreds or thousands of messages to show the frequency of key words demonstrating, for example, friendly or unfriendly phrases. Even when such analyses are put into computers, this has not proven productive for policymakers working on current issues. The most significant communications are often the most secret. Some are oral and are lost to history and to the public, unless they turn up in memoirs or archives many years later. Even if they appear in current news reports, and many do, it takes a keen analyst to weigh them against other statements, which is a task that computer clerks or computers cannot do. Particularly in a crisis situation, some information may not get through, or get distorted, and lower levels may operate without clear direction from the top.

Many organizations are involved in foreign affairs, and political moves of governments are complicated by contests that occur between agencies and top officials of important nations. (See Figure 7-1.) Professors and analysts often puzzle over moves of policymakers that appear inconsistent with a general line of policy. With the competition of powerful agencies and opinionated leaders in a government, it is a wonder there is as much consistency as there is. Moreover, officials of a treasury agency or a military organization have a great deal of technical knowledge and they may have more in common with similar officials of foreign governments than they have with their own foreign offices. Treasury officials of different countries tend to speak a common language, read the same material, and take relatively conservative positions often at variance with those of their respective foreign offices. Military representatives abroad often tend to take a hard line that is far from the diplomatic and negotiating lines of their respective foreign offices. They sometimes conceal military moves from diplomats which could provoke reactions leading to a crisis.

Because of the contests among all these factions at home and in other countries, it is very difficult for an ordinary secretary of state to coordinate and take initiatives in foreign policy that involve military or economic issues. Secretary Kissinger was able to achieve dramatic breakthroughs by short circuiting the process through personal diplomacy — traveling for weeks visiting prime ministers and national leaders. At the same time, he made an equally strenuous effort to maintain support of the President as well as of Congress and news media. Many of the old line diplomats looked with jealousy and sometimes horror at these personal initiatives outside of regular government channels, and policymakers in the Department of State had difficulty picking up the pieces after him. This type of personal diplomacy, however, may be the only way in which a secretary of state or leader can complete negotiations in the face of entrenched positions of powerful military, commercial, and intelligence organizations. Kissinger could never have completed the Vietnam negotiations or Mideast negotiations without bypassing these organizations.

With the growing influence of the news media observers have suggested that we have entered an era of public diplomacy or media diplomacy in contrast with the old-fashioned secret negotiations. There is truth in this, particularly if confrontation is involved. We have noted that TV coverage of the Vietnam War and of the demonstrations against it helped pressure President Nixon to withdraw U.S. troops. Since then the use of portable TV cameras and satellite connections for newscasts have brought daily diplomatic crises to the living room TVs.[17] Sadat's cultivation of reporters and liberal use of media interviews enhanced his prestige and helped build up domestic support for his peace-with-Israel initiatives. The Iranian and Afghanistan crises of 1979-1980 were major media events. The coverage of the hostages in Iran forced President Carter to keep that crisis at the top of his agenda, and incidentally helped him win the Democratic primaries. In the Afghanistan crisis he pressured the Soviets in the U.N. forums and boycotted the Olympics to deter further aggression. The Panama Canal Treaty ratification debates of 1978 were major news events, and President Carter managed to get a victory in the Senate and in public opinion on this issue. Diplomats as well as politicians are more and more judged by their public diplomacy and their images in the media. A corollary of this is that we should analyze their ideas and ideologies to obtain a basic understanding of international politics.

Contests involving leaders, government agencies,

legislatures, the media, public opinion, and elections help determine foreign policy, particularly in democracies. The heads of government assisted by policymakers try to steer a course in the best interest of their countries and try to build up public support and avoid policies which would be rejected by the system. With all the confusion and pressures, bad judgment and inconsistency can result. The media helps as an accelerator at times and as a regulator at other times. It features the drama, mistakes, and discrepancies, and can, therefore, create frictions. It also encourages caution, or at least discourages inconsistencies by spokesmen for a government.

The Policymakers' Point of View

We are now at a point where we can make a few broad generalizations about the general point of view of diplomatic policymakers with the aim of helping make sense out of their actions in international politics. The viewpoints of such policymakers can be contrasted with those of reporters and professors who are major observers and critics of foreign policies.

A number of forces converge to encourage caution by policymakers. Many of them realize a wrong move by their government could bring catastrophe. International politics is not like a game where a team can lose a few contests and still end up in the Super Bowl. One serious error by a government could bring about war, which could be a disaster for participants and even for a large part of the world. Less serious errors could bring about major political and economic losses. Diplomats, therefore, soon learn to be cautious, particularly when a policy could involve force and the possibility of escalation.

The previous section noted powerful political pressures which surround foreign policy issues, and the reporters who are ready to highlight conflicts and headline sensitive information which could make problems harder to solve. Diplomatic policymakers soon learn by experience about complexities of foreign policy and that it is difficult or impossible to predict most international events. Perhaps one reason former officials do not write texts on international politics is that they have resisted analysis based on broad generalizations and on probabilities. Diplomats are trained to take actions on specific problems and analyze particular situations. For example, it is not helpful for officials who work on the Middle East affairs watching a tense situation develop between Israel and Syria to use as a guide a theory that war is less likely in a multipolar world of several major power centers than in a bipolar world with two superpowers. Instead, such officials will want to know as much as possible about the views of the leaders making the decisions in each country, the status of their armed forces, and details on the degree of support that these leaders enjoy domestically and internationally.

Many professors would be happy if they found political or economic factors that would give them a 70 percent positive correlation with past decisions by states on certain issues.[18] However, a policymaker would be a failure if they carried out policies that were right only 70 percent of the time, particularly if they involved issues of war or peace. Such officials would soon have their country at war, which could be a disaster. Diplomatic officials have to take risks, but they make every effort to avoid making critical decisions that have only a 70 percent or even a 90 percent chance of success. They do make mistakes, of course, as illustrated by the sad history of wars and conflicts.

Perhaps this realization of uncertainty in international politics accounts for the caution of diplomats that is often criticized by outside observers as a bureaucratic attitude. These policymakers realize that leaders with whom they deal are sometimes irrational, show poor judgment, and have human failings. Thus, diplomats cannot rely on a game theory that assumes the other side will make a rational or predictable response in its best interest. Moreover, officials know that even with the best information, accidents can bring about an unexpected result. For example, the death of Nasser of Egypt and his replacement by Sadat enabled temporary settlement of a dangerous dispute with Israel through the mediation of the United States.

Another basic problem of policymakers that often is not reflected in textbooks or news reports is the constraint of time under which officials work. Diplomats often have to make a decision on a day-to-day basis and go on record with their view either within their own government or in front of the news media. Diplomatic policymakers hesitate to make predictions and instead they qualify statements, because if they are proven wrong by events, they face hostile editorials and severe criticisms by opponents in the political process and by the news media. Diplomats should maintain a reputation for truthfulness and reliability if they are to work effectively with their own government and with foreign officials. Secretary Kissinger was severely criticized for his "peace at hand" statement on Vietnam in November, 1972, which to some implied a truce in a few days or weeks. The fact that the truce came about a few months after his statement did not mollify many reporters who suggested that the statement was made originally for the presidential election.

Policymakers, like all human beings, are biased to some extent and are influenced by images created or reinforced by the news media. Diplomats who have lived abroad for extended periods, however, can more readily discern their own countries' prejudices since they have dealt with foreign leaders and been exposed to the foreign press and public. Ambassadors and other diplomats have been accused of being parochial and oversold on the point of view of foreign countries. They are often chided about this and they should guard against losing their perspective. Nevertheless, they are involved in the problems of their areas and they can observe first hand the results of policy decisions. Diplomats are close to the facts and tragedies involved in war and disasters that may result from policy decisions. The consequences may not be as clear to policymakers, reporters, and academicians thousands of miles away.

Normally, officials are forced to take an interdisciplinary approach and to integrate economic, political, and other factors in a decision. The oil crisis, worldwide inflation, violent changes in grain prices, and the international monetary crisis have brought economics to the foreground of the minds of political policymakers. Many have been forced to accept reduced aid and military programs for their areas because of economic factors. Economic officials have always been forced to recognize politics in their decisions. Diplomats operate in an interdisciplinary world, more so than reporters or professors who teach in a particular discipline. This text attempts to show the importance of economics in today's world and the importance of politics to economists.

A policymaking approach is similar to a decision making approach to foreign policy, but there can be significant differences. A major advantage of the policymaking approach is that it looks for individuals or groups working on problems or supporting certain ideas. This could be a President or a Secretary of State, but in large and powerful countries a group of policymakers or agency or even a legislature may be directly responsible for certain policies. The policymaking approach, therefore, can jump back and forth among several levels of government and policy analysis. Policymakers instinctively focus attention on other officials or groups of officials who are their counterparts and who must clear policy papers, even though this may not be the top official or decisionmaker who formally approves an instruction. Such top officials may sign messages because they have confidence in their subordinates even though they do not understand the details of a policy and all its implications.

For example, to understand the U.S. position on the Strategic Arms Limitation Talks (SALT), one should understand the views of top policymakers and also officials in the Pentagon, the Department of State, the Arms Control and Disarmament Agency, and key members of Congress. The President, who is the decisionmaker authorizing any agreement, may understand the major issues, but at most he may have negotiated only a few issues in the agreement, and those issues at the prompting of subordinates. On SALT issues officials in the Pentagon often come up with a uniform view, although it is also quite possible the Secretary of Defense and the three services originally may differ depending on whether the proposal is to limit an Air Force, Navy, or Army weapon.

Fortunately for the students much information is available on the views of competing groups. Hundreds of reporters around the world are engaged in trying to unearth policy conflicts and to air them for their readers. The disputes among groups and leaders are much more interesting to the public than straight-forward, unexciting accounts of constructive acts in foreign affairs. Officials leak information to the press to undermine their opponents and even their superiors. The Xerox machine, as illustrated by the *Pentagon Papers,* has been a boon to the media. Officials write memoirs and articles after they leave office in order to throw light on their actions and to support a goal they failed to achieve while in office. Congressional investigations and former agents have exposed even the secrets of the CIA. There are few secrets left.[19]

In large democratic governments policy instructions on issues such as arms limitation are usually prepared after days or months of debate among officials of different offices. Policymakers involve the media through planned and unplanned briefings and leaks to reporters. Constitutional processes and political pressures normally encourage careful consideration by legislatures, all of which act to reveal the controversies to the public.

An understanding of crisis politics requires an analysis of ideas of leaders and policymakers more than the analysis of structures of governments. In other words the substance of policy ideas is more important than the policy process. The competition of policymakers to get political support for ideas is the basis for international politics. The complicated political game at the national level is carried forward with politics among policymakers at the international level.

We will now apply the framework of analysis developed in the first seven chapters to international politics in the superpower system, which has dominated the world since World War II.

Summary

It is important to analyze the policymaking structure and process, because it is here that factors affecting policies converge and the winning policies emerge. There are unique organizational factors for each government but it is possible to make a few generalizations.

Heads of governments are forced to lead in foreign policy, because the existence of the state depends on their policies and they must obtain support of parliaments, ruling groups, or the public to implement policies. Foreign offices and Department of State officials carry out important day-to-day business. Crisis decisions usually rise to the top of the government structure and involve other agencies, particularly the military. The military with its huge resources, channels of communication, and control of weapons is the most influential element in most crises.

Ambassadors can play key roles in diplomacy, although they often are at a disadvantage in comparison with officials in the capitals. Other important agencies in making decisions are the Treasury, CIA, and aid and commerce officials. Legislatures exert leverage principally through the control of the purse. This was particularly true in the United States after the Vietnam War. The news media also influence international affairs. They tend to distort the picture by featuring controversies rather than positive accomplishments. It is difficult in a democracy for an entirely consistent policy to emerge from the interaction of the Executive Branch, the Congress, and media, but different elements of the policy process tend to restrain and check on each other. Only the press has no major institutional critic.

Diplomats have a healthy respect for the policy process and are forced to be cautious in their public statements to avoid public criticism. In our approach to foreign policy analysis we will focus on major centers of influence and determine how ideas and ideologies are used in the process.

FOOTNOTES

1. J. Robert Schaetzel and H.B. Malmgren, "Talking Heads," *Foreign Policy,* Summer, 1980, pp. 130-142; J. Robert Schaetzel, "The Pull of the Past," *Washington Post,* January 7, 1977.

2. Sir Harold Nicolson, *Peacemaking* (New York: Houghton-Mifflin and Company, 1933), and *Diplomacy* (New York: Harcourt and Brace, 1939).

3. Cited by Charles W. Thayer in *The Diplomat* (New York: Hawker and Brothers, 1959), p. 109. See also J. Robert Schaetzel, "The Pull of the Past," *Washington Post,* January 7, 1977.

4. Harry S. Truman, *Years of Trial and Hope* (Garden City: Doubleday and Company, 1956), p. 550.

5. Henry Kissinger, *White House Years, op. cit.,* pp. 27-28, 887.

6. Department of Defense Comptroller, Information Operations and Control, May 18, 1977.

7. John Newhouse, *Cold Dawn, The Story of SALT* (New York: Holt Rinehart and Winston, 1973); Kissinger (1979), *op. cit.,* pp. 130-138.

8. Department of State, *Newsletter,* November, 1977, pp. 3-4.

9. See Roy C. Macridis, Editor, *Foreign Policy in World Politics* (Englewood Cliffs, New Jersey: Prentice Hall, Inc., 1972), Chapter 5.

10. Victor Marchetti and John D. Marks, *The CIA and the Cult of Intelligence* (New York: Dell Publishing Co., 1974).

11. Loch K. Johnson, "Controlling the Quiet Option," *Foreign Policy,* Summer, 1980, pp. 143-153.

12. John Barron, *KGB* (New York: Bantam Books, 1974).

13. *Ibid.,* and Anwar el-Sadat, *In Search of Identity* (New York: Harper & Row, 1978), Chapter 8.

14. Bernard C. Cohen, *The Press and Foreign Policy* (Princeton: Princeton University Press, 1963), pp. 28-29.

15. Amos Yoder, "The News Media and One World," *Political Communication and Persuasion,* 1981.

16. This is the thesis of an unpublished Ph.D. dissertation by Dixie Ehrenreich, University of Idaho, entitled "Newspapers, Public Opinion and Neutrality 1935-1939." I confirmed these conclusions in samples of foreign news coverage of 147 Northwest newspapers from 1935 to 1939 and 1975 to 1978. *Ibid.* See also Christine Ogan and others, "The Changing Front Page of the *New York Times,* 1900-1970," *Journalism Quarterly,* Summer, 1975, p. 341.

17. Michael Mosettig and Henry Griggs Jr., "TV at the Front," *Foreign Policy,* Spring, 1980, pp. 67-79.

18. The 70 percent "correlation" is not used in the sense of a correlation coefficient. A .7 correlation coefficient actually only accounts for 49 percent of the variance (.7 x .7).

19. See for example: Victor Marchetti, *The Cult of the CIA* (New York: Dell Publishing Company, 1974); The New York Times, *The Pentagon Papers* (New York: Bantam Books, 1971); Robert F. Kennedy, *Thirteen Days* (New York: W.W. Norton & Company, 1969); John Barron, *KGB* (New York: Bantam Books, 1974); United States Senate, *Alleged Assassination Plots Involving Foreign Leaders* (Washington, D.C., U.S. Government Printing Office, 1975); John Newhouse, *Cold Dawn — The Story of SALT* (New York: Holt, Rinehart and Winston, 1973).

PART THREE
The Superpower System

We will now use the terms and concepts of the
first seven chapters to analyze power politics in
the superpower system. We will look at how the
Cold War developed out of the debris of World
War II and at how attempts were made to
promote detente. The most dangerous crises
occurred in Eastern Asia and in the Middle East
where the two superpowers reacted to rather
than controlled conflicts involving new power
centers of China, Vietnam, Israel, Iran, Egypt,
and other nations.

CHAPTER

8

Superpower Politics in Europe

International politics today involves three interacting systems — the superpower system, the multipolar system, and the United Nations System. (See Figure 8-1.) The superpower system is based on interactions of the governments of the Soviet Union and the United States and their allies. The superpower system is the most visible of the three, because the news media usually picture almost any world crisis as affecting the position of the United States and Russia, the two superpowers. As rivalry increases it is seen as the Cold War. As tensions relax the situation is pictured as detente.

The superpower system grew out of the natural ideological antagonism between communism and liberal democracies, which dominated European politics before World War II. The resulting suspicions helped delay threatened nations from cooperating to forestall aggression of the Axis powers. However, the Western and Russian "Grand Alliance" defeated the Axis and formed the U.N. System to keep the peace. As a rift again developed between Russia and the West after the War, U.S. leaders formed NATO and other alliances against what they saw as the Russian Communist threat, while the Soviets countered with the Warsaw Pact.

Meanwhile, the massive growth of international interaction since World War II expanded the U.N. System. It managed to keep the two superpowers in the U.N. and to include almost all the states of the world. However, the superpowers have engaged in disputes about issues before the U.N. more than they have cooperated.

With a nuclear standoff deterring war and the use of nuclear weapons, new power centers have arisen outside the superpower system. Their power has been based largely on economics. The growing economic interdependence of the world and the dramatic increase in the economic power of the petroleum powers is causing them to interact in a multipolar economic system. This system includes more than the system generally recognized as the Third World. For purpose of analysis I have also included non-state entities, such as OPEC, the European Community, and multinational firms as a part of this system. (See Figure 8-1.)

We will first examine the operations of the superpower system in Europe and Asia, and then analyze the other two systems.

Cold War

The Pivot of U.S. Policy. The strongest foreign policies are those that have the firmest hold on the minds of policymakers and which they have sold to their governments. By this measure the U.S. alliance with Western Europe against the Soviets is the "cornerstone" and "pivot" of United States foreign policy. Statements along these lines have been proclaimed by every Secretary of State since World War II. President Carter in his first trip abroad reaffirmed this policy in his speech before the North Atlantic Council on May 10, 1977, stating that the United States "will continue to make the alliance the heart of our foreign policy."

The long and close relationship of the United States

Figure 8-1 Major Elements of the United Nations, Superpower, and Multipolar Systems

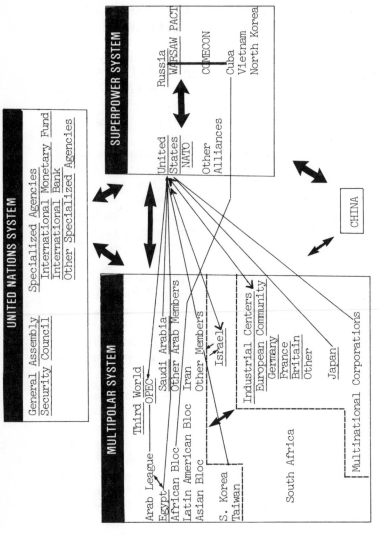

* Major power centers are underlined.
  ———— Strong influence (power)
  ———— Strong interaction

with Western Europe is based on historical and cultural factors and also the economic fact that over 20 percent of U.S. trade is carried on with that area. Moreover, it is easy for policymakers to see Western Europe helping achieve a balance of power against the Soviet Union. This concept is reinforced by ideological differences — the Communist totalitarian and revolutionary ideology versus that of the liberal democracies of Western Europe. Russian military intervention in Eastern Europe since World War II (Czechoslovakia, Poland, East Germany, and Hungary) and the Communist leaders' support of revolution against the "capitalist-imperialist" systems of the West have reinforced balance of power and anti-Communist ideas in the U.S.

At the end of the war much of Europe was in a shambles. The Soviet troops quickly took over control of Eastern European countries and installed regimes friendly to, and later subservient to, the Soviet Union. Russia's moves to take control of these countries by its forces, which in American eyes ignored Soviet commitments under the Yalta and Potsdam Agreements about free elections, initiated the Cold War. This term covers the diplomatic conflict of the United States and its allies with the Soviets and their Communist allies after World War II. The Cold War involved power politics short of overt military action and usually did not involve breaking off of diplomatic relations.

The United States demobilized quickly, but it could not escape responsibility for the West German zones of occupation. The United States and British military occupation authorities were pragmatic. They realized they could not let the Germans in Western Europe starve or remain on the dole by suppressing the German economy, so finally, against the opposition of the Soviets, the United States and Britain unified their zones and established a common currency.[1] The Soviets, whose major aim was to control the Ruhr and its economic potential with the good of limiting the military potential of Germany, responded in March 31, 1948, to the moves to strengthen Germany with the Berlin Blockade. This Russian realpolitik dramatized the Cold War for the United States. It gave strength to those who wanted to create an alliance of Western Europe to create a balance of power against the Soviet Union, which had taken over and controlled Eastern Europe.

In the two years after the end of World War II the United States had provided $15 billion in loans and grants for relief of Western Europe. As these wartime and emergency programs came to an end, economists had estimated that Europe faced an import deficit of $7 billion annually largely due to its loss of investments and the destruction of the war. Secretary of State George Marshall on June 5, 1947, at Harvard's commencement proposed a European recovery plan to be drawn up by Europeans themselves as a basis for United States assistance to Western European recovery. Secretary Marshall had cleared the idea first with Senator Vandenberg, and as a result Democrats and Republicans were able to support the program in the United States.[2] Internationalists, moralists, and advocates of power politics joined in its support. The Europeans led by the British Prime Minister quickly called a conference and drew up a plan; and the United States launched a five year plan eventually totalling $15 billion in assistance that put Europe well on the way to recovery by 1952, when the plan came to an end.

Senate Republican Minority Leader Vandenberg initiated the move toward the NATO alliance by obtaining approval of a Senate resolution in June, 1948, by a vote of 64 to 4. It was aided through the Senate by reaction to the Berlin Blockade and the Russian invasion of Czechoslovakia of that year. The resolution called for an association of the United States by constitutional processes with "regional and collective arrangements based on mutual aid," a reference to the Brussels Pact of 1947. A drafting of the initial text of the NATO Treaty was done in Washington by Secretary of State Acheson and the ambassadors of Canada and the Brussels Pact countries (the United Kingdom, France, Belgium, the Netherlands, and Luxembourg) in close consultation with Senator Connally, the Democratic leader, and Senator Vandenberg.[3]

On July 21, 1949, the U.S. Senate ratified the North Atlantic Treaty (NATO) by 82-13, well above the two-thirds majority required. The key language of that pact commits each party to take action "as it deems necessary" including the use of armed force to restore and maintain the security of the NATO area. The Soviets countered with the Warsaw Pact and consolidation of the East European buffer. These actions set the stage for the Cold War.

The Russian View. Diplomats often try to look at problems from the other side's point of view in order to understand issues and to try to devise solutions. It is revealing to look at the above developments from the Soviet leaders' perspective, who typically used power politics to achieve their aims.

Stalin and Russian leaders had an overriding fear of Germany, which had devastated Western Russia two times in this century. This fear was reinforced by fundamental tenets of Communist ideology that the capitalist system generates war and aggression. The ideology holds that the German fascist system of the 1930s was a historical result of the workings of the capitalist system. During World War II, moreover, Stalin had kept asking for a second front. Unfortunately, President Roosevelt indicated to Stalin that the United States expected to form a second front in 1942, but it was not until two years later that the second front was actually established.[4] The British were against an early second front for sound military reasons: the American forces were just beginning to be mobilized, and the British did not think their troops were adequate. This delay, however, helped create a suspicion in the Russian minds that the Allies wanted Russian forces chewed up by the Germans, particularly since the Russians were taking very heavy casualties from the German attack.

After World War II the Soviets had tried to obtain four power control of the Ruhr and thus control Germany's warmaking potential. With their Communist view of the importance of economic factors in politics, they hoped to use this control as leverage to prevent Germany from ever again becoming a threat. The United States and Britain, faced by the pressures and responsibilities of keeping the Germans alive and wishing to restore the health of Western Europe, unified their two occupation zones and took steps to give Germany back its economic and political sovereignty. Stalin, in a power move, responded by blockading access to Berlin, which threatened its starvation unless the Western Powers yielded. The Allies, led by President Truman, countered with the dramatic air lift to Berlin over the zonal boundaries. (See Map 5-1.)

Meanwhile, the drama of the blockade sped up the formation of the Western Alliance. Faced by the allied success in supplying Berlin by air, the failure of the Berlin Blockade to obtain a reversal of Western policy, and the blockade's encouragement of the NATO Alliance, the Soviet lifted the blockade within a year.

The fear of a revived Germany was the basis for the Soviets' Eastern European policy of creating the East European buffer against Germany. The Cold War started between Russia and Britain over this issue. Britain had entered World War II because of Hitler's invasion of Poland and therefore was concerned about its future. To the Soviets, Poland geographically was an essential part of the buffer against a German threat. In the meetings before Yalta, Churchill was insisting that the conservative Polish regime under Mikolajczyk with headquarters in London should have a 50-50 balance in a new Polish government against the group of Lublin Poles, who were dominated by the Soviets. No clear understanding was reached on this point, but in February, 1945, at Yalta the three powers agreed to establish the provisional Polish boundaries that exist today.[5] Under this arrangement Poland took over areas of Eastern Germany and gave up part of Eastern Poland to the Soviet Union.

The text of the Yalta agreement of March 24, 1945, stated that three governments would assist the East European people to form "interim governmental authorities broadly representative of all democratic elements in the population." With this wording, the Soviet Union consolidated its control with Communist leaders trained in the Soviet Union and used the Soviet armed forces as a lever to impose regimes dominated by Moscow. Within a few years the Soviets had firmly established all through Eastern Europe a series of friendly Communist governments under Soviet domination. Prime Minister Churchill on June 4, 1946, dramatized the situation by his famous phrase, "the iron curtain," which had descended between Eastern Europe and the West.

Khrushchev's memoirs give a frank account of how Russia dominated the East European governments after

World War II. Stalin personally selected the leaders of Poland with the assistance of Khrushchev and other Soviet officials using as the major criteria whether the new leaders shared Soviet goals and would be "faithful" later on. Elections were rigged during the years after the War as the Communist leaders took over control of the state apparatuses in Eastern Europe.[6]

The breaking away of Yugoslavia in 1947 from the Eastern Bloc provided a shock to the Eastern European system, but it increased the determination of the Soviets to consolidate their control of other East European countries. Thus, the East German revolt of 1953 was put down with Soviet troops, and East Germany has remained one of the most subservient states of the entire bloc.

Another major shock to the Soviet East European system came with Khrushchev's denunciation of Stalin in February, 1956. Although Khrushchev made no reference to "the peoples' democracies," he shattered the myth of Stalinist infallibility. The United States covertly published the speech and helped spread it throughout Eastern Europe including Poland. Many Communists interpreted the speech as heralding a relaxation of Soviet domination of Eastern European governments. This helped encourage the Polish workers of Poznan to protest about low wages, and failing to get satisfaction from a mission to Warsaw, they rioted. The Polish government put down the revolt with its armed forces in June, 1956, but it later made concessions to the workers. Unrest spread a few months later to Hungary, and in late October, 1956, a revolution broke out led by students and workers. Imre Nagy, the leader, proclaimed Hungary's neutrality and demanded that Soviet troops be withdrawn. Within a few weeks Khrushchev ordered Soviet troops to intervene to arrest the leaders. Despite protests of U.N. bodies, where the Soviets were outvoted, the Soviets arrested Nagy and executed him.

The East European system was stable for 12 years after the Hungarian revolution, but in August, 1968, nationalist pressures erupted again when Czechoslovakian officials demanded liberalization. The Czechoslovakian government, under the leadership of Dubcek, set goals of developing toward a socialist type of democratic system; however, Chairman Brezhnev moved Soviet and Eastern European troops into Czechoslovakia announcing that the U.S.S.R. was determined to defend the interests of the "Socialist Commonwealth," and that Russian and East European troops would give mutual assistance to countries where the existence of "socialism" is threatened.[7] This became known as the "Brezhnev doctrine." Under the Soviet occupation Dubcek was forced out and replaced with a government that agreed to the stationing of Soviet troops.

Although at the end of 1978 Romania openly challenged Soviet demands to increase the Warsaw Pact budget, the East European countries along the historic invasion route of northern Europe have not challenged Soviet dominance. The Warsaw Pact and the economic arrangements of CMEA provide the treaty framework for continued Soviet control.

The Rival Alliances. The major aim of the NATO alliance is to defend Western Europe, but it was sold with the idea of a unified command that would integrate German forces so closely with other forces that war between Germany and France would not be feasible. Secretary of State Acheson in urging German rearmament as early as 1950 on French Foreign Minister Schuman stressed this argument as well as one of creating a balance of power against the Soviets. The formation of NATO led to an inflow of United States military aid that amounted to $16 billion compared to the $15 billion of Marshall Plan economic aid. (See Figure 8-2.)

The United States no longer dominates NATO as it did after World War II, although NATO considers United States troops as essential for the defense of Western Europe. A major element in strengthening the European part of the alliance was the political reconciliation of France and Germany that developed under the Schuman Plan of 1950, which merged the steel and coal industries of Western Europe. (See Chapter 11.)

The United States took the lead in negotiating agreements for restoring German sovereignty and in admitting it as a full fledged member of NATO in 1955. In the ABC Agreement of 1955, which was part of the bargain, Germany pledged not to develop atomic, bacteriological or chemical weapons of mass destruction. This reassured France and other NATO partners.

The NATO organization is impressive with its ceremonies and its Council of Ministers, which meets twice a year. Its high level military bodies include the headquarters in Belgium, a Nuclear Planning Group, and the various joint commands which are subordinate to the Allied Command in Europe (ACE). Most of their proceedings are secret, but enough information is released to permit a large number of military experts and reporters to evaluate their activities. Table 8-1 gives a brief summary of key military and economic data for the NATO alliance compared to the Warsaw Pact, which is discussed below.

The NATO countries have a much larger population than the Warsaw Pact and about twice the GNP. However, the Warsaw Pact outnumbers NATO in soldiers, particularly in the critical northern and central area, and it outnumbers NATO tanks and aircraft by over two to one. On the other hand NATO has about twice as many "tactical" nuclear warheads. In terms of conventional warfare, the Soviets have a superiority in weapons and firepower. (See Table 8-1 and Figure 8-4.) NATO planners, therefore, year after year call for increased NATO efforts to match the Soviets. From an overall strategic point of view, which implies using tactical and strategic nuclear weapons, there is a balance of terror. (See Figure 8-3.)

NATO planners, to offset the conventional weapons inferiority, plan to use tactical nuclear weapons in the event of a major Russian attack. Many arms control experts, however, say it would be impossible to draw the line between the use of tactical and strategic nuclear weapons in such a conflict, and they predict an all-out war would result.

NATO suffers from another conventional disadvantage since the French withdrawal from the NATO military commands. The International Institute for Strategic Studies report for 1976-1977 on the military balance, notes that the most powerful forces of NATO, the U.S. forces, are in Southern Germany, while NATO forces are less powerful in the north German plain, where invasions normally take place. This pattern of deployment has left the U.S. forces relying on logistic lines running north and south to Bremen close to the border of Eastern Germany. The U.S. forces at present no longer use French supply

Figure 8-2   United States Collective Defense Arrangements

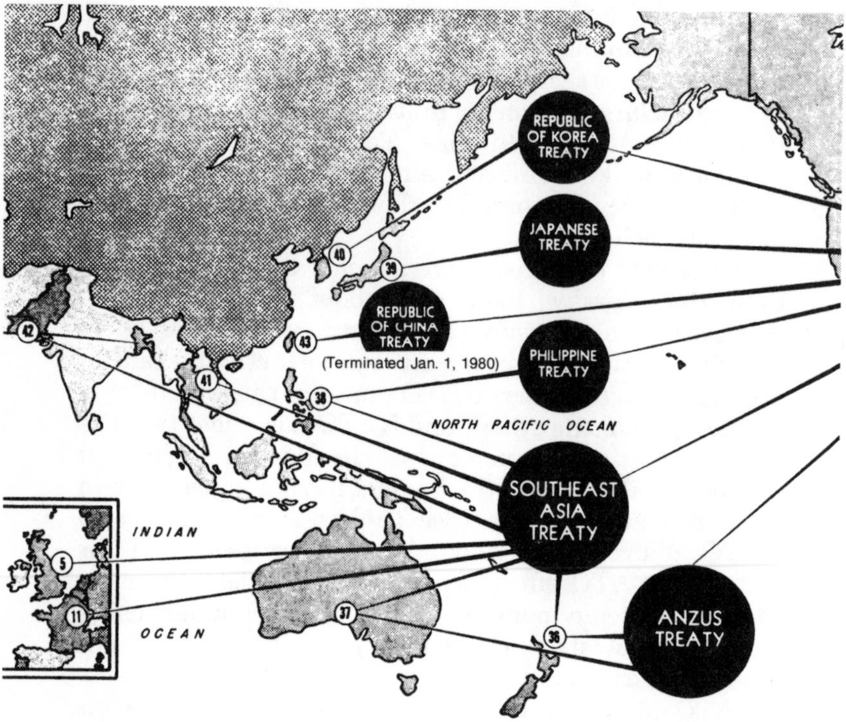

NORTH ATLANTIC TREATY
(15 NATIONS)
1 UNITED STATES
2 CANADA
3 ICELAND
4 NORWAY
5 UNITED KINGDOM
6 NETHERLANDS
7 DENMARK
8 BELGIUM
9 LUXEMBOURG
10 PORTUGAL
11 FRANCE
12 ITALY
13 GREECE
14 TURKEY
15 WESTERN
   GERMANY

RIO TREATY
(21 NATIONS)
1 UNITED
   STATES
16 MEXICO
17 CUBA
18 HAITI
19 DOMINICAN
   REPUBLIC
20 HONDURAS
21 GUATEMALA
22 EL SALVADOR
23 NICARAGUA
24 COSTA RICA
25 PANAMA
26 COLOMBIA
27 VENEZUELA
28 ECUADOR

29 PERU
30 BRAZIL
31 BOLIVIA
32 PARAGUAY
33 CHILE
34 ARGENTINA
35 URUGUAY
42 TRINIDAD
   & TOBAGO

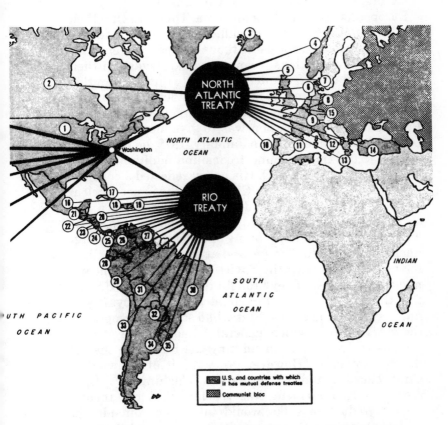

ANZUS (Australia—New
Zealand—United States)
TREATY
(3 NATIONS)
  1 UNITED STATES
36 NEW ZEALAND
37 AUSTRALIA

PHILIPPINE TREATY
(BILATERAL)
  1 UNITED STATES
38 PHILIPPINES

JAPANESE TREATY
(BILATERAL)
  1 UNITED STATES
39 JAPAN

REPUBLIC OF KOREA
(South Korea) TREATY
(BILATERAL)
  1 UNITED STATES
40 REPUBLIC OF KOREA
    (SOUTH KOREA)

SOUTHEAST ASIA
TREATY
(8 NATIONS)
  1 UNITED STATES
  5 UNITED KINGDOM
11 FRANCE
36 NEW ZEALAND
37 AUSTRALIA
38 PHILIPPINES
41 THAILAND
42 PAKISTAN

REPUBLIC OF CHINA
(Formosa) TREATY
(BILATERAL—TERMINATED)
  1 UNITED STATES
43 REPUBLIC OF CHINA
    (FORMOSA)

lines because of French withdrawal of forces from the NATO unified command. In a conventional war, therefore, U.S. forces would be vulnerable.

Europeans are faced by a dilemma. They fear that their conventional arms are not sufficient to stop or deter a Soviet invasion. At the same time they fear that even the use of tactical nuclear weapons would devastate their countries. Figures 8-3 and 8-4 illustrate the problem that NATO military planners face as the Soviets improve their medium range nuclear weapons targetted at Europe. President Carter's solution was to give more priority to conventional forces, and in January, 1978, he pledged to assign 15,000 more ground troops and additional F-111 fighter-bombers to NATO. His policy reflected a concern, like that of Schelling's in Chapter 2, that once nuclear weapons are used it would be difficult to draw a line against escalation. The European solution has evolved to agreeing to a further upgrading of the U.S. medium range nuclear missiles in Europe, and at the same time calling for negotiations with the Soviet Union to "limit theater nuclear weapons." They brought pressure on the U.S. for this through NATO and in collateral diplomacy. It was not easy since the United States had stalled on reopening the SALT talks, which generally had been seen as a prelude to agreement on limiting the European theater nuclear weapons. However, as a result of the visit of Chancellor Schmidt of Germany to Washington D.C. in April, 1981, agreement was reached that the theater nuclear reduction talks would take place outside the SALT process with the results being included in the SALT.[8]

As noted above, the Warsaw Pact of 1955 had been the Soviet balance of power response to NATO. The preamble of the Pact makes clear the reason for it was the entry of West Germany into NATO. All the East European countries were members of the Pact except Yugoslavia. It is a mutual defense treaty, reinforced by similar bilateral treaties between the members. Observers generally state that it is more an instrument for Soviet domination of Eastern Europe than a treaty for mutual decisions. The Soviets station their forces in Poland, East Germany, Hungary, and Czechoslovakia under the Treaty, provide military advisers to the member states, and standardize

Table 8-1 The Military Balance of NATO and the Warsaw Pact, 1976*

	NATO	U.S. Share	Warsaw Pact	U.S.S.R. Share
Population	550,000,000	(216,000,000)	360,000,000	(250,000,000)
Gross National Product	$2.8 trillion	($1.6 trillion)	$1 trillion	($ .7 trillion)
Northern and Central Europe				
Combat Forces (Ground)	782,000	(193,000)	935,000	(475,000)
Tanks	6,730	(2,000)	16,200	(9,250)
Aircraft	1,344	(335)	3,075	(1,300)
Tactical Nuclear Warheads	7,000	(7,000)	3,500	(3,500)

*See the International Institute for Strategic Studies, *The Military Balance—1976-1977* (London: 1976), pp. 99, 102; *The Military Balance 1979-1980* (London: 1979); Ruth Sivard, *World Military and Social Expenditures 1977* (Leesburg, Va.: WMSE Publications, 1977); and *World Military and Social Expenditures* (WMSE Publications, 1979). Tactical nuclear weapons are of shorter range than the other nuclear warheads.

the weapons of the alliance on the basis of Soviet materiel.

The treaty follows the NATO pact in a number of key provisions, and it, like NATO, is loosely tied to the U.N. Article 11 has an interesting balance of power provision for dissolving the Warsaw Pact when an all-European collective security treaty is signed. This implies that if U.S. forces from Europe were withdrawn, the Warsaw Pact and its provisions for stationing troops throughout Eastern Europe would be terminated.

Since 1969 the obvious Soviet domination of the Pact has been relaxed and the East European ministers of defense are no longer subordinate to the Russian commander-in-chief. The ministers now form a council of defense ministers to advise the Pact. The joint high military command, however, is controlled by Soviet officers.

The two treaties provide a framework for military confrontation in Europe. The confrontational aspects were eased, however, by the provisions of the Conference on Security and Cooperation in Europe (CSCE) of 1975 which permits observers from each of the pacts to observe military maneuvers involving over 25,000 troops. This lessens chances of misinterpretation of practice maneuvers. Also there have been desultory discussions of Mutual Balanced Force Reductions (MBFR) in Europe between officials of the two alliances. With the ingrained suspicions of military leaders of the other side's intentions, there is not much hope for force reductions, unless strong civilian leaders take charge.

In 1949 the Soviets had also set up the Council for Mutual Economic Assistance (CMEA) as a counter to the Western initiative of the Marshall Plan, but CMEA was not actually activated until five years later, after Stalin's death. The same countries as the Warsaw Pact are members, with other Communist countries as observers. The CMEA embraces 300 million people including 250 million Soviets. All members of the CMEA theoretically are equal and all decisions are unanimous, and it has not developed the type of supranationality that the European Community has. Despite the broad aims of CMEA, its main accomplishments have been trade agreements among the members and provisions to strengthen the

Figure 8-3   A Strategic View of Balance of Power — NATO and the Warsaw Pact

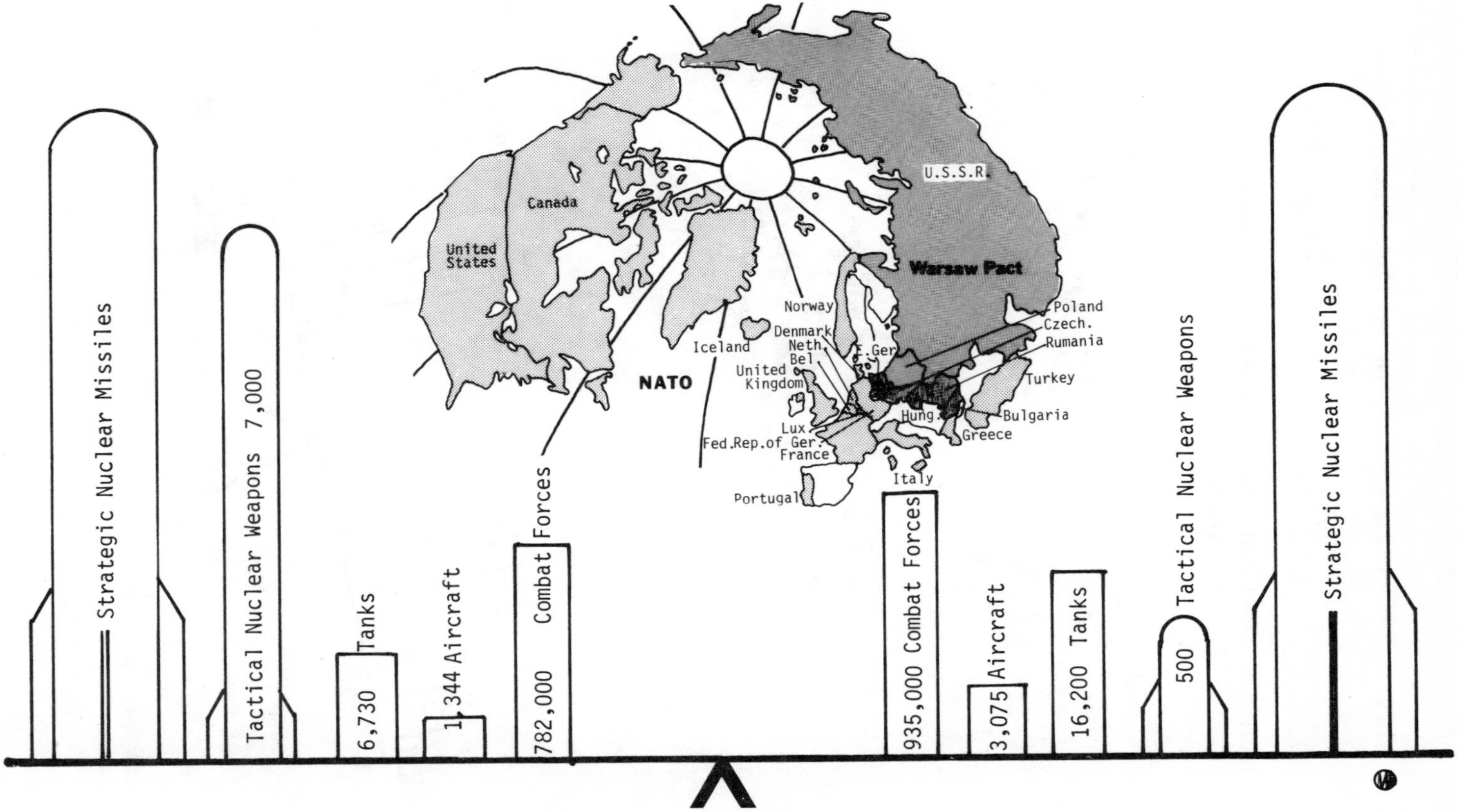

Strategic Nuclear Missiles

500   Tactical Nuclear Weapons

16,200 Tanks

3,075 Aircraft

935,000 Combat Forces

782,000 Combat Forces

1,344 Aircraft

6,730 Tanks

Tactical Nuclear Weapons 7,000

Strategic Nuclear Missiles

U.S.S.R.

Warsaw Pact

Poland
Czech.
Rumania
Turkey
Bulgaria
Greece
Hung.
E.Ger.
Italy

Norway
Denmark
Neth.
Bel.
United
Kingdom
Iceland
Lux.
Fed.Rep.of Ger.
France
Portugal

NATO

Canada

United
States

**Figure 8-4   The Balance of Power of Northern Europe
in Conventional Weapons**

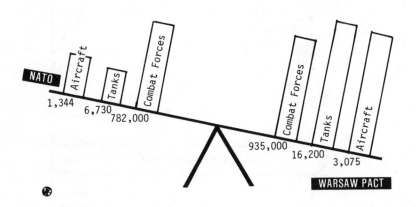

ruble as an instrument for clearing trade balances between the various countries. Although one of its aims is to coordinate economic plans of the Eastern European countries, reportedly it has made little progress.

Detente with the Soviet Union

Detente is a French word which means a relaxation of tension, and not a comprehensive settlement of issues. Coexistence is a similar term in the Communist dictionary. In essence they are pragmatic survival policies of Russia and the United States overriding conflicting ideologies and foreign policy strategies.

United States observers often place the beginning of detente with the 1970 Kissinger negotiations to reach agreement on limiting nuclear weapons in SALT. The Europeans see detente more as settling European issues with the Russians through the German *Ostpolitik*. (See Chapter 3.) The Soviets are enthusiastic about both *Ostpolitik* and SALT.

There is no agreed chronicle of detente or its opposite, the Cold War. Most Americans regard detente as a development of the 1970s, but in a sense detente began after Stalin's death in 1953 and Khrushchev's taking control of Soviet foreign policy. In the years after Stalin's death Soviet and Western policymakers concluded a series of agreements including the Korean War Truce in 1953, the Geneva Agreement on Indochina in 1954, and the Austrian Treaty, which had been under negotiation since the end of World War II. Khrushchev not only withdrew troops from Austria in connection with the Treaty, but he did the same in Finland and reduced Russian troops in Eastern Europe. His motives seemed to be pragmatic — to reduce causes of friction with East European allies and to reduce the expense of maintaining these forces.[9] His later nuclear detente with the U.S. seemed based on a genuine fear of the potential of these terrible weapons.

Detente received a setback with the revulsion in the United States and Europe over the 1956 repression by Khrushchev's troops of the Hungarians' revolt against Soviet political and military control. In 1958 Russia supported China in a statement against the United States during the Chinese off-shore island crisis, but Mao's threatening statements about nuclear weapons, as indicated below, helped create the split between Peking and Moscow; this split more than a decade later permitted the detente between the United States and Peoples' Republic of China. Khrushchev restored better relations during his 1959 visit with Eisenhower at Camp David, but this was shattered by the Russian's shooting down of an American U-2 spy plane over the Soviet Union in 1960.

The Cold War was intensified with Soviet pressures on Berlin and the Cuban Missile Crisis of 1962. Graham Allison in his perceptive study looking at the missile crisis from various points of view concluded that probably the major motive of the Soviet action was to try to catch up with Americans in long-range strategic missiles. Placing Soviet intermediate range missiles in Cuba would have brought American cities within range of a much larger number of Soviet missiles and in one dramatic move the Soviets would have narrowed the gap with the Americans in long-range missiles.[10] This was a high point of the Cold War.

The Soviets were taken aback by the strength of the United States response to their move in Cuba. For a while the world seemed to teeter on the brink of a nuclear war. United States policymakers mobilized support of Latin American nations in the Organization of American States and the backing of other allies. With carefully escalated power politics, including partial mobilization and a blockade of Cuba designed to cut off shipments of nuclear weapons, and with the informal assurances to the Russians by his brother Robert Kennedy[11] that the U.S. would remove its missiles from Turkey, President Kennedy managed to get the Soviets to withdraw their missiles. This is considered by most observers as a triumph of American diplomacy. However, the Soviets intensified their development of long-range missiles and within 10 years had redressed the balance of power with larger and more terrible weapons of destruction.

In 1963 there was a brief revival of a trend toward detente with Ambassador Harriman's conclusion of a partial nuclear test ban treaty. Most laymen regarded the treaty as designed to keep nuclear fallout out of the

The Cuban Missile Crisis

We have lived so long with nuclear weapons we have forgotten how close we have been to a nuclear holocaust. In the weekend before President Kennedy announced that the Russians were installing nuclear missiles in Cuba I was duty officer for the State Department's Bureau of Far Eastern Affairs. One highly classified message was delivered to me, and in glancing at it I saw that the Russians were installing nuclear missiles in Cuba. I immediately informed Assistant Secretary Averill Harriman, who read the message and hurried up the hall to discuss it with George Ball, the Undersecretary of State.

On Monday when President Kennedy announced the action to the American public I began following developments from the news tickers near the State Department's press room. I did not have access to policy messages on the subject, but the news tickers gave a factual picture of the deepening crisis. That week I arranged for my family to travel to a cousin's farm in Ohio, while in the evenings I built a temporary bomb shelter at my home in the suburbs of Washington, D.C. In retrospect, I may have overreacted to the crisis. However, Secretary of Defense Robert McNamara later stated that at one point he was not sure that he would see the sun rise next morning, and Prime Minister Macmillan of Britain said it was the greatest period of strain which he faced in several decades of public service, including the whole of World War II. See Robert F. Kennedy, *Thirteen Days* (New York: W.W. Norton, 1969), Introduction.

atmosphere, but it had perhaps an even more important side effect of limiting the testing of large new weapons. There was also the "hot line" agreement during this period, but detente soon was submerged in the escalation of the Vietnam War under President Johnson in 1965. The Soviets were a major supplier of arms to the North Vietnamese, and the Cold War intensified, while the hot war in Southeast Asia became a focus of conflict. Detente became a household word only in the early 1970s as Kissinger pursued the SALT negotiations and negotiated an end to the Vietnam War.

Henry Kissinger was a prolific author before becoming President Nixon's Assistant for National Security Affairs, and he had been best known for his books and articles on nuclear weapons. Two threads dominate many of his writings — that to create a deterrent the United States should be willing to use tactical nuclear weapons in a limited defensive war, and that it is necessary for the survival of civilization to conclude agreements to limit strategic nuclear arms.

In 1972 he reached agreement with the Russians on limiting ICBMs, ABMs, and Sea-Launched Ballistic Missiles (SLBMs) under SALT I but the agreement did not include bombers and Multiple Independently-targeted Reentry Vehicles (MIRVs). The agreement called for a series of ongoing discussions of subsidiary agreements and for a subsequent comprehensive agreement. President Ford in November, 1974, at Vladivostok reached an oral agreement with General Secretary Brezhnev on the outline of a comprehensive agreement to also cover bombers and MIRVs, but he did not conclude a written agreement by the end of his term. Meanwhile, in 1975, detente continued in other fields by the signing of the Final Act of the Conference on Security and Cooperation (CSCE) concluded at Helsinki, Finland, by 32 Eastern and Western European countries plus the United States and Canada. The Act includes prior notification of military maneuvers, exchanging observers, increasing cooperation in the cultural and scientific fields, and promoting respect for human rights and fundamental freedoms. The Western European countries, as well as the East European nations, strongly supported the CSCE agreement.

President Carter in his May, 1977, speech to the North Atlantic Council in London reaffirmed the interest of the United States in carrying out the provisions of the Final Act of the CSCE and in pressing forward in negotiating mutual and balanced force reduction (MBFR) agreements for the mutual withdrawal of NATO and Warsaw Pact armed forces from Central Europe. At the same time he suggested that we should draw the nations of Eastern Europe into "cooperative undertakings," not with the aim of turning the region against the Soviet Union, but for enlarging the opportunities to work together with them to meet the challenges of modern society.

President Carter appeared a lot more determined than Secretary Kissinger to pursue detente and SALT talks with the Soviet Union. One of the few specific points made in his inaugural address was a pledge to pursue these talks and to move a step toward the "ultimate goal: the elimination of all nuclear weapons from this earth." He also resumed negotiations with the Soviets for ending nuclear testing and limiting arms exports. However, the human rights issue complicated Carter's policy of detente with Russia. President Carter appeared driven by a moral compulsion to pressure the Soviets on their human rights commitments under the CSCE. Although not explicitly stated, he probably believed that if all major world powers accepted the political and social rights listed in the U.N. Universal Declaration of Human Rights, this would establish a firm foundation for world peace.

The principles of human rights, however, are at odds with the tight totalitarian controls of the Russian society. While the Soviets can handle the pressures for human rights within their own country, the human rights issue caused them considerable uneasiness in Eastern Europe. The nationalists of Eastern Europe resent Soviet dominance over their societies, and the human rights issue provides them with internationally recognized slogans to attack such controls. The human rights issue also affected the Western European Communist parties, which since 1976 had been demanding a fundamental change in the Soviet position on this issue.

In the preparations for the 1976 Berlin meeting of Communist parties, the French and Italian Communist parties had issued a "Eurocommunism" manifesto calling for independent roads to communism and listing liberal democratic rights. They indicated their sincerity later by criticizing Soviet treatment of dissidents and abuse of prisoners in labor camps. In March, 1977, leaders of the Spanish, French, and Italian Communist parties agreed on the Declaration of Madrid, again calling for respect of universal suffrage, political plurality, and individual freedoms. The host of the meeting, the Spanish Communist Party leader Santiago Carrillo, publicly said the meeting was not meant to be a challenge to anybody, but a prominent Czechoslovak party member labelled the Eurocommunists as traitors.[12] Moscow waited until after the Spanish elections to attack Carrillo, knowing full well the Spanish as well as the other Communists would get the message. The Soviet *New Times* attacked Carrillo's proposal for an independent Europe and his vague call for a European defense arrangement as supporting the imperialist policy of arming Western Europe against world socialism.[13]

The year 1977 also saw the beginning of President Carter's human rights campaign, which made the Soviets even more sensitive to the Eurocommunists' statements about political freedoms and human rights. In the summer of 1977 the European and U.S. committee that was formed to report on the implementation of the Final Act of the Conference on Security and Cooperation in Europe met in a preliminary session at Belgrade to set the agenda and make arrangements for the full-dress meeting later that year. The Soviets made a sharp attack on the Carter statements on human rights, saying they undermined detente and accusing the West itself of human rights violations. They also stepped up arrests and action against Soviet dissidents who were demanding the Soviets live up to obligations under the Final Act. The Soviet leaders obviously saw Eurocommunism and the human rights campaign as challenges to their own totalitarian system and a threat to their East European buffer through encouraging Eastern European leaders and people who want to achieve independence from Soviet domination. President Carter denied that human rights were linked to detente and negotiations with the Soviets, but they resented his 1977 actions to request Congress to double funds for Radio Free

Europe and Radio Liberty, which daily broadcast into the Soviet Union and Eastern Europe.

The human rights campaign did not prevent pragmatic progress toward SALT. On June 18, 1979, President Carter and President Brezhnev signed the SALT II Treaty in Vienna, and on June 22, President Carter presented it to the Senate for their advice and consent to ratification. In speeches he emphasized this treaty would not end competition with the Soviet Union, but his embrace with President Brezhnev at the Vienna ceremonies dramatized the hope for an extension of detente to other areas. In comments to the press Carter indicated that he would not be the one to resume the arms race even if the Senate did not approve the treaty. This implied as Commander-in-Chief he would respect the SALT II limits as long as the Soviets did. This angered some senators and complicated the Senate approval process, but it was further evidence of Carter's determination to pursue SALT and detente.

In the closing days of 1979 and early 1980, prospects for detente and ratification of the SALT suffered a severe setback when about 100,000 Soviet troops entered Afghanistan to put down a rebellion against a new Marxist leader, reportedly installed by Soviet troops. The United States, its Western allies, neighboring countries, and other governments objected strenuously. Although technically a case could be made under international law that a sovereign government can invite Soviet assistance, reports of Soviet intervention in the coup itself and the massive and rapid entry of its forces into Afghanistan indicated an imperialistic type of power politics that was in a different category than its previous indirect support to "national liberation" and revolutionary movements in the Near East and Africa.

President Carter took the lead in mobilizing condemnation of the Soviet aggression. His major psychological move was to bring about a U.S. boycott of the Moscow Olympics in the summer of 1980. Germany, Japan, Arab countries, and a total of 60 countries joined the boycott. Although many European and other Olympic committees decided to participate, the athletes of 16 of these nations refused to fly their nations' flags at the ceremonies. Other moves joined in varying degrees by other governments included sharply curtailing grain exports and Soviet fishing privileges, suspending scientific and cultural exchanges, and restricting exports of high technology and other strategic items through consultations among the Western industrial nations. President Carter also withdrew the request for Senate approval of the SALT agreements, which was doubtful in any event, but the President still made clear the United States would continue to observe the SALT limits unless the Russians moved first to exceed them. Meanwhile news reports indicated the Afghanistan people were mounting massive resistance to the Russians including demonstrations and guerrilla action even though they were outgunned by modern Soviet weapons.[14]

By the middle of 1980 the Russians and the Americans had slipped back into Cold War rhetoric and postures. The Western European nations, while also demanding a withdrawal of Russian troops from Afghanistan, continued diplomatic approaches to persuade the Soviets to withdraw. As usual the Western Europeans held back and let the United States take the lead as the world policeman. However, they gave support to the U.S. pressure policies against the Soviets, and they agreed to take more of the burden of NATO defense to ease the burden of the U.S. buildup in the Persian Gulf area.

The reaction of many important world leaders against the Soviet invasion of Afghanistan set the stage for the Polish workers' major challenge to the Communist systems of Eastern Europe. In mid-August, 1980, the workers in the Polish shipyards of Gdansk and other Polish cities struck in protest against a sharp rise in meat and other food prices and for improved working conditions. Mr. Lech Walesa, an unemployed electrician who had helped lead the 1976 strikes for higher wages and work councils, assumed leadership of the strikes and put at the forefront demands that the Polish government should recognize the right to strike and the right to form unions independent of the government. He and his workers insisted on "free trade unions, independent from parties and employers" as the first demand in order to give permanent leverage against the government, which in the previous strikes had failed to maintain the value of concessions it had granted. After weeks of confrontation while strikes spread to the vital coal mines of Silesia and the economy suffered, Prime Minister Gierek granted the major demands of the workers. Six of the 19 members of the Polish politburo were replaced during the crisis.

The negotiations were in public view and widely publicized by radio in Poland and in the Western news media. The United States, Germany, and Western European countries initially refrained from comments, fearing to encourage Russian intervention to prevent concessions to the strikers, that would undermine the Communist Parties' controls in Eastern Europe. After the strike was over, Prime Minister Gierek was replaced because of a heart attack, that could have been in part political. The Russian news media grumbled and threatened, but Russian troops and authorities did not openly intervene.

After a year of confrontations demanding democratic reforms of Poland's political and economic system, at the end of 1981 Poland was deep in debt and the Communist Party was in disarray. In December when the Solidarity Union demanded a referendum on the political system, General Jaruzelski, as Minister of Defense and not as Communist Party leader, imposed strict martial law and outlawed strikes. It appeared the man with the guns would not back down without a struggle and that the country was headed for turmoil.

If Russia allowed new centers of union authority to erode the totalitarian system of Poland, this could have a major impact on other East European systems, including that of Russia itself. Thus, not only in Western Europe's Eurocommunism movements but in the Polish unions of Eastern Europe, the Communist model and ideology faced fundamental challenges at the beginning of the 1980s. Adding to these Soviet troubles was the loss of prestige from the costly and vicious war waged against their occupation troops by the Afghanistan patriots.

During most of the 1970s the Russian propaganda had stressed how harmoniously the Council of Mutual Economic Assistance was working in the Socialist Commonwealth of Eastern Europe, although reminding the members to remain vigilant against a resumption of the Cold War. It stressed the importance of detente for consolidating peace. The Afghanistan rebellion in 1980 triggered resumption of the hostile rhetoric of the Cold

War, and the Soviet media pictured Carter and the United States as villains in all the crisis areas of the world.[15]

As Russia became more and more mired in the fighting in Afghanistan and as economic and political retaliation led by the United States increased the pressure, detente receded. The Reagan Administration pointed to the events as confirming their worst suspicions of the nature of the Soviet regime. The internationalists clung to their hope that pressures short of military action would help bring about changes in Russian policies, particularly if the aging Brezhnev should step down. The other threads of superpower relations affecting the world scene cannot be unraveled without examining the patterns of Chinese relationships with the Soviet Union and the United States.

Summary

The superpower system is the most visible of the world systems because observers generally picture world crises as affecting the position of the United States and Russia. The pivot of U.S. policy is the NATO alliance of Western Europe against the Soviet Union. The Cold War, which gave birth to that alliance, grew out of the Soviet invasion of Czechoslovakia, the Berlin Blockade, and other Soviet power moves to establish a buffer of satellites in Eastern Europe. Western Europe and the United States saw this as a threat to their countries. The Soviets were motivated by fear of a German revival and a Communist ideology that considers capitalist nations as natural enemies and a threat to peace. The U.S. support for Europe was reinforced by close historical and economic ties.

The course of detente which has moderated the Cold War has had many ups and downs. It began after Stalin's death when Khrushchev supported truces in the Korean War and Indochina and withdrew troops from Finland and Austria. There were serious setbacks to detente by Khrushchev's ruthless suppression of the Hungarian revolt, by the Cuban Missile Crisis, and by the Vietnam War, but detente came to flower in the 1970s with negotiations to control nuclear weapons. At the end of 1979 Russia and the United States seemed within reach of a basic SALT treaty despite Soviet resentment of Carter's human rights campaign, but hopes were shattered in 1979 when the Soviets invaded Afghanistan and set up a puppet government. President Carter responded by mobilizing opposition to the moves including organizing a boycott of the Moscow Olympics in the summer of 1980 and restrictions on trade with the Soviets. Thus, the 1980s began with a major swing back into the Cold War.

FOOTNOTES

1. Lucius D. Clay, *Decision in Germany* (Garden City, N.Y.: Doubleday & Company, 1950).

2. Dean Acheson, *Present At The Creation* (New York: W.W. Norton & Co., 1969), pp. 226-235.

3. *Ibid.*, pp. 276-277.

4. See Robert E. Sherwood, *Roosevelt and Hopkins: An Intimate History* (New York: Harper, 1948), p. 577.

5. Winston S. Churchill, *Triumph and Tragedy, op. cit.,* Chapter 3, pp. 227, 365-402.

6. *Khrushchev Remembers, The Last Testament,* translated and edited by Strobe Talbott (Boston: Little, Brown and Company, 1974), pp. 173, 197-250.

7. Russians refer to their system as socialism. Western writers usually refer to their system as Communism, and reserve the word socialism for a social democratic system.

8. Frankfurter Allgemeine Zeitung, April 11, 1981, cited in *The German Tribune,* April 26, 1981.

9. *Khrushchev Remembers, The Last Testament, op. cit.,* pp. 250-262, 279-298.

10. Graham T. Allison, *Essence of Decision: Explaining the Cuban Missile Crisis,* (Boston: Little, Brown & Company, 1971).

11. Robert Kennedy, *Thirteen Days: A Memoir of the Cuban Missile Crisis* (New York: 1969).

12. James O. Goldsborough, "Eurocommunism After Madrid," *Foreign Affairs,* July, 1977, p. 801.

13. Article by Victor Zorza in *Washington Post,* June 29, 1977, editorial page.

14. U.S. Department of State, Bureau of Public Affairs, "Soviet Dilemmas in Afghanistan," Special Report No. 72, June, 1980. (Reports by the State Department's Bureau of Intelligence and Research and by the Department of Defense.)

15. Trends of Soviet propaganda can be followed in *The Current Digest of the Soviet Press* and in daily accounts by the Foreign Broadcast Information Service. The latter U.S. Government publication is made available to many libraries.

CHAPTER

9

Superpower Politics in Asia and the Middle East

The Cold War dominated European diplomacy for most of the period after World War II. In Asia, China increasingly took a major role in international politics, which centered on defining China's relationship with the two superpowers. The 1950s were marked by a cold war type of hostility between China and the U.S. In the 1960s China's splitting away from its close alliance with Russia was one of the most dramatic and important developments of the post World War II era. This cold war in the Communist orbit had a major impact on world politics and led eventually to normal relations between China and the United States.

In the 1970s during the phasing down of the Vietnam War the major crisis area shifted to the Middle East. The superpowers found themselves reacting to, more than controlling developments in the Middle East. The political conflicts there continued to be dominated by ideologies, particularly those of conflicting nationalisms. Action was increasingly influenced by the new petroleum powers and the economics of oil.

The Sino-Soviet Split

Chinese nationalism and nuclear weapons policy have had a major impact on China's relationship with the Soviet Union. Many of the present Chinese Communist leaders still resent how Russian Communist advisers tried to dominate them during the 1920s. At that time there were factional conflicts between the Chinese Communists, and particularly between a group led by Mao and one by Moscow. Mao built much of his appeal on Chinese nationalism, and this ideology came into conflict frequently with policies of Russian Communist advisers, whose goal was to strengthen Moscow as the center of world Communism and support those Chinese who looked to Moscow for advice.

The United States established relations with the Republic of China in 1928, when it was clear that President Chiang Kai-shek exercised *de facto* control of the Government of China. He attained this position after fighting with Communists and purging them from his party while battling the Chinese warlords. Chiang's running battle with Communist forces under Mao continued during much of the 1930s. In 1936 Chiang was kidnapped by Communist sympathizers in Sian in western China, but after a strong message from Moscow, the Chinese Communist leaders, over Mao's objection, released Chiang and agreed to cooperate with Chiang in fighting the Japanese. Stalin's nationalist motive was to build an anti-Japanese coalition in China that would reduce the Japanese threat to Siberia. Stalin at that time was worried about the growing power of Hitler and did not want to divert troops to defend Siberia from Japan, which was allied with Germany.

Since World War II there have been periods of close cooperation between the Soviet Union and the Chinese Communists, but most of the period since the formation of the Peoples' Republic of China in 1949 has been characterized by strife. At the close of World War II the Soviets were primarily interested in better access to the Pacific through control of railroads in Manchuria and concessions in Port Arthur. For this reason and with United States encouragement they completed a treaty of friendship with Chiang Kai-shek's Nationalist Government. However, when Russia accepted the surrender of the Japanese troops in 1945 in Manchuria, the Russians secretly handed over surrendered arms to Chinese Communist forces under Mao. Thus, the Russians were getting concessions from the official Chinese government, and taking out insurance by supporting the Communist rebels.

The period of 1949-1957 was the high point of Sino-Soviet cooperation. The Soviets were the first to recognize the new Chinese Communist regime that was set up in 1949 after Chiang Kai-shek and his remaining forces fled to Taiwan. The Soviets even refused to participate in U.N. Security Council meetings in 1950 during the first part of the Korean War, because the Chinese Nationalist Government still represented China in the United Nations Security Council. This was a tactical error, however, since it permitted the Western powers led by the United States to mobilize the United Nations machinery to oppose the aggression of North Korea against South Korea. Since North Korea had been occupied by the Soviet Union after World War II, had numerous Soviet advisors, and had been heavily supplied with Soviet arms and equipment, it was clear that Soviet leaders had approved the invasion. The Soviets, however, carefully avoided involving their troops in the Korean War.[1]

Just before the outbreak of the Korean War, Chairman Mao Tse-tung spent three months in Moscow. During this visit Mao agreed to Kim Il-sung's plan[2] to attack South Korea, and the Sino-Soviet Treaty of Friendship and Assistance was revised so that if either state was attacked by Japan "or any state allied with it," the other partner would immediately render military and other assistance "by all means at its disposal." This extended defensive coverage of the Treaty to an attack by the United States, which was allied with Japan. When China felt itself threatened as the U.N. forces led by General MacArthur approached the Yalu River boundary between Korea and China, hundreds of thousands of Chinese "volunteers" came across the Yalu to drive back the American and U.N. troops. China saw its action as protecting its borders, but it was pulling Russian chestnuts out of the fire by preventing a defeat of Russia's North Korea protege.

China was covered in the new Treaty by the Russian guarantee of assistance if the United States (an ally of Japan) had attacked China.

The North Korean attack on South Korea in June, 1950, had a far reaching effect on the power politics of the Far East. President Truman interpreted the open aggression of North Korea as a move of the Communist powers to expand their influence by aggression, and he mobilized the United Nations System under the flag of collective security. Many nations responded and the aggression was repelled after a bitter and costly war.

President Eisenhower and his Secretary of State John Foster Dulles created a series of formal alliances around the periphery of the two Communist giants to deter future aggression of this type. The selective security system included the alliance with Japan (1951), Korea (1953), the Republic of China on Taiwan (1954), and the SEATO or Southeast Collective Defense Treaty (1954) which included the United States, Australia, Britain, France, New Zealand, Pakistan, the Philippines, and Thailand. The treaty texts were similar to the NATO Pact, but the Asian pacts have not come close to NATO in the strength of commitments. (See Figure 8-2.) Some observers blame the Eisenhower-Dulles containment policy against Communist China on their overreaction to Senator Joseph McCarthy's propagandistic attacks on the State Department for harboring Communist sympathizers, but such a view seriously underestimates the political impact of the Korean War.

In the early 1950s, the Soviet Union provided hundreds of millions of dollars of aid through loans, grants, and technical assistance to Communist China. The Soviet steel and machinery plants were the basis of industrialization in the first five year plan of China, which permitted China to rebuild its industry after the terrible destruction of the Chinese Civil War. Early in 1955 the Soviet Union began assisting the Peoples' Republic of China in nuclear energy through providing an experimental reactor and training its scientists at Dubna in the Soviet Union. China, in fact, helped finance this major nuclear research center. By October, 1957, China had made an agreement with the Soviet Union[3] for it eventually to provide China with a sample atomic bomb and technical data for its manufacture.

Also in 1957 the Soviet Union tested its first intercontinental missile, and on October 4 it put Sputnik I into orbit. The Americans were dismayed and the Chinese were delighted. Mao journeyed to the Soviet Union in November, 1957, to celebrate the 40th anniversary of the Russian revolution. In his speech at the Moscow airport he praised Soviet achievements in space, thanked them for their generous assistance, and stated that "there is no force on earth which can separate us."[4] Soon thereafter, in meeting with a group of Chinese students studying in Russia, Mao stated that the launching of the Russian satellite marked a turning point in the struggle between the socialist and communist camps and that now the "East wind prevails over the west wind."[5]

In this speech Mao said that the Communist countries would not be the first to unleash a nuclear war, but if one were started by the imperialists and "worse came to worst and half of mankind died, the other half would remain while imperialism would be razed to the ground and the whole world would become socialist. Then the victorious people would very swiftly create on the ruins of imperialism a civilization thousands of times higher than the capitalist system and a truly beautiful future for themselves."[6] He put this position more crudely during the Conference in terms of the Chinese producing more babies. Implications of these statements were profoundly disturbing to Soviet leaders and foreign observers.[7]

At this time the Chinese were secretly asking for a sample of a nuclear bomb, but the Soviets stalled. This was a reasonable position on their part; even the United States does not turn over nuclear weapons to its allies without retaining ultimate control over their use.

In 1957 most experts and observers perceived the Sino-Soviet alliance as solid, cemented not only by the leaders' Communist ideology, which saw Communist countries threatened by a hostile capitalist world led by the United States, but also cemented by economic interests, in which the strong Russian heavy machinery capacity could help Communist China build a base for industries paid for by Chinese shipments of raw materials. Even without this ideological and economic cement, they could have allied on strictly balance of power terms against the United States. However, within two years this unity was to be shattered, and experts are still not agreed on which were the principal reasons for the split. The cracks started to show during the 1958 Offshore Islands crisis after Mao's "East Wind-West Wind" speech.

In August, 1958, Communist China started a heavy bombardment of the offshore islands close to the mainland of China but still held by Nationalist China. During this period the American press carried stories of the U.S. military buildup in the Taiwan area including nuclear capabilities. American naval ships helped convoy supply ships up to the last three miles of territorial waters of the offshore islands with Chinese nationalist forces taking the supplies the rest of the way under fire.

On September 6, 1958, Premier Chou Enlai announced that Communist China had no desire for war with the United States and proposed a resumption of the Sino-American Ambassadorial Talks in Warsaw. The following day Khrushchev for the first time intervened with a statement that an attack on the Peoples' Republic of China would be regarded as an attack on the Soviet Union. On September 19, in an even stronger stand in a formal note to the United States, the Soviets stated that "our side" also has nuclear weapons — a reply to reports in the American press that nuclear weapons might be used to defend the offshore islands.[8] Years later when the Chinese Communists and Soviets were trading abuse and referring to the offshore island crisis, the Chinese asserted that the Khrushchev statements were too late to do any good; nevertheless, the Chinese did not suspend bombardment of the offshore islands until October, 1958, a month after the Soviet statements of support were made. Many analysts take the Chinese assertions about Khrushchev at face value, but in view of the propagandistic nature of the later exchanges that occurred in the 1960s, it is reasonable to assume the Chinese were attempting to play down the importance of the Soviet statements of support in 1958. This is supported by the fact that on January 28, 1959, Premier Chou Enlai referred to "unbreakable unity" of the Communists, the "correct leadership" of Comrade Khrushchev, and the "fraternal assistance" of the Soviet Union.[9] In February,

Eisenhower   Dulles

Secretary of State Dulles and International Law

Secretary of State Dulles' foreign policies are associated with "massive retaliation," a doctrine announced in early 1954, when President Eisenhower was saying Vietnam could be the first of other falling dominoes in Asia. The Dulles doctrine implied a foreign policy of power politics with little regard for international law and similar restraints on policy. He was a good poker player, and no one called his hand to see if he was bluffing. Many observers fail to stress that he had a long background as an international lawyer. This helps explain his early support for an international order under the United Nations (see box on page 000), his opposition to the British and French attack on the Suez Canal, and the network of mutual defense treaties he created.

International law also played an important part in the Offshore Islands crisis of 1958. In that crisis U.S. warships convoyed supplies up to three miles from the islands, and then the Nationalist Chinese forces took the supplies for the last stretch under heavy fire from Chinese Communist coastal batteries. I served on the State Department's China Desk from 1960 to 1964, working on political military affairs, including issues involving the Offshore Islands. In checking back files I was impressed with the fact that Secretary Dulles personally established the three-mile policy in recognition of international law, which at that time designated areas beyond three miles as international waters.

1959, the two countries signed a long-term trade agreement including technical assistance which was their largest economic agreement to that date.[10] In retrospect the Soviet support during the offshore island crisis of 1958 in view of the possible nuclear confrontation with the U.S. was impressive despite the Chinese belittling of Russian support.

In any event, the Chinese Communists did not attempt to cash in on the Soviet support of September, 1958, and on October 5, 1958, they announced a one week cease fire, that was later changed to shelling the islands on odd-numbered days. The islands in 1978 were still subjected to bombardment with propaganda shells, but in 1979 this ended after the U.S. recognized China.

By the middle of 1959 Sino-Soviet relations were fractured when in June the Soviet Union secretly tore up the agreement on "new technology" for national defense and refused to provide China with a sample of a nuclear bomb and technical data concerning its manufacture.[11] In October, Khrushchev attacked economic policies of the "Great Leap Forward" and "arrogant" leaders in the Chinese Communist camp. These Soviet actions occurred at the time Mao was purging the top military leader, Peng Teh-huai, who was friendly with Moscow.

By July, 1960, tensions and pressures had developed to such a point that Khrushchev abruptly terminated the Soviet economic aid agreement recalling all 1,390 Soviet scientists and technicians from China within a few weeks. Trade was cut back. The effect on the Chinese economy was disastrous because ambitious plans of the Chinese had depended on imports of Russian capital, equipment, and technical advice. This, joined with abortive economic policies of the Great Leap Forward and a poor harvest, led to a Chinese depression.

The next crisis in Sino-Soviet relations occurred in the 1962-1964 time frame over the negotiation of the partial nuclear test ban treaty, and when the dust had settled, Chairman Khrushchev had been deposed. At the end of 1962 the Soviets informed the Chinese of their intention to negotiate a nuclear test ban treaty with the United States. The Chinese were furious since one of the articles of the treaty, which was ratified in 1963, foreclosed Soviet nuclear weapons assistance to the Chinese.

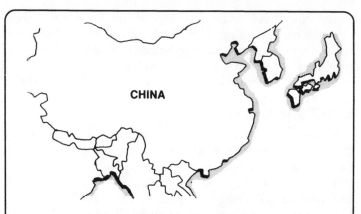

Experts' Views on China

Someone has defined experts as persons who can give good reasons for why they were wrong. China experts are no exception.

From 1959 to 1964 I served on the China Desk as an economic officer under John Holdridge, who later became Secretary of State Kissinger's chief advisor on China. I was a novice in Chinese affairs transferred there from Tel Aviv, Israel. In 1959 and 1960 John Holdridge and a few other China experts were a small minority of the China experts who took seriously the developing split between the Soviet Union and China. I had reservations about the seriousness of the split, even though I had access to the U.S. government's reporting on the matter. It was not until Russia withdrew its technicians in late 1960 that many of the China experts believed the split was real.

By late 1959 I was convinced that Chinese economic statistics were greatly exaggerated and that it was in serious economic difficulties as a result of the Great Leap Forward. John Holdridge and I were among the few in government who believed this, and we had a running bureaucratic battle with the CIA and the Bureau of Intelligence and Research of the Department of State whenever this issue came up. It was years before many China experts of the U.S. government and outside the government recognized the serious economic problems in China, caused in large part by Great Leap Forward policies.

The Chinese pressed forward with developing their own nuclear arsenal and on October 16, 1964, exploded their first atomic device. Significantly, a few days before this Khrushchev had been deposed, and one of the accusations against Khrushchev by the Central Committee was "hare-brained scheming." In the Communist dictionary this could have covered plans for a preemptive strike.[12]

Chinese nuclear weapons progress accelerated after the first test. On October 27, 1966, the Chinese Communists fired a medium range missile with a nuclear warhead, and on June 17, 1967, they exploded their first hydrogen bomb. The Soviets countered with moving strategic missile units into Outer Mongolia, within range of the area where the Chinese carried out their tests.[13]

The dispute in 1969 entered a critical phase that later led directly to the Chinese move for a detente with the United States. During this period reports circulated in the press and among the Communist parties of Europe that the Soviet Union was seriously considering a strike against China to forestall its developing fusion weapons that could threaten European Russia. It is even reported that the Soviet Union approached the United States in 1969 to explore what its attitude would be if the Soviet Union carried out such a strike, but that it was discouraged by the United States.[14] This was soon after the Soviets invaded Czechoslovakia with Eastern European satellite troops to put down a liberalization tendency in Czechoslovakia and announced the "Brezhnev Doctrine" proclaiming the right of the Soviet Union to intervene where it judged the cause of "socialism" to be in danger. In the latter part of 1969 the Chinese carried out more tests of thermonuclear weapons culminating in the successful test in December, 1969. On August 28 a Pravda editorial had stated:

> The military arsenals of the Maoists are filling up with all the latest weapons, and a war, should it break out in present day conditions, what with the existing weapons and lethal armaments and modern means of delivery, would not spare a single continent.

A Soviet weekly at the same time was claiming the Chinese were building fortifications in Manchuria for war with the Soviet Union. It accused the Chinese of a reckless, adventurous policy and warned that "any attempts to speak with the Soviet Union in the language of arms to encroach on the interest of the Soviet people, which is building Communism, will meet with a firm rebuff." The Chinese people are being alerted for possible nuclear war and border clashes are part of a chain of "hostile actions by the Peking leadership which does not cease its absurd territorial claims on the Soviet Union."[15]

The Chinese retort in October accused the Soviet Union of intending to launch a nuclear war against China. They stated they would never be intimidated by threats and that there would be war should a "handful of maniacs dare to raid China's strategic sites in defiance of world opinion."[16] It is clear from the above that Chinese leaders saw Soviet statements as threats of a preemptive strike, and that the dispute over nuclear weapons was at the heart of the split.

Historians and political scientists continue to debate the many other issues underlying the Soviet split with China. Many observers stress competition for leadership of the world Communist movement. The Soviet Union, since the Great October Revolution of 1919, has seen itself as the leader of the "socialist camp." Mao Tse-tung and the Chinese Communists, however, also aspired to lead the world Communist movement. Both sides have competed for influence in Vietnam, Laos, Cambodia, and many of the Communist parties of the world. Moreover, there have been numerous border disputes and clashes along the 5,000-mile border between the Soviet Union and China. Major military forces of the Soviet and Chinese face each other along this border.[17]

The Sino-Soviet split is a fact of international life and has achieved a great deal of momentum, but some observers regard it as a split that can be mended. Perhaps the leaders succeeding Mao Tse-tung on the Chinese side and Brezhnev on the Soviet side may renew cooperation between these two great Communist powers. The Soviet Union at times makes gestures of reconciliation which are rebuffed by the Chinese, but this does not mean that they will always be rebuffed. Just as the Sino-Soviet split surprised most academic and government observers, a reconciliation would also catch them off balance. If forces of reason prevail, the two countries would complement each other economically and ideologically. If

Figure 9-1   The Sino-Soviet Split

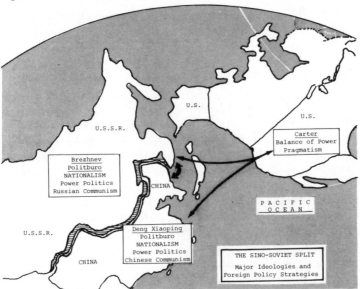

nationalistic jealousies prevail, the split will continue to the benefit of world stability, which would be threatened by a powerful and militant Communist bloc. (Figure 9-1.)

U.S. Recognition of Communist China

Although Europe is regarded as the pivot of American foreign policy, the United States has been deeply involved in Asian affairs. During the lifetime of present top policymakers the United States has waged three major wars in East Asia. Japan's attack at Pearl Harbor, which arose from U.S support of China, brought the United States into World War II and started a chain of events leading to the age of nuclear weapons. The Korean War involved war with Chinese forces. The Vietnam War, the longest U.S. war, involved a tragic defeat and generated political turmoil within the United States. The present focus of U.S. Asian policy is on China and Japan, but United States leaders are also deeply concerned about Korea, Taiwan, and Southeast Asia.

After Pearl Harbor the United States focused on the European War, but it continued to support the Chinese Nationalist Government. The U.S. had supported Chinese independence since the beginning of the century. Moreover, China kept Japanese troops occupied, so strenuous efforts were made to supply China through Burma and by flights "over the Hump" from India into China.

After World War II China was racked by a vicious civil war. In 1946 and 1947, the United States, through General George Marshall, attempted to mediate, but finally gave up trying to find a basis for trust and compromise between President Chiang Kai-shek and Chairman Mao that would permit the building of a coalition government. During this period the United States continued to provide economic and military aid to Chiang Kai-shek's forces, so after the victory of the Chinese Communists in 1949 the United States was at the top of the list as an enemy of the new Chinese Communist regime.

The Chinese Nationalist Government fled to Taiwan, and the United States withdrew its military mission from Taiwan and was not providing military aid to it at the outbreak of the Korean War. Although, in 1949 and 1950, 14 non-Communist governments wanted to establish diplomatic relations with Communist China, it established formal relations immediately with only six. The initial Chinese Communist attitude toward Western missions was one of contempt. They seized American property belonging to the American Consulate in Peking and mistreated and arrested the American Consul, Angus Ward. As a result, the United States withdrew all official personnel from China.

The Korean War was part of the avalanche that established a course for United States foreign policy that was not changed for 20 years. The Korean War came from a Russian-North Korean initiative, but there was evidence, also reported in the Hong Kong press, that the Chinese Communists were assembling boats to invade Taiwan, so President Truman "neutralized" the Taiwan Strait with the Seventh Fleet immediately after the outbreak of the war. Peking reacted with angry propaganda against the United States, and in a cable to the United Nations, accused the United States of armed aggression against the territory of China.

The Chinese Communists warned in a public statement on September 30, they would not supinely tolerate seeing their neighbor, North Korea, invaded by imperialists and later relayed a direct warning through the Indian Ambassador in Peking of the intention to intervene if Americans crossed the 38th parallel into North Korea. After the U.N. troops under General MacArthur drove into North Korea, Chinese Communist troops appeared as "volunteers." In November, 1950, hundreds of thousands of Chinese "volunteers" helped drive the United States and U.N. forces back beyond the 38th parallel into South Korea. After severe fighting the front was finally stabilized near this line close to where the fighting began. Meanwhile, the United States took the lead in the U.N. in organizing a strict trade embargo, and it led the fight in the United Nations year after year to keep Communist China out of the United Nations. Moreover, the United States provided large amounts of military and economic aid to Taiwan, its U-2 spy planes flew over mainland China, and its Seventh Fleet patrolled the Taiwan Strait, although the neutralization of the Strait by the Seventh Fleet was officially terminated after the Korean War.

As the war in Vietnam heated up, U.S. relations with China continued to be hostile with many American leaders and most of the American public seeing North Vietnam as a satellite of the Russians and/or the Chinese. More perceptive observers and most of the State Department policymakers, with whom I worked by the time of escalation of the war in Vietnam, realized that North Vietnam was obtaining aid from the two great Communist powers, China and the Soviet Union, and playing them off against each other. Meanwhile, Chinese propaganda attacks against the United States continued unabated, and there appeared to be little chance under President Nixon for an improvement of relations.

Thus, it was an incredulous world which received the announcement on July 15, 1971, that President Nixon had sent his Assistant for National Security Affairs, Dr. Henry Kissinger, to Peking to meet with Premier Chou Enlai on July 9 through 11. The amazement continued when President Nixon visited Peking February 21 through 28, 1972, with TV cameras and full coverage of the news media. In retrospect it appears the Chinese invitation for the visit was motivated by Chinese fear of the Russian threat of their northern border and by a fear of a Russian nuclear strike as noted in the previous section.

The February, 1972, communique established the basic framework for "normalization" of relations between the United States and the Peoples' Republic of China. The dilemma of reconciling basically different ideologies and views toward Taiwan and toward Far Eastern policies in general was finessed in the Shanghai Communique, by setting forth in diplomatic language each side's view of these issues, and then indicating agreement on some general principles. The areas of agreement included a desire to work toward "normalization" of relations, to reduce the danger of war, and not to seek "hegemony" in Asia. The Chinese side stated the Communist line that the nations want liberation and the people want revolution as an irresistable trend of history and that the Chinese firmly support oppressed people — including the people of Vietnam, Laos, and Cambodia. The U.S. in the communique made it clear that it wanted a negotiated solution to the Vietnam problem and that it would maintain its close ties and support for the Republic of Korea, its friendly relations with Japan, and that it wanted a peaceful settlement of the Taiwan question by the Chinese themselves.

President Carter, on July 1, 1977, reaffirmed the Shanghai Communique and stated that he hoped the United States could work out an agreement with the Peoples' Republic of China for "full diplomatic relations" and still make sure of maintaining the "peaceful lives of the Taiwanese."[18] Intensive and secret negotiations with the Chinese were carried out in 1978, and at the end of the year President Carter announced that the United States would establish full diplomatic relations with the Peoples' Republic of China on January 1, 1979, breaking off diplomatic relations with Taiwan. He also announced U.S. intentions of abrogating the mutual defense treaty with Taiwan in one year, in accordance with the termination clause of the treaty. Background news reports indicated that the Chinese request to terminate it immediately had been the sticking point in the secret talks, and that the new Chinese Government, apparently controlled by Deng Xiaoping, had finally yielded on this point.

During the weeks that followed, Chinese government statements indicated that, although it did not rule out an invasion of Taiwan, the government was in no hurry about resolving the matter. U.S. statements also made clear that the United States would continue to sell arms to Taiwan, and that the United States still was interested in a peaceful solution of the Taiwan problem. Although American critics accused the Carter Administration of selling out Taiwan, supporters of the policy pointed out Taiwan was in an excellent defensive position with 100 miles of ocean between it and the mainland, and that it was unprecedented for a country like China to agree to another country (the United States) selling arms to a regime (Taiwan) that claimed to be the legitimate government.

In regard to the United States' moral and treaty commitments to Taiwan, the United States made clear its continuing interest in Taiwan's welfare, and that the United States did not foreclose future direct assistance if Taiwan should be threatened. Hong Kong, a Nineteenth Century British colony, had coexisted peacefully with the Communist regime for 30 years, and presumably Taiwan could also coexist if it did not pursue its claim to be the legitimate government of all of China.

The U.S. policy was consistent with traditional foreign policy strategies. As indicated in Figure 9-1, the most obvious aim was to help maintain a balance of power. If Russia and China joined hands against the United States, the U.S. would be faced with an alliance of the two largest and potentially most powerful countries in the world, both with a revolutionary and hostile ideology. Opening up diplomatic, trade, and cultural relations with China could help prevent formation of such a hostile bloc. Meanwhile, Deng Xiaoping's government has broken with Mao's tradition of suspicion, hostility, and isolation, and it is getting U.S. support — including U.S. investments, technology, and even lethal weapons.

Southeast Asia Before and After Vietnam

The Korean War conditioned U.S. policymakers to look at North Vietnam's attacks against South Vietnam as another Communist challenge to the security of Asia. President Truman tried to help French forces stop the spread of Communism in Indochina by providing major financial and equipment support to France in the early 1950s. General Eisenhower pictured South Vietnam as a domino that, if it fell, would topple other Asian governments to Communist pressures. As we noted in Chapter 3, however, Ho Chi Minh's use of the ideas of nationalism and Communism were major factors in his continued attacks on South Vietnam, and most of the world saw the struggle in this framework rather than in balance of power terms and a superpower confrontation.

Ho Chi Minh's initial victories against the French were due more to support from China than from the Soviet Union, although later the Soviet Union provided most of his material support. His forces in the early 1950s were supported from Chinese sanctuaries and by Chinese military equipment and training. After the 1954 Geneva Conference, which recognized Ho's North Vietnam, the French withdrew from the South under pressure of its President Diem. The United States military eagerly took over the job of training and equipping the South Vietnamese forces.[19]

Soon after President Diem assumed power, there was a vicious circle of terrorism by Communist insurgents countered by suppression by the Diem government. By 1960 the North Vietnamese were openly supporting the insurgents. The United States supported Diem until 1964, when his police elements killed Buddhist priests during a Buddhist demonstration and outraged U.S. policymakers. Following a coup secretly encouraged by U.S. officials, in which Diem was killed, there were a series of military governments. Later, President Johnson, convinced that Asian stability depended on U.S. support to South Vietnam, increased U.S. troop strength there from 16,000 in 1964 to almost 540,000 by 1967. This, as much as any fact, demonstrates the extent the U.S. took over a role of world policeman in Vietnam.

Early in 1968 the Vietcong mounted the "Tet offensive," and its waves threatened the U.S. Embassy in Saigon before the Vietcong were forced back with heavy casualties. American officials claimed a military victory, but the media coverage and political impact of heavy attacks on American and South Vietnamese positions led to President Johnson's withdrawal from the presidential race.

After President Nixon took office in 1969, Secretary of Defense Laird withdrew U.S. troops with the announced aim to stabilize the area by strengthening the South Vietnamese capability to fight. (See Box.) Secretary Kissinger finally concluded a truce with the North Vietnamese at the beginning of 1973 after strong pressure by the United States, including bombing of North Vietnam and blockading of its ports. This was a classic use of realpolitik. South Vietnamese and North Vietnamese units continued skirmishes after the truce, and North Vietnamese continued to reinforce its troops in flagrant violation of its provisions. In 1975 its regular military units completely defeated the South Vietnamese forces and took over control of the South, forcing the remaining U.S. civilian advisers and masses of Vietnamese to flee the country.

The war created deep divisions in the U.S. society; demonstrations and strong congressional opposition to the war became a major factor in Nixon's final decision to withdraw U.S. forces.[20] Major issues of the war can be defined by looking at the approaches to it by the policymakers and their critics. The Vietnamese aggression to President Johnson seemed to be a part of the pattern of the Communist aggression initiated by North Korea in the Korean War and Communist insurgent attacks in Malaysia, Burma, the Philippines, Indonesia, and Thailand.[21] President Johnson and his top policymakers initially escalated the U.S. military commitments to help in the defense of South Vietnam under the Tonkin Gulf Congressional Resolution, which included provisions for maintaining collective security under the U.N. Charter and under the SEATO Treaty. The United States, however, soon slipped into the role of being a world policeman in that part of Asia with virtually no support from allies.

Two Secretaries of Defense:
McNamara and Laird

From 1969 to 1971 during the major withdrawal of forces from Vietnam I was attached to the Air Force in the Pentagon as a Department of State political advisor. Although I was not concerned with Vietnam, which was under a military command, I had informal discussions with military officers about the issues involved. It impressed me that there was widespread support for Secretary of Defense Laird despite the fact that during this period he made a major cutback of military forces and funds. In contrast, many officers still criticized Robert McNamara and his 'whiz kids,' although during the period he had been Secretary of Defense there had been major increases of the military budget and U.S. forces. The relatively favorable view of Laird persisted, even though many military officers resisted his withdrawal of U.S. forces from Vietnam.

It appeared to me that the military had resented the way McNamara and his civilian advisors intervened in military-type decisions and had told the military how it should spend funds to be cost effective. Laird, in contrast, eliminated the whiz kids. In cutting back on the operations in Vietnam he would give the military a numerical quota and let the generals and admirals decide where and how the cuts should be made.

This is a further illustration of how jealously the military guard their responsibilities for military matters. This makes it very difficult for the State Department to intervene in military decisions which have a major impact on foreign policy.

One fundamental issue is whether the war was one of revolution or aggression. If the conflict in South Vietnam were a locally inspired insurgent movement, the Executive Branch could not have justified getting support from Congress to intervene in a Vietnamese "civil war." Also, from the point of view of internationalists, intervention in civil wars is not justified under the U.N. Charter, since they are within the domestic jurisdiction of states (Article 11.7). If, on the other hand, the conflict grew out of aggression by military forces under the command of the state of North Vietnam, the United States and other allies could justify helping the state of South Vietnam as a collective security policy under Article 51 of the U.N. and under the SEATO Treaty. There was no doubt in my mind during the 1969-1971 period, when I was reading many intelligence reports on Vietnam, that the fighting was controlled and supplied from North Vietnam. However, in the earlier period from 1957 to 1960 the relative importance of attacks of the South Vietnamese insurgents and North Vietnamese Communist cadres versus President Diem's purge of Communist elements in initiating the conflict in South Vietnam is still not clear.

By 1975 the U.S. Congress was tired of supporting a world policeman role in Southeast Asia, and it drastically cut military and economic aid to Vietnam. This encouraged the North Vietnamese in their final offensive. The United States had borne almost the entire burden of trying to help South Vietnam with only minor support from Australia, New Zealand, Thailand, and Korea. The European allies were conspicuous by their non-support and criticisms of the United States.

After the North Vietnamese victory over South Vietnam, the withdrawal of U.S. forces removed a deterrent to aggression by the powerful forces of North Vietnam. In conventional balance of power terms North Vietnam seemed to dominate Southeast Asia. Few observers anticipated China would later enter the balance of power equation against Vietnam, since China had helped Vietnam in its war against South Vietnam and the United States.

In 1975 an extreme Communist group under Pol Pot, who acknowledged support and inspiration of China, took over Cambodia. Pol Pot's regime repeatedly clashed with

Thailand's Nationalism

Most of the bombing of North Vietnam during the Vietnam War was by American aircraft from Thai bases. Some of the Thai bases in the Northwest were only 50 to 100 miles from the Ho Chi Minh Trail, the Communists' major supply line to Vietnam, yet Thailand was an island of stability during the war. The bases were protected by Thai paramilitary units, and at Thailand's request there were no armed American soldiers in Thailand to protect them. The bases came under attack only three or four times by small groups of infiltrators.

The most serious attack was against the Udorn air base about 50 miles from Laos at the end of July, 1968. I happened to be the weekend duty officer at the Embassy in Bangkok the Sunday it occurred. On the way home from the swimming pool with my family I received a buzz on the portable radio from the marine guard asking me to stop by the Embassy. Within five minutes I was there and the marine guard informed me he had received a commercial phone call from the U.S. Air Force unit in Udorn that the base had been attacked. About seven guerrillas had wounded a few Thai guards and four Americans and damaged two planes. Two guerrillas had been killed and one captured. The Air Force unit had phoned the Embassy because the communications were not working to JUSMAG, the U.S. military advisory group of about 1,000 personnel in Bangkok.

Since this was a military matter and not directly an Embassy responsibility, I phoned the military duty

Vietnam along the border areas. Communist elements who acknowledged friendship with Vietnam took over Laos.

Thailand, after the precipitate withdrawal of U.S. forces from Vietnam, began to normalize its relation with Vietnam and with China. Spurred on by student demonstrations against U.S. forces in Thailand, the Thai authorities acceded to the Vietnamese request to get U.S. troops to withdraw from Thailand in order to remove that officer at JUSMAG. The major on duty had not heard the report and assured me there was nothing to worry about and that the report was probably false. (This is an example of the "Pearl Harbor" mentality.) Nevertheless, I sent in a flash reporting cable to Washington, D.C., alerted the Ambassador and the Political Counselor, and stationed a marine guard at the Ambassador's residence that night as a precaution. Subsequent reports confirmed the original Udorn report. It was about a year, however, before another similar probe was attempted against an air base.

Although there were 50,000 U.S. Air Force and related military personnel in Thailand plus hundreds of U.S. AID and Peace Corps officials in Northeast Thailand near Laos and the Ho Chi Minh Trail, none of the Americans was molested during the Vietnam War. There were skirmishes between Thai units and Communist insurgents in the Northeast mountain areas, however. I travelled through the Northeast several times and stayed with the U.S. Consul General who lived with his family in an unguarded compound in Udorn. I can only explain this peaceful situation for Americans by the fact the Thai authorities took the responsibility for protecting "Thai" bases where U.S. military were stationed. The Thai people revered their King and had pride in their nation, and the Thai farmers probably tipped off the police about the few attempts at infiltration. There was no major geographic obstacle since the Mekong River could have been easily crossed by boat.

obstacle to resuming normal diplomatic relations with Vietnam. Thailand obviously wanted United States support in Southeast Asia, but Thailand realized it could not rely on the United States after its precipitate withdrawal from Vietnam.

The United States only slowly and carefully reaffirmed its interest in maintaining a balance of power in Asia. In 1975 President Ford reaffirmed the importance of Asia and particularly the Philippines and Indonesia to U.S.

foreign policy but there was no strong commitment to Thailand. Secretary of State Vance on June 29, 1977, in the Carter Administration's first major address on Asia focused on East Asia. He stated an intention of reducing U.S. ground forces in Korea, but added that the U.S. was considering additional military aid. He stressed the U.S. would remain an "Asian and Pacific power." At the same time he called for diplomatic relations with Vietnam, although he rejected the idea of any reparations payments to Vietnam.

During this period the world was horrified by reports of mass killings and starvation under the Communist regime of Cambodia that came to power at the end of the Vietnam War. This new regime engaged in border skirmishes with Vietnam. During 1979 and 1980 Vietnam gave major troop support to so-called Cambodian insurgents against the new regime headed by Premier Pol Pot. This coincided with closer relations of Vietnam with the Soviet Union, including a treaty of friendship and cooperation. China responded to the Vietnamese attack on its ally, Cambodia, with an invasion of the northern border of Vietnam. Deng Xiaoping, the new Deputy Prime Minister, announced that the Chinese aim was to punish Vietnam and get it to withdraw troops from Cambodia. Tensions rose in 1980 as Russia reinforced troops along its border with China, and for a time the war took on the air of confrontation between the two major Communist powers, China and Russia, as well as Vietnam against China and Cambodia. After punishing Vietnam, China withdrew its troops and began peace talks, but it did not succeed in getting Vietnam to end support to the new regime it installed in Cambodia. Further tension developed between Vietnam and China when Vietnam expelled hundreds of thousands of its Chinese. After the 1979 Chinese attack Vietnam doubled the size of its armed forces to 2,600,000 a number larger than the U.S. armed forces.

In 1980, therefore, the situation was murky. The major conflicts involved Asian Communist powers, with war between Vietnam and Cambodia, and between Vietnam and China, and tension between China and Russia. Southeast Asian friends of the United States doubted the reliability of the United States support and were trying to establish a non-provocative stance toward their powerful and belligerent Communist neighbors.[22]

In East Asia, where the United States reinforced its alliance with Japan and South Korea while promoting normal relations with China, the situation was more stable. However, South Korea was alarmed at the build-up of North Korean forces and its continued hostility, and the United States postponed its scheduled withdrawal of forces from South Korea to maintain the balance of power there.

It appeared that, despite continued U.S. interest in the area, the United States would no longer be the prime mover in East Asia. Major conflicts were arising within the Communist world, and the U.S. no longer had troops on the mainland to counter threats to the non-Communist nations. If the uneasy equilibrium were to be maintained or reinforced, other countries, particularly those in the area, would have to take initiatives to strengthen their position vis-a-vis the new Communist powers.

The Middle East Maelstrom

Pre-1973 Arab-Israeli Conflicts. A major danger spot for international politics lies on the western edge of Asia in an area commonly known as the Middle East. Superpower politics and ideological and economic pressures are involved here as well as on the eastern edge of Asia.

As indicated in Chapter 3 the 1948 Arab-Israel war originated primarily from conflicting nationalist claims. The State of Israel that was consolidated behind the 1949 armistice lines controlled both the Jewish and much of the Arab portions of the original U.N. partition plan. Arab-Israeli hatreds and suspicions arising from the 1948 war were reinforced by the 1956 conflict, which ended in a draw. U.N. forces were organized as a buffer to police the Israel-Egyptian border area.

The third war occurred in 1967 and set the stage for the Mideast crises of the 1970s. President Nasser mobilized Egyptian forces in the Sinai in May, 1967, to threaten Israeli forces and succeeded in getting the U.N. forces to withdraw. In part Nasser's action was in response to false reports by the Soviets that Israel was planning an attack. He then blockaded the Red Sea to Israeli shipping, which cut off Israel's commerce to Asia. The Egyptian aggressive blockade and action to mobilize threatened Israel and caused it to call up reserves by stripping factories and farms. After about three weeks of tension, Israel attacked in the Six Days War and again gained and retained the Sinai plus the West Bank of the Jordan and the Golan Heights of Syria. (See Map 3.) After a cease fire was arranged, Egypt rebuilt its military strength with Soviet aid and pressured Israel with a build-up of military strength and surface to air missiles (SAMs) along the Suez Canal cease fire lines. No serious negotiations about withdrawal of Israel from Arab territories took place before the 1973 war.

Except for Arab nations, Israel was recognized by most nations of the world, and most countries considered its right to exist as a nation as beyond question. Israel insisted as a condition of negotiations over the Sinai, the West Bank, and the Golan Heights that the Arab countries also recognize Israel as a nation and agree to end their state of belligerency against Israel. Major demands of the Arab countries included restoration of the pre-1967 boundaries, Israel's acceptance of a new Palestinian state on the West Bank, and restoration of Palestinian land and property seized by Israel. The tensions and distrust from previous wars reinforced the Arab refusal to carry on face-to-face negotiations, and experts in 1973 agreed that no settlement of the Arab-Israeli dispute was in sight.

The 1973 War. October 6, 1973, was one of Israel's most solemn religious holidays — Yom Kippur, the Day of Atonement. During this holiday businesses are shut down and religious Jews do not even travel in automobiles. With a large element of strategic surprise, Egyptian forces attacked and initially advanced across the Suez Canal with a salient in the Sinai. Syrian forces attacked in the Golan Heights. The Israeli forces rallied, and as reserves mobilized and rushed to the front, Israeli forces regained lost territory. One element under General Ariel Sharon pushed across the Suez Canal into Egypt and caused havoc back of the Egyptian lines, cutting off the Egyptian salient in the Sinai. Meanwhile, Secretary of State

Kissinger applied pressure to establish a truce, and world opinion as expressed through United Nations Security Council resolutions called for a cease fire. (See Chapter 12.)

A cease fire was established by October 25th, less than three weeks after the fighting had started. Slow and painful negotiations followed, resulting in a temporary agreement with Egypt establishing truce lines along the Canal and later with Syria on the Golan Heights. As indicated below Israel and Egypt eventually were able to reach agreement on a treaty that involved giving Egypt back the land Israel had taken in the 1967 war. There was no peace along Israel's northern borders, however, as PLO units mounted attacks from Lebanon. These attacks and Israel's retaliation helped trigger a civil war in 1976 which involved extreme Palestinian nationalists, Lebanese forces, and Christian militants. Syrian Palestinian armed units and smaller units from other Arab states entered Lebanon to try to enforce a truce. By 1980 the "Arab Deterrent Force" in Lebanon was almost entirely Syrian, and its units from time to time were involved in the civil war. Israel supported Christian units in southern Lebanon to help provide a buffer against the Palestinian units, which attacked Israeli targets across the border at every opportunity. The U.N. also set up a force to patrol the Israel-Lebanon border to keep the war from spreading. In the spring of 1981 Israel saw Syria's installation in Lebanon of surface-to-air missiles (SAMs) as a threat to Israel's Christian allies, and Israel threatened to attack them. The United States sent Philip Habib, a veteran diplomat, to mediate, and he began the type of shuttle diplomacy between capitals that Secretary Kissinger had used to settle the 1973 war. The shuttle diplomacy, at least temporarily, was successful in deterring a major conflict.

Policymaking Elements of the Arab-Israel Dispute. Probably no one can understand the strength and direction of political currents of the Middle East maelstrom, but tracing the more obvious ones helps in understanding positions of major leaders and their difficulties in settling the issues.

In July, 1972, President Anwar Sadat of Egypt expelled Soviet military advisers and ended his close connections with Russia in a reaction to Russian KGB efforts to undermine his government.[23] This opened the way for Secretary Kissinger during the 1973 truce negotiations to reestablish friendly relations between Egypt and the United States.

In December, 1977, Sadat astounded the world by a trip to Jerusalem, breaking the Arab diplomatic boycott of Israel. He assumed the role of spokesman of the Arabs in negotiating the Middle East dispute. Other Arab states, including most of the moderates, boycotted the negotiations and isolated Sadat.

Superpower confrontation in the Middle East in 1981 involved strong U.S. backing for Israel and friendly relations with the moderate Arab states — Egypt, Jordan, and Saudi Arabia — while Russia backed the radicals, including Syria, Iraq, and Libya.

The Palestine Liberation Organization (PLO) is a major force to be reckoned with in any negotiations. It is an alliance of Arab nationalist Palestinian groups, which include radical groups that have maintained a campaign of terrorist attacks against Israeli citizens. In 1975, backed by the Arab oil producers, the PLO gained a major political victory when its leader, Yassir Arafat, spoke before the U.N. General Assembly, which endorsed its right to take part in Mideast peace talks. The PLO insists on a separate Palestinian state on the West Bank, with an implication that the boundaries would include all of Israel.

President Sadat's original peace initiative of 1977 was carried forward by President Carter in September, 1978, when he, President Sadat, and Prime Minister Begin of Israel met at Camp David to hammer out the outlines of a peace agreement. The formal treaty was signed on March 26, 1979. It provided for an interim withdrawal of Israeli forces from most of the Sinai over a period of nine months followed by the resumption of normal diplomatic relations between Israel and Egypt. The final withdrawal from the rest of the Sinai was set at three years from ratification. United Nations personnel were to be stationed in buffer zones between Israel and Egypt and not to be withdrawn without the affirmative vote of the five Permanent Members of the Security Council unless Egypt and Israel agreed otherwise, an obvious guarantee against the sort of precipitate withdrawal of U.N. forces that preceded the 1967 war. In an attached understanding, Israel and Egypt agreed to negotiate a settlement of the West Bank and Gaza strip issues with the aim of reaching agreement within a year on setting up self-government in the area and withdrawing Israeli forces to specified security locations over the following four years. Following the treaty the Israeli Government permitted further Jewish settlements in the West Bank area, which infuriated Arab groups.

Israeli officials, with their long experience with Arab attacks, have made concessions only with great reluctance and are determined not to give up important buffer zones until assured that Israel can have peaceful relations with its Arab neighbors. The hard-line elements in Israel were not prepared to give up the West Bank and the Golan Heights, which act as buffers to protect Israel, and they continued to encourage Jewish settlement in the West Bank.

On the Arab side, leaders who favor negotiations with Israel have been in a precarious position with hatred generated from wars with Israel and reinforced by propaganda of extremist groups. Some of the governments are subject to nationalist pressures from the military, the men with the guns.

The crux of the matter is that PLO leaders, who have strong emotional support of the people and leaders of many Arab states, do not trust Israeli leaders. Under the Camp David formula Israeli forces stationed in West Bank areas could intervene and arrest PLO and other Arab leaders if there were terrorist attacks. Such incidents would be likely because PLO aims extend into Israeli areas of Palestine beyond the borders of the West Bank. In 1981, therefore, negotiations were stalemated.

The Soviet Union has historically and ideologically looked to the Middle East as an area for expansion of its influence. In the eyes of the Russian Communists, many of the governments of the Middle East are feudalistic and capitalistic and ripe for the historical forces of Communism to take over. Reportedly, the KGB was influential in a plot to overthrow President Sadat, and it is possible that the hardliners of the Russian KGB dominate Russian policymaking for the Middle East.[24]

Meanwhile, Russians have had influential positions as advisers in Syria and Iraq, and the speeches of some national leaders reflect Marxist ideology, even though the governments are not Communist regimes. The Soviets resented the growing influence and friendship of the United States with Egypt and other Arab countries in the area, much of it at the expense of the Soviets who were forced to withdraw almost completely from Egypt and who had relatively little influence outside Iraq, Syria, and Libya.

On the United States side, it has a long tradition of support for Israel which is reinforced by the Jewish lobby of the United States. Many Jews in the United States strongly support Israel, and they make their views known by legitimate democratic means through many letters and approaches to their congressmen.[25]

Military leaders in the United States often see the conflict as one of power politics between the forces of Western democracy against the forces of Communism, which they feel dominate many governments in the area. These military elements back the sale of arms to Israel and to Arab states as a means of balancing Communist influence in the area.

Support for Israel has diminished in the United States as many U.S. officials have become concerned about maintaining a source of supply of oil from Arab countries which resumed friendly ties with the United States. These Arab countries could easily turn against the United States if it did not pressure Israel to settle its conflict in a manner satisfactory to Egypt and Syria. Figure 9-2 illustrates major pressures exerted in the area.

The situation became even more complicated in 1980 after the Soviet invasion of Afghanistan. All the Arab countries except the close Russian allies — Libya, Syria, and "Democratic Yemen" — condemned this invasion of a fellow Moslem country. Almost all Arab countries withdrew their Olympic teams from the 1980 Moscow Olympics. However, they could not bring themselves to welcome openly the U.S. military presence in the Persian Gulf because of deep opposition to the Camp David agreements and the related U.S. support for Israel and Egypt. Moreover, Iran had embraced the PLO and continued its campaign of hatred against the United States.

Figure 9-2 Ideologies and Strategies in Mideast Conflicts

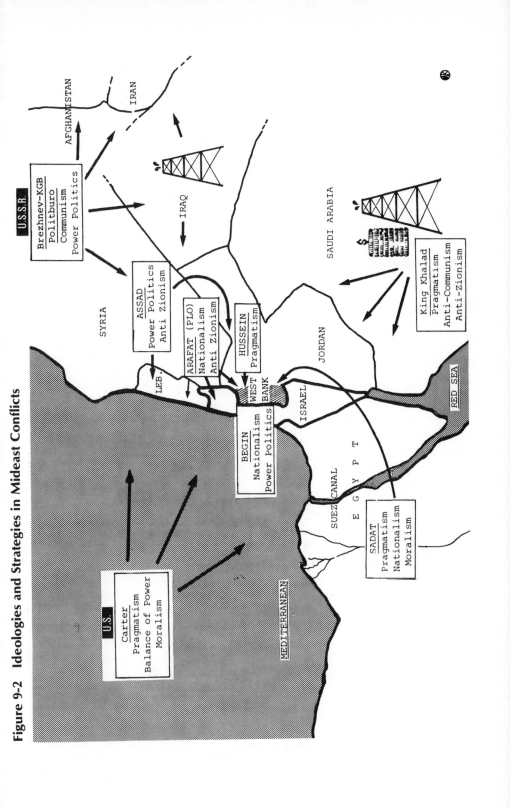

The U.S. could gain considerable influence at the expense of the Soviets and help Egypt regain its position *if* the U.S. could bring about a settlement of the Arab-Israel dispute, which centered on the West Bank and Jerusalem issues. This would tend to relieve political, religious, and economic pressures in the area which continually threatened to erupt. That was a big "if," however, and the realistic prospect at the beginning of the 1980s was for more turbulence and conflicts in the Middle East. At worst they would threaten to escalate into a world war, and at best continue the slow strangulation of oil supplies.[26]

Erosion of Superpower Politics

During the period since World War II diplomats, reporters, and academicians viewed international politics as centered on the diplomacy of the two superpowers. In crises involving allies of the superpowers fears would arise that a collision of policies could lead to war and world disaster. Asia and the Middle East were major arenas of action with occasional confrontations in Africa and in Cuba. In recent years there has been a tendency to view world politics as involving more centers of power. There are fewer bipolar confrontations and superpower domination of world politics has been eroded.

The United States. At the end of World War II the United States was thrust into world leadership, and its leaders gladly took up this role; some hoped to establish a system to prevent another world war, which they realized might be the last because of the terrible potential of nuclear weapons. United States policymakers took a leading part in creating the United Nations System, including the World Bank and the International Monetary Fund. The U.N. organizations are assuming more world responsibilities and in the process are reducing the comparative importance of the superpower system. (See Chapters 12 to 14.)

Similarly, the United States was the leader in reconstructing Europe and building the NATO alliance. This permitted the growth of the European Community, now another major center of power. Its economic strength rivals that of the United States. The European Community not only has developed a common point of view on economic matters, but its members are cooperating more closely on political issues. Germany, in particular, has emerged as a major economic power.

United States leaders mobilized the U.N. to repel aggression in Korea in 1950 and then formed a network of alliances to contain the spread of Communism in the Far East. These alliances were a disappointment. Several SEATO allies did not help in the Vietnam War, and the United States and its South Vietnamese ally suffered a humiliating defeat. As a result of the defeat Thai and Philippine leaders lost confidence in the ability of the United States to exert military power in Southeast Asia, and they brought about the termination of the SEATO military organization under the Southeast Asian Defense Treaty, hoping to mollify their Communist neighbors. President Carter, in establishing full diplomatic relations with the Peoples' Republic of China, terminated the bilateral defense treaty with Taiwan. In South Korea President Carters' policy of withdrawing U.S. ground troops made the South Korean leaders doubtful about the strength of the U.S. commitment. Thus, U.S. backing of Asian alliances by traditional power politics eroded.

United States diplomacy after the mid 1970s focused on the Mideast. Presidents Carter and Reagan continued Kissinger's policy of supporting Israel, mediating the Mideast conflict, and trying to make friends with the Arab states. They also cultivated Saudi Arabia, a new center of financial and diplomatic power, which now plays a major role in Middle East politics. The policy was characterized by mediation and cultivation — not domination.

Russia. Late in the 1960s and during the 1970s detente developed, and as the Soviets caught up in nuclear weapons, the Soviet Union and the United States concluded a series of arms limitation agreements. This occurred at the same time as Willy Brandt's *Ostpolitik,* which helped the Soviets achieve a major post World War II aim, that of confirming the boundaries established at the end of that war.

Meanwhile, the Soviet dispute with the Chinese had come to flower in the early 1960s and persisted. In 1969, there were hints by the Soviet Union it was considering a nuclear strike against China to wipe out its developing nuclear threat against the Soviet Union. The crisis subsided but during the 1970s there were no signs of a healing of the split.

The Soviet Union carried out a pragmatic policy of detente to ease tensions with the capitalist world and at the same time bitterly criticized the Peoples' Republic of China, a Communist government. Soviet coexistence with the West was a recognition of the overriding fact that a nuclear war could be disastrous not only to the Soviet Union but probably to most of the world. It also reflected the economic pressures in which the Soviet Union must limit military spending, import large quantities of grain, and obtain access to Western technology if it is to meet many of the material demands of its people.

In the mid 1970s the West European Communist parties instituted a major challenge to Soviet leadership of the European Communist movement by their Eurocommunism ideology. This call for a move in the direction of democratic rights blurred the differences between their ideology and that of social democracy. The major effect from the viewpoint of international politics was to weaken the ties of the Soviet alliance system by encouraging dissident groups in Romania, Czechoslovakia, and other satellites to oppose the rigid, Soviet-dominated system of Eastern Europe.

However, the Brezhnev doctrine continued to prevail with the Soviet and East European invasion of Czechoslovakia in 1968 still in the minds of East European policymakers. The Eastern European leaders apparently operated on the assumption they could not reform their system to a democratic form of socialism without inviting the intervention of Soviet troops. Many leaders did not want such reforms because they benefited from their entrenched and privileged position.

The Soviet leaders saw substantial gains in power in the past two decades as they closed the gap with the United States in the overall strength of their nuclear weapons. They attained a major goal in the CSCE agreement which recognized their territorial gains made in World War II.[27] They also backed a winner in Vietnam.

Nevertheless, their nuclear weapons are useful only if they are willing to cause or risk a world holocaust. In other important respects they lost power. Instead of an ally in China, they had a potentially dangerous enemy growing continually in nuclear strength along their 5,000 mile border. They lost powerful friends in the Middle East, including Egypt, and they were on the sidelines in its diplomacy. In Eastern Europe Polish trade unions challenged the rigid Communist system and, indirectly, the Soviet leadership itself. Many West European Communist leaders seemed closer to United States' assertions of human rights than to tough statements of Russian Communist media. Internal economic pressures caused the Soviets to import huge quantities of grain, and Soviet leaders realized its cumbersome economy was far behind that of the Western capitalist nations in terms of technology. If the Russian Communist system becomes more open, more of its people will also come to this conclusion.

Kremlinologists speculated the Brezhnev era was nearing its end in 1981 because of his poor health. No protege or successor was evident to these observers. Conceivably there could be a marked change of policy with a new leader, but a continuation of Soviet policy in the same directions seemed more likely. Brezhnev did not markedly change Russian foreign policy, and there was little prospect of change in the aging top echelons after he took over.[28]

Soviet policymakers are likely to continue to take advantage of weak spots in global politics and to give aid to potential friends, such as the leftist regimes of Africa and the Middle East. Assuming the new Russian leader comes from the present conservative leadership, further agreements could be reached in the SALT negotiations, and the forces of reason and profitable trade could reinstitute detente with the West despite conditions and sharp differences in ideologies of the two superpowers. However, if the Soviets persisted in the imperialistic policy demonstrated in early 1980 in Afghanistan, the prospect was for an intensified Cold War and a further loss of friends. Perhaps power moves against neighbors could gain temporary advantages for Russia, but over the long run such policies would more likely generate a loss of respect and influence (power) on the international scene.

China. Asia faces a dangerous future that depends to a

great extent upon its new leaders. There seems to be little argument that Communist China will advance to the rank of a superpower by virtue of improved nuclear weapons and its dominant power position in Asia. Depending on Chinese policies, this will have a profound effect on world politics.

Most observers expected the deep split between the Soviet Union and China to continue, and for the Soviet Union's strength and policies to help restrain China. It is normal, however, for experts and observers to be heavily influenced by past trends and history and not to foresee possibilities of personal and political changes. One strong leader emerging in the post-Mao period could act to bring the two major Communist powers back together. This would not be as surprising as the 1972 detente with and subsequent U.S. recognition of the Peoples' Republic of China.

The Peoples' Republic of China supported indirectly by propaganda and other means the insurgent movements in northeast Thailand, in Malaysia, and in Burma. It was elbowed out of North Vietnam by the Soviet Union after the fall of Saigon, and out of Cambodia by Vietnam. In Laos, the Russian advisers appeared to have more influence than the Chinese Communists, although Chinese Communist engineering batallions had built and maintained roads in Northwest Laos. These roads connecting with China posed a military threat to Thailand. The Communist power politics in Southeast Asia were obscure, but it was clear that there was rivalry for influence between the Chinese and Russian Communists. The Communist rivalries helped maintain a balance of power and dampen superpower influence in the area.

Japan, no longer a dominant power in Asia, stayed aloof from most of the superpower politics, although Russia and China whipsawed it in negotiating separate treaties to settle World War II issues. Japan stayed closely aligned with the United States, and what influence Japan exerted in Asia was largely based on its exploding economy. While the world is distracted with the power games of the superpowers, Japan may regain a dominant position in Asia with its economic strength.

Meanwhile, with an equilibrium in Asia and a nuclear

standoff in Europe, there was a major conventional crisis in the Middle East. Here countries practiced the traditional realpolitik based on competing nationalisms, conventional military forces, and petroleum power. The superpowers in the 1970s did not control events but reacted to crises, trying to keep them from spreading by supporting cease fires and truces. Until 1980 the major movers of policy were the Arab countries and Israel with Saudi Arabia playing an increasingly important role.

At the end of 1979 the Soviets surprised the world by a thinly veiled intervention and invasion of Afghanistan. This intensified the turmoil in the area and stimulated a build-up of U.S. military power in the Persian Gulf area to protect oil fields vital to the U.S. and world economy. Thus, the new decade opened with a renewal of the Cold War, now focused on the Middle East maelstrom.

We will now take a closer look at the new world centers of power and particularly the oil rich nations.

Summary

Superpower politics in Asia has been dominated by the changing three-way relationships among China, the United States, and the Soviet Union. In the 1950s during the aftermath of the Korean War, there was a cold war type of hostility between China and the U.S. which was replaced in the 1960s and 1970s by a similar split between China and Russia. The Sino-Soviet split grew out of Chinese leaders' alarm over Russia's attempt to dominate them and resentment over Russia's refusal to trust the Chinese with nuclear weapons. By 1969 there was a threat of a preventive nuclear war by Russia against China. This laid the basis for U.S. recognition of the Peoples' Republic, initiated by President Nixon and consummated in January, 1980, by President Carter. The U.S. broke off diplomatic relations with the Republic of China (Taiwan), but the U.S. continued military and political support to Taiwan is an unsettled issue with China.

President Johnson's decision to act as the world policeman in Southeast Asia and resist aggression organized from North Vietnam kept Southeast Asia and the United States in turmoil during the latter part of the

1960s. U.S. massive support to Vietnam was no match for the Communist-nationalist ideology and geographic advantage of Ho Chi Minh's forces. North Vietnam won the war in 1975. After the war the Communist nations of the area — Vietnam, China, Cambodia, and Laos — began warring among each other and the 1980s opened with the area in turmoil. The superpowers seemed to have lost control, and the outcome appeared to depend on actions of countries in the area.

By the late 1970s the major areas of world conflict shifted to the Middle East. Since World War II conflicting nationalisms have been at the root of the wars between Israel and its neighbors. President Sadat's dramatic initiative to make peace with Israel in 1978 removed the immediate threat of war at the end of the decade, but the unsettled demands of the PLO nationalists for a nation on the West Bank of Jordan kept the area in political turmoil. The Soviet invasion of Afghanistan added to the tensions and threats of major conflicts in the Middle East, which controls most of the world's oil.

Many conflicting ideas and ideologies in the Middle East and Asia undermined the control of the superpowers over these situations, and by the beginning of the 1980s the centers of action and influence there had shifted to other nations.

FOOTNOTES

1. *Khrushchev Remembers, op. cit.,* Vol. 1, pp. 271-272.

2. *Ibid.*

3. Morton H. Halperin, *China and the Bomb* (New York: Frederick A. Praeger, Publishers, 1965), pp. 79-80; *Peking Review,* August 15, 1963, p. 14. Edward E. Rice, *Mao's Way* (Berkeley: University of California Press, 1974); Chapter X has a good summary of nuclear developments of this period. Also see *Khrushchev, op. cit.,* Vol. II, p. 306.

4. Stuart R. Schram, *Political Thought of Mao* (New York: Praeger, 1969), p. 436.

5. William E. Griffith, *The Sino-Soviet Rift* (Cambridge: The MIT Press, 1964), Document 8, pp. 371-387 and *Peking Review* VI, 36, September 6, 1963, pp. 7-16.

6. *Peking Review* VI, 37, September 13, 1963, pp. 13, 21-22.

7. *Khrushchev Remembers, op. cit.,* pp. 290-291.

8. *New York Times,* September 20, 1958, p. 1.

9. *Peking Review,* February 3, 1959, p. 6.

10. *Peking Review,* February 10, 1959, p. 12.

11. Griffith, *op. cit.,* p. 351; and *Peking Review,* VI, 33, August 16, 1963, p. 12.

12. This possibility is suggested by Edward Rice who was U.S. Consul General in Hong Kong during this period; this was the major U.S. reporting post for Communist China. See Rice, *Mao's Way,* p. 474, *op. cit.*

13. *Ibid.,* p. 475.

14. Harold C. Hinton, *Three and a Half Powers: The New Balance in Asia* (Indiana University Press, 1975), p. 108.

15. *New York Times,* August 29, 1969, pp. 1 and 4.

16. *Peking Review,* XII, October 10, 1969, pp. 3-4.

17. George Ginsburg, *The Sino-Soviet Territorial Dispute 1949-1964* (New York: Praeger/Holt, 1978).

18. *Washington Post,* July 1, 1977, p. A-12.

19. See *The Pentagon Papers* (New York: New York Times, 1971), Key Documents #2-14.

20. Richard Nixon, *RN — The Memoirs of Richard Nixon* (New York: Grosset & Dunlap, 1978), pp. 392-395.

21. The New York Times, *The Pentagon Papers* (New York City: Bantam Books, Inc., 1971), pp. 127-130.

22. Robert A. Scalapino, "Asia at the End of the 1970s," *Foreign Affairs 1979,* pp. 693-737; *Washington Post,* June 26, 1980, p. 1; William S. Truley and Jeffrey Race, "The Third Indochina War," *Foreign Policy,* Spring, 1980, pp. 92-116; The International Institute for Strategic Studies, *Strategic Survey 1979,* pp. 56-72; "The Peoples' Republic of China, 1979," *Current History,* September, 1979; *Time,* July 21, 1980, pp. 32-33.

23. Anwar el-Sadat, *In Search of Identity* (New York: Harper & Row, 1977), pp. 215-231.

24. John Barron, KGB, *The Secret Work of Soviet Secret Agents* (New York: Bantam Books, 1974).

25. *Washington Post,* November 23, 1974, pp. 1, 10.

26. Stanley F. Reed III, "Dateline Syria, Fin De Regime," *Foreign Policy,* Summer, 1980, pp. 176-190; Malcolm Kerr, Nathan Leites, and Charles Wolf Jr., "Inter-Arab Conflict Contingencies and the Gap Between the Arab Rich and Poor," (Rand: Santa Monica, Calif., 1978); Denis Healy, "Oil, Money and Recession," *Foreign Affairs,* Winter 1979-1980, pp. 217-223; Claudia Wright, "Iraq — New Power in the Middle East," *Foreign Affairs,* Winter 1979-1980, pp. 257-277; William B. Quandt, "The Middle East Crisis," *Foreign Affairs — America and the World 1979,* pp. 540-562; Walter J. Levy, "Oil and the Decline of the West," *Foreign Affairs,* Summer, 1980, pp. 999-1015; Fouad Ajami, "The End of Pan Arabism, *Foreign Affairs,* Spring, 1980, pp. 355-373; International Institute for Strategic Studies, *Strategic Survey 1979* (London: 1980), pp. 24-28 and 73-83.

27. Leonid I. Brezhnev, *Leonid I. Brezhnev — Pages From His Life* (New York: Simon and Schuster, 1978).

28. For example, 89 percent of the 1971 Central Committee, the major

governing body, was reelected in 1976 and 100 percent in 1981. The average age of the Central Committee increased to 60 in 1977 compared to 52 in 1961. Jerry F. Hough, "The Brezhnev Era," *Problems of Communism,* March-April, 1976, pp. 1-17. See also William G. Hyland, "Brezhnev and Beyond," *Foreign Affairs,* Fall, 1979, pp. 51-66.

PART FOUR
The Multipolar System of States and Non-State Power Centers

In Part Four we look more closely at the economic dynamics of the multipolar system. I include developing nations in this system as well as industrial nations and organizations outside the superpower system, such as the European Community and multinational corporations. By the 1970s more and more national leaders were using economic leverage as a major element of power to achieve their goals. We will examine their international politics involving oil, raw materials, and economic development.

10

OPEC and the Developing World

After over 25 years of a nuclear standoff between Russia and the United States, many world leaders outside the superpower system take the deadlock for granted and assume they do not need to get deeply involved in superpower politics. Many of these leaders worry more about their own country's political and economic position in the international arena than they do about the problems that worry the superpowers. We can regard the non-superpowers as operating in a multipolar system with OPEC in a key position. Economics, particularly of oil and its financial power, dominated the system in the latter part of the 1970s and early 1980s like military strength dominated the superpower system.

Part of the multipolar system consists of the developing world; the other part consists of industrial centers of power including the European Community, other industrial states, and multinational corporations. Leaders in the system focus on issues such as trade and investment problems, military aid, raw material supplies, and similar issues that directly affect their country's international position. Many of the leaders of the developing world are highly critical of the nuclear arms race, and their representatives often join European powers in calling for nuclear arms limitation and disarmament.

Within the multipolar system the European Community, with Germany, France, and Britain as leading centers of industrial power and influence, has created close economic ties with the developing world. European integration issues and economic relations with the rest of the world draw more attention in Europe than the threat posed by the Communist forces of Eastern Europe.

After 1973, when oil prices skyrocketed, Saudi Arabia, and to a lesser extent, Iran, gained a great deal of wealth and economic power. Saudi Arabia dominated OPEC and used its economic power to influence Mideast political issues, much like the superpowers used military strength to back their policies.

Saudi Arabia and OPEC

It would have been difficult in the early 1970s to see OPEC and Saudi Arabia as major world power centers. Saudi Arabia was a backward desert kingdom of about 6 million people. It had no legislature or political parties. It was known to have the largest oil reserves on earth, but outside the pipes and ports to move oil to fleets of tankers, there was relatively little development. Its influence on Middle Eastern politics was not particularly strong. Saudi Arabia's relations with Egypt had been strained during the 1960s as they supported opposite sides in the Yemeni Civil War.

Saudi Arabian forces did not participate in the 1967 Israeli-Arab war, but after the war it provided subsidies in excess of $100 million annually to both Jordan and Egypt to help them recover from the war. However, after 1973 Saudi Arabia acquired such tremendous financial resources it was almost forced into the game of realpolitik, and it played the game with skill.

Table 10-1 Economic Profile of Superpowers and Major Power Centers — 1977

	Pop.	Gross National Product			Trade		Reserves	Petroleum		Military*		% School Age Pop. in School‡
	(Mil.)	(Bil. $)	% Growth	Per Cap.	Exp. (Bil. $)	Imp. (Bil. $)	(Bil. $)	Exp. (mbd)**	Gov. Oil Rev. (Bil. $)	Manpower (000)	% GNP	
Superpowers												
United States	218	2,100	4	9,650	144	183	20			2,022	5	85
Russia	261	1,250	3	4,800	52	50	15			3,658	12	59
China	1,000	444	12	440	10	11				4,360	10	56
Other Power Centers												
European Comm.	260	2,000	3	7,500	462	463	119					
(Germany)	61	640	3	10,440	142	122	54			509	3.4	67
(France)	53	470	3	8,820	79	82	14			365	3.3	69
(Britain)	56	310	3	5,540	72	79	17			323	4.7	88
(Italy)	57	235	2	4,150	56	56	15			365	2.4	63
Japan	115	970	6	8,430	98	80	34			241	.9	72
OPEC												
(Saudi Arabia)	6.3	65	3	10,320	38	24	19	8.1	34.5	44	15	29
(Iran)	35	88	.2	2,500	23	19	12	4.5	18.7	413	11	50
(Nigeria)	72	35	5.5	480	10.4	8.5	1.9	1.8	8.5	193	8	22
(Indonesia)	145	48	7	330	11.6	6.7	2.6	1.4	5.0	239	3.4	38
Egypt	40	11.7	8	290	1.7	6.7	.6			395		43
Israel†	3.5	13.3	5	3,800	2.4	6.0	1.2			166	30	62
India	656	101	4	150	6.4	7.4	6.8			1,096	3.2	42
Brazil	121	150	6	1,230	12.7	15	12			281	1.0	53
Taiwan	17	24	13	1,410	12.7	11	1.5			539	7.7	63
South Korea	39	46	12	1,200	12.7	15	2.8			619	5.6	63
North Korea	17									672	11.4	61

*1976 figures. Source: The International Institute for Strategic Studies, *The Military Balance 1979-1980* (London).
†Source: Ruth Leger Sivard, *World Military and Social Expenditures* (Leesburg, Va.: World Priorities, 1979).
‡Ages 5-19.
**A million barrels a day. Source: National Foreign Assessment Center, *Handbook of Economic Statistics* (Springfield, Va.: National Technical Information Center).

OPEC was also a relatively weak organization in the 1960s. It was founded in Baghdad, Iraq, in 1960 largely at the initiative of Dr. Alfonso of Venezuela. Its chief accomplishment of that decade was to maintain the income of oil producing countries in the face of declining world market prices. This was not particularly difficult, because by OPEC's insisting that oil payments be based on "posted prices" instead of world market prices, the oil companies were able to count such payments as "taxes," and the American oil companies received credits for such payments on their U.S. tax returns. Thus, the oil countries and oil companies maintained their revenues despite fluctuations in market prices, and the U.S. Treasury lost revenue.

From 1970 to 1973 the multinational oil companies were whipsawed in a series of negotiations between Libya on the Mediterranean and Iran and Saudi Arabia on the other side of the Middle East. Colonal el-Qaddafi took over Libya in a military coup in 1969, and his government exerted strong pressure on the oil companies for higher prices. With Libyan high quality oil that was easily accessible to Europe, he was able to obtain a premium price. Moreover, he exerted strong pressure on the oil companies by nationalizing British Petroleum in Libya and later the other foreign oil companies. OPEC nations carried on a series of parallel negotiations on Persian Gulf oil, and the posted price of oil there was raised from $1.80 to $3.01 per barrel in the fall of 1973.

Both economic and political factors played a part in the dramatic price explosion that followed. Up until 1973 the international oil cartel of private oil companies had managed to keep crude oil prices relatively low in comparison with the cost of other forms of energy. This was of great advantage to the governments of the industrial countries, which levied taxes many times the original cost of $1.20 to $1.80 a barrel. (A barrel equals 42 gallons, which gave a cost of only three cents a gallon at $1.20 a barrel.) The United States imposed a complicated system of controls designed to limit imports of cheap foreign oil and protect the price of domestic oil, but by 1973 U.S. reserves had been drawn down so it could not readily expand production to make up for a drastic cutback in foreign supplies.

Qaddafi of Libya, with his Marxist leanings, and his followers were determined to cut ties with what he saw was a colonial type of control over the Libyan economy. His government demanded that the United States leave the Wheelus air base in Libya, and it began nationalizing foreign oil firms, while pressing for higher prices for Libyan oil. The lesson was plain to OPEC. They, too, could pressure the oil cartel. Saudi Arabia and Iran then got OPEC to increase the price of Persian Gulf oil in October, 1973, to $5.11 a barrel and then to $11.65.

The private oil cartel was in a vulnerable position. It could not find alternative supplies of oil. Refusing to buy the Middle East oil at this high price could have caused economic disaster in Europe and hardship in the United States. Also, the small, independent oil companies would have been glad to move in and purchase the oil at the higher price and end the virtual monopoly of the big oil companies. Moreover, the big oil companies, to the extent possible, wanted to maintain good relations with OPEC nations and discourage the trend toward nationalization of their properties.

On the other hand, by cooperating with the OPEC governments, and particularly the moderates such as Saudi Arabia, the oil companies passed price rises along to consumers and earned undreamed-of profits. In 1974 it is estimated the oil companies made about $15 billion in profits, about double the amount in 1972.[1]

Saudi Arabia was the key to OPEC's success in maintaining high oil prices. OPEC could not have maintained the price structure unless it could have prevented its members from using their excess capacity to chisel on prices, which are many times the cost of production. Saudi Arabia was in a unique position to control output and prices. Having a small population yet providing almost 30 percent of the world's exports, Saudi Arabia had far more oil income than it could spend. It, therefore, could afford to cut back drastically on production as necessary to maintain high prices and incidentally conserve on its oil reserves.

Thus, it dominated OPEC. In 1975, when Libya and other oil producers wanted to raise prices further, Saudi Arabia refused for fear of the disastrous effect this would have on Europe and threatened to increase production if the other OPEC members did not agree. As a result the price increase was limited to about 10 percent.

Sheik Yamani, Saudi Arabia's Oil Minister, is quoted in the *New York Times Magazine* of September 14, 1975, as saying:

> We can produce as much as 11 million barrels a day ... This makes us a power to be reckoned with both by producing and consuming countries. To ruin the other countries of OPEC, all we have to do is produce to our full capacity; to ruin consumer countries we only have to reduce our production. In the first case the price would fall noticeably; in the second, the price would rise not by 35, but by 40, 50, or even 80 percent. We can dictate our conditions to all, even within the OPEC.

In 1975 Saudi Arabia's production fell to about half of its capacity, and high prices were maintained.

Saudi Arabia's control of a large part of the world's oil supply and the income from this oil provide the leverage for its realpolitik. Saudi Arabia's King Faisal and his successor of 1975, King Khaled, were ardently anti-Communist and anti-Zionist. Saudi Arabia did not have diplomatic relations with the Communist states. It would have cut back oil to exert pressure against Israel in the 1973 Mideast War even if the higher oil income were not the result. In the spring and summer of 1973 King Faisal had warned the United States there would be a reduction of oil shipments to the United States unless U.S. policy changed. President Nixon, in a press conference on September 5, stated in reply that the United States is not pro-Israel and not pro-Arab and "we are not any more pro-Arab because they have oil and Israel hasn't."[2]

King Faisal and his close advisers also warned the President of Aramco in May, 1973, that Communists and Zionists were on the verge of "having American interests thrown out of the area" and that Sadat might have to embark on war. The oil companies took the warning seriously and raised their production and stocks in anticipation of trouble.[3]

Despite Saudi Arabia's anti-Israeli position and the United States' strong support for Israel, the anti-Communism of Saudi Arabian leaders pressed them toward an alignment with the United States, even during the period they were pressuring the United States with an oil embargo during the 1973 war. In 1973 King Faisal took the lead in cutting off oil supplies to the United States and Holland, and he did not agree to lift the embargo until March 18, 1974, well after the truce was arranged with Sadat.

Secretary of State Kissinger, during his shuttle diplomacy in the fall of 1973 to establish a truce in the Mideast War, made a point to inform King Faisal of the progress of the negotiations, to enlist his support, and to try to get the embargo lifted. The key to his diplomacy was to convince both Arab and Israeli leaders he could be trusted and would not favor one side over the other. President Nixon made a special point to visit Saudi Arabia in June, 1974, shortly after the embargo was lifted. During the visit King Faisal warned President Nixon of Zionist and Communist conspiracies. At the departure ceremonies the King pledged his friendship saying "Therefore, we beseech Almighty God to lend His help to us and to you so that we both can go hand in hand, shoulder to shoulder in pursuance of the noble aims that we both share, namely those of peace, justice, and prosperity in the world."[4]

Saudi Arabia's close association with the United States was cemented by more than anti-communism and trust in U.S. leaders such as Henry Kissinger. Saudi Arabia's leaders wish to protect its tremendous wealth, and the United States as a superpower is an obvious source of support. The United States has sold it advanced military equipment and services. More than half of these military sales were military contracting services to oversee the construction of ports, communications, and even an entire city for 60,000 people. This construction and U.S. technology plus its reserves are a basis for Saudi Arabia's rapid economic development, and a source of future prosperity.

U.S. intentions toward the Saudis were put to a test in the spring of 1978 when President Carter presented to Congress a package arms deal involving the sale of advanced fighter aircraft to Israel and Saudi Arabia along with defensive aircraft to Egypt. After an agonizing debate in the Senate Foreign Relations Committee and intense pressure from Jewish and Arab groups, the Foreign Relations Committee in a tie vote passed the question to the full Senate. In May, the Senate voted by a strong majority 54 to 44 in favor of the sales.

The *Washington Post's* May 16, 1978, front page commentary is revealing:

> Three years ago this month, in a moment of diplomatic tension between the United States and Israel, 76 U.S. senators signed a letter to President Ford strongly backing Israel and bringing to an end, for all practical purposes, the Ford-Kissinger Middle East Policy 'reassessment.'
>
> In the Senate yesterday, at another crucial time for U.S. policy in the Middle East, Israel and its domestic supporters were able to muster only 44 votes to kill warplane sales to Saudi Arabia and Egypt. For the first time in many years, Israel lost a high-priority, high-visibility test on the floor of Congress.
>
> The two incidents were different in detail, but the political shift was plain to see. Last time, there was little or no countervailing argument in the Senate against a signature or a vote for Israel. This time, there is a powerful one. The word is a short one, and it was cited often yesterday: Oil.
>
> Senator Abraham A. Ribicoff (D-Conn.), a longtime supporter of Israel and a prominent American Jew, spoke of the changed circumstances as 'these new realities.' These are that Saudi Arabia has emerged as a world power with grave impact on the U.S. national interest and that Egypt under President Anwar Sadat, has profoundly changed the Middle Eastern scene. Ribicoff argued that a strong and secure Israel is dependent on a strong United States, and 'without a stable, predictable supply of oil from Saudi Arabia and the Persian Gulf, the West could face the worst depression of the industrial era.' (Senator Ribicoff voted for the sales.)[5]

One year earlier the London *Economist* (April 2, 1977), in elaborating on why Saudi Arabia is the "Arab superpower," noted its authority began with the embargo of U.S. supplies in 1973, and that later the Saudis bribed the South Yemeni government to stop its rebellion in Oman, supported Somalia against Ethiopia, and persuaded Syrian, Egyptian, and Lebanese leaders to sign the Riyadh peace plan ending the 1976 civil war in Lebanon. This influence was bought with billions of dollars of oil revenues.

The leverage of Saudi Arabia increased toward the end of the 1970s as its reserves mounted, and as the United States struggled with inflation and financial strains on the dollar. At the end of 1978 the United States was forced to mobilize $32 billion in loans from Europe, Japan, and the International Bank to back the dollar, which was falling in their money markets. Saudi Arabia and other OPEC nations had already invested $130 billion in dollar-denominated investments, which had strengthened the dollar. This put Saudi Arabia and the OPEC nations in a position where they could pull the rug on the dollar and the international financial system and cause a monetary panic. They did not because they, too, would lose the value of their dollar investments.

Saudi Arabia's huge investments had paid off politically in the package arms deal noted above by which the United States continued to supply the Saudis with advanced military and construction technology. The investment also paid off in behind-the-scenes pressure on the Israeli-Egyptian peace treaty negotiations. Press reports indicated the Saudi leaders were pressing Egypt to take a firmer stand against Israel on linking a settlement of the issue of Palestinian rights on the West Bank. The United States drift toward the Egyptian position in the latter part of these peace treaty negotiations may well have reflected U.S. concern about the Saudi's stand on this matter. At the same time the Saudi's approval of a 17.5 percent OPEC oil price increase for 1979 seriously set back anti-inflation efforts in the United States and amounted to another turn of the screw of economic-political pressure. The United States could not raise too much of a fuss, because other OPEC nations were pressing for higher price rises to protect their dollar investments.[6]

The Shah's overthrow in Iran and the subsequent taking of U.S. hostages in Teheran resulted in the U.S. cutting off of oil imports from Iran. A precarious petroleum supply situation developed in the United States. OPEC took advantage of the tight petroleum supplies in 1979 to institute massive increases in oil prices, even greater in dollar terms than the 1973 increases. Saudi Arabia again took a moderate position keeping its prices below those of Libya and other producers. The Saudis also agreed to increase their petroleum production which helped ease the gasoline shortage in the United States. This was an important step, since the PLO and some of the radical Arab States were demanding that the Arab countries use their oil power to the fullest to bring an end to the Egyptian-Israeli peace treaty. In this way the moderate Saudi diplomacy allowed the Saudis to have undreamed-of-profits and still maintain close relations with the United States.[7]

Saudi Arabia's leaders were constrained by ties to other Arab countries to denounce the treaty and related Camp David Agreements, but close relations with the U.S. continued. In October, 1981, these relations were tested again when Congress voted on President Reagan's proposals to sell them Aircraft Warning and Control (AWACs) radar planes to help protect their oil fields. Despite strong opposition by the pro-Israel lobby, the sale passed by 52 to 48 in the Senate after strong personal lobbying by President Reagan.

Saudi Arabia, with the gifts of geography and the strength of its economic position, has the international power to help maintain stability in the Mideast. Its political structure is not modern, however, and its absolute monarchy is not restrained by a legislature. With its strong anti-Communist posture and conservatism, its views are far from the radical, pro-Soviet members of OPEC and from most of the Arab League. Barring a radical revolution or a new outbreak of war in the Middle East, Saudi Arabia should continue to dominate OPEC and help maintain stability among the many newly rich oil countries of the Persian Gulf.

Iran

Iran was also an unlikely candidate for great power status in the 1960s. Iran developed one of the earliest civilizations, but its history includes accounts of invasions and domination by other powers. After World War II Russian forces which had occupied Iran's northern provinces during World War II to ensure an Iranian supply route refused to withdraw, apparently hoping to support a revolt in that area. The U.N. Security Council, however, at the U.S. initiative pressured Russia to withdraw from Iran's northern provinces of Azerbaijan and Kurdistan, and Russia complied.

In 1951, the Anglo-Iranian oil company, which controlled Iran's oil production, was nationalized at the instigation of Muhammed Musaddiq. At that time he was a member of the Iranian parliament, and his action proved so popular that he became premier. The Shah tried to oust him by decree, but failed and then fled as mobs smashed his statues in Teheran. Meanwhile the oil cartel, which at that time controlled the international market, maintained an embargo on purchases of Iran's petroleum, and Iran's oil exports dropped from $400 million to less than $2 million. The military supporters of the Shah rallied and in bloody street fighting moved in and restored the Shah to the throne in 1953. The American CIA assisted the Shah clandestinely.[8] The Iranian government kept ownership of the refineries, but the oil companies continued to have effective control of the refinery operations, and they received 50 percent of the profits.

The United States and Iran maintained close relations after the political crisis of the early 1950s. Under an agreement of 1959 the United States was committed to assist Iran in accordance with U.S. constitutional processes in the event of aggression by a Communist state. The United States provided technical assistance and military assistance during the 1960s. Military sales rose rapidly after the oil price rises of 1973, so that Iranian purchases matched those of Saudi Arabia. By 1975 Iran had $10 billion of military items on order.

Iran's oil reserves and oil production were second to Saudi Arabia's in the Persian Gulf Area. Just as in the case of Saudi Arabia, Iran's friendship with the United States did not prevent it from pressing for an oil price rise. In 1973 Iran took the lead in OPEC in the second dramatic price rise of oil from $5.11 to $11.65 per barrel.[9] Iran, however, maintained that oil should not be used as a political weapon, and it supplied Israel with oil up until 1979 despite Iran's close association with the Arab nations.

The Shah seemed well on the way to leading Iran to a prominent position among the great powers of the world. At the beginning of 1979, however, his government was overthrown by massive demonstrations led by the Muslim religious leader, Ayatollah Khomeini. The religious demonstrators objected to the Shah's authoritarian government, the repression of the secret police, his extravagant spending, particularly on military goods, and his lack of regard for the religious customs and traditions of his people. The civilian government that assumed control ended the Shah's modernization program, cut back on oil exports, and began a socialist policy of taking over many of the large foreign and domestic enterprises.

In November, 1979, a group of students and radicals stormed the American Embassy in Teheran and took over 50 hostages, mostly diplomatic personnel, demanding that the United States return the Shah to Iran for trial for his crimes. The Shah, who had been denied permanent residence in the United States, at that time was temporarily in a New York hospital being treated for a serious case of cancer. President Carter refused the captors' demands on the basis that the Iranian government, under international law, was committed to protect diplomats and that hostages should not be used for blackmail.

Over the next few months millions of Iranians demonstrated in favor of the captors and against the United States. Khomeini indicated support for the captors because of his hatred of the United States for its intervention in 1953 and support for the Shah. The hostage issue was used by the religious leaders or mullahs to strengthen the grip of their Islamic Republican Party on the government. By the summer of 1980 the mullahs and their party controlled the commanding heights of the political system, including the Revolutionary Council, the revolutionary courts, the Revolutionary Guards (an elite force to maintain order), the national radio-TV network, and a majority of seats in the parliament, which was elected in the spring of 1980. Bani-Sadr, the elected president, indicated a desire to return the hostages, but he could make no headway against the entrenched political power of the mullahs.[10]

The new government, in its revolutionary and religious fervor, alienated many of the minorities who made up over one-third of Iran's population. The most serious revolt was by the Kurds, who were supplied from Iraq. The Iranian leaders blustered and threatened their neighbors as well as their minorities. Khomeini's creed included a call on Muslims of the world to "wake up and liberate Islam and Islamic countries from the yoke of imperialists and their supporters."[11] His speeches made it plain he was referring to Iraq and conservative Arab regimes and kings friendly to the United States, such as Saudi Arabia,

Egypt, and Oman, and also Lebanon.[12] The situation became more tense and threatening after the Russian invasion of neighboring Afghanistan in December, 1979. Khomeini and his supporters gave a nod to the Russian threat on their borders but still castigated the U.S. as the main enemy.

In September, 1980, Iran's confrontation with Iraq erupted into a full scale war. President Saddam Hussein of Syria, which has only one-third the population of Iran, apparently took Khomeini's threats against his regime seriously and decided to move against Iran while it was weakened by internal strife and lack of military supplies for its military machine, which was based on U.S. equipment. Iraqi forces invaded the east bank of the Shatt-al-Arab waterway which borders the two countries. It is Iraq's lifeline to the Persian Gulf and its control has long been disputed between the two countries. Iraq also invaded the adjoining province of Khuzestan (Arabistan), which contains almost all of Iran's oil production and blocked off the strategic highway between Baghdad and Teheran. Iraq's attack quickly put Iranian oil fields and refineries out of production, and Iran responded in kind with bombing raids. As 1980 ended, Iraq dominated the vital waterway of Shatt-al-Arab, although determined resistance in Iran's refinery city of Abadan prevented complete control. Both countries were being weakened economically by the war which shut off their oil production and revenues.

The conservative countries led by Saudi Arabia sympathized with Iraq because of the threats against their regimes by Khomeini, but only Jordan openly gave assistance to Iraq. The radical Arab nations led by Syria and Libya backed Iran. The motives were not clear in the maelstrom of politics and religion, but they included Syria's historic distrust of Iraq and unwillingness to see it assume a leading role in the Mideast by the defeat of Iran. The war threatened to spread, and the other Islam nations and the U.N. attempted to mediate and confine it.

The United States was faced with difficult choices — it did not want to see Iran weakened and made vulnerable to the local Communist movement, which might be backed by Soviet intervention. However, the U.S. was still the "Great Satan" of Khomeini's regime and found its hands tied by the hostage issue. Options for U.S. policy in 1980 could be grouped under concepts we have been using as follows:

1. *Internationalist.* The United States took the internationalist route during the first months of the crisis, taking the issue to the U.N. Security Council, the General Assembly, and the International Court of Justice. On November 9, November 26, December 4, and December 31, 1979, the Security Council demanded the release of the hostages. (See box.) On December 15, 1979, the International Court of Justice ordered the immediate release of the hostages by a unanimous decision. (See box.) On December 17, 1979, the U.N. General Assembly adopted without a vote a Convention Against Hostage-Taking, which prohibits hostage-taking under any circumstances and calls on states to punish or extradite offenders.[13] The U.N. Secretary General went to Iran to try to negotiate their release, and later sent a special mission with the same objective. None of these moves succeeded in getting Khomeini to order the captors to release the hostages, but the U.N. actions did give the United States legal backing for its action to freeze about $8 billion in Iranian government funds and to mount a trade embargo against Iran. The measures also helped the U.S. to mobilize economic sanctions by the European Community and other nations against Iran.

2. *Power Politics.* In November, 1979, and subsequently the United States reinforced its military presence in the Persian Gulf area with two aircraft carriers and support ships, and later began adding transport ships in the Indian Ocean with equipment designated to supply a combat unit that could be flown to the area. The United States did not threaten to attack Iran, but it did signal an intent not to let Iran cut off oil supplies through the strategic Straits of Hormuz, through which most of the world's oil trade flows. These forces were also a signal to the Soviet Union, which had invaded Afghanistan at the end of December, 1979.

In April, 1980, President Carter amazed the world by mounting a raid to free the hostages. The attempt aborted when three of the nine helicopters malfunctioned. Except for the rescue attempt the power politics used by Carter were consistent with the internationalist policy and

Excerpts From Order of International Court of Justice on U.S. Demand for Release of American Hostages in Teheran
(December 15, 1979)

There is no more fundamental prerequisite for the conduct of relations between states that the inviolativility of diplomatic envoys and embassies, so that throughout history nations of all creeds and cultures have observed reciprocal obligations for that purpose.

Continuance of the situation, the subject of the present request, exposes the human beings concerned to privation, hardship, anguish, and even danger to life and health and thus to a serious possibility of irreparable harm. . . .

The court, unanimously, indicates, pending its final decision in the proceedings instituted on November 29, 1979, by the United States of America against the Islamic Republic of Iran, the following provisional measures:

A. (1) The Government of the Islamic Republic of Iran should immediately insure that the premises of the United States Embassy, chancery, and consulates be restored to the possession of the United States authorities under their exclusive control . . .

(2) The government of the Islamic Republic of Iran should insure the immediate release, without any exception, of all persons of United States nationality who are or have been held in the Embassy of the United States of America or in the Ministry of Foreign Affairs in Teheran, or have been held as hostages elsewhere, and afford full protection to such persons, in accordance with the treaties in force between the two states, and with general international law.

(3) The Government of the United States of America and the Government of the Islamic Republic of Iran should not take any action and should insure that no action is taken which may aggravate the tension between the two countries or render the existing dispute more difficult of solution.

B. Decides that, until the court delivers its final judgment in the present case, it will keep the matters covered by this order continuously under review.

could easily have been defended under international law. Critics of the Carter Administration, however, called for stronger power politics such as bombing Iranian power plants and other targets.

3. *Moralistic Approach.* Two days after the hostages were taken, former Attorney General Ramsey Clark and Mr. William Miller, a U.S. Senate committee staff officer, left for Teheran carrying a message from the President to negotiate the release of the hostages. Khomeini rejected talks with them and they returned empty handed. In May,

1980, Ramsey Clark on his own initiative accompanied other Americans to a conference in Iran on "American Intervention in Iran" which was organized by President Bani-Sadr. During the conference most of the delegates, although critical of the U.S., opposed holding of hostages. Ramsey Clark, on his return to the United States, announced that he would set up a commission to determine the extent of U.S. intervention in Iran. Clark acknowledged the disorder in Iran and lack of a central authority that could speak on the hostage issue, and he asserted the hostages' fate depended on Iranian public opinion. Clark believed that a formal hearing to determine American guilt in the crimes of the Shah could swing the balance in the new Iranian parliament and in Iranian public opinion for releasing the hostages.[14] The United States should do this, he said, because it is "right" and we should "not always think in terms of bargaining."

President Carter, thus, was faced with a "trilemma" on which three policies to choose. The internationalist approach had not worked against a band of fanatics who took their cues from old Khomeini, the supreme ruler, who was filled with hate toward the American government and its President. Moreover, Khomeini saw most governments supporting the United States on the hostage issue as being under the influence of imperialism, and he had no respect for U.N. resolutions. The power politics policies of trade and economic sanctions against Iran also had not worked. A basic element of Khomeini's creed was that Iran should develop industries that are not dependent on imports from the corrupt modern world, and that Muslims should live a simple, austere life.[15] Moreover, an element of the Shiite Islam faith is a desire to emulate the martyrdom of the founders of their religion. On the United States side it did not want to undermine Iran's economic and political life to the extent chaos would develop and present an opportunity for the Iranian Communist party, which was one of the few remaining coherent political groups in 1980.

The moralist approach might work but this was doubtful and it could invite humiliation of the United States by additional demands from Khomeini and other centers of political power. Khomeini, early in the crisis, taunted Carter for not having the "guts" to carry out

**Excerpts From Security Council Resolution
of December 31, 1977
(approved 11 to 0)***

The Security Council . . .

Gravely concerned over the increasing tension between the
Islamic Republic of Iran and the United States of America caused
by the seizure and prolonged detention of persons of United States
nationality who are being held as hostages in Iran in violation of
international law, and which could have grave consequences for
international peace and security. . . .

Conscious of the responsibility of States to refrain in their
international relations from the threat or use of force against the
territorial integrity or political independence of any State, or in
any other manner inconsistent with the purposes of the United
Nations. . . .

1. *Reaffirms* its resolution 457* (1979) in all its aspects.

2. *Deplores* the continued retention of the hostages contrary to
Security Council Resolution 457 (1959) and the Order of the
International Court of Justice of December 15, 1979 (S/13697);

3. *Urgently calls,* once again, on the Government of Iran to
release immediately all persons of United States nationality being
held as hostages in Iran, to provide them protection and to allow
them to leave the country;

. . .

5. *Requests* the Secretary-General to report to the Council on his
good offices efforts before the Council meets again;

6. *Decides* to meet on January 7, 1980; in order to review the
situation and in the event of non-compliance with the resolution,
to adopt effective measures under Articles 39 and 41 of the Charter
of the United Nations.

* Bangladesh, Czechoslovakia, Kuwait, and the U.S.S.R.
abstained on this resolution because of paragraph 6 which called
for effective measures such as trade restrictions against Iran.
These countries had approved similar resolutions including
resolution 457 which did not call for such measures. Russia on
January 13, 1980, vetoed the resolution calling for sanctions.

military reprisals against Iran.

In the spring of 1980 Carter resorted to a traditional
State Department option, that of stalling or "letting it
fester." Iran appeared to be in desperate straits. It was
faced with insurrections of Kurds and other minorities,
huge unemployment, inflation, and a sharp drop in
exports and imports. Oil production was down from
around five million barrels a day to well under one million.
Iran's military equipment was deteriorating rapidly
without American spare parts. Russia's invasion of

neighboring Afghanistan also threatened Iran. Iran's economic and military situation could have been alleviated by the simple release of 53 American hostages. The Iranian President seemed to recognize this, although he was stymied by the mullahs.

The Shah's death and the Iraqi invasion of Iran later in 1980 helped start negotiations for release of the American hostages. Iran needed military spare parts and the $8 billion of assets frozen by the United States. The Iranian prime minister faced a cool reception when he brought charges in the U.N. against Iraq for invading Iran, because Iran had ignored repeated demands by the U.N. to release the diplomatic hostages. Iran's delays in releasing the hostages until after the 1980 elections helped defeat President Carter, but this did not help Iran's position. As 1981 began, Iran faced a new U.S. President pledged to take a hard line against countries such as Iran humiliating the United States.

It was clear that Iran, in its dispute with the United States, had drastically undermined its international and domestic position and forced it to discard the Shah's aim of making it a major world power. The attempts of its leader Khomeini to challenge the international system and gain power (influence) through petroleum and hostage politics and appeals to foreign Muslim groups appeared to have foundered in 1981.

The Third World

Prior to 1973 the OPEC countries had not acquired their vast oil wealth and were considered a part of the developing world. They were active members of the developing world caucus in the U.N. System. During the oil crisis of 1973 the OPEC countries assumed a leadership role that has not been matched since that date. With the strength of their oil weapon they gave the Third World's drive to establish a "new international economic order" a momentum that has brought about changes in the international system, although the changes are far less drastic than those originally proposed.

The "Group of 77," which in 1980 included over 120 members, was the major group which coordinated positions of the Third World for U.N. meetings. It was formed originally for the first U.N. Conference on Trade and Development (UNCTAD), which met in India in 1964 and thereafter every four years. The Group of 77 met periodically to prepare positions for the UNCTAD Conferences and for other major meetings of the U.N. on development issues. A subset of about 92 nations calling themselves the "non-aligned" also coordinated positions for these meetings. This latter group was founded by India and Yugoslavia, which called conferences to demand an end to the Cold War as well as radical solutions to the world's economic and political problems.

Very little is written on what goes on behind the closed doors of the meetings of the Group of 77. It is essentially a caucus without a permanent secretariat. The Group maintains a remarkable unity despite the fact that their ideologies range from the Communism of Vietnam on the left to the conservatism of Saudi Arabia on the right. Before the 1973 crisis this unity was their major leverage since they could use their voting power to force through resolutions in the General Assembly and other parts of the U.N. System.

In 1973 and 1974 they were enthusiastically united on their demands for a "new international economic order," including the slogan of "permanent sovereignty over natural resources," and demands for international commodity agreements. In their speeches they elaborated their ideas as follows: "The old order permitted the wealthy industrial countries to obtain huge profits through control over the oil and natural resources of developing countries. As a result prices of raw materials were depressed, and the prices of manufactured goods were too high. This exploitation of the developing world prevented it from developing its full potential, and the gap between it and the wealthy industrial countries continued to widen."

The Group of 77 backed by the OPEC countries maintained the right of governments to take over control of foreign investments as a form of "sovereignty" over their natural resources. Representatives of developed countries in replying to this position often acknowledged the right of developing countries to expropriate foreign investments, but insisted that international law called for prompt, adequate, and effective compensation. They also warned that such expropriation would scare away foreign investors who had the ability to create the business organizations which could profitably mine and sell such resources.

At the beginning of 1974 President Houari Boumedienne of Algeria, acting as a spokesman of OPEC and of the non-aligned countries, called the Sixth Special Session of the General Assembly to approve a program of action for the new international economic order. Another special session was subsequently approved for 1975.

The tactic of Algeria and the oil producers during these special sessions was to convince the developing countries that their problems could be solved if they followed the example of OPEC by organizing to raise prices of commodities. Such arguments were well received by those with a social democratic or communist philosophy, who believe the capitalist system naturally generates a drive to obtain cheap raw materials in poor countries. The developed countries countered the above arguments by arguing that cartels such as OPEC could only hinder and restrict world trade and hurt the developing countries, which also are major buyers of raw materials, including oil.

The developing countries, which normally coordinated their positions with the OPEC nations, had a strong incentive to follow the lead of the newly rich oil countries at these special sessions. The industrial countries were also coerced by the power of the oil producers. Moreover, in 1974, Secretary Kissinger needed Arab support for his Middle East negotiations and was consulting on Middle East issues with President Boumedienne during the 1974 Special Session of the General Assembly. After this meeting with Boumedienne, Kissinger gave strong support to the major resolutions of the Special Session of the General Assembly.

A major compromise on the new economic order was a 1974 General Assembly resolution calling on the Secretary General of UNCTAD at the 1976 UNCTAD Conference to make recommendations on international arrangements for setting prices of commodities. The developing countries regarded UNCTAD, which is under the U.N. General Assembly, as a sympathetic organization under their voting control, and went along with this compromise. There were other components of the compromise, including trade and development policies, which are discussed in Chapter 14.

Negotiations proceeded under U.N. auspices after that date to establish a fund to stabilize world commodity prices. The developed countries took a sympathetic view on the record, but their delegates knew the political and economic difficulties of establishing such a fund. In the past, individual commodity agreements had taken years to negotiate because of the many consumer and producer interests that needed to be reconciled. With 150 countries involved, the difficulties of establishing a worldwide system of commodity arrangements appeared almost insurmountable.

After the 1976 UNCTAD Conference, it was not until January, 1978, that the first new commodity agreement, which was on sugar, was approved. Fifty-three exporting countries and 34 consumer countries were represented in the agreement with 1,000 votes for each group. (The OPEC agreement has no consumers represented.) In the same month UNCTAD sponsored meetings to negotiate agreements on tea and jute. In 1979, an UNCTAD committee reached agreement in principle to establish a Common Fund to stabilize prices of important world commodities. At the 1980 UNCTAD Conference in Manila which ended June 3, voluntary contributions to the Fund of $87 million were pledged. On June 27, 1980, representatives of 101 countries at another UNCTAD Conference reached agreement on the charter for the Fund. Developing countries were disappointed at the small resources of the Fund ($750 million) compared to its ambitious goals. However, the financially powerful International Monetary Fund pledged that the IMF would "cooperate in every possible way with the new institution." Capital for the "first window" of $470 million would be provided as governments joined. By June 27, $200 million had been pledged to the second window, which is designed to help in commodity research and development.[16]

Some of the sense of urgency behind the new international economic order was lost after the high point of 1974-1975. It was becoming obvious that the leaders of the most powerful oil producer countries were not willing to disrupt the international order in order to press forward with the ideas of drastically changing the system. Saudi Arabia, the key power, had too much at stake. It depended on purchases of advanced weaponry from the United States and other industrial nations for defense. It and other OPEC countries had tens of billions of dollars invested in the financial centers of the industrial world which would be lost if the structure collapsed. They counted on the income from these investments to guarantee their prosperity as long as the financial system existed. They were importing and using the latest in civilian technology. Their average per capita income was overtaking that of the West.

As early as 1976 Cuba and Jamaican leaders of the Group of 77 were pointing out the paradox of the poorest of the earth being championed by those oil countries living in opulence. Nevertheless, the OPEC countries continued to assist the developing countries in negotiations on raw material agreements under U.N. auspices and in the rhetoric of resolutions on the "new international economic order." Also, major oil countries and the Third World obtained more voting power in the international financial institutions and made their increased economic power felt in changes, or reforms, in the international economic order. (See Chapter 14.) The OPEC countries by and large used their wealth to encourage reforms and to permit the international economic system to cope with the strains in a way observers a few years earlier would not have thought possible.

There were a number of other power centers in crisis areas of the developing world which were using their growing economic power successfully to support their position in the international arena. (See Table 8-3.) Their extensive trade and investment relations with the rest of the system buttressed their position even though they were at odds with certain countries on international issues. Taiwan and South Korea were two countries of this type which lived under the threatening shadow of their neighbors but which appeared to be in no near term danger, largely because of a firm economic foundation. Indonesia and India were other nations in unstable areas of Asia that seem destined for a leading role. Other potential leaders in Africa and South America are only mentioned in this brief survey because during the 1970s they were not directly involved in major world crises.

Taiwan and South Korea. Taiwan and South Korea have two of the most remarkable records of economic expansion since World War II. Investors from the developed world and from the Chinese communities of the Far East have financed enterprises that have given Taiwan a GNP growth of about 10 percent a year, one of the fastest growing economies in the world. With a population of only about 17 million, Taiwan has matched the trade volume of mainland China with a much greater population of about one billion. Japan, Taiwan's former colonial master, broke formal diplomatic relations with it in 1973, but this did not seriously set back trade. In Chapter 9 we noted how the United States followed suit at the end of 1978. The United States pledged to maintain commercial and other unofficial relations with the aim of continuing to encourage the economic well-being of Taiwan.[17]

Taiwan's skilled and energetic working force and industrial base promised to support its large volume of trade with other Far Eastern countries and the United States. This same industrial base supported its 500,000 armed forces and permitted it to continue to buy modern weapons. As of the beginning of 1981 there was no indication that the Peoples' Republic of China intended to invade Taiwan, and military observers suggested if it did, there would be a hell of a fight. Not only do 100 miles of ocean separate Taiwan from the mainland, but there were implications, when the United States made the December 15 announcement, that it would support Taiwan despite the U.S. recognition of the Peoples' Republic of China. Thus, although in 1980 only about 23 nations recognized Taiwan as the Government of the Republic of China, Taiwan's basic economic strength gave its government a strong position.

It is possible that Taiwan might develop a relationship with the mainland something like that of Hong Kong. Hong Kong was ceded to Britain in perpetuity, and China has made no threats against it, although Britain governs Hong Kong like a Nineteenth Century colony on an island and on a peninsula of China. China sends $2 billion of

U.S. Policy Toward South Korea

In a debate on U.S. policy toward Korea on June 25, 1980, on the MacNeil/Lehrer TV Report Ernest Lefever of the Ethics and Public Policy Center of Washington, D.C., proposed supporting the present regime and quietly encouraging it to broaden the base of its support. Donald Ranard of the Center for International Policy proposed to forcefully and openly make the government move in the direction of democracy. Senator John Glenn, of the Senate Foreign Relations Committee, concluded the discussion as follows:

Let's get away from this idea that we can dictate what happens all over the world, and that people automatically have to drop in line like little ducks behind a mother and follow the United States. Those days are gone. Post World War II days, we set out not to create a colonial empire. We set out to help other nations. We helped Korea, we helped Japan, West Germany, Taiwan, all these places to recover and get going. It's one of the great success stories of history, and we forget that. Now, we've been so successful, that these places are largely economically independent of us, and they no longer have to follow us like little ducks, and every time we ring a bell, they do something out there. That day is past. It's one of the difficulties of foreign policy these days. We have the greatest flow of wealth in the OPEC nations. Europe has recovered. The Far East has recovered. We now have half a dozen major economic centers around the world, of which Korea happens to be one. And I think, to think that we can just dictate things is not right. We have to begin working with them rather than saying that they should automatically follow our lead. And I think that's the case in Korea. We can't dictate what happens in these places. We have to be more of a cooperative leader instead of a coercive leader.

exports to Hong Kong every year, and this accounts for over one-fourth of China's export earnings. China would be reluctant to end such a profitable relationship. Perhaps over the years Taiwan can reestablish a profitable economic relationship with mainland China.

South Korea's position is similar to that of Taiwan — it has had rapid economic expansion coupled with a strong military position supported by United States equipment and aid. However, South Korea has kept diplomatic relations with most of the countries of the world, and in 1980 the alliance with the United States was firm. The Carter Administration in 1977 had announced that the large U.S. military contingent in Korea would be gradually reduced. This caused an outcry in South Korea, but the fact that its population is twice as large as that of North Korea and that its economy and military forces are strong gave it strong insurance against an attack. Nevertheless, President Reagan, as one of his first acts, welcomed President Chun Doo Hwan to Washington D.C. and assured him the U.S. had no plans to withdraw troops.

Although North Korea continued to threaten to force unification with the South, there was no indication that Russia or China would assist in such an effort, and the basic situation on the Korean peninsula appeared stable.

Indonesia. Indonesia with a huge population of 136 million and a rapidly rising petroleum production in 1980 appeared destined to become a major power in Southeast Asia. For two decades after World War II it was held back by internal economic and political difficulties including a threat of Communist takeover, but after 1965 a conservative coalition led by the military strengthened the country and attracted assistance from the Western world and international financial institutions. As its economic base strengthened, Indonesia began to make its diplomatic voice count for more in Southeast Asia. It also embarked on an active diplomatic campaign to renew cooperation in U.N. institutions and to strengthen the Association of Southeast Asian nations (ASEAN).[18]

India and Other Nations. India's huge population has helped strengthen its voice in Asia despite its relatively slow-speed economy. Indian officials have hosted conferences for the developing world and have worked actively throughout the U.N. system. Moreover, it drastically reduced the military position of its chief rival, Pakistan, in the 1971 war, which ended in the formulation of a new state, Bangladesh, from West Pakistan. (See Chapter 12.) Because of India's huge population and potential power it has been the world's major recipient of economic aid. Although someday India may be a great power, in 1980 it had neither the economic or financial resources for this status.

Other potential powers in the developing world include Brazil, the strongest economic power in South America with 112 million people, Nigeria, a rising petroleum power in central Africa with a population of 75 million, and Mexico with vast new oil reserves.

The above nations do not approach the superpowers in international power and prestige. None of them, with the exception of India, which has exploded a nuclear device, is a nuclear power, and even India has not developed a nuclear arsenal of recognized strategic importance. They have, however, buttressed their international position or made their weight felt in the international area by virtue of their economic position.

The politically and economically most powerful of the developing nations base their strength on oil and financial strength. Oil and its related financial power seem destined to dominate the structure and the politics of the multipolar system in the forseeable future. Also, until the Middle East maelstrom is quieted by an Arab-Israeli peace settlement, the world's attention will probably be centered on the politics of that area.

Saudi Arabia has exerted influence on Middle East issues through its tremendous financial power. Both it and Iran have also given a great deal of momentum to the attempts of developing countries, particularly in the U.N. System, to revise the old international economic order. Even without this pressure for negotiations in the U.N. System on major policy issues, which are described in Chapter 14, major reforms would have been demanded by the financial strains put on the system by the skyrocketing prices of oil.

The internal politics of Saudi Arabia, Iran, and other wealthy oil states of the Persian Gulf area will be a key to how the multipolar system evolves. Saudi Arabia has the facade of development, but its political system has changed little from the model it used when it was an undeveloped country of desert tribes. Its people have undreamed of prosperity, particularly those at the top, but there is little popular participation in government. Iran has had some past experience with democratic government, but the Shah's one party system was authoritarian. The Shah's regime embarked on ambitious land and social reforms, but it alienated large numbers of

its students, including those for whom it generously
financed university educations. The Islamic revolution of
1979 which deposed the Shah and confronted the United
States contributed to internal turmoil and to a weakening
of Iran's world position.

The situation in the Middle East continued to be
unstable with the invasion of Afghanistan, turmoil
around Iran, and the unsettled Arab-Israeli disputes. The
disintegration of Iran's government or a radical coup in a
country such as Saudi Arabia could upset the uneasy
balance in the area. A confrontation of Middle East
nations with the industrial nations of the multipolar
system with resulting rises in oil prices or cutbacks in oil
exports could undermine the world economic system. We
will now look at the industrial sector of the multipolar
system and how it has related to the other parts of that
system.

Summary

With the nuclear standoff between Russia and the
United States, other countries and non-state units operate
in a multipolar system using economic factors to
dominate the action.

In the developing world Saudi Arabia during the 1970s
became a powerful nation on the basis of its huge oil
reserves and financial power. Saudi Arabia, Iran, and
other new oil power centers used OPEC to control the oil
market and drastically raise oil prices. Saudi Arabia and
the United States maintained close relations based on
their anti-Communism and close economic ties despite
major differences on the Arab-Israel conflict. The United
States maintained similarly close ties with Iran until 1979
when a radical Islamic revolution overthrew the Shah.
Relations with the United States were fractured after a
group of students and radicals stormed the American
Embassy taking Embassy officials as hostages and
demanding the U.S. return of the Shah, who was
temporarily in the United States for treatment of cancer.
The United States refused on the basis such action
flagrantly violated international law. The U.S. mobilized
support in the U.N. and among its allies to return the

hostages and retaliated with strong economic sanctions against Iran.

In 1980 a war broke out between Iraq and Iran, which undermined the Iranian economy and wrecked its military potential, which was based on U.S. equipment. This plus economic and political pressures finally forced Iran to negotiate the return of the hostages. In 1981 Iran was so weakened by the war and economic sanctions, it was no longer a major power in the Middle East. Even the loss of its huge oil exports to the world market was no longer a major power factor, since Saudi Arabia, another neighbor Iran had alienated, maintained high oil production to offset the cutting off of Iranian oil supplies.

During the 1970s the Third World countries were supported in the U.N. by OPEC delegations in their demands for a new international economic order based on international commodity agreements and other reforms of the international economic system. Reforms were made in the system, but not as extensive as those demanded by the activists. Other centers of Third World power included Taiwan, South Korea, Indonesia, and India, which also were preoccupied more with economic problems than with superpower politics.

FOOTNOTES

1. John M. Blair, *The Control of Oil* (New York: Vintage Books, 1978), p. 312.

2. Richard Nixon, *RN — The Memoirs of Richard Nixon* (New York: Grosset and Dunlap, 1978), p. 984.

3. Blair, *op. cit.,* p. 268.

4. Richard Nixon, *op. cit.,* p. 984.

5. *Washington Post,* May 11, 1978, p. 1.

6. *Washington Post,* December 16, 1978, pp. A-17 and A-19.

7. "Democracy Itch," *The Economist,* April 5, 1980, p. 30.

8. Kermit Roosevelt, *Countercoup — The Struggle for the Control of Iran* (New York: McGraw-Hill, 1979).

9. Blair, *op. cit.,* p. 264.

10. Series of four articles by William Branigin, *The Washington Post,* June 15 to June 18, 1980, and *The Economist,* May 31, 1980, p. 39.

11. Consulate General of the Islamic Republic of Iran (San Francisco), "Ayatollah Khomeini: On Issues Related to the Struggle of the Muslim People of Iran," "Imam Khomeini's Message to Liberation Movements," November 27, 1979, and Embassy of the Islamic Republic of Iran,

"Imam's Message Marks Mobilization Week." February 22, 1980; *Washington Post,* November 13, 1979.

12. "How to Lose Arab Friends and Madden Almost Everybody," *The Economist,* April 12, 1980, pp. 23-24; *Washington Post,* April 9, 1980, p. A-18.

13. *U.N. Chronicle,* January, 1980, p. 85.

14. Ramsey Clark on the MacNeil/Lehrer Report, June 19, 1980.

15. "Iran: Sanctions Force Oil Export Cut," *Washington Post,* June 13, 1980, p. A-30; Consulate General of the Islamic Republic of Iran, *op. cit.;* "Imam Khomeini's Speech to the Revolutionary Guard, December 15, 1979, and "Imam Defines His Stance in Respect to Embassy Occupation," November 10, 1979; "Interview with the correspondent of *Le Monde,* May 23, 1978.

16. Secretary of State Muskie and Senator Percy in the Senate Foreign Relations Committee hearing, February 16, 1981.

17. *U.N. Chronicle,* January, 1978, pp. 30-31; *U.N. Chronicle,* July, 1979, pp. 44-53; *IMF Survey,* June 18, 1979, pp. 1, 186; *IMF Survey,* July 7, 1980, pp. 213-214; and *Development Forum,* June-July, 1979, p. 16.

18. *Washington Post,* December 16, 1978, p. 1.

11

Industrial Centers of the Multipolar System

The major non-Communist centers of industrial power outside the United States are located over the coal and steel resources of Western Europe, and in the dynamic industrial islands of Japan. Their economic activities are controlled by the nation states of these areas, by the multinational corporations, and by the supranational European Community. These industrial centers are the economic heart of the multipolar system.

The European Community was founded on the idea that permanent peace between Germany and France would come about through economic integration followed by eventual political unity in Western Europe, rather than by reliance on military guarantees. The European Community institutions have made great progress in economic integration, and they operate in an economic system largely separate from the military alliances of NATO and the superpower system. The Community speaks with one voice in trade negotiations with the

United States, and in dealing with development issues it often finds itself in the middle between the United States and the developing world.

Germany, France, and England dominate the European Community like Saudi Arabia dominates OPEC. There are policy differences among leaders of the Community, and we will examine them to help in understanding the dynamics of European development.

"Trilateralism" is a new concept in international affairs implying three connected policy poles of power — The European Community, the United States, and Japan. Japan's relations with the other two poles of power will be examined.

The multinational corporations (MNCs) are on a separate organizational level within the multipolar system with their activities crossing national boundaries. They play a key role, the nature of which is controversial, and we will look at their activities from different ideological angles.

Some analysts see the interactions within the multipolar system as reducing the powers of sovereign states and thereby bringing about a fundamental change in the world's political structure. We will examine this issue, described as functionalism by some and supranationalism by others, to evaluate the evidence for such changes.

The European Community

The origin of the European Community illustrates the importance of leaders and ideas in international politics. Before World War II the great iron and steel center of Western Europe was controlled by an international steel cartel, Entente Internationale de L'Aciers (EIA), which included the steel producers of Germany, France, Belgium, Luxembourg, and the Saar. After World War II broke up this cartel, the occupation authorities replaced it with the International Authority for the Ruhr which was designed to control the coal and industrial power of Germany, which was centered in the Ruhr. The Ruhr Authority gave Germany only three out of 15 votes in allocating exports of coal and it became a center for confrontation rather than cooperation as the Western European members and the United States argued over who should get Germany's coal.

Jean Monnet, author of the five year plan for the recovery of France, realized the weakness of this system, which was imposed on Germany as a conquered nation. He was convinced that institutions with supranational power were necessary for world peace, and for peace between Germany and France, in particular. His experience as Deputy Secretary of the League of Nations after World War I had convinced him that "Goodwill between men and between nations is not enough. One must also have international laws and institutions."[1]

Monnet, after discussions with academic associates, drafted a detailed plan for a single market for coal and steel for all of Western Europe with a supranational institution in which Germany would have an equal voice with other Western European nations. He obtained Foreign Minister Schuman's support, who formally announced it at a press conference on May 9, 1950.

During the early 1950s French public opinion favored European union in principle, and public polls showed percentages ranging from 55 to 70 percent favorable. In only two polls, taken in 1955, did less than 50 percent favor a European union.[2] The unification of the coal and steel markets proceeded so well that its momentum supported the drive for a Common Market of all goods. The aim of the Common Market was to liberalize all trade and eliminate tariffs and barriers among movements of capital and labor in West Germany, Italy, France, and the Benelux countries. The European Economic Community (EEC) Treaty was put into effect on January 1, 1958.

By January, 1959, when General de Gaulle, an ardent French nationalist, took over as President of the Fifth Republic, the French recovery and economic progress under the coal and steel community and the EEC were so promising and there was so much public support for the idea that de Gaulle chose to work with it. However, by 1965 when the Treaty called for increasing commitments to supranationality and achievement of a Common Market by 1970, President de Gaulle instructed his ministers to withdraw from the Council of Ministers of the

Origins of the European Community

Plans for the European Coal and Steel (ECSC) and the European Community unquestionably originated with Jean Monnet of France and his associates. In the period before and after Monnet proposed the "Schuman Plan" for the ECSC, there were bitter arguments between French and German delegates over allocations of coal under the International Authority for the Ruhr, which was set up after World War II specifically to control Germany's coal and steel, the basis for its industrial strength.

Policymakers of the United States and Britain made strenuous efforts to encourage French and German cooperation in the Ruhr Authority, as well as in the Organization for European Economic Cooperation, which was set up to make a plan for Marshall Plan aid. At that time I was a junior officer on the German Desk of the Department of State, and I was responsible for preparing and clearing instructions for the Ruhr Authority meetings. (My Ph.D. dissertation was on the Ruhr Authority.) At one point we informally had to move negotiations on coal allocations to the occupation authorities in Bonn to break a deadlock in the Ruhr Authority, even though it was responsible for coal allocations.

American policymakers, therefore, were astounded at Jean Monnet's initiative to give Germany an *equal* voice with France in setting up a *supranational* authority under the "Schuman Plan" over *all* coal and steel resources in Western Europe! There was at first some suspicion in the media of American and British behind-the-scenes pressure. However, I was privy to the reporting cables and views of policymakers involved as the Ruhr Authority was gradually phased out and the ECSC took over, and it was clear that Monnet's plan was entirely a French initiative. Because of French national pride, his internationalist initiative probably would not have gotten off the ground if it had been even slightly tainted with American or foreign pressure, and conversely its great success is due to the fact it was a French initiative.

European Economic Community, and he attacked its supranational character.

The other countries resisted the idea of changing the aims and ideals of the Treaty, so they continued meetings with the policy of the "empty chair" for France, which amounted to stalling in the hopes that France would change its policy and return to the Council of Ministers.

General de Gaulle left the government on April 28, 1969, during a series of economic and political unheavals in France. President Pompidou took over in June, and he indicated France would end the boycott of the European Economic Community meetings. Not only did he end the boycott, but in April, 1972, he sought and obtained approval from the French people by a national referendum for British, Irish, and Danish entry and participation in the Common Market.[3]

Major European Economic Organizations

A. European Community (Communities) — 1967

1. Major Organs

    a. Council of Ministers. Foreign Ministers of Belgium, Denmark, France, Germany, Ireland, Italy, Luxembourg, Netherlands, and the United Kingdom.

    b. The Commission. Fifteen members supervising a staff of 7,500, which executes laws and policies.

    c. European Parliament. Membership of 355 directly elected in 1979.

    d. Court of Justice. Nine judges who interpret treaties and implementing legislation.

2. Major Operating Bodies in the European Community (EC)

    a. European Coal and Steel Community (ECSC). Established in 1952 to create a common market in coal and steel in Western Europe.

    b. European Economic Community (EEC) (Common Market). Established in 1958 to create a common market of all goods in Western Europe.

    c. European Atomic Energy Community. Established in 1958 to pool efforts in peaceful nuclear development.

    d. European Political Cooperation. Consultation for common position on foreign policy.

B. Organization for Economic Cooperation and Development (OECD), formerly Organization for European Economic Cooperation. Established in 1961 to promote economic growth in member and nonmember countries.

Membership: Australia, Austria, Belgium, Canada, Finland, France, Germany, Greece, Iceland, Ireland, Italy, Japan, Luxembourg, Netherlands, New Zealand, Norway, Portugal, Spain, Sweden, Switzerland, Turkey, United Kingdom, United States.

OECD ✗

Limited participants: Commission of the European
Communities and Yugoslavia.

C. U.N. Economic Commission for Europe. (ECE)
Membership: All countries of Eastern and Western Europe plus
the United States and Canada. Other countries such as Japan
and Israel participate on matters of concern to them.
This regional U.N. organization under the U.N. Economic and
Social Council devotes itself to problems of trade, transport,
agriculture, environment, and other problems of industrial
societies.

In May, 1974, Giscard d'Estaing as President formed a
new cabinet in France. In December, 1974, at a Summit
Meeting of the nine governments of the EC held in Paris,
he agreed to the direct election of a European Parliament
by the peoples of the EC "Nine" and renounced with the
other heads of state the "unanimous consent" procedure,
thereby allowing for a qualified majority to make
decisions. Since that meeting the Nine have consulted on
foreign policy questions under the framework of
"European Political Cooperation," and there has been a
growing tendency for them to take common positions on
foreign policy questions affecting Europe.

The economic accomplishments of the European
Community are widely acclaimed, and the Community
has achieved a combined economic power comparable to
that of the United States. The European Coal and Steel
Community and the European Economic Community
have achieved their aim of abolishing custom duties on
trade among the members, who have agreed on a common
external tariff. Workers can work anywhere within the
Community, and restrictions on investment have been
removed. Trucks, trains, and automobiles move across
national borders with only a cursory check. One of the
unanticipated bonuses of the system has been the
attraction of investment from abroad. Multinational
corporations investing in France, for example, have
access to the entire Common Market of over 250 million
people, larger than that of the United States. This
investment has supported the economic boom in Western
Europe under the Community.

The European Community's economic relations with
certain countries of the developing world could be
compared to the United States' military relations with its
allies in the superpower system. The Community has

negotiated agreements for associate membership in the Community with Greece (1962), Turkey (1964), as well as with Tunisia, Morocco, Malta, and Cyprus. In 1963 and 1968 it made similar agreements with 20 African states, most of which were former French colonies. The Community regards the agreements as a form of aid to these areas. The United States at first objected to these preferential arrangements but finally under pressure from the developing world adopted similar preferential tariffs for developing countries. In February, 1975, the Community signed the Lome Convention with 46 African, Caribbean, and Pacific states with preferential arrangements. Britain's Commonwealth partners in a May, 1975, formal resolution expressed a positive attitude toward British membership in the European Community hoping Britain would help them get preferences for entry of their tropical goods and financial aid to stabilize their export earnings. Under Britain's Accession Treaty to the Community the Commonwealth countries were offered this opportunity.

In the U.N. System the European Community often speaks for the Community as a whole in the dialogue between the developing and the developed countries. It was my impression that the European Community delegate naturally assumed a leading role in U.N. meetings because of his having the advantage of staff backing from economists of the European Community that the diplomatic delegates from the nine individual countries could not match. At these U.N. meetings the European Community spokesman and the West European delegates were often more receptive to new ideas of the new international economic order than were U.S. delegates. On the U.S. side we were often held back by the conservative views of our Department of Treasury and Department of Commerce officials who cleared the instructions. Despite the strong efforts to negotiate policy differences with the developing countries, we sometimes found ourselves in a small voting minority not including the European Community members. The Community position could be explained in part by France's and Britain's close relationship with their former colonies. It may also at times have reflected Western Europe's greater dependence on Arab oil and their desire not to confront the Arab delegates. Secretary of State Kissinger was a powerful figure who came to have a conciliatory view on development issues, but in the early 1970s he was spread thin and did not bring his political views to bear on these issues. By the mid 1970s he was taking a greater interest and helping to compromise development issues.

At the 1976 Conference on International Economic Cooperation the European Community succeeded in getting an agreed position on the idea of a Common Fund to support certain world commodity prices.[4] This was a fundamental concession to the developing countries for their new international economic order. The Community's agreement to this idea helped put pressure on American policymakers, who later accepted the idea.

It is fashionable to criticize the European Community as losing its momentum and to highlight the obstacles to progress in coordinating financial and budgetary policies. Observers should not, however, underestimate the forward momentum toward integration that now is affecting foreign policies. At the June, 1980, Common Market meeting in Venice, which was devoted mostly to economic issues, the "Nine" European Community leaders took issue with the United States and Israel by calling for "self-determination" for the Palestinians, and "association" of the PLO in the Mideast peace settlement (the Camp David process). They offered to participate in guarantees "on the ground" for a settlement, implying troop guarantees. A month later French President Giscard d'Estaing in a visit to Germany emphasized France's close ties to Germany and said: "Now we must undertake common action to restore Europe its influence in the world." This shows the Nine were moving forward together on important political issues as well as in the economic realm.[5]

There has been tremendous progress in economic integration since 1950, when France's major aim in foreign policy appeared to be to keep Germany suppressed. As we have seen, the European institutions have achieved a major momentum, and a reversal to the old order of independent national economies seems out of the question. It is helpful in appraising the future of European integration to look more closely at the policies of leading states and their leaders.

France. Two major ideas have affected the French position as a center of power in the European Community and the Multipolar System. The first has been the persisting urge for national greatness (*grandeur*) typified by General de Gaulle, and a related fear of a revival of a German threat. The second idea has been the French leaders' determination to maintain close connections with France's former colonial empire.

Jean Monnet's European Coal and Steel Community has so much momentum and public support that by the time General de Gaulle, a fierce French nationalist, assumed the presidency in 1958 he decided not to oppose the Community but use French membership to dominate the organization. For this reason he opposed British membership in the Community. He also resented United States power in Europe, and in April, 1966, he carried this to the extent of withdrawing forces from the NATO command. These Gaullist ideas still influence French political groups and lie behind some of the difficult day-to-day negotiations of political and economic issues within the Community.

General de Gaulle's major contribution to French stability, and unexpectedly to the power of the European Community, was a peaceful settlement of the French colonial question. Before World War II France's empire was second only to Britain's. France controlled almost one-third of Africa and the large colonial area of Indochina. Just after being forced out of Indochina in 1955, a rebellion broke out in Algeria. Much of the French army from Indochina was put into the Algerian conflict, which later became a Trojan horse to help in the final demise of the French Fourth Republic.

Tunisia and Morocco received their independence in 1956 after wars of independence and terrorism, and they subsequently provided help to the rebels of Algeria. With the large French presence in Algeria, backed by the army from Indochina, the Algerian War intensified with dim prospects of settlement. By 1958 France was actually threatened with a civil war and coup backed by the French Algerian army that had been alienated by the French Government's Algerian policy. De Gaulle was the only national symbol that appeared to be an alternative to an army coup.

De Gaulle, then, in a series of brilliant political moves, won acceptance from the National Assembly for his government and support of the French Army in Algeria, which regarded him as a trustworthy symbol of national unity and a reliable supporter of French *grandeur* and the Empire. The Socialist Party realized that de Gaulle was the only alternative to a military coup. De Gaulle insisted on and obtained full powers for six months while a new constitution was being drafted.

It took four years for de Gaulle to settle the questions of Algeria and the remainder of the French empire. De Gaulle sought and obtained the support of the French armed forces and the Algerian people by the force of his personality and by vague rhetoric. One of his first major acts was to visit Algeria, and his first address appealed to them to help in the pacification of Algeria so it would always be "body and soul" with France. In touring Morocco he pledged that all men would be equal.

The new constitution, reflecting de Gaulle's influence, provided that overseas territories, if they ratified it, would be associated in a "community of common interests." The new countries would enjoy autonomy, but the Community would deal with foreign affairs, defense, currency, and international economic problems. The French colonies were given the right in a referendum to stay in the French Community or to be completely separated. The referendum on the constitution won by 80 percent in France and in all territories including Algeria, except Guinea in French West Africa. France then immediately granted Guinea independence, which was headed by a leftist, Sekou-Toure.

Fifteen independent countries were established in Africa from the French empire and admitted to the U.N. These were Chad, Congo, Gabon, and the Central African Empire from French Equatorial Africa; Benin, Guinea, Mali, Ivory Coast, Mauritania, Niger, Senegal, and Upper Volta from French West Africa; Comoros, Djibouti, and Madagascar. These countries negotiated special agreements, which were ratified by the French National Assembly, providing for economic, military, and social cooperation, but not French domination of foreign policy, defense, and international economic policy as originally planned.

France has provided large subsidies and economic and administrative help to the former colonies and assisted them in negotiating special trade arrangements and other arrangements with the European Community.

France's close association with its former colonies gave it an understanding of their problems and a strong motivation to accommodate to their problems of development. This helps to account for the European Community's strong support for policies of the developing world in comparison with the position of the United States.

Germany. Germany by virtue of its resources and rapid economic expansion has been a power center of the European Economic Community. The first step toward unity under the European Coal and Steel Community was by a speech of Chancellor Adenauer in 1949 proposing a union of coal and economic resources of Western Europe. Adenauer was a Catholic Christian Democrat who was oriented toward the West away from the Prussian Protestant Junkers of East Germany. Adenauer's speech stimulated Jean Monnet to initiate the Schuman Plan, which became formalized in the European Coal and Steel Community.

If the European Community does someday establish a close relationship with Eastern Europe, it could owe such ties to the economic strength and political initiatives of Germany. Before World War II the Ruhr was a major source of machinery for Eastern Europe, and Western Germany imported large quantities of food from Eastern Europe.[6] Since World War II and the lowering of the "iron curtain," Eastern Europe's trade has been directed toward the Soviet Union, but economic forces together with political detente may rebuild Western Germany's former trade volume with Eastern Europe.

Since 1970 the Federal Republic has developed closer political and economic ties with Eastern Europe under the framework of *Ostpolitik* (Eastern Politics — See Chapter 3).

The *Ostpolitik* of Germany tends to contrast with United States relations with Russia, which have been characterized by confrontations over Berlin and U.S. encouragement to NATO to build up its strength against the threat from the East.

Great Britain. Britain has traditionally played a leading role in international organizations. This grew naturally out of its pre-World War I colonial interests that were replaced after that war by Commonwealth ties. The pervasiveness of the English language in former Asian and African colonies, and its spread by the United States in areas of U.S. influence after World War II have made it easy for British diplomats to maintain their leadership positions in international organizations. The English language today is the primary language used in the U.N. and most international organizations.

British private groups and the British Foreign Office provided the major initiative in plans for the League of Nations, and Britain gave strong support for the United Nations. It is a permanent member of the U.N. Security Council. The many close contacts of British policymakers with Commonwealth allies, the United States, and the European Community allow them to make contributions to the multipolar system that are greater in proportion than Britain's economic strength.

In a meeting of the Socialist Fabian Society in Blackpool on September 29, 1975, Foreign Secretary James Callaghan, who later became Prime Minister, set forth a strategy to take account of basic changes in world diplomacy caused by the withdrawal of United States from Vietnam and Britain's new dependence on international economic relationships. He said modern world power was shared among the United States and various international groupings including OPEC, the European Community, the Eastern Communist Bloc, as well as political groupings of the Third World. The main thrust of Britain's policy, he added, would be to find solutions to world problems in a multilateral context. He was concerned about confrontation with developing countries in the U.N. and stated Britain had decided to work on solutions to problems based on international interdependence and partnership rather than domination. He explained that the Labor Government, by associating itself with the European Community and other international organizations, was developing a policy of building bridges among them, which would allow Britain to make a contribution out of proportion to her size.

The European emphasis represented a new direction of Labor Party policy. The Labor Party had opposed entering the European Economic Community on the terms negotiated by the Conservative Government but had been overridden by a Conservative Party majority in 1972. In 1974 Prime Minister Wilson, in a new Labor Government, was faced with the problem of strong opposition in his Labor Party to retaining membership with the European Community. Wilson, however, desired entry and solved the dilemma by "renegotiation" of terms of Britain's entry into the European Community, to take account of objections of the Labor Party, and he then obtained support in a national referendum. The Labor Party members were removed from "party discipline" for the votes on this issue. This meant they could "vote their conscience" without implying a no-confidence vote for the government, which would result in a new election. Wilson won the election dramatically, showing how one leader could affect foreign policy even against his party.

In earlier years the issue of joining the Common Market had been pictured as one of developing relations with the European Economic Community at the expense of giving tariff preferences and ties with the Commonwealth. However, as already noted, in May, 1975, Commonwealth members favored British membership in the European Community in order to get free entry for certain tropical goods and financial aid to help stabilize their export earnings.

It will be difficult for British industries to compete in the Common Market. Economic observers in Britain, however, for many years have said that it will be necessary for it to solve its problems of inflation and productivity if it is to survive. On the other hand, Britain's balance of payments situation improved dramatically after 1977 with increased petroleum supplies from the North Sea.

With Britain's long experience in diplomacy and close ties with the Commonwealth and the European Community, British policy can be expected to exercise a stabilizing influence by building bridges between international groups including those of the developed and developing countries. These policies have enough momentum and support to continue whether a government is Labor or Conservative.

Japan

Japan's economy dominates East Asia in trade and economic relationships, but it has not achieved the political spin-offs developed by Western Europe through the integration movement and cultivation of former colonial ties. Also, Japan has not developed close economic ties with Western Europe as implied by the concept of trilateralism.

Before World War II Japanese imperialists argued that because of its small size — about the size of California — and its large population — about half that of the United States — Japan was forced to establish an empire. Japanese militarists had already conquered Korea, Taiwan, and Manchuria, and after Pearl Harbor the armed forces took over most of Asia. After World War II Japan was forced to give up its empire and be confined to its small home islands, but here it achieved probably the most remarkable economic expansion in the Post World War II era. It was aided by a friendly American occupation and an effective, democratic government. The relatively small Japan has achieved a GNP four times that of China with only one-eighth the population. Japan's per capita GNP has risen above the European average. Most observers have been forced to the conclusion that Japan has succeeded economically largely because of its skilled, educated population with a strong work ethic.

Japan has been a feared competitor in Europe. The European Community for this reason has not embraced a close relationship with Japan.[7] In the 1970s the U.S. and the European Community criticized Japanese commercial policies and pressured it to reduce its export surplus to the European and United States markets, even though Japanese trade accounted for less than five percent of the Community's imports.[8] Trilateralism has been a catchy slogan implying a three-way intimate relationship between Japan, the United States, and the European Community, but it does not give an accurate picture of the economic relationship.

Japan is more a separate island of strength in the Far East, respected and feared as a competitor, rather than a partner. Japan's major trading partner is the United States, which accounts for 25 to 30 percent of its total trade. Japan buys large quantities of U.S. agricultural products and ships high quality electronic and industrial goods in return. Japan has also managed to maintain a high trade volume with both the Peoples' Republic of China and the Republic of China on Taiwan despite an abrupt change of political ties. From 1970 to 1974 trade with both areas increased about three- to four-fold, although in 1972 Japan established diplomatic relations with the Peoples' Republic of China and was forced to break off diplomatic relations with the Republic of China on Taiwan. Japan maintained consular and commercial relations with its former colony, Taiwan. Trade with mainland China accounted for only a little over three percent of Japanese trade in 1975; however, China obtained one-third of its imports from Japan and sent it one-fifth of its exports. In other words, Japanese trade was much more important to China than vice versa. Japan rapidly increased its imports of high-grade crude oil from China, but it also investigated the possibility of helping develop the Russian oil fields in Western Siberia.

Japan took advantage of its reparations payments to the countries of Asia, which it had occupied and exploited in World War II, by paying them in exports and development projects. This provided a base for an expansion of its commercial trade, including spare parts, with Asia. Also, aside from reparations it had an active aid program, including private lending, amounting to almost one percent of its GNP, compared to about .6 of one percent for the U.S. About 80 percent of Japanese aid was devoted to Asia, which also provided a basis for future commercial trade development.

Japan's foreign policy is oriented toward economics, and Japanese government initiatives have helped the private sector achieve one of the most remarkable economic expansions in the world. Observers with both jealousy and admiration have tagged the Japanese system as "Japan Incorporated."[9] In evaluating Japanese foreign policy one should realize that diplomatic discussions usually center on commercial matters rather than subjects of international power and diplomacy that preoccupy the superpower system.

Japan's role in the multipolar system of states, therefore, is one of an island of economic power with extensive trade with the developing countries, a heavy dependence on OPEC oil, and a heavy dependence on trade with the United States. China, since its split with Russia, is dependent on Japan for much of its technology and trade, but Japan has such a powerful economy this trade constitutes only a small proportion of Japan's total trade. In fact Japan trades almost as much with the small area of Taiwan as it does with all of mainland China. There is no economic rival to Japan in the Far East, and although Japan has little military power, it is gaining more prosperity and influence by peace than it gained by war in World War II.

The Multinationals

Multinationals companies (MNCs) are private business firms operating in more than one country.[10] There has been much controversy over the part multinationals play in international politics. To those with Communist views, and to some with socialist views, the multinational corporations are the root of evil in international politics. Communists and many socialists see them as dominating the politics of nation states and striving to dominate foreign governments and foreign markets and to obtain control over sources of cheap raw materials. These observers believe the capitalist system does not create home markets adequate to absorb the production of the MNCs, so they must operate abroad in order to survive. They assert this process is a major cause of war and of civil strife. Much of the drive to establish a new international economic order that was described in Chapter 10, reflects to some degree a belief that the international system allows too much power to the MNCs, and that governments should intervene in the world markets and with international organizations to limit the power of private business.

Many market economists, on the other hand, would say that multinational firms are the most effective instruments of economic development. These firms, they say, mobilize the financial, technical, and marketing skills of the most advanced industrial countries and bring these assets to the developing world. These economists assert the MNCs mobilize local resources that no other organization could do as effectively, including local labor, financial, and managerial skills. Moreover, the MNCs do this at a low price, unless the local government decides to let the firms produce in a protected high-price market. The market economists would assert that state-owned firms could not mobilize resources as efficiently, in part because they have an irresistable temptation to use governmental power to produce at a high price in a protected market. The multinational firms, the argument goes, have succeeded by virtue of the fact they have learned to produce at prices that meet world competition.

Much of the rhetoric of debates on MNCs which fill shelves of U.N. libraries consists of elaboration of the above theories, and they throw little light on specific problems of development. Both sides have legitimate points to make.[11]

It is clear that the multinational corporations are huge and powerful. In 1970 more than 200 MNCs had surpassed a sales value of $1 billion. Writers often exaggerate their size by using their gross sales figures rather than value added,[12] but even by using value added figures, the output of each of the top 10 multinational corporations in 1971 was over $3 billion, or greater than the GNP of over 80 countries. The value added of all MNCs in 1971 was about $500 billion or one-fifth of the world's GNP, not including the Communist economies.[13] From one point of view this is an index of their tremendous power and influence. From another, it reflects the fact that most of the world economies are based on the market system where industrial products are produced by private corporations, which often trade and operate abroad.

The Communist view that multinational corporations are a major cause of war is not accepted by non-Communist historians. Wars have occurred since the beginning of history, thousands of years before multinational corporations were conceived. Since World War II there have been about 70 wars. In only one war, the Congo War of 1960 to 1965, the Belgian Government intervened to protect a powerful multinational mining company. There have been a number of colonial wars since World War II — Algeria, 1945; Indonesia, 1945-1949; Indochina, 1945-1954; Tunis, 1952; Kenya, 1952-1954;

Algeria, 1954-1962; Angola, 1962; and Mozambique, 1965. These wars, however, were waged by governments for protecting their overall economic and political interests in colonies, not for protecting *multinational* firms, which by definition operate outside a colony in more than one country.

On the other hand, historians would agree that Communist governments and their ideology, which is the antithesis of capitalism, played a major role in many wars; e.g., Korea, 1950-1954; Chinese Civil War, 1946-1949; offshore islands conflicts in China, 1954 and 1958; Hungary, 1956; Laos, 1959-1962; Vietnam, 1961-1975; China-U.S.S.R. border, 1969; Indonesia, 1965-1966; Vietnam-Cambodia, 1978-1980; Laos, 1975; China-Vietnam, 1979; and Afghanistan, 1979. Communist historians proudly call some of these conflicts wars of national liberation. It is a travesty for Communist historians to blame wars on multinationals.

Professor George Modelski, in analyzing this problem, has compared the intensity of corporate activities with a list of countries where major armed clashes occurred after World War II. He concluded "high corporate activity goes hand in hand with low conflict incidence; low corporate activity correlates with higher frequency of conflict." He notes that obviously this is because world business tends to avoid areas of instability which would threaten their investments.[14]

We have noted in Chapter 10 that the international oil cartel until 1973 exercised tremendous power, and at one point was able to cause an economic crisis in Iran which weakened a revolutionary regime and helped restore the Shah to power. The cartel controlled world oil prices before 1973 and was able to create a price structure that allowed the governments where the product was sold to impose taxes on oil many times the original price for the oil. We have also noted, however, that this private oil cartel after 1973 was tamed by the militarily weak and undeveloped Middle Eastern states. It was forced to agree to OPEC's tremendous increase in world oil prices that caused fundamental difficulties for the economies of the most powerful nations of the world. These advanced governments, which had overwhelming military strength, according to the Communist doctrine were dominated by the oil cartel and other MNCs, but the doctrine does not explain why they made no move to take back control over the oil fields from the weak nations that challenged their control. In fact, these governments and the private cartel meekly acquiesced in the take-over and assisted the Middle East governments in spending and investing their vast new wealth. Communist doctrine does not explain why the powerful nations would yield to pressures of weak nations on such an issue.

The critics of MNCs use as a favorite example of the power of the MNCs the operations of the International Telephone and Telegraph (ITT) Company in Chile. ITT from 1970 to 1972 conspired with American Central Intelligence Agency (CIA) agents first to oppose the election as President of Salvadore Allende, who had campaigned on a program to nationalize foreign firms including large investments of ITT in Chile. ITT provided funds to opposition newspapers and at one point offered the CIA $1 million to block the election and even help in his overthrow after the election. Later it urged a program of economic sanctions against Chile to undermine Allende's government. In March, 1972, Jack Anderson of the *Washington Post* uncovered the scheme by publishing texts of ITT letters which he secretly had obtained. The case soon became a favorite horrible example in U.N. debates of the abuse of power of multinational corporations. ITT documents were widely published in Latin America.[15] On September 11, 1973, Allende was overthrown in a military coup. A subsequent U.S. Senate investigation that criticized ITT and CIA opposition to Allende was not able to show that CIA or ITT support for his opponents had a direct bearing on the success of the coup.[16]

The other major series of scandals implicated big airplane companies, such as Lockheed, which bribed former Japanese Prime Minister Tanaka and other government officials to the tune of about $8.7 million to support the scale of their products. Tanaka and other officials were indicted, and the Liberal Democratic Party after many years of dominating Japanese politics came close to losing an election because of the scandal. The new Liberal Democratic Prime Minister Miki led his party to victory after arresting the former Prime Minister and bringing him to trial. A similar series of scandals rocked

Italian politics, and another involved Prince Bernhard, the husband of the Queen of the Netherlands. These scandals were not in the usual ideological framework of Socialist or Communist attacks on exploitation of developing countries, however, because they involved developed countries. Moreover, most of the companies making the bribes were not *multinational* in the sense of having production operations in the country where the bribes occurred, but they were American-based firms selling American products abroad. The scandals led to congressional investigations and U.S. legislation to deter such payments in the future.

In the period of 1972 to 1974 the U.N. established a commission and research center on MNCs. One of the commission's major tasks has been to draft a code of conduct for MNCs. (See box.) The Organization for Economic Cooperation and Development, which includes the major industrial nations of the world, on June 21, 1976, approved such a code which included a set of voluntary guidelines defining standards for good business conduct in the OECD area. It includes provisions for respect for contracts, refraining from improper political activities, and recognition of the right to unionize. The U.N. code, of course, would be broader in its area of application by including all countries of the world.

The World Bank has recognized problems of MNC operations by establishing the International Center for the Settlement of Investment Disputes. To date relatively few investment disputes involving developing nations have been submitted to it.

There are numerous ways in which the activities of the multinationals, which are controlled by foreign interests, impact on developing countries and would be covered by such a code. They include the following:

1. The MNCs make decisions on extracting non-renewable resources such as oil and minerals for use abroad.
2. They introduce machine-made goods which displace local producers.
3. They can use their financial power to influence the domestic political process.
4. They implant different life styles and much higher standards of living, which can cause friction.
5. They can avoid exchange controls through setting

The U.N. Commission on Transnational Corporations

Three policymakers — Ambassador Bernard Zagorin of the U.S. Mission to the U.N. and Ambassador Hernan Santa Cruz, Chile's U.N. Ambassador, along with U.N. Undersecretary de Seynes — were mainly responsible for the establishment of the U.N. Commission on Transnational Corporations. The compromise was made in UNCTAD and ECOSOC in 1972 despite the fact that at that time the American multinational firm, International Telephone and Telegraph (ITT), was a favorite horrible example in Chile and Latin America of an MNC intervening with the CIA to try to defeat the election of Chile's President Allende.

Ambassador Zagorin believed that U.N. examination of the MNC issues would permit constructive action and prevent the MNC issue from continually being used as a whipping boy in U.N. debates. Ambassador Santa Cruz, the leader of the developing country caucus, wanted to use the leverage of the U.N. to curb MNC abuses. Despite their different ideologies — socialist on the one hand and market economist on the other — the two agreed to establish the U.N. Commission on Transnational Corporations in 1972. Included in the deal was an increased voice of developing countries in international monetary reform and in GATT trade negotiations. (See Chapter 14.)

I was responsible as a U.S. State Department Officer for preparing instructions and backstopping the 1972-1974 U.N. meetings that set up the U.N. organizations for the MNCs. Normally it would have been virtually impossible to get the U.S. Treasury to approve such instructions because of its deep-seated conservatism and suspicion of the motives and influence of the developing countries in the U.N. in setting up such U.N. machinery. Ambassador Zagorin, however, was a former high official of the Treasury and with his backing, I was able to get Treasury and other Washington clearances on instructions to our U.N. delegations approving this initiative.

"transfer prices" of sales between a parent and subsidiary.

6. They can avoid taxes by various accounting procedures including transfer prices.

Thus, the multinational corporations can create tensions and conflicts with national policies of the host countries.

On the other hand, the corporations are vulnerable to a variety of host country controls that can hinder operations including:

1. Permits and licenses for their operations.
2. Laws against foreign land ownership.
3. Laws against entering certain economic fields.
4. Laws about local equity ownership, and setting time periods to divest a proportion of ownership to local interests.
5. Taxation.
6. Exchange controls and controls on remitting profits.
7. Import licensing.
8. Expropriation of foreign concerns.

It becomes obvious there is a full menu for negotiating a code of conduct for multinational corporations operating in foreign countries. It is significant that both developed and developing countries support establishing such guidelines. The MNCs are an integral part of the world economic system and the economic development process, and it is probably for this reason that they continue to expand and grow in economic power despite the many attacks levied against them, including expropriation and government investigations.[17]

Their avowed ideology of market and enterprise economics has little appeal in the developing countries, but the way in which the MNCs can produce does have appeal. The MNCs will probably continue to dominate the world economy and be a major instrument for development for many years, if they can avoid further notorious abuses of their power. A U.N. Code of Conduct could be of considerable help in such a process.

Supranationalism

The success of the European Community in integrating the economies of Western Europe has stimulated many studies of the process and speculation about whether other areas of the world will follow its example. David Mitrany has used the word functionalism to describe the process of specialists increasingly performing technical, "non-political" tasks facing government. He believes such functional activities can bring about increasing economic and political integration.[18]

We noted above that Jean Monnet's original plan for the European Community was based on his aim to establish a "supranational" authority over states which would first unify Western Europe's heavy industry and increasingly bring about the political unification of Europe. A United States of Europe was his ultimate goal. Amitai Etzioni, writing about the European Community and other international organizations, described the "spill over" effect in the unification process in which an increased flow of goods, persons, and communications within a system such as the European Community helps bring about further integration of other parts of the system including the political sector.[19]

George Ball, former Undersecretary of State (U.S.), in *Fortune* in 1967 made an extreme statement often quoted about the expanding activities of the multinational corporations; the nation-state, he said, has become "a very old-fashioned idea."[20]

Does the analysis above indicate support for these ideas? Certainly the European Community is an impressive example of a supranational organization integrating Western Europe's economy and absorbing functions of national governments. In the process it has achieved a major aim of its founder, Jean Monnet, of creating the basis of a lasting peace between France and Germany. His leadership backed by popular support for his ideas in France and Western Europe prevailed against the opposition of a powerful French leader, President de Gaulle, whose name is a symbol of French nationalism.

The fact that the Monnet plan succeeded against what appeared a trend of French-German friction in the opposite direction and against General de Gaulle's policies suggests that the personal leadership element and timing are extremely important, and more important than trends that could be uncovered in an exhaustive analysis of political forces. Similarly, the British participation in the Common Market showed a similar impact of an individual leader, Prime Minister Wilson, who went against his party to keep Britain in the Common Market. The timing was important because the entry occurred when another leader, President Pompidou of France, was ready to accept British entry. Both the British and French leaders gave their electorate a chance to make this decision in a referendum.

Is the European Community a unique occurrence? Many observers have analyzed that unification process to determine how it occurred and if the process could spread to other areas of the world. The European Community would have great difficulty in spreading to Eastern Europe. The gulf between the two parts of Europe is the center of attention of the Superpower System and tends to be maintained by military elements of its two alliances. Germany, with its *Ostpolitik,* and the Economic Commission for Europe have only made a beginning in breaking down the barriers between East and West, and in trying to achieve a normal trade relationship.

There is closer interaction between the European Community and many developing countries than there is with Eastern Europe or with the United States.[21] The colonial experience of most developing countries, however, makes them suspicious of any suggestion of integration with European countries through government institutions. Much of the close association of the European Community with African nations is due to the unexpected actions of one leader, General de Gaulle. The direction of his policies was not predicted in advance by analysts, again underlining the importance of leadership and ideas in foreign policy.

The multinational corporations show little promise of taking over functions of states, although MNC activities have stimulated international cooperation to control them. The MNCs have no military force at their disposal or organization to speak and act for them. Illusions of MNC power were undermined by their retreat and appeasement of the OPEC nations when these militarily weak nations challenged what was probably the world's most powerful private cartel and took over ownership of its members' oil properties. OPEC, a weak, loosely knit international organization without a permanent secretariat, was the instrument used in this victory. Behind OPEC was the power of two weak nation states which happened to have enough oil production to control prices on the international market.

In another major part of the multipolar system Japan acts as a national island of economic power. It is dependent on U.S. trade and OPEC oil for its prosperity, but it has no strong organizational links with the United States or Europe that could be compared to U.S. ties with the European Community. Trilateralism is a catchy slogan, but it has little practical meaning in terms of economic and political integration of the Japanese government institutions with those of the United States and Europe. Only in recent years has the Japanese government even permitted close investment relationships between Japanese MNCs and those of the United States and Europe. Its trade and investments are becoming increasingly oriented toward the developing world.

An obvious reason not always appreciated for the success of the European Community in Western Europe has been general acceptance of democracy and related values by Western European nations.[22] Theoretically, the United States might be encouraged to draw closer to Western Europe on the basis of these common values and increasing economic interaction. However, French nationalism and suspicions of foreign domination are more than matched in strength by similar feelings of the U.S. public, which would pull away from a close embrace involved in joining together in European Community institutions.

Unless there is a major world crisis to change established patterns of ideas, or unless strong leaders appear unexpectedly like Jean Monnet, who can set a new course, the working of the multipolar system will probably continue to encourage economic contests and compromises through meetings of nation states rather than dramatic moves toward integration and supranationalism. The type of close integration of Western Europe has only barely begun in other areas of the world, and the other 140 states of the world seem to cherish national independence.

Meanwhile, economic processes help bring about closer

cooperation between industrial states and developing nations. Those developing nations that are most closely involved in trading and investment relationships with the industrial nations have developed the strongest economies, which in turn have buttressed their international position. In the case of Taiwan its position has been supported by economic forces, even though its claim to represent all of China has been undermined diplomatically and has faded away. On the other hand, extensive economic relations with the rest of the world are not necessary for military strength, as demonstrated by the powerful Communist countries. These military powers are outside the working of the multipolar economic system and have based their economic policies largely on the ideas of economic self-reliance.

The multipolar economic system is relatively independent of the superpower military system on economic policy matters. The multipolar system does work closely, however, with the U.N. System on economic issues. We will now look at the U.N. System, where states meet to compromise and resolve security and economic problems.

Summary

The economic centers of industrial power of the multipolar system are the industrial nations of Western Europe and Japan. After World War II the French took the initiative in political reconciliation of Germany and France by establishing the European Coal and Steel Community, which later was broadened to establish a common market for all goods under the European Community. This Community has achieved an economic power comparable to the United States. It has also reached out and created close ties with former colonial areas of the developing world. This includes reaching agreement with them on programs for their new international economic order. Japan is another major center of economic power which has developed extensive trading relations with China and Asia as well as with the United States.

The role of multinational firms in international affairs

is controversial with some observers blaming them for wars and corruption of international society. Others see them as major instruments for economic development. In any event, they are a central part of the world economic system. The United Nations is involved in a major effort to draft a code of conduct to make them more acceptable to some of the developing countries that have reservations about their operations.

The growth of the supranational European Community and expanding activities of MNCs have led some political scientists to question the staying power of the nation state. The growth of supranationalism or functionalism is regarded as an irresistable trend by some, but evidence points to nationalism and the nation-state system as being the winner in the foreseeable future.

FOOTNOTES

1. Merry and Serge Bromberger, *Jean Monnet and the United States of Europe* (New York: Howard McCann, Ind., 1968), p. 19.

2. Roy C. Macridis (ed.), *Foreign Policy and World Politics* (Englewood Cliffs: Prentice-Hall, Inc., 1972), p. 91.

3. Norway was also included in the French referendum but it later declined to join.

4. Stephen Taylor, "EEC Coordination for the North-South Conference," *World Today,* November, 1977, pp. 433-441; Andrew Shonfield, "The World Economy 1979," *Foreign Affairs,* 1979, pp. 596-621.

5. *Economist,* June 21, 1980, pp. 13-14, 61-62; *Washington Post,* June 14 and July 8, 1980.

6. The prewar trade statistics are in the following sources: a) *League of Nations, International Trade Statistics* (Geneva: League of Nations, 1938); b) Statistisches Reichamt, *Statistik Des Deutschen Reichs,* Binde 522 I, 522 II, 523. (Berlin: Verlag Paul Schmidt, 1938). These are analyzed in my Ph.D. dissertation, "The Problem of the Ruhr in the Peace Settlement," University of Chicago, 1949.

7. Werner J. Feld, *The European Community in World Affairs* (Alfred Publishing Company, 1976), pp. 199-201.

8. *European Community,* May-June, 1978, p. 45; *Washington Post,* May 8, 1978, p. A-22.

9. Eugene J. Kaplan, *Japan Incorporated* (Washington, D.C.: U.S. Government Printing Office, 1974).

10. United Nations, Multinational Corporations in World Development (United Nations: 1972), Document ST/ECA/190. Annex II has a list of definitions by various authors.

11. *Ibid.* See for example Joan Edelman Spero, *The Politics of*

International Economic Relations (New York: St. Martin's Press, 1977), Chapter 4.

12. See Chapter 6.

13. U.N., *Multinational Corporations in World Development, op cit.,* p. 11.

14. See George Modelski (ed.), *Multinational Corporations and World Order* (Beverly Hills, Calif.: SAGE Publications, 1972), pp. 14-20. For a more critical view see chapter by Jonathan F. Galloway, "The Military-Industrial Linkages of U.S.-Based Multinational Corporations," pp. 89-107 in the same book.

15. Some Chilean observers noted to me, however, that the documents created relatively little impact in Latin America because they were mild in comparison to the accusations that had been levied about MNC activities.

16. U.S. Senate, Select Committee to Study Governmental Operations with Respect to Intelligence Operations, "Alleged Assassination Plots Involving Foreign Leaders," November 20, 1975.

17. Amos Yoder, "U.N. Monitoring of Transnational Corporations," *Towson State Journal of International Affairs,* Spring, 1980.

18. David Mitrany, *A Working Peace System* (Chicago: Quadrangle Books, 1966).

19. Amitai Etzioni, *Political Unification* (New York: Holt, Rinehart and Winston, 1965).

20. George Ball, "The Promise of the Multinational Corporation," *Fortune,* June 1, 1967.

21. *European Monthly,* a bimonthly publication of the European Community in May-June 1978 reported the following statement of Sir

22. Christopher Soames, until 1977 the Vice President of the European Commission in charge of external affairs, at a conference at Pomona College, California said: "I can assure you that if any member country of the Community ever got itself a government which ceased to follow precepts of a pluralist democracy and the freedoms that evolve, then that country could no longer remain a member of the Community." *European Community,* May-June, 1978, p. 44.

PART FIVE
The United Nations and an Interdependent World

World leaders often bring the major conflicts and issues of international politics into the United Nations System. Many observers have criticized the U.N. for its inability to prevent war, which is its major function under the U.N. Charter. Others see the U.N. as the world's best hope for achieving peace. We will try to get perspective by evaluating U.N. actions on wars and related issues, including arms limitation. We will also examine the actions of the U.N. System on international economic development issues, which absorb most of its resources.

12

The UN System and Peacemaking

The contests in the Superpower System and its interactions with the rest of the world have dominated international politics since World War II. The most critical issues were related to the Cold War of the superpowers, and many of the problems were brought before U.N. bodies for debate or action. The U.N. System is often regarded as just a forum or an instrument to be used by the superpowers or other nations in these disputes. For many years after World War II many viewed the U.N. as dominated by the United States, with the Russians on the defensive using their veto to block U.S. initiatives. A common view of recent years is that the U.N. is dominated by the Asian and African developing countries, with their strong voting power derived from a trebling of U.N. membership since it was founded. Other observers, including internationalists, see the U.N. as developing its own momentum with an increasing potential to settle disputes and provide economic assistance.

To get more perspective on the work of the U.N. we will look at what the system has produced on some of the major issues of peacemaking and economic development. This pragmatic approach will permit us to judge how different parts of the U.N. System generated their own momentum, or supranationalism. This will give us data to evaluate what impact the U.N. System is having and is likely to have on the other two major world systems — the Superpower System and the multipolar system of states and non-state power centers.

The preamble and first article of the U.N. Charter state its purposes: "to save succeeding generations from the scourge of war" and to "maintain international peace and security." The main elements of the U.N. System work on a wide range of economic and social issues, but peace and war are its major concern. The success or failure of the U.N. is being and will be judged on this basis.

The drafters of the U.N. Charter had the League of Nations experience very much in mind and designed the U.N. to avoid the flaws that led to the death of the League. They, therefore, wrote into the Charter stronger provisions for the U.N. to take action against an aggressor. The Charter was drafted during World War II at the height of Great Power cooperation, and for a short time it seemed possible that they would stay united to maintain the peace. As the Cold War developed, these hopes were shattered, and the power brokers saw the U.N. only as conference machinery or a forum. We will first briefly look at the League experience that impressed the founders of the U.N. and the policymakers who followed. In this evaluation of the League and in judging the U.N. it is helpful to look at the organizational possibilities as falling somewhere on a continuum between the two separate poles of possibilities.

Conference Machinery   **World Government**

The League of Nations

Historians generally agree that World War I arose from misunderstandings and blunders rather than from a plot by German leaders to conquer Europe.[1] In the century preceding that war European crises had been considered by a "Concert of Europe," which was a series of conferences of major European powers convened periodically to settle territorial disputes, colonial problems, and other major issues. The Concert had its origin at the close of the Napoleonic Wars in the Quadruple Alliance of 1815 designed to maintain the status quo of the treaties ending that war and to suppress revolution. The Concert during the Nineteenth Century arranged for military intervention in certain European countries, primarily to suppress revolutions.

On the eve of World War I European powers mobilized to support their alliance systems and to get a jump on rival alliances. Sir Edward Grey, the British Foreign Secretary, frustrated in an attempt to call a conference to prevent the war, declared on the eve of its outbreak that world statesmen should work together to create an international system to prevent such crises in the future. Prime Minister Asquith shortly after the war broke out declared that a league of nations to preserve peace was one of the war aims of the British people. Although President Wilson is regarded by many Americans as the founder of the League, British leaders such as Sir Edward Grey and Lord Robert Cecil did most of the preparatory work on the League. They had an important influence on Wilson's speech of May, 1916, when he first publicly announced support for the idea. In January, 1918, President Wilson proposed a League of Nations as one of the Fourteen Points, later accepted as a basis for the Paris Peace Conference.

Colonel House, President Wilson's principal advisor, in exploring ideas for the League of Nations in a letter to Lord Robert Cecil of Great Britain, wrote the following:[3]

> One of the most essential features of any league seems to me to be the installation of a moral standard such as that maintained among individuals of honor. Even before Germany smashed the international fabric, reprehensible action was condoned under the broad cover of patriotism;

actions which in individuals would have been universally condemned and the perpetrators ostracized from society.

I believe the most vital element in bringing about a worldwide reign of peace is to have the same stigma rest upon the acts of nations as upon the acts of individuals. When the people of a country are held up to the scorn and condemnation of the world because of the dishonorable acts of their representatives, they will no longer tolerate such acts.

This expresses the essence of how an international organization can work toward a peaceful world order among sovereign nations. Leaders of sovereign nations have not yet yielded important elements of national sovereignty to a world organization. The success of such an organization in achieving peace, therefore, should be measured by how it mobilizes political and material support to maintain peace and facilitates compromise, rather than how it enforces peace, which is a task that is very difficult or perhaps impossible in today's world.

The British, American, and other experts who drafted the League of Nations Covenant were determined to establish an organization that could prevent the type of blunders that led to World War I. Their major concept was to create a permanent organization which could be convened quickly to deal with an emergency. The principal organ for such crises was the League Council, which was designed as a permanent organization to represent five great powers with permanent seats, and four lesser powers with non-permanent seats. Important decisions under the League Covenant were by unanimity of members. This and the failure of the U.S. to join weakened the League, but aside from this it is doubtful in the 1930s the major powers would have opposed Japanese, German, and Italian aggression. The attempt of the League to oppose their aggression was countered by their withdrawal. The Secretary General dissolved the organization in 1940 at the beginning of World War I. The sad history of the 1930s does not illustrate just the failure of the League to act against aggression, but the failure of sovereign nations to use the League organization for that purpose.

The Founding of the U.N.

As a result of the failures of the League in the 1930s to

stop aggression President Roosevelt and other leaders of the alliance during World War II began planning for a new and stronger organization to keep the peace. At first Roosevelt, Prime Minister Churchill, and Marshal Stalin favored a system based on regional organizations to enforce the peace, but Secretary of State Cordell Hull insisted on a universal organization based on the League of Nations model. He won Roosevelt over to the idea, and then formed a broadly based committee of government, congressional, and private sector representatives to prepare a first draft of the charter of the organization that later became the U.N.[4] Roosevelt supported the idea and gave it the impetus necessary to become a reality a few months after his death, but during the war most of Roosevelt's energies were devoted to waging the war and military planning, so there is little on record of his specific ideas about a new world organization. After Roosevelt's death, President Truman enthusiastically took up the cause.[5] Dean Acheson, later Truman's Secretary of State and a brilliant practitioner of power politics, shepherded the Charter, which by then had a tremendous momentum, through Congress. He was just doing his job because he personally felt the U.N. was "impracticable" and a "legacy of the Nineteenth Century."[6] Just as Foreign Secretary Grey and President Wilson were leading policymakers who promoted the League of Nations, President Roosevelt and Secretary of State Hull were the leaders who gave the United Nations a major impetus.

Today it takes years to organize international conferences and draft major conventions. With the bitter lessons of World War II as an incentive, the drafting and approval of the U.N. Charter was accomplished in only a year. The Dumbarton Oaks Conferences of Britain, the United States, Russia, and China working mostly on a draft from the advisory committee set up by Hull approved the first draft of the U.N. Charter in two months. Less than a year later, delegates from 50 nations met in San Francisco and approved the final charter on June 26, 1945. Within five weeks the United States Senate approved American membership by a vote of 89 to two, and on October 24, 1945, the United Nations was formally established.

The United Nations like the League of Nations is

Early Preparations for the U.N.

Department of State officials carried on extensive consultations with Congress and the public in planning for the United Nations. Dr. Leo Pasvolsky, one of the principal authors of the early draft of the U.N. Charter, was active in public relations. For example, in March, 1942, as a student I attended the National Study Conference of the Federal Council of Churches of Christ held at Ohio Wesleyan University. Dr. Pasvolsky, John Foster Dulles, later Secretary of State, and Carl J. Hambro, President of the Assembly of the League of Nations, gave talks and helped work out a program which was endorsed by the Federal Council of Churches. Their program stressed the "interdependence" of nations and the need for a world organization after the War. (See *Time*, March 14, 1942, pp. 44-48.) I was very impressed by the idealism and internationalist views of these speakers, and the resolutions of the Conference illustrate the broad base of public support that was developing for a world organization.

designed for worldwide membership. Its Security Council can be convened in hours to act on an emergency. There are two major parts of the U.N. System: (1) the U.N. proper, which I refer to as the U.N., and (2) the U.N. Specialized Agencies, which have their own separate charters and secretariats. The major purpose of the U.N., stated in its preamble and Article 1 of its Charter, is to maintain international peace. The most important bodies of the U.N. are the Security Council, patterned after the League Council to maintain peace, the General Assembly, the Secretariat, and the International Court of Justice. Other bodies under the Secretariat include military groups to supervise truces, and organs to carry out social and economic functions. (See Figure 12-1.)

Figure 12-1   The United Nations System

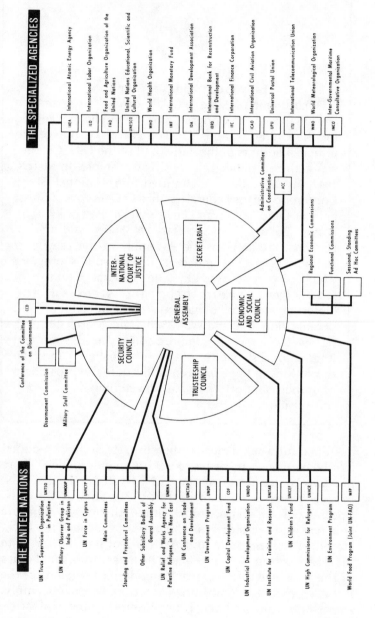

In this chapter we will concentrate on the peacekeeping functions of the Security Council and the General Assembly and on the role of the Secretary General. In Chapter 13 we will examine arms limitation agreements and then in the next chapter analyze the economic and social work of the U.N. and the Specialized Agencies. The Specialized Agencies have their own secretariats, charters, and budgets, but they work closely with the U.N.

The wartime alliance against Germany and Japan was called "The United Nations," and Roosevelt, Churchill, and Stalin originally hoped that it would continue to enforce peace through regional organizations. The United Nations Charter as finally drafted reflected this idea by recognizing regional organizations and by including proposals to put armed forces at the disposal of the Security Council.[7] Chapter VII of the Charter provides for a Military Staff Committee, composed of representatives of the five permanent members (the United States, Russia, Britain, France, and China) to direct armed forces placed at the disposal of the Security Council. To protect the sovereignty of the permanent members any one of the five can veto actions by the Security Council, other than procedural matters and measures for the peaceful settlement of disputes. The Cold War broke out soon after the end of World War II, and the military enforcement units were never formed, although U.N. "peacekeeping" forces have been established outside the above framework, as will be described below.

Often observers conclude the U.N. has failed because it has no powerful military units to enforce its decisions. They are diverted from appreciating the peacemaking accomplishments of the U.N. by the cumbersome political way in which it operates.[8] It is easy to criticize U.N. rhetoric and the time wasted on minor issues. Delays and speeches are an important part of political processes, however, and the U.N. process involves about 150 governments. In fact the U.N. Charter in Chapter VI calls for use of this type of political process as the first step in settling a dispute including "negotiation, inquiry, mediation, conciliation, arbitration, judicial settlement, resort to regional agencies or arrangements, or other peaceful means of their own choice." This process of talks and delay is designed to allow tempers to cool and permit mobilization of world opinion against aggression. It is not designed to avoid the issues.

Article 51 is a key article which states that "Nothing in the Charter shall impair the inherent right of individual or collective self-defense if an armed attack occurs against a Member of the United Nations, until the Security Council has taken measures necessary to maintain international peace and security." Under this article friendly nations and allies can rush to assist a member which is attacked by another nation. This does not authorize intervention in civil wars, however, and Article 2, paragraph 7, states that nothing in the Charter shall authorize the United Nations "to intervene in matters which are essentially within the domestic jurisdiction of any state." The General Assembly in 1974 in order to prevent aggression under a facade of a civil war approved a definition of aggression which included prohibiting a state from sending armed bands across a border to attack another state.

To evaluate the U.N. political process of peacemaking we will first look at the important peacemaking efforts of the 1970s as well as the Korean War, the most highly publicized case. We then will examine the recent major crisis put before the U.N. — the invasion of Afghanistan by Soviet troops — and evaluate its action and lack of action there and in the Vietnam conflicts and Iran-Iraq war.

U.N. Peacekeeping

The three major wars addressed by the U.N. in the 1970s were the India-Pakistan war, the Israel-Arab conflict, and the Cyprus conflict. In each of the crises there was a large area of consensus on U.N. resolutions between the developed and developing countries. This contradicts a popular image that U.N. action is being hindered by bloc voting of the developing countries.

The India-Pakistan War. In December, 1970, the Awami League of East Pakistan won an overwhelming victory in an election in which the major issue was autonomy or independence for East Pakistan. When President Yahya Khan, to avoid partition, postponed convening Pakistan's national assembly, a civil war broke out. The repressive measures of the Pakistan government resulted in hundreds of thousands of deaths and the flight of about 10 million East Pakistan refugees to India. In the following year the Indian Prime Minister, Indira Gandhi, emphasized her concern about the burden of supporting 10 million refugees by public statements and a visit to the United States. The U.N. Secretary General, fearing that war might break out if the refugee problem were not solved, tried to forestall war but could not get the cooperation of Pakistan.

Failing to get a solution to the refugee problem, Indian forces openly joined those of the Bangladesh rebels in East Pakistan. Pakistan, goaded into war, launched a surprise attack on Indian forces on December 4, 1971. At that time I prepared a brief report on the war as a political advisor to the U.S. Air Force. The officials on the Pakistan and Indian desk at the State Department with whom I consulted were pessimistic, realizing that India and Pakistan were historic enemies and fearing the war would escalate into an all-out conflict or that it would lay the basis for continuing conflict in the region.[9] Russia backed India while China issued an official warning to India, which added to tension. The United States dispatched a nuclear aircraft carrier, the Enterprise, into the Bay of Bengal. It was obviously a warning signal to India, although ostensibly it was sent to help evacuate Americans, if necessary. This move made the Indians furious and drew widespread criticism in the United States.

The war was brought before the U.N. Security Council on December 4, 1971. A resolution calling for a cease-fire obtained an 11-2 vote, with only Poland and Russia (India's major supporter) opposing. After further debate the question was passed to the General Assembly. On December 7, it called for a cease-fire by an overwhelming vote of 104 to 11, with only India, Bhutan, and the Communist Bloc opposing. During the next several days the debate continued in the U.N., but on December 16, the West Pakistan army surrendered to the commander of the Indian and Bangladesh forces. The issue by that time was back in the Security Council which adopted by a vote of 13-0, with Poland and the U.S.S.R. abstaining, a resolution calling for a cease-fire and withdrawal of the armed forces to their respective territories as soon as possible. India complied, having crushed the Pakistan forces in East Pakistan and having left the rebel forces in control of what became recognized as a new state of Bangladesh in former East Pakistan.[10]

Observers differ on why Prime Minister Indira Gandhi withdrew Indian forces promptly from Bangladesh. Few Americans give the U.N. action much credit for influencing her decision. Many, after the crisis was over, concluded that her objectives had been limited only to establishing an independent Bangladesh, which could take back the 10 million refugees who had fled to India. Serious doubt was cast on this interpretation, however, by President Nixon's May, 1977, interview with David Frost when the former President said the U.S. "tilt" toward Pakistan and against India in that crisis arose from a "completely reliable" report of Indira Gandhi's cabinet deliberations that India was prepared to attack West Pakistan following the conflict between the two countries in the east.[11] "Completely" reliable implies a transcript or audio tape of the cabinet proceedings. This statement would support some observers' fears at the time that India's objective might have included crushing Pakistan and not only relieving the refugee problem. Significantly, Nixon's and later Kissinger's allegations about the CIA report caused a major political flap in India and were not denied by Mrs. Gandhi.[12]

Other observers have suggested the threats of the great powers noted above influenced Indira Gandhi's decision. However, few if any believed the United States' gesture of sending an aircraft carrier to the region, ostensibly to help evacuate Americans if necessary, had much effect. The United States was reeling from the heavy human and material costs of intervening in the Vietnam War, and there would not have been internal political support for intervening militarily to help Pakistan. Observers did not take China's pro-Pakistan statements very seriously because of the difficulty China would have had in using its military forces in that area far from its base of supplies. Moreover, China was fearful of the Russian threat on China's northern border, and was in the process of opening a detente with the United States because of that fear. One possibility is that Russia, which supported India during the crisis, might have influenced India to exercise restraint. This is supported by President Nixon's and Dr. Kissinger's memoirs.[13]

Why then did Indira Gandhi order a prompt withdrawal before making certain it had a regime installed it could dominate? We may never know for sure unless the story comes out in reliable memoirs, or in another form. I would suggest the U.N. action helped pressure her into such a decision. She must have been impressed by the 104 to 11 vote against her policy in a resolution that demanded prompt withdrawal of Indian forces. This showed that if the war did escalate and perhaps involve major powers, India would have no support except possibly from Russia and its satellites.

In any event, the U.N. performed a remarkable task in assisting resettlement of the 10 million refugees and making a reconciliation possible between India and Pakistan. Although it has received relatively little credit, the U.N. mobilized over $1 billion in aid for the refugees, largely from the United States. Both India and Bangladesh accepted the neutral U.N. presence in this operation. U.N. organs which assisted included the U.N. Relief Operation in Dacca, the U.N. High Commissioner for Refugees, and UNICEF — all under the U.N. Secretary General — the World Health Organization, and other U.N. Specialized Agencies. It would have been impossible to find another organization with the resources of the U.N. to do this task.

Most observers were in despair over the short term and long term prospects arising from the conflict. Few, if any, anticipated the speed with which the conflict was ended and the refugees resettled. Within three years the U.N. organizations were able to terminate their emergency assistance to the refugees.

To sum up, a very difficult political, military, and refugee situation was settled expeditiously with the U.N. playing a major role. Moreover, this was done with a large area of agreement in the U.N. between all elements including the developed and developing countries.

The Arab-Israeli War of 1973. The Arab-Israeli conflict has been a major concern of the United Nations since 1947, when General Assembly approval of a report by the U.N. Special Committee on Palestine played the crucial part in establishing the state of Israel. The background of the 1973 war is in Chapter 9. The initial truce was established as a result of an October 24, 1973, resolution by eight nonaligned members of the Security Council, who authorized a U.N. Emergency Force to separate the combatants. Secretary of State Kissinger played a key role in negotiating the truce, and this would not have been possible without the U.N. forces to supervise it. The overwhelming support by the developing countries for a cease-fire, for a withdrawal of forces, and for financing the peacekeeping forces expressed in Security Council and General Assembly resolutions helped to mobilize U.N. resources. Again, there was unanimity between the developing nations and the developed countries on this pressure for a cease-fire.

The Cyprus Conflict. On July 16, 1974, Secretary General Kurt Waldheim called a Security Council meeting to report on information received through the commander of the U.N. force in Cyprus that a coup had been staged against President Makarios by the Cyprus National Guard, a force set up there by the Greek government. U.N. forces also had been stationed there since 1964 to prevent the Greek and Turkish communities from fighting. On July 20, Turkish forces invaded the island with the announced purpose of protecting the Turkish community on Cyprus. Greek and Turkish forces mobilized, threatening a war between the two nations. During weeks of complicated negotiations the Security Council adopted eight resolutions for a cease-fire, showing a wide area of unanimity between the great powers and developing countries. On November 1, the General Assembly unanimously adopted a resolution supporting the Security Council's action by urging the withdrawal of all foreign armed forces from Cyprus and requesting the Secretary General to continue providing humanitarian assistance. It also authorized him to strengthen peace-keeping forces if necessary.

Diplomats, including Secretary Kissinger of the United States and the Secretary General of the U.N., carried on important collateral negotiations to help settle this conflict. Secretary of State Kissinger received a large part of the credit in the American press, but it should be stressed that the truce would not have been possible without U.N. peacekeeping forces to monitor the truce. In the following years it could easily have been broken without the U.N. Secretary General's help to settle prisoner of war and other difficult issues between the two sides. The situation in 1981 was still unresolved with a *de facto* partition imposed on Cyprus.

The Korean Enforcement Action. On the surface the action by members of the Security Council and the General Assembly to repel the North Korean invasion of South Korea in 1950 was a high point of U.N. enforcement activity coming close to the concept in which forces under a U.N. command would take action by force to restore peace. However, there were certain unique features permitting Security Council action in this crisis that are not likely to occur again.

Korea was divided at the 38th parallel after World War II in a U.S.-Soviet agreement in which the Soviets occupied the North and the United States the South. The United States was not able to reach agreement with the Soviets on unifying Korea, so it submitted the problem to the General Assembly. In line with recommendations of a temporary commission set up by the General Assembly, the United States permitted elections in August, 1948, which established a government in South Korea; a separate government was established in the North. The General Assembly recognized the Republic of Korea as the only legal government on December 12, 1948.[14] The General Assembly did not recognize the government in the North because that government refused to permit United Nations observers for an election to establish a unified government. Both the United States and the Soviet Union in 1949 withdrew their forces in line with General Assembly recommendations.

On June 25, 1950, the United Nations Commission on Korea and the United States Government informed the U.N. Secretary General that North Korean forces had invaded South Korea along the 38th parallel. (See Chapter 9.) President Truman, as soon as he was informed, requested a meeting of the U.N. Security Council. That same day the Security Council voted nine to one that the attack was a breach of the peace and called for withdrawal of the North Korean forces. Under Article

51 of the Charter U.N. members may help others in "collective self defense" against armed attack until the Security Council has taken such action as it deems necessary. By June 27, after a further report from the U.N. Commission on Korea, the Security Council called for support to South Korea by all U.N. members. The Soviet Union was not present at the Security Council meetings to veto the resolutions because it had objected to the attendance of the Republic of China (Taiwan) at the Council instead of the Peoples' Republic of China.

On August 1, the Soviet representative resumed his seat at the Council, but by that time the Security Council had set up a unified U.N. command under the command of the United States Commander — General MacArthur. Military units were provided by 16 member states: Australia, Belgium, Canada, Columbia, Ethiopia, France, Greece, Luxembourg, the Netherlands, New Zealand, the Philippines, Thailand, Turkey, the Union of South Africa, the United Kingdom, and the United States. Five other nations supplied medical units.

On November 30, 1950, the General Assembly, in a "Uniting for Peace" resolution proposed by the United States Secretary of State Dean Acheson, increased U.N. power to act in a crisis. This resolution provided that if the Security Council, because of lack of unanimity of the permanent members failed to exercise its responsibility when there appeared to be aggression, the General Assembly could make recommendations for collective measures including the use of armed forces. The legality of this has been questioned, but on balance it appears not to violate Article 12 of the Charter which only prohibits General Assembly action when the Security Council is exercising its functions in respect to a dispute.

After U.N. forces recouped from the original attack and crossed the 38th parallel into North Korea, about 400,000 Chinese Communist "volunteers" entered the war and drove the U.N. forces back across the 38th parallel. The line was stabilized, after bloody fighting, just north of the original border.

An armistice was signed on July 27, 1953, by the commanders of the U.N. Command, the North Korean forces, and the Chinese Volunteers. There was a further outbreak of hostilities followed by further negotiations at a June, 1954, Geneva Conference with no settlement of the Korean problem as such, but with the armistice remaining in effect.

The Korean War was a dramatic and bloody war. Supporters of the U.N. praise its role in mobilizing U.N. forces to repel aggression. This type of action was close to that envisaged in the Charter. Critics of the U.N., on the other hand, point out the Security Council action was accidental since it would not have occurred without the absence of the Soviet Union. Stalin had encouraged the aggression in the first place (See Chapter 9), and the Russian representative obviously would have vetoed Security Council resolutions and action if he had been present.[15] The rebuttal to this is that the U.S. through the "Uniting for Peace" resolution could have transferred action to the General Assembly, which strongly supported the U.S. position.

The U.N. System in that crisis was flexible enough to permit the United States and many other nations to support South Korea under the U.N. flag and the U.S. command. It opened the door for the General Assembly to take future initiatives of this type when blocked by a Security Council veto, if members had the political will to act.

The Afghanistan-Iranian Crisis. In the middle of the Iranian hostage crisis, described in Chapter 10, Soviet troops in the last week of 1979 invaded Afghanistan and installed as President Babrak Karmal, a Communist leader from Afghanistan who had been exiled by the previous regime to Eastern Europe. About 50,000 Soviet troops entered in the first weeks rising to about 100,000 in later months. Soviet advisors were placed in key positions throughout the government.[16]

The U.N. Security Council met at the request of 52 countries to consider the situation in Afghanistan and its implications for international peace and security. During six meetings of debate it considered a draft resolution sponsored by Bangladesh, Jamaica, Niger, the Philippines, Tunisia, and Zambia calling for the immediate and unconditional withdrawal of all foreign troops. The resolution failed because of the Soviet veto with a vote of 12 in favor and two against including the Soviet veto. During the debate there was bitter condemnation of the Soviet action. On January 9, the Council adopted a procedural resolution calling an emergency special session of the General Assembly, because the veto prevented the Council from exercising its primary responsibility for the maintenance of peace and security. During the General Assembly debates the Soviet invasion was condemned by all speakers except those from the East European Communist Bloc and eight other Communist oriented countries. The General Assembly resolution passed by a vote of 104 for, 18 against, and 18 abstaining.[17] It called for the "immediate, unconditional, and total withdrawal of the foreign troops from Afghanistan." (See box.)

The Soviet invasion challenged the basic principles of the U.N., and the Security Council kept the issue alive after the Soviet veto by transferring action to the General Assembly. Although the condemnation there was overwhelming, the members were not willing to include economic and political sanctions. The unexpressed fear of the delegates that the Soviets would withdraw from the U.N. if the U.N. mounted strict sanctions was probably the major factor limiting the scope of the resolution to a verbal condemnation only.

Meanwhile, the Afghanistan people mounted a massive resistance to the Soviet invaders. Most Moslem countries condemned the Soviets, and news reports indicated that some sent arms to the rebels. In June, 1980, the Soviets acknowledged these pressures by announcing a partial withdrawal of troops and tanks. Whether the Afghanistan resistance and combined pressure of world opinion would ultimately bring about a complete Soviet withdrawal was not clear at the end of 1981. However, the associated power moves of the United States and statements of its NATO allies indicated there would be a much sharper reaction, probably involving military force, if the Soviets moved beyond Afghanistan toward the strategic oil resources of the Middle East or into Pakistan.

To sum up, the U.N. operated at near maximum capacity in the Korean War, and it repeated this activist role in 1961-1965 during the war in the Congo despite varying degrees of opposition from permanent members of the Security Council.[18] During the 1970s the U.N. System operated effectively with support of the five

Excerpt From General Assembly Resolution January 14, 1980

The General Assembly,

Taking note of Security Council Resolution 462(1980) of January 9, 1980, calling for an emergency Special Session of the General Assembly to examine the questions contained in document S/Agenda/2185,

Gravely concerned at the recent developments in Afghanistan and their implications for international peace and security.

Reaffirming the inalienable right of all peoples to determine their own future and to choose their own form of government free from outside interference,

Mindful of the obligations of all States to refrain in their international relations from the threat or use of force against the sovereignty, territorial integrity, and political independence of any State, or in any other manner inconsistent with the purposes and principles of the United Nations,

Recognizing the urgent need for immediate termination of foreign armed intervention in Afghanistan so as to enable its people to determine their own destiny without outside interference or coercion, . . .

1. Reaffirms that respect for the sovereignty, territorial integrity, and political independence of every State is a fundamental principle of the Charter of the United Nations, any violation of which on any pretext whatsoever is contrary to its aims and purposes;

2. Strongly deplores the recent armed intervention in Afghanistan, which is inconsistent with that principle; . . .

4. Calls for the immediate, unconditional, and total withdrawal of the foreign troops from Afghanistan in order to enable its people to determine their own form of government and choose their economic, political, and social systems free from outside intervention, subversion, or coercion or constraint of any kind whatsoever; . . .

7. Requests the Secretary-General to keep Member States and the Security Council promptly and concurrently informed on the progress towards the implementation of the present resolution;

8. Calls upon the Security Council to consider ways and means which could assist in the implementation of this resolution.

permanent members in the major wars in Cyprus and in the 1973 Arab-Israeli War, and also in the India-Pakistan conflict of 1971 despite a veto of the Soviet Union. However, the U.N. played only a belated and peripheral role in the Vietnam conflicts, and by the end of 1980 had not succeeded in obtaining a Soviet withdrawal from its invasion of Afghanistan. The U.N. also failed at least initially to mediate the Iraq-Iran War that broke out in the fall of 1980.

To understand the successful U.N. role in the former conflicts and its lack of decisive action in the latter wars, we must understand that the U.N. is designed for a political role among sovereign nations rather than for a legal or executive role. The U.N. cannot enforce peace among the permanent members of the U.N. although it can help them compromise differences. Similarly it usually acts politically in conflicts involving close allies of the Great Powers. If the antagonists or their Great Power allies do not want U.N. action, the possibilities for U.N. intervention are limited. If two outlaws are fighting, U.N. members may hold back before authorizing U.N. intervention, as long as the conflict does not threaten to spread.

The U.N. was only on the periphery of the Vietnam War, primarily because North Vietnam and the United States did not want U.N. intervention at the outset of the conflict. It was not until January 31, 1966, when the war was well underway, that the U.S. brought the matter before the Security Council, asking it to call a conference to help settle the war. However, Secretary-General U-Thant's suggestions for helping peace negotiations, including cessation of bombing of North Vietnam, were not heeded. Key U.N. members realized the U.S. was not prepared to give up its role of policeman in Southeast Asia; also U-Thant in his report to the U.N. pointed out the absence of North and South Vietnam and of China from the U.N. made it impossible to compromise the conflict. Secretary-General Kurt Waldheim soon after assuming office in April, 1972, offered his good offices to the parties, but they did not accept his offer. In this case the U.N. could not go beyond the wishes of its members and of the antagonists, and it did not intervene.

After North Vietnam's victory the conflicts continued. North Vietnam invaded Kampuchea (Cambodia), and a Soviet veto blocked Security Council action. Five members of the ASEAN members in Southeast Asia brought the issue before the General Assembly, which faced a dilemma. Should it support Pol Pot's government of Kampuchea which had been invaded? That government was a repressive regime reportedly responsible for over a million deaths of its people after the Vietnam War. Or should the General Assembly support the puppet government set up by Vietnam after its invasion? The General Assembly took a legalistic view calling for the withdrawal of foreign troops from Kampuchea and continuing to recognize the repressive Pol Pot's seat in the U.N., rather than recognizing the government set up by aggression. Meanwhile, the U.N. Commission on Human Rights denounced the massive violation of human rights by the Pol Pot Government.[19]

The U.N. faced a similar dilemma in the fall of 1980 when Iraq invaded the southern provinces of Iran with the announced aim of controlling the Shatt-al-Arab waterway with its access to the Persian Gulf. Iraq was an outlaw for initiating the attack. Iran was also an outlaw as noted in Chapter 10, for ignoring resolutions of the Security Council and the General Assembly and orders of the International Court to release the American hostages it was holding. It had also mounted propaganda attacks against the U.N. and neighboring Arab regimes including Iraq. The dilemma of U.N. members not wanting to choose between two outlaws helps explain the U.N.s failure to take decisive action, although it did attempt to mediate the dispute.

To conclude: During the past 10 years the U.N. successfully helped bring about truces in the India-Pakistan conflict, the Arab-Israeli War, and the Cyprus War. The U.S. failed to use the U.N. during the Vietnam War, but the U.S. suffered a humiliating defeat. At the beginning of the 1980s the conflict in Kampuchea was dragging on without successful U.N. intervention but at least the war was not spreading. At the beginning of 1981 Soviet attacks in Afghanistan were continuing despite fierce resistance in Afghanistan and overwhelming U.N. condemnation; this was embarrassing to Russia, and mobilization of world opinion and warnings from the U.S. and other powers helped prevent that conflict from spreading. The U.N. made efforts in the fall of 1980 to settle the Iran-Iraq war while reports indicated some members were not pressing for U.N. intervention hoping the antagonists would tire of their battle. Thus, even where the U.N. was failing to halt wars, its condemnation or disapproval played a part in containing them.

The Secretary General as a Policymaker

The U.N., like the League of Nations, depends on the instructions of its members, and is more of an instrument which they can use for peacekeeping than a superior world organization. Nevertheless, the Secretary General and key members of the Secretariat can take initiatives in a crisis, either under a specific Charter provision or by virtue of not being challenged when they do act. To the extent the Secretary General takes initiatives and Secretariat officials shape the final action, they are performing policymaking functions and the U.N. is acquiring a degree of supranationality.

Under Article 99 of the Charter the Secretary General may bring to the attention of the Security Council any matter which may threaten international peace and security. This article is seldom used, but it does give the Secretary General the prestige to intervene in disputes he or she considers dangerous. The Secretary General has played a major role in helping to settle disputes and wars in many ways not specified in the Charter.

He has a tremendously difficult and complex job. His responsibilities cover many bodies with many functions as can be seen from the left side of Figure 12-1. He frequently attends and sits at the right hand of the Chairmen of important international meetings, including that of the Security Council and General Assembly, and he is expected to be able to offer advice on procedural and substantive matters. He is often brought in to informal meetings to help resolve the critical issues that arise in the formal meetings.

The management job alone is burdensome. He is under constant pressure in filling over 8,000 positions to keep a reasonable balance among the 150 or so nations represented. He has established a standard and unified budget for the many U.N. bodies including the Specialized Agencies. This budget includes not only assessments, but many types of voluntary contributions. The U.N. has been under a financial cloud for many years because of peacekeeping actions in the Congo and the Middle East, which were done without the full financial support of all permanent members of the Security Council, and Russia particularly, so that there has been a chronic shortage of funds. He has had to solicit voluntary contributions and to float loans to cover this deficit. Making the complicated financing arrangements is an essential part of peacekeeping.

He is responsible for the reporting of the Secretariat, which is called on to produce reports and statistics on all aspects of economic and social development as well as on controversial security issues considered by the Security Council. He should keep the confidence of delegates of the many nations and ideologies represented in the U.N., so the U.N. reports are generally bland, but they are also factually sound. Moreover, the reports and records of important meetings and decisions must be produced quickly in the six working languages of the U.N. The reports from U.N. units were a key to U.N. action in the Korea and Middle East crises because they provided on-the-spot accounts uncolored by propaganda.

The most important peacemaking function has been to recruit and manage the peacekeeping forces stationed in Egypt, Syria, Lebanon, and Cyprus and observer units in Pakistan, India, Bangladesh, and other areas. In the 1973 war Secretary General Waldheim mobilized units within 48 hours to separate warring forces.[20]

Secretary General Waldheim was a key figure in mediating the Cyprus dispute, which involves Cypriot political factions, Turkey, Greece, and Great Britain, which has forces stationed on the island. He traveled a great deal to meet with officials and to visit areas where U.N. peacekeeping forces are stationed.

The Secretary General's ability as a policymaker to influence events can be shown by contrasting Lie's and Hammarskjold's actions with those of their successor, U Thant. In the 1967 Middle East crisis Secretary General U Thant was widely criticized for withdrawing U.N. peacekeeping forces from the Sinai on the request of President Nasser. About three weeks after these forces left, the 1967 war broke out. Critics suggested that he could have stalled and perhaps averted the war. Although his defenders would point out in the weeks preceding the pullout the Secretary General had warned the great powers about the dangerous situation, and they did not heed his warnings, nevertheless, the U.N. lost a great deal of prestige as a result of his decision to withdraw.[21] (See Chapter 9.)

The first U.N. Secretary General, Trygve Lie, was so active in policy matters that the Soviet Union, at the end of his term, refused to cooperate with him and ultimately brought about his resignation. Early in 1950 he had challenged the U.S. when he advocated seating the Chinese Communist delegation in the U.N. A few weeks later, however, he had strongly supported the American action under the Charter to mobilize support to repel aggression by North Korea. Reports of U.N. observers under him helped generate overwhelming support in the Security Council and the General Assembly against North Korean aggression and helped turn the Soviets against him.

Secretary General Hammarskjold, also an activist, as a matter of principle tried to gain authority for his initiatives from the Security Council or the General Assembly. At times, however, he took initiatives when the Security Council was deadlocked, which drew fire from permanent members of the Security Council. Particularly during the Congo crisis, when he managed the U.N. forces and tried to achieve order among warring units supported by different Security Council members, he at times offended most of the permanent members. After his action against revolutionary groups in the Congo crisis, the Soviets demanded his resignation, but the General Assembly gave him a vote of confidence of 83 to 11; and he stayed on until his death in a plane crash in the Congo.

The above activities of the Secretary General and of the U.N. Secretariat represent a significant form of supranationalism. Such initiatives, however, require support by the major powers and can easily backfire. The two Secretary Generals since Hammarskjold have not confronted the superpowers on major issues.

The International Court of Justice

The International Court of Justice is the principal judicial organ of the United Nations. Its 15 judges sit at the Hague, as did its predecessor during the era of the League of Nations. The Court has received little attention from the public. Cases are seldom submitted to it, and even when it does make a ruling, the ruling is sometimes ignored. There are no provisions for enforcement of its rulings, and in practice states do not consider themselves bound to submit cases to it. Nevertheless, it rules on about one contentious case a year, and supporters of the court would say that if it has managed to settle even one dispute that could have led to a war, it would have more than justified its existence.

The sources of international law as set forth in Article 38 of the Court's Statute, which is part of the U.N. Charter, are international conventions, international custom, general principles of law, and teachings of highly qualified publicists. The General Assembly has initiated through its International Law Commission, and bodies subsidiary to it, draft studies and law codes for adoption by members of the U.N. The General Assembly has also initiated conferences to draw up codes on matters of international concern. One of the successful ones was the Vienna convention on diplomatic relations, which came into effect in 1964. U.N. bodies began working on a Law of the Sea convention and concluded some initial agreements in the early 1960s. However, these did not settle all the controversial issues, including those of mining and fishing rights, and an international conference continued working on these issues into the 1980s.

The substantive core of international law is its respect for sovereignty of nation states. A corollary of this is its opposition to war. The League of Nations Charter had elaborate provisions for the international community to act against aggressors, the Briand-Kellog Pact of 1928 "outlawed" war, and the U.N. Charter states that its foremost aim is "to save succeeding generations from the scourge of war" and to "maintain international peace and security." The General Assembly on December 14, 1974, reaffirmed these principles and adopted a definition of aggression that included sending of armed bands and irregulars, blockade, and other forceful acts.[22] Realistically the International Court cannot enforce this international law, and the U.N. has had to rely on the peacemaking procedures described above and supportive political action by the international community.

President Carter, in accordance with his internationalist views supporting the United Nations, placed the case of Iran's holding U.S. diplomats as hostages before the Security Council and also before the International Court. Normally the Court is reluctant to rule on cases if both parties do not appear, but in this case Iran's flouting of international law was so flagrant, the Court took the case.

The U.S. Attorney General argued that Iran had violated three diplomatic conventions, including the Vienna convention mentioned above, and a treaty of amity between Iran and the United States. These conventions and the treaty provided for submission of disputes on their provisions to the International Court. The tribunal deliberated for four days and on December 16, 1979, issued a unanimous opinion, including that of the Russian judge, that Iran should immediately release the hostages and return the embassy to U.S. control. "There is no more fundamental requirement than the inviolability of diplomatic envoys," said the Court's president, Sir Humphrey Waldock of Great Britain. Although the Court had no enforcement machinery, its clear and unambiguous ruling gave political backing to the United States in rallying support from other U.N. members to put pressure on Iran to return the hostages to the United States.

The Court, just like the U.N. itself, depends on political support from U.N. members. Its action in the Iranian case indicated that the Court is available, and that its lack of use has not been due to a weakness of the institution so much as to the weakness of the will of sovereign nations to submit cases to it for judgment.

Negotiation Versus Enforcement

Although the action of the Security Council and the General Assembly in the Korean crisis was more dramatic and forthright than U.N. action on wars of the 1970s, which were discussed above, this does not diminish the relative worth of the U.N. machinery in these later crises. Ending the three wars of the 1970s quickly was not as exciting as mobilizing forces to fight the Korean War, but perhaps the successes of the 1970s deserve more praise. Quick truces were arranged in the 1970s before large scale casualties occurred. The U.N. machinery registered an overwhelming majority of nations disapproving of the conflicts. Major powers used bilateral diplomacy to reinforce the U.N. resolutions. It is true, however, in the Korean conflict of 1950 the North Korean leaders probably would have paid little attention to such disapproval and were more impressed with military action.

The effectiveness of negotiations under the U.N. could be measured if it could be determined what influenced the leaders involved to stop the fighting. Indira Gandhi has not written her memoirs, and there is little on the record about her personal views on the 1971 war. Prime Minister Golda Meir in her memoirs admits frankly it was U.S. pressure and the fact the United States was Israel's only friend in the 1973 war that brought about an early ceasefire.[23] President Sadat was apparently ready to quit. His forces were surrounded and his objective, he claims, was achieved: that is to demonstrate Egypt's ability to fight to regain lost territory.[24] In the Cyprus crisis, Greek and Turkish leaders were subject to strong pressure and persuasion from the United States, Britain, and other NATO allies.

Registering of the overwhelming disapproval by U.N. delegates weighs heavily in such war and peace issues. President Sadat claimed that his December, 1977, initiative to visit Jerusalem grew out of pressure from his people and others for peace. The votes of the Security Council and the General Assembly gave a good reflection of the views of the world community on conflicts, and they served as a warning of lack of support or at least as a face saving device to help persuade him to bring the war to an end.

The U.N. normally does not receive much credit from reporters, particularly those of the United States. They mostly see only debates and resolutions. Talk is less exciting than confrontations, and when the U.N. is successful, it avoids the big news stories and crises of bilateral diplomacy. The travel of national leaders from one capital to another gets the headlines and the TV coverage, whereas the quiet trips of the U.N. Secretary General receive much less attention, although he has played an important part in settling disputes mentioned above.

Although the American news media give relatively little attention to the United Nations, the U.N. peacekeeping efforts receive widespread political and financial support from many other countries. The process is economical. The United States, for example, has spent $3,000 on its own military budget for every $1 it has spent in supporting U.N. peacekeeping operations since 1970.

The U.N. in the above crises provided a forum and the machinery to settle disputes and mobilize pressure against aggressors. I would suggest, as a minority view, that the U.N. has moved since the 1965 Mideast crisis toward the middle of a continuum, between the conference machinery and world government terminals. Most observers would probably place it nearer to the conference machinery side than I would, in part because they attach less importance to the results the U.N. has obtained from opinion registered by governments and by other non-military measures.

Strengthening the U.N. process of peacemaking would require a sustained commitment by the United States and other major powers, as well as a willingness of national leaders to risk letting others, including the Secretary General exercise initiatives. President Carter seemed included to rely on the U.N. more than President Reagan. At the end of 1979 in the crises over U.N. hostages held in Iran and the Soviet invasion of Afghanistan, Carter supported Security Council meetings on these issues, and he referred the hostage issue to the International Court. He also agreed to the Secretary General attempting to mediate in Iran. President Carter paralleled this by strong statements and by movements of U.S. military forces into the Persian Gulf area. The action in the U.N., the power moves, and statements of support from European allies demonstrated that world powers and the U.N. would not stand idly by if the Soviets threatened Iran and the highly strategic oil reserves of that area.

In a world of sovereign nations peace depends on convincing a potential aggressor to desist. The slow and undramatic process of debate and delay such as occurred in the India-Pakistan War, the Mideast, and the Cyprus wars was educational for those involved. It permitted the pressures of world opinion to help convince policymakers and leaders to stop conflicts or at least to keep them contained. The precedents of these peacemaking efforts is a major hope for avoiding major wars among sovereign nations.

Summary

The major purpose of the U.N. as stated in its Charter is to maintain international peace and security. The U.N. Charter was designed to be stronger than the League of Nations Covenant by having regular armed units at the U.N.'s disposal, but this was never implemented because of the frictions of the Cold War.

In this decade the U.N. provided a forum to register world demands to end the India-Pakistan War, the Arab-Israeli War of 1973, and the Cyprus conflict of 1974. U.N. resolutions backed by both developed and developing nations, and by Communist and non-Communist nations helped persuade leaders of warring nations to end the fighting. Although U.N. discussion and police action were not so dramatic as combat of U.N. troops in the Korean War, these wars of the 1970s were ended quickly with relatively few casualties.

The important limits to U.N. action have been illustrated again in the Afghanistan invasion when one of the major powers vetoed the Security Council resolution, but the U.N. Security Council and General Assembly did register overwhelming condemnation of the action and provided a political basis for economic and political sanctions outside the U.N. These actions plus collateral power moves of the United States and its allies were designed to deter further aggression and encourage Russian withdrawal from Afghanistan. Similarly the U.N. disapproval of Iran's holding American hostages and sanctions against Iran may have had a major impact on Iran's leaders. These actions did not satisfy power brokers who demanded quick, forceful solutions.

The U.N. Secretary General plays an important role in peacemaking, particularly in commanding peacekeeping forces. The International Court has played a relatively minor role in world crises.

In the peacekeeping process the U.N. has been acquiring more authority and starting to move along a continuum from being merely a forum toward obtaining authority of a world government organization.

FOOTNOTES

1. See for example the classic studies of World War I: Sidney Fay, *The Origins of the World War* (New York: MacMillan, 1933); Luigi Albertini, *The Origins of the War of 1914* (London: Oxford University Press, 1952); and Barbara Tuchman, *The Guns of August* (New York: MacMillan, 1962).

2. Charles Seymour, *The Intimate Papers of Colonel House* (Boston: Houghton Mifflin Company, 1938), Volume 4, Chapter 1.

3. *Ibid.*, p. 18.

4. Cordell Hull, *The Memoirs of Cordell Hull* (New York: The MacMillan Company, 1948), Part Eight, pages 1625-1648. Dr. Leo Pasvolsky, Special Assistant to Secretary Hull, and a group of other State Department policymakers prepared the draft in consultation with the committee. He and other public leaders actively promoted the idea of the world organization during the war. Edward Stetinius, Secretary of State during the San Francisco Conference, also claims credit for helping found the United Nations, but in my view Secretary Hull, President Roosevelt, President Truman, Dr. Leo Pasvolsky, and Senator Vandenberg are the policymakers who deserve the principal credit for the American participation. See also Thomas C. Campbell and George C. Herring, *The Diaries of Edward R. Stetinius, Jr.* (New York: New Viewpoints, 1975).

5. Harry S. Truman, *Memoirs by Harry S. Truman* (Garden City, N.J.: Doubleday and Company, 1955). Chapter 2.

6. Dean Acheson, *Present at the Creation* (New York: W.W. Norton & Company, 1969), pp. 38 and 111.

7. *Everyone's United Nations* (New York: U.N. Office of Public Information) plus the *U.N. Chronicle* are excellent initial sources for details on U.N. actions such as votes and texts of resolutions. Also, the annual *U.S. Participation in the U.N.* report by the U.S. State Department gives details on action in the many U.N. organizations and on the U.S. role. To get more detailed U.N. reports one should check with the reference librarian.

8. Ralph B. Levering, *The Public and American Foreign Policy 1918-1978* (New York: William Morrow and Company, 1978), pp. 160-161.

9. See, for example, "Brinkwomanship," *Economist* (London), December 4, 1971, pp. 13-14; "Into the Net," *Economist,* December 11, 1971, pp. 11-13; "Carry on Fighting," *Far Eastern Economic Review,* December 11, 1971, p. 3; T.J.S. George, "Can Mujib Survive Victory?" *FEER,* December 11, 1971, p. 5; "Holy War Boosts Morale," *Ibid.;* "Armageddon Awaits," *Ibid.,* p. 6; A. Hariharan, "Nixon: Not so Much Pro-Pakistan as Anti-India," *FEER,* December 25, 1971, p. 6; Michael Malloy, "Indira: An Armed Bid for Hegemony," *Ibid.,* p. 7; *Newsweek,*

December 13, 1971, pp. 39-40; and *Newsweek,* December 20, 1971, pp. 34-38.

10. Robert Victor Jackson, *South Asian Crisis: India, Pakistan, Bangladesh* (Praeger: New York, 1975).

11. Richard M. Nixon, *R.N. — The Memoirs of Richard Nixon* (New York: Grosset and Dunlop. 1978), pp. 525-531, and Kissinger, *op. cit.,* pp. 901-913.

12. *Hindustan Times,* November 29, 1979, p. 1.

13. Nixon, *op. cit.,* pp. 901-913.

14. The Soviet Union, however, vetoed the admission of South Korea to the U.N.

15. The Security Council actions to mobilize support were probably illegal under a strict interpretation of the Charter. Article 27 requires the affirmative vote of the five permanent members on non-procedural matters, and the Russians probably thought their absence would amount to a veto. Although technically illegal under such an interpretation, the actions were consistent with the major aims of the Charter to repel aggression, and the Council has accepted the practice of requiring a country to vote no to exercise a veto.

16. *Washington Post,* January 2, 1980, pp. A 1-A 2, and January, 25, p. A 20.

17. *U.N. Chronicle,* March, 1980, pp. 5-17.

18. *Everyone's United Nations* (New York: United Nations Publication, 1979), has brief summaries of U.N. actions in the Congo conflict and other conflicts.

19. *New York Times,* April 5, 1980.

20. Indar Rikhye, *The Thin Blue Line* (New Haven, Conn.: Yale University Press, 1974).

21. Arthur Lall, *The U.N. and the Middle East Crisis of 1967* (New York: Columbia University Press, 1970).

22. For text of General Assembly Resolution see *U.N. Monthly Chronicle,* May, 1974, pp. 86-89.

23. Golda Meir, *My Life* (New York: G.P. Putnam's Sons, 1975), Chapter 14.

24. Interview with NBC, December 2, 1977.

13

Arms Limitation Agreements

One of the major achievements of the U.N. System has been to encourage arms limitation agreements. About a dozen agreements for limiting nuclear weapons and controlling crises were either begun by U.N. organs or have been negotiated in the U.N. system. The media and other observers tended to overlook most of these agreements, in part because the media focused on the more dramatic SALT talks, which involve only the United States and Russia. Even in these SALT talks, however, the two superpowers acknowledged their obligation under the U.N. Non-Proliferation Treaty to pursue such talks in good faith. We will evaluate these agreements and particularly the "good faith" aspects. (See Figure 13-1.)

Another part of the public apathy about the arms limitation agreements, particularly among the younger generation, is due to the lack of active civil defense and public education programs about these weapons. This is not surprising because most public officials and experts accept the fact that there is no feasible defense against nuclear weapons. For the older generation the lack of interest may reflect a callousness resulting from living with the nuclear threat for so long. However, the leaders who are burdened with the terrible responsibility of command over nuclear weapons seem awed and anxious to control them, more so than lower levels of experts and legislators who bargain and debate over details of the agreements.

The dimensions of the nuclear threat are awesome. The Soviet Union with one rocket could cause "near total destruction" of Washington, D.C., and all suburbs within a radius of 12 miles. One U.S. submarine with its rockets carries enough nuclear power to devastate every city in the Soviet Union with a population of over 150,000.[1] In 1979 the United States had 9,500 strategic nuclear warheads, any one of which could destroy a major part of a large Russian city. The Soviet Union was catching up in numbers with an estimated 8,200 strategic warheads.[2] Approximately 200 city areas in the United States and about 400 cities in the Soviet Union contain over half the population of these nations. The present stocks of warheads, even assuming many missiles miss their targets, could in a surprise attack immediately destroy most of the population of the other superpower many times over. Even more terrible to contemplate is the fallout from a major nuclear war which could kill many more people or, as some scientists estimate, fatally contaminate the northern hemisphere and fatally upset the world's environmental balance through destruction of the ozone layer that protects the earth from the sun.[3] Nevertheless, the race to develop more powerful warheads continues.

In addition to the above threat, in 1975 the United States had about 7,000 tactical nuclear warheads in Europe (in addition to the 9,500 strategic warheads). The average power of each U.S. "tactical" warhead reportedly greatly exceeded that of the weapon that destroyed Hiroshima.[4] A 1967 United Nations study by 12 recognized world experts reported that if several hundred of the tactical weapons were used against military targets in Central Europe, including targets such as rail centers, the effect would be no different than a major nuclear war with strategic weapons in which millions of people would be killed.[5]

Secretary of State Kissinger in answer to a reporter's asking if the United States was falling behind the Russians in the arms race, exclaimed, "One of the questions we have to ask ourselves as a country is: What in the name of God is strategic superiority? What is the significance of it? What do you do with it?"[6]

The SALT Agreements

In the latter part of 1968 President Johnson made a strenuous effort to get strategic arms limitation talks started with the Russians.[7] He announced at the signing of the U.N. Treaty on Nuclear Non-Proliferation (NPT) on July 1, 1968, that Russia and the United States had agreed to enter discussions on limiting strategic arms in the near future. The Soviets considered the NPT a precondition of SALT negotiations, and Soviet SALT negotiators stressed that the Germans in particular must not have access to nuclear weapons.[8]

Article VI of the NPT commits the parties to pursue negotiations on ceasing the arms race at an early date. The Russian invasion of Czechoslovakia in 1968, however, offended U.S. opinion, and President Johnson decided to postpone the talks. Several months later in November, 1968, the Russian Ambassador to the United Nations announced his government was ready to begin the talks, but at that point President-elect Nixon discouraged President Johnson from opening negotiations just before President Nixon would assume office. On the day Nixon took office the Soviet Foreign Minister again indicated the Soviets were willing to begin discussions.

The formal negotiations began in November, 1969, in Helsinki, Finland, alternating in Geneva,[9] and they were finally transferred entirely to Geneva. There were heated bureaucratic battles in preparing the U.S. positions for the SALT talks, and during the negotiations Henry Kissinger, the President's Advisor on National Security Affairs, took control of the discussions by instituting a highly secret series of negotiations with Brezhnev parallel to the formal negotiations between delegations in Geneva.

Secretary Kissinger saw the SALT process as an essential part of detente between the two superpowers that should be linked to other issues. Other United States spokesmen referred to SALT as a process, implying that a major aim was to continue discussions on new agreements as a way to lessen the chance of confrontation and conflict.

President Nixon and Chairman Brezhnev signed the first SALT agreements in Moscow on May 26, 1972, at a summit meeting. There were two major parts — "interim" agreements limiting the number of long range missiles, not including those in bombers, and an Anti-Ballistic Missile (ABM) Treaty. The interim SALT I Agreement was approved overwhelmingly in a joint Senate-House resolution and the ABM Treaty by a similar vote, with only two in opposition. The Supreme Soviet of the U.S.S.R. ratified for the Russians.

Table 13-1 sets forth a summary of the agreements. The ceilings and subceilings are complicated, but only in terms of elementary arithmetic, not higher math. Under SALT I the United States was limited to a total of 1,710 intercontinental missiles (ICBMs) and sea-launched ballistic missiles (SLBMs) with an option to substitute new submarine missiles for old land missiles. The Soviets had a higher ceiling of 2,358 ICBMs and SLBMs with an option for a similar substitution. Opponents of the agreements attacked them on the basis they allowed the Soviet Union more and bigger missiles. Defenders pointed out that the United States had more warheads on bombers and on multiple independently targeted reentry vehicles (MIRVs) with a higher destructive power. Bombers and MIRVs were not covered by SALT I. Moreover, the U.S. submarines were quieter and harder to detect, and the submarine missiles had a longer range. SALT II is discussed below.

A technological breakthrough that permitted conclusion of the agreements involved satellite photography which can capture details of missile silo construction, the missiles themselves, and submarine construction.[10] This is called monitoring by "national means," and the agreements specified that Russia and the United States should not attempt to interfere with this process. This finesses the difficult problem of on-site

Table 13-1 The Strategic Arms Balance, 1979

	United States		Either Side		Soviet Union	
	Allowed by 1972 SALT	Actual End of 1978	Vladivostok Agreement	SALT II Treaty	Allowed by 1972 SALT	Actual End of 1978
ICBMs	1054 or 1000*	1054			1618 or 1408*	1,398
SLBMs	710†	656			950†	950
Bombers	(not covered)	574				156
Total	1,710	2,284	2400	2,250 (by 1981)	2,358	2,504
(Subceilings)						
MIRV weapons and airplanes with missiles			(1320)	(1320)		
(Subceilings)						
MIRV Ballistic Missiles		—		(1200)		—
Land-based Ballistic Missiles with MIRVs				(820)		
Russian Heavy Ballistic Missiles				(308)		—
Actual Missiles in 1979		Approx. 9,500				8,200

*The U.S. could trade in 54 older land-based ICBMs, and the Soviets 210 ICBMs for newer submarine-based missiles. The Soviet Union is allowed 62 modern ballistic missiles submarines while the United States is allowed 44.
†These levels are allowed if the ICBMs are dismantled as indicated above.
Source: The SALT II Agreement, United States Department of State, Document No. 12A, June 18, 1979.

inspection to check ceilings. Military authorities, and particularly the Russians, have opposed letting foreigners inspect their most highly advanced weapons systems.

The other major part of the SALT agreements was a treaty limiting each country's defensive system to two anti-ballistic missile (ABM) sites. An alleged purpose of this limitation was to deter both sides from an initial nuclear attack by leaving almost all of an aggressor's population and land-based missiles unprotected by ABMs, a policy of mutual assured destruction or "MAD." This also was a recognition that it is impossible to develop an ABM system that would be effective against thousands of incoming rockets. Moreover, defense would be futile since both the Soviet Union and the United States have developed submarines which could launch nuclear missiles from many directions which could destroy enemy cities, even if the defense could destroy incoming intercontinental missiles launched from enemy land sites.

In November, 1974, President Ford met with General Secretary Brezhnev in Vladivostok, and they agreed orally on the framework for negotiating a further SALT agreement to limit the number of strategic nuclear weapons and delivery vehicles through 1985. The explanation to the press indicated that such an agreement would, for the first time, include ceilings on long-range heavy bombers and on the number of missiles with MIRVs. Subsequent explanations indicated that satellites would be used to detect testing of missiles, which would permit the United States and the Soviet Union to keep track of the number of MIRV-potential missiles and warheads being tested. A test of a certain type of missile with a MIRV would result in an assumption this type of missile was MIRVed, and it would be counted as such.

By the beginning of 1978 the Soviet Union and the United States negotiators had agreed on an outline of a new SALT agreement, which would be in the form of a more permanent "treaty" lasting until 1985 rather than an "interim" agreement. Officials briefed the press on progress in the talks, which was a change from the previous negotiations which had started out in deep secrecy and which had leaked to the press.

The SALT II Agreement, which was presented to the Senate by President Carter on June 22, 1979, set an overall ceiling on strategic nuclear delivery systems at 2,250 for the end of 1981, including non-MIRVed missiles and bombers without cruise missiles. There were subceilings, but the treaty permitted substitution of submarines, bombers, and ICBMs within these ceilings. (Table 13-1.)

Supporters of the treaty stressed the treaty required Russia to reduce strategic offensive arms to 2,250 by the end of 1981, that it limited the number of MIRV warheads, that it provided for non-interference with verification, and above all that it provided for continued negotiations to limit nuclear weapons. Supporters also said the treaty did not require the United States to change plans to develop weapons like the cruise missile or mobile MX ICBM which, subject to verification, could be substituted for other weapons under the treaty. Opponents said it did not go far enough in limiting nuclear weapons, that it legalized a dangerous Soviet superiority in weapons after it MIRVed its heavy missiles, and that verification provisions were not adequate. After the invasion of Afghanistan by Russia at the end of 1979, President Carter and Senate leaders postponed Senate debate on the treaty. He indicated, however, he intended to abide by the draft treaty as long as the Soviets acted with similar restraint.[11] The Soviets by notifying the U.S. of nuclear tests gave a similar indication. Thus, during 1980 SALT II was in effect without formal ratification. Moreover, during the 1980 campaign Governor Reagan criticized the SALT II Treaty and pledged to reopen negotiations if he were elected. In November, 1981, President Reagan proposed that the U.S. and the Soviets eliminate mid-range nuclear missiles in Europe, and he confirmed opening of new strategic arms reduction talks (START) in early 1982. Significantly, his actions in 1981 resulted in continuing observance of SALT II by Russia and the U.S., although the treaty had not been ratified.

Other related agreements already approved by the U.S. and Russia under the SALT process included the following:

1. In 1976 the Ford Administration submitted a treaty to the Senate that would limit nuclear tests underground to 150 kilotons or less. Although the

Senate did not act on the treaty, both the United States and the Soviet Union have treated it as binding.[12]

2. Another agreement providing for controls on peaceful nuclear explosions was signed on May 28, 1976, and submitted to the U.S. Senate, but had not been approved by the fall of 1981.

3. A Protocol to the original ABM Treaty came into force May 24, 1976, limiting ABM systems to one rather than two sites. The United States subsequently deactivated all but the radar part of its one ABM emplacement near Grand Forks, North Dakota, in recognition of the impracticality of the systems.

4. The Hot Line Agreements of 1963 and 1971 established a quick and secure communications link between the President of the United States and Moscow.

5. During Secretary Brezhnev's visit to the United States on June 22, 1973, he and President Nixon signed an executive agreement that their objective was to avoid nuclear war and the use of nuclear weapons, with a provision to consult in a nuclear confrontation.

Nuclear Non-Proliferation Treaty and Other Treaties

Problems of preventing non-nuclear powers from developing nuclear weapons concerns policymakers about as much as the nuclear arms race between Russia and the United States. As noted above, Russia began the SALT talks on the condition that Germany should not obtain nuclear weapons. President Carter indicated his great concern with the non-proliferation problem by trying to get congressional and international agreement not to use plutonium as a fuel for power plants because of the opportunities it might give to other countries and terrorist groups to obtain weapons material.

The Nuclear Non-Proliferation Treaty (NPT). The NPT originated in an Irish resolution in the General Assembly which was approved unanimously on

December 4, 1961. The Treaty itself was negotiated in the
U.N. Eighteen-Nation Committee on Disarmament in
Geneva. The negotiations depended on agreement among
the nuclear powers, since a key provision was that they
should not share their nuclear weapons technology. It
came into effect in 1970 when 40 states signed it in
addition to the United States, the United Kingdom, and
Russia. China, France, and a number of other countries
have not signed it including Israel, Egypt, the Union of
South Africa, Pakistan, Brazil, Taiwan, and South Korea.
By 1981 about 114 states had approved it.

Most non-nuclear states insisted as a condition of their
approval of the Treaty that the nuclear powers commit
themselves to reduce their nuclear arsenals and to press
forward with general measures of disarmament. In
addition many of the non-nuclear states insisted on a
security guarantee. This was accomplished by a U.N.
Security Council Resolution of June 19, 1968, recognizing
the Security Council would have to act immediately in
accordance with U.N. obligations in the event of a nuclear
threat against non-nuclear powers and welcoming the
expressions of support by the United States, Russia, and
the United Kingdom for the victim of such an act or threat
of aggression. (Articles 2 and 3.)[13]

The 1963 Partial Test Ban Treaty. The Treaty
Banning Nuclear Weapons Tests in the Atmosphere, in
Outer Space, and Under Water (Partial Test Ban Treaty)
took about eight years of agitation in the General
Assembly and in the world media before the superpowers,
and particularly the United States, could be brought
around to accept it. "No arms control measure — prior to
SALT, in any event — enlisted so intensely the sustained
interest of the international community."[14] Pressure
mounted when the U.S. exploded in 1954 a test bomb
about 600 times the yield of the Hiroshima bomb. The
crew of a Japanese fishing vessel, *The Lucky Dragon,* 80
miles from the Bikini blast was caught in the fallout and
severely blistered. One of the fishermen died from the
fallout. The lethal area for the fallout extended 120 miles
downwind. Some of the contaminated fish from the boat
were sold before the Japanese government could stop the
sales, which caused a wave of panic. Many Japanese
people temporarily stopped eating fish and demanded a
ban on atomic weapons.[15]

Figure 13-1   Arms Limitation Agreements

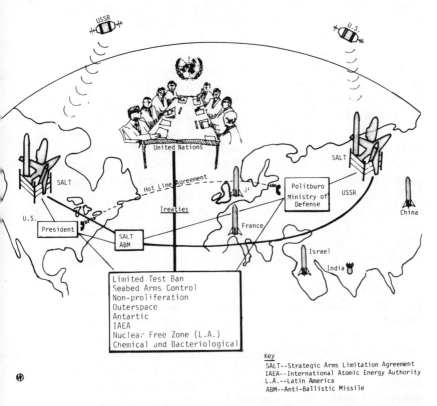

Key
SALT--Strategic Arms Limitation Agreement
IAEA--International Atomic Energy Authority
L.A.--Latin America
ABM--Anti-Ballistic Missile

In 1955 the Soviet Union proposed a test ban as part of a plan to reduce armaments. The General Assembly year after year by overwhelming majorities advocated test bans. The Soviet Union claimed that existing technology could permit monitoring of the tests, but the Western countries alleged they were not convinced this was adequate. Moreover, U.S. policymakers of the Atomic Energy Commission claimed it was necessary to continue to develop nuclear weapons "which are so essential to our freedom and actual survival."[16] At one point after the Soviet Union agreed to inspection posts, a group of international experts recommended 180 inspection posts; the American government then demanded 6,000 noting that its tests showed underground explosions were very difficult to detect.

After Khrushchev agreed to a partial ban which would permit underground tests, rather than a complete test ban, President Kennedy selected Averill Harriman, a man of vast experience including that of Ambassador to Moscow at the close of World War II, to head the negotiations. He and a British colleague completed the negotiations in 10 days, and two months later the U.S. Senate had approved the Treaty by a vote of 80 to 19. Most of the world's nations quickly added their approval. France, and particularly Communist China, attacked the Treaty. The Chinese were bitter because one of the provisions prevented a party to the Treaty from assisting others in testing, which foreclosed Soviet nuclear assistance to China. By 1980 over 100 members of the U.N. had signed or acceded to the Treaty.

Although the partial test ban Treaty originated in a popular fear of fallout, the Treaty is significant from the arms limitation viewpoint, because it limits testing of new weapons. It is not feasible to develop reliable weapons without testing.

The parties to the Treaty undertake not to carry out any nuclear explosion in the atmosphere, under water or in outer space, or in any environment where the debris would go beyond the borders of the state conducting the explosion. Thus, the treaty permitted underground tests to continue if radioactive dust did not get carried to another state, and the United States and the Soviet Union continued active programs of underground testing. The Treaty is of unlimited duration.

Since 1968, periodic discussions have continued to try to prohibit all nuclear tests. As part of the SALT negotiations the United States and the Soviet Union agreed to ending tests above 150 kilotons, and in November, 1977, started negotiating in the U.N. to ban all nuclear weapons tests.

The International Atomic Energy Agency (IAEA). The International Atomic Energy Agency had its origin in President Eisenhower's address to the General Assembly of December 8, 1953, in which he suggested a world organization devoted to the peaceful uses of atomic energy. Three years later its statute had been negotiated and approved at a special U.N. Conference in New York and signed by 80 nations. It came into existence on July 29, 1957.

In the first years of its existence the IAEA mainly assisted in establishing research reactors and technical assistance in isotope research. With the signing of the Nuclear Non-Proliferation Treaty, however, the IAEA was assigned the key task of monitoring the use of fissionable material in nuclear installations in order to prevent diversion to weapons. This involved stationing inspectors on the territory of states with nuclear plants and giving them the right to make complete inspections of physical facilities and plant records. Diversions are to be brought to the attention of the U.N. Security Council for appropriate action. In a fundamental sense this process represents a yielding of a portion of a state's sovereignty to the IAEA inspectors.

Non-nuclear states were concerned that the IAEA safeguards might place them at a commercial disadvantage, so the United States agreed in 1967 to place all nuclear facilities in the United States under IAEA safeguards excluding only those with "direct national security significance." The United Kingdom also agreed to this, but the Soviet Union did not.

The IAEA is essential to international security through helping control commerce in radioactive materials. For example, thousands of pounds of plutonium are created annually in peaceful nuclear power plants. This incredibly poisonous substance when enriched can be used to develop nuclear weapons. If a terrorist group should gain control of a few pounds of it and manufacture a nuclear weapon, the group could have a powerful blackmailing capability against any country. One weapon detonated in a major city of the United States could kill a million people in the worst single catastrophe in history.

Other Arms Limitation Agreements. The following listing of other major arms limitation agreements gives perspective on the extent of the network and the widespread acceptance by nations of the need to try to control the terrible technology of war.

1. The Geneva Protocol to Prohibit the Use of Poison Gas and Bacteriological Warfare is the only holdover from the League of Nations in the list. The Geneva agreement was not approved by the U.S. Senate until 1975 — 50 years after it was negotiated. In addition President Ford ratified a convention on January 22,

1975, to prohibit production of bacteriological weapons. A basic problem with the convention is that an inspection system is not feasible, since such weapons can be made in a small room converted to a laboratory. The Treaty depends on the good faith of the signers, although a country violating its provisions would risk losing its credibility for all arms limitation agreements if a key scientist defected and reported a violation. About 115 countries have acceded to the Treaty.

2. The Anarctic Treaty of June 23, 1961, demilitarized the Anarctic Continent. A unique provision agreed to by the 19 interested countries, including the Soviet Union, is that any installation there must be open for inspection by any of the parties.

3. The Treaty on Outer Space of 1967 began with a Soviet initiative in 1962, and the General Assembly approved it by acclamation in 1963 and 1966. It prohibits a country from placing weapons of mass destruction in orbit or in outer space.

4. The Treaty to Prohibit Nuclear Weapons in Latin America provides for a nuclear free zone in the countries ratifying the Treaty. The nuclear powers have ratified the Protocol which commits parties not to introduce nuclear weapons into the nuclear free zone established by the Treaty. Cuba and Argentina have not yet ratified the Treaty, and Brazil held up final action to make its ratification dependent on Argentina's approval.

5. The Treaty to Prevent Emplacement of Nuclear Weapons on the Seabed came into effect on May 18, 1972. The initiative, started by Ambassador Arvo Pardo from Malta in 1967 in the U.N., was consummated in 1972. As a result of the Treaty, five-sevenths of the earth's surface is free of emplaced nuclear weapons. At the end of 1977 88 countries had signed the Treaty, but not the nuclear powers China and France.

Compliance Versus Cheating

As we have noted, the common pattern in arms limitation agreements is for spokesmen of small nations to get endorsement in the General Assembly of action in certain areas of arms control. Then the major nuclear powers usually spar for years and finally reach agreement on major issues. The other countries then fall into line and an agreement is concluded. France and China seldom adhere to the agreements not wishing to have their national sovereignty impaired.

The ratification process is slow, involving in the case of the democracies, approval by the parliaments. It is helpful in understanding nuclear weapons policy and pressures for compliance to look at the other policymaking levels which are involved. The decision on the use of the weapons is entrusted to the head of state or at most a very small group of officials. In the United States the President as Commander in Chief controls their use. For the Soviet Union it appears to be the General Secretary of the Communist Party, and possibly a small group in the Politburo including the Minister of Defense and possibly the KGB; for the United Kingdom it is the Prime Minister consulting with his Cabinet if possible; in France it is the President consulting with the Premier and Cabinet if possible; and in China before his death it would have been Mao Tse-tung, Chairman of the Central Committee and possibly a small group of the Military Commission under the Politburo.[17] Precise information is impossible to get because it is a highly secret matter, but is clear that the top governmental leaders keep a tight control on these awesome weapons.

Below these few top leaders of the superpowers is the military establishment which controlled the design, manufacture, and deployment of the highly complex nuclear warheads and their delivery vehicles. These weapons are at the frontiers of nuclear and engineering technology. They include highly complex computers for the weapons systems, rocket propulsion, nuclear technology for fission and fusion, and nuclear power units for submarines.

Many military officers who control this process are highly motivated — they are willing to give their life for their country — but they are also highly demanding for financing new weapons systems. The U.S. Army has a weapon that travels 8,000 miles with an accuracy less than one mile and 50-100 times the strength of the weapon that destroyed Hiroshima. Nevertheless, it has been spending billions to increase the accuracy and put multiple warheads on the missile, each with the strength of many times the Hiroshima weapon. The U.S. Navy is spending billions to increase the range and strength of its nuclear submarines each with 16 nuclear missiles, which now have multiple warheads, some of which can be fired over 3,000 miles. The Air Force is still testing the B-1 supersonic stratospheric bomber that starts in the stratosphere and then comes down close to ground level to penetrate the antiaircraft defense.

The original purpose of developing weapons systems for a reasonable deterrent has become immersed in politics and competition among the Army, Navy, and Air Force to promote their own strategic weapons systems. The deterrent has long passed the point of strength to bring about world disaster. The policy of letting each of the three military services develop strategic missiles has been sold with the image of the "Triad" — three effective, invulnerable delivery systems.

The maxim of General George C. Marshall, U.S. Chief of Staff during World War II about the military is revealing — always give them half of what they are asking and double their missions.[18] The warning of General Dwight Eisenhower, Supreme Allied Commander, is also often quoted where he warns against powerful lobbies of the "military industrial complex" that "spring up to argue for even larger munitions expenditures. And the web of special interest grows."[19]

The large constituencies of military establishments in democracies must also be recognized in considering the problems of limiting and controlling nuclear weapons. They include not only millions of military personnel, but also the many contractors, the hundreds of thousands of workers making the weapons, as well as congressional supporters who have military bases in their districts and have come to believe that the United States must stay ahead or at least not get behind in the arms race to maintain its security.

The third level of policymaking is the civilian arms control experts and diplomats who want to create a network of agreements to limit the arms race and thus lessen tensions that could lead to war. They have no enthusiastic constituency; the diplomats need the leadership of a strong president or secretary of state to convince the defense establishment and its supporters. Thus, heads of state such as John Kennedy, Chairman Khrushchev, Presidents Johnson and Nixon, and Chairman Leonid Brezhnev, as well as Secretary of State Kissinger have played a major role in concluding agreements such as the limited test ban treaty, the non-proliferation treaty, and SALT. These top civilian leaders generated the support for such agreements, and not the military establishments.

There is a contest between the civilian leaders who want tight controls over these weapons and the military who have created them and naturally want to use them to deter or, if necessary, to win a war. They often want as few restrictions on their use as feasible. A general in command of one of our important nuclear installations once expressed his exasperation to me that military commanders would not be able to use nuclear weapons in an emergency because of the safeguards put on them. Of course, the purpose of the safeguards is that they be used only with presidential authorization and as a last resort. The SALT ceilings and related restrictions have not stopped improvement of nuclear weapons, and the military on both sides press for improvement of weapons to the maximum extent allowed by their provisions.

The fourth level of policymaking is the U.S. Senate which may make the critical policy decisions on the SALT Treaty. In the Senate Foreign Relations Committee hearings on the SALT Treaty in 1979 Senator Frank Church played a central role in obtaining a favorable committee report and in fighting off killer amendments, which if approved would have upset the careful balance achieved in years of negotiations with the Soviet Union and would have made the Treaty unacceptable to the Russians. In the midst of the debate Senator Church released evidence to the press that a Cuban combat unit had been in Cuba for several years in violation of U.S.-Russian understandings reached at the end of the Cuban missile crisis of 1962. This caused a public and media flap that threatened the ratification. Senator Church then obtained Committee approval of a condition to the resolution of ratification that required the President, prior to ratifying the Treaty, to affirm that the Soviet military forces in Cuba are not engaged in a combat role and will not become a threat to any country in the Western hemisphere. This condition was acceptable to the Administration.[20] Then another obstacle arose — the insistance of a sizable number of Senators that there be a marked increase in the Defense Budget. Just when a compromise was close on this issue, the Soviets invaded Afghanistan. Senator Byrd and Senator Church then, at the request of the President, decided to withdraw consideration of the Treaty by the Senate. In this case, as already noted in the debate on the Panama Canal, Senator Church and key Senators were playing policymaking roles on critical foreign policy issues. (Figure 13-2.)

The basic guarantee against cheating in these agreements is that if only one major violation of a nuclear power's commitment were discovered, this would undermine confidence in the entire system of SALT and NPT agreements, and in fact the other agreements noted above. Experts are satisfied that satellite photography is adequate to check on the number of land based missiles and the number of submarines constructed. They cannot be 100 percent certain of 100 percent compliance, but they believe any major move to exceed the ceilings stands a high likelihood of being quickly detected. Both sides stand to gain in terms of deterring war and limiting the expensive arms race. In other words, the arms limitation agreements are designed to be a game in which both sides can win, or both lose everything, rather than a zero-sum game where one side can win by cheating at the expense of the other side's losing.

A similar reasoning applies to the non-proliferation treaties. It would be very difficult for non-nuclear powers to build and test a weapon without being detected. If they were detected, this would probably set off a nuclear arms race by their neighbors. Moreover, as long as they do not have nuclear weapons, they could avoid being threatened by nuclear devastation if a nuclear war broke out among the great powers.

Until President Reagan all the U.S. presidents since World War II had supported an active U.N. role in arms control. These men with the terrible responsibility of "the

Figure 13-2   The SALT Negotiation Process

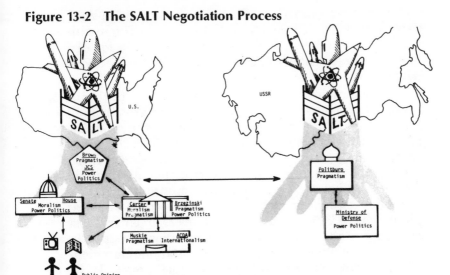

trigger" realized dimensions of the nuclear threat and pushed for international control. Progress has been slow but cumulative with an impressive list of agreements now in effect.

Those who oppose arms control agreements usually regard the arms competition as a zero-sum game, or a race in which only the power which stays ahead can maintain security. Supporters of the agreements, on the other hand, accept the fact that effective control depends on agreement and cooperation among the superpowers even more so than in the case of conflict settlement under the U.N. System. Cheating in the arms control agreements by a superpower could plunge the world into a frightening arms race, heighten tensions, and increase the risks of nuclear war. There would be no net gains for a surprise attack. Superpower strategy is based on keeping enough excess weapons to deliver a massive nuclear retaliation after a surprise nuclear attack.

There is no authority strong enough to enforce the network of arms control agreements, and no specific penalties are prescribed, but the agreements depend on national leaders voluntarily abiding by the agreements. For this reason many observers fear that the system is weak. However, with the advanced monitoring devices by satellites and other devices, it is unlikely countries could violate the agreements without being caught. In fact, there have been no major violations proven. The Indian explosion of a nuclear device in 1974 was a violation of a bilateral agreement with Canada not covered in the above network of agreements.

The voluntary compliance with international commitments on arms control parallels the growth of an attitude opposing aggression noted in the previous chapter that in the past has helped the U.N. settle conflicts and has given it more authority in peacemaking.

Part of the U.N. arms control system, the International Atomic Energy Agency, has further eroded nationalism and achieved supranationality in its inspection of nuclear plants. The U.N. inspectors are free to enter these countries and their nuclear installations. With the expansion of nuclear power, the supranational functions of the IAEA may expand. For example, proposals are under consideration to establish international centers under the IAEA to reprocess nuclear fuel for power plants.

Indirectly the superpowers under the SALT agreements have yielded up sovereignty in the skies above them by allowing spy satellites to photograph their territory, and they have even agreed not to try to conceal certain installations such as submarine pens. Over 100 countries have agreed not to make nuclear weapons under the Non-Proliferation Treaty.

The U.N. Secretary General also has had supranational power as commander of the peacekeeping forces which have had military control over areas of Syria, Egypt, Lebanon, and Jordan, and U.N. observers have been given the right to travel and report on developments in other countries. These developments represent a significant erosion of nationalism and a growth of supranationalism based on a desire of national leaders to cooperate in order to survive.

Summary

The U.N. System has sponsored over a dozen international agreements for limiting nuclear weapons and controlling crises. Only a beginning in the process has been made because the remaining weapons of the great powers could devastate the world. The SALT agreements, which have received the most attention, include ceilings on nuclear weapons and delivery systems. The U.S. and Soviet Union use satellite photography and other means to insure the SALT provisions are not being violated even though the provisions of the 1979 agreements were not formally ratified through 1981. Other important agreements include:

1. An Anti-Ballistic Missile (ABM) Treaty limiting the U.S. and U.S.S.R. to one ABM system against incoming missiles.
2. The Nuclear Non-Proliferation Treaty (NPT) ratified by over 100 states who pledged not to make nuclear weapons.
3. The Partial Test Ban Treaty banning large scale tests and tests where fallout would cross national borders.
4. The International Atomic Energy Authority (IAEA) to promote peaceful uses of nuclear energy and control trade in nuclear materials.
5. Treaties to prohibit nuclear weapons in the Antarctic, outer space, on the seabed, and in Latin America.
6. The Hot Line Agreement to establish emergency communications between the United States and Russia.

Although no specific penalties are prescribed for non-compliance, there has been no reported important violation of the above agreements. Nations are deterred from violating any one of them for fear of undermining the system that has prevented a deadly arms race.

FOOTNOTES

1. U.S. Department of State, *The SALT Process* (Publication 8947, June, 1978), p. 1.

2. One of the best sources of information on military strength is the International Institute for Strategic Studies (IISS) *The Military Balance 1979-1980* (London: IISS, 1979). Figures are from U.S. Senate, Committee on Foreign Relations, *The SALT II Treaty* (Report of the Committee on Foreign Relations, November 19, 1979), pp. 94-101.

3. U.S. Arms Control and Disarmament Agency, "Worldwide Effects

of Nuclear War — Some Perspectives," (Washington, D.C., ACDA, 1976); Office of Technology Assessment, U.S. Congress, *The Effects of Nuclear War* (U.S. Government Printing Office, May, 1979).

4. International Institute for Strategic Studies, *The Military Balance 1976-1977* (London, 1976), pp. 16, 103. These are generally accepted figures but they probably understate the numbers. Milton Leitenberg in *Foreign Affairs Newsletter* of December 1, 1975, notes the U.S. has "tens of thousands" of nuclear warheads in many countries, and that the Soviet figures are subject to a wide margin of error.

5. United Nations, *Basic Problems of Disarmament* (New York: United Nations, 1970), pp. 75-98.

6. Moscow Press Conference of Secretary Kissinger, July, 1974.

7. Lyndon B. Johnson, *The Vantage Point* (New York: Popular Library, 1971), Chapter 20.

8. John Newhouse, *Cold Dawn, The Story of SALT* (New York: Holt, Rinehart and Winston, 1973), pp. 104, 136. This gives an excellent account of the politics and policymakers involved in the SALT negotiations. The test of related U.N. agreements and a brief history of their negotiations is given in U.S. Arms Control and Disarmament Agency, *Arms Control and Disarmament Agreements* (Washington, D.C., June, 1980).

9. Newhouse, *op. cit.;* Kissinger, *op. cit.,* pp. 1216-1246.

10. Ted Greenwood, "Reconnaisance and Arms Control," *Scientific American,* February, 1973.

11. President Carter's address to American Society of Newspaper Editors, April 10, 1980, *Department of State Bulletin,* May, 1980, p. 5.

12. Paul Warnke, former director of the U.S. Arms Control and Disarmament Agency in the *Washington Post,* January 29, 1980, editorial page. Details on provisions of the agreements are given in ACDA's *Arms Control and Disarmament Agreements* (1980 edition).

13. Keesings Research Report, *Disarmament, Negotiations, and Treaties 1946-1971* (New York: Charles Scribners and Sons, 1972), pp. 253-255.

14. U.S. Arms Control and Disarmament Agency, *Arms Control and Disarmament Agreements* (Washington, D.C., August, 1980), pp. 34-47.

15. Herbert F. York, *Arms Control Readings from Scientific American* (San Francisco: W.H. Freeman and Company, 1973), p. 73.

16. Cited in John G. Stoessinger, *The United Nations and the Superpowers: China, Russia, and America* (New York: Random House, 1977), p. 166.

17. U.S. Congress, Committee on International Relations, Subcommittee on International Security and Scientific Affairs, "Authority to Order the Use of Nuclear Weapons" (U.S. Government Printing Office, December 1, 1975).

18. David Halberstam, *The Best and the Brightest* (Greenwich, Connecticut: Fawcett Publications, Inc., 1972), p. 391.

19. Dwight D. Eisenhower, *Waging Peace* (Garden City, N.Y.: Doubleday, 1965), pp. 614-616.

20. United States Senate, Committee on Foreign Relations, *The SALT II Treaty,* 96th Congress, Report of the Committee on Foreign Relations, November 19, 1979, p. 47.

14

The International System and Development

The founders of the United Nations ranked solving economic and social problems as a major aim of the Charter. They believed that economic and social progress by the entire world community would strengthen the basis for friendly relations and peace. More than 90 percent of U.N. resources are devoted to economic and social problems. Delegates of the developing nations support this emphasis with their voting power, while developed nations also support this policy realizing the U.N. System can provide aid and advice more effectively than uncoordinated efforts of many countries.

Delegates work on economic resolutions and policy guidelines in interminable meetings and conferences. Many of the meetings, if they are covered at all, are reported in a few local or specialized media. Experts make important international financial decisions behind closed doors and often explain them in such highly technical terms that it is doubtful presidents, prime ministers, and possibly even secretaries of the treasuries understand some of their implications. Many of these discussions are not a matter of public record. Positive accomplishments, therefore, tend to be overlooked by the news media, which focus on drama and confrontations of international politics.

We will look at the politics of important economic organs of the U.N. System and how their decisions have affected nation states. In this analysis we will see familiar ideological contests between developed and developing countries, between social democrats and more conservative market economists, as well as between supporters of nationalism and internationalism.

ıe United Nations Programs

The top U.N. body for setting economic guidelines and acting on economic and social issues is the General Assembly and under it the Economic and Social Council (ECOSOC) and the U.N. Conference on Trade and Development (UNCTAD). The U.N. Secretariat, which assists these organs, directly administers a number of other organizations which take action in the field of development, including the U.N. Development Program and relief organizations. The above are the bodies of the U.N. proper. Action may also be taken in the U.N. Specialized Agencies, which have separate charters and different rules of voting. Many of the U.N. Specialized Agencies were acting on international problems before the U.N. was formed, but they voluntarily associated with the U.N. Together the above organizations make up the U.N. System. (See Figure 12-1.)

There is often a bargaining process at different levels of the U.N. System to revise guidelines. Policy guidelines in one body affect the issue in another body, since policymakers of a country taking a position in one organ of the U.N. would feel obligated to have their countries' delegates take a consistent position in another U.N. organ. The process is usually voluntary and countries not agreeing to a policy in one of these organizations may decide not to contribute or cooperate with the policy.

Following is a survey of activities of major U.N. bodies acting on economic and social issues and an analysis of major world issues they address. These efforts are not as dramatic or as well known as settlement of political disputes in the U.N., but such efforts may be as important for peace in the long run.

The General Assembly. The General Assembly with permanent representatives from about 150 nations meets in a regular session for about two and a half months beginning in September of each year, and in additional special sessions which have been averaging about one a year. The General Assembly approves the U.N. budget, passes resolutions with goals and guidelines, approves world conferences, and organizes the U.N. System to work on economic and social issues. The General Assembly is too unwieldy and meets too short a time, however, to resolve the really difficult economic issues or take over action responsibilities on them. It is a political organ, a place to let off steam and to influence public opinion, but it also has budgetary power and authority to reorganize institutions if their performance does not satisfy a majority of the delegates.

Resolutions railroaded through the General Assembly and other U.N. bodies with a numerical majority but without agreement of major nations have had little consequence and limited political utility. However, the developing nations have been supported by powerful OPEC nations and their challenge of the developed nations has produced policy changes, particularly in the 1970s. It would be difficult to show exactly where the erosion of the developed countries' policies took place, but we noted in previous chapters how developed countries made compromises on establishing a framework for international commodity agreements, granting tariff preferences, and beginning to negotiate a code of conduct for multinational corporations. In this chapter we will note how the U.N. System acted on other parts of the "new international economic order" including granting the developing countries more of a voice in international monetary reform and providing more economic assistance plus action on programs considered important to the developed countries. General Assembly resolutions and decisions played a part in all these issues.

The Economic and Social Council (ECOSOC). Under the U.N. Charter ECOSOC has broad responsibilities for economic and social functions. It has expanded administrative functions under Article 63 through agreements with the Specialized Agencies, but these agencies, and particularly the World Bank and the International Monetary Fund, have retained policy independence.

The original membership of ECOSOC was 18, but it was increased to 27 and then to 54 in 1973. The policymakers of the large powers realized that if they did not allow larger representation on ECOSOC, more and more of the action on development questions would pass to the U.N. Conference on Trade and Development (UNCTAD), a special body set up under the General Assembly to handle development questions and which is dominated by developing countries.

The 54 member ECOSOC works surprisingly well in part because the same delegates work together on problems year after year, and also because there is tight discipline within the geographic caucuses. The developing countries are tightly organized, the Eastern European members vote as a bloc, and the developed countries work together fairly well. Since ECOSOC meets four times a year, it is in a much better position than the General Assembly to coordinate the subsidiary bodies of the U.N. and to do preparatory work of debating issues, considering reports, including those from the Specialized Agencies, and making recommendation to the General Assembly for further action.

The U.N. Conference on Trade and Development (UNCTAD). UNCTAD grew out of an idea of Raul Prebish, a prominent Latin American economist and statesman. He believed that the major problems of the developing world centered on foreign trade, and that if developing countries could be given adequate access to the markets of the industrial countries and if they obtained a fair price for their commodity exports, they would not need huge amounts of aid. As a result of his influence, the General Assembly in December, 1962, authorized a world conference which was held in 1964 to establish UNCTAD. The UNCTAD Conference, or governing body, meets every four or five years to consider problems of trade and development. In the interim, the issues are considered by its Trade and Development

Board and subsidiary committees which meet mostly in Geneva to work on these questions. These bodies are supported by a large UNCTAD secretariat under the Secretary General appointed by the U.N. Secretary-General.

UNCTAD and its subsidiary committees set broad policy guidelines on development issues and propose action on development problems. It is dominated by the developing countries. As in the General Assembly, the developed countries seriously consider the positions of the developing nations and often respond to their pressures. Considering the controversial issues involved, the spirit of the meetings is businesslike. For example, in the 1972 meeting at Santiago, Chile, during the Vietnam War, Cuba, the Peoples' Republic of China, and certain other countries made speeches criticizing the United States and proposed a critical resolution on Vietnam, but by a vote of 50 to 26 with 17 abstentions the Conference supported a motion by the United States declaring the Vietnam issue not within UNCTAD's competence. The Conference returned to trade and development issues.

The programs initiated in UNCTAD are often regarded as radical by developed country delegates, but many get accepted in a watered-down and revised form within five or 10 years after they are first proposed. As already noted UNCTAD was used in pressing for trade preferences for developing countries, establishing arrangements to stabilize world commodity prices, and negotiating a code of conduct for multinational firms. UNCTAD has also played a leading role in demands for providing more aid to the least developed countries, in giving developing countries more voice in the international monetary reform, and other issues. The above issues were on the agenda of the 1979 UNCTAD Conference in Manila but there were differences in the final resolutions in comparison with previous conferences. The demands at Manila were for institutions already established to take better care of these problems, or for new institutions to take their place.[1]

The U.N. Development Program (UNDP). One of the most effective of the U.N.'s action organizations is the U.N. Development Program, the world's largest program of grant technical assistance, which is under the U.N.

Details on the U.N. Development Program

In February, 1974, while traveling to and from a meeting of the U.N. Economic Commission for Asia and the Far East, as a U.S. State Department official I visited several UNDP projects to get a first-hand impression of UNDP officials and their work. The visit included:

1. Bangkok: Resident Representative, Thomas Power; the Committee for Coordination of Prospecting for Minerals in Asian Offshore Areas; the project to help Thailand's Ministry of Industry establish standards for certain industrial goods; and the Southeast Asian regional population officer for UNDP.

2. Dacca, Bangladesh: The Resident Representative, Mr. D'Astugues, and the UNDP advisor for public health workers in family planning.

3. New Delhi, India: The Resident Representative, Mr. McDiarmid; the Ground Water Survey project; the Indian Agricultural Research Institute project headed by Dr. Frederiksson of the University of Uppsala, Sweden, with Dr. Rawitz of Israel (an expert in radioactive tracers), Dr. Farkas of Hungary (an expert on micro-organisms), and Dr. Lang (an Australian veterinarian); and the UNDP population officer for India.

My major conclusion was that these officials were very competent and seemed well in control of their programs despite a small staff and low overhead. Some of the problems I noted included the desirability of more authority for the Resident Representatives to monitor some of the U.N. Specialized Agency programs, and a need for more interchange between the New York Headquarters of UNDP and the field. The visit, of course, only scratched the surface of the 8,000 projects of UNDP in over 140 countries, but the small sample was impressive.

Secretariat. The United States has been the major contributor. In the 1970s its annual contribution dropped from about $90 million to about $80 million. The U.S. share as a percentage of the total declined from about 30 percent to 20 percent by 1977, but in 1979 the Carter Administration increased the appropriation to $126 million for UNDP operations.

In informal recognition of the size of the U.S.

contribution and its active interest in the organization, past Administrators of UNDP have been Americans, and the United States has been one of the permanent members of the 48 member governing council.

The UNDP draws on experts from the U.N. System in many fields including agriculture, industry, public administration, and education. It has about 8,000 projects underway in 150 countries and territories. Recipient governments generally provide a little over half the project costs. Support of development has remained a major aim of U.S. policy, and this U.N. program has been an instrument for mobilizing a cooperative effort of both developed and developing nations.

The "Resident Representatives" of UNDP are recognized as senior representatives of U.N. operations in the various countries and not only coordinate technical assistance but act to coordinate relief activities of the U.N. and the Specialized Agencies in an emergency. These Resident Representatives by and large are highly respected among aid officials and are largely responsible for the U.N. organs being able to operate as a system in each country. Many countries prefer to channel their aid funds through the administrative structure of the UNDP system to save administrative costs.

World Food Program and Emergency Relief. United Nations organizations that play a major relief role include the World Food Program, the U.N. Disaster Relief Office, the U.N. High Commissioner for Refugees, the U.N. Relief Office in Dacca (UNROD),[2] the World Health Organization (a specialized agency), and the U.N. Childrens' Fund (UNICEF). Since 1970 the major U.N. international relief efforts have been in Bangladesh. By the middle of 1972, about $670 million was pledged by U.N. members with $215 million from the United States. By the end of the relief program in 1975 aid efforts totalled over $1 billion, with the United States the largest single contributor. These aid programs, supported by the resolutions of the U.N. Security Council, were supported strongly by the United States to defuse the India-Pakistan conflict (see U.N. Peacekeeping section above). Similarly, there has been a perennial focus of U.N. refugee relief to assist Palestine refugees originally displaced in the Arab-Israeli War, which also is an emphasis that suits U.S. foreign policy priorities of pacifying the Middle East.

The General Assembly set up the U.N. Disaster Relief Office (UNDRO) in 1971 to coordinate relief efforts for disaster situations. The U.S. Agency for International Development (AID) has a teletype service with the UNDRO office in Geneva. The United States found this coordination so useful that Secretary of State Kissinger in his U.N. speech on September 23, 1974, called for strengthening the office and offered a voluntary contribution of up to $750,000 to strengthen its administration. (This was not Kissinger's original idea, but that of one of his policymakers — John McDonald — my immediate superior.) The General Assembly approved the U.S. sponsored resolution on this matter in 1974.

The World Food Program is a joint undertaking of the United Nations and the Food and Agriculture Organization, which is a Specialized Agency, to provide food aid. Its budget is around $200 million annually, but this only accounts for about 10 percent of the world's total food aid; the remainder is provided through direct arrangements. The European Community in recent years has become a substantial direct supplier of food aid to developing countries from the large surplus of grains and dairy products created by high prices maintained under the Community's common agricultural policy.

The Specialized Agencies

The other part of the U.N. System consists of the Specialized Agencies. These bodies have made special agreements with ECOSOC for coordinating their administrative practices. Most of them also coordinate their substantive policies with those of the United Nations. The Specialized Agencies have their own charters, governing bodies, and budgets. The International Monetary Fund and the World Bank in their agreements negotiated with ECOSOC stress that they are not subject to policy guidance from the United Nations on substantive matters. Nevertheless, representatives of Specialized Agencies attend important substantive meetings of the United Nations and cooperate closely with the U.N. bodies, as well as coordinate their administrative practices with the rest of the System.

Although the Specialized Agencies are not subject to policy direction from the General Assembly or ECOSOC, the Specialized Agencies take resolutions of these bodies seriously since the same governments that sit in the major bodies of the U.N. also control the Specialized Agencies. The International Monetary Fund (IMF) and the International Bank (IBRD) have weighted voting, it is true, but when important economic resolutions are passed in the U.N., they are likely to have the general approval of governments which have the most weight in IBRD and IMF votes. Executive directors who represent member governments in the IMF and IBRD rarely contradict policies supported by their governments in other parts of the U.N. System.

The International Bank Group. The International Bank and its close relative, the International Monetary Fund, reflect the determination of the Allied Governments not to make the same mistakes that were made in the World War I peace settlement. In 1919 John Maynard Keynes, a prominent British economist, wrote a study on the economic consequences of the peace correctly predicting disaster from the heavy reparations payments imposed on Germany. During World War II he and Harry Dexter White of the U.S. Treasury collaborated in producing the plan for the International Bank and the International Monetary Fund to permit management of world currencies and loans so that the world economic system would not be subject to the panic and disruption that occurred in the 1930s. The articles of agreements for these organizations were approved in July, 1944, and they began operations in 1946. Through agreements approved by the General Assembly in 1947 they became Specialized Agencies and part of the U.N. System. Bank & Fund

In over 30 years of experience these organizations have acquired the prestige and expertise that have helped the world economic system to weather many crises. Thus, they have acquired an aura of supranationalism. The United States Treasury and treasury representatives from other nations instruct the delegates and set general policies of these institutions. This with a fair degree of success has insulated them from political pressures. Most of the Board of Governors and executive directors are banking types and financial experts. The debates on the most controversial issues, which often center on concessions to the developing nations, are on a high technical plane, rather than in the plain language and give-and-take that occurs in the U.N. policy organs. The insulation from outside politics is not perfect, but it has resulted in a conservative economic cast to the institutions; nevertheless their liberal founders would probably like their record.

The International Bank for Reconstruction and Development (IBRD) and its associate, the International Development Association (IDA), are the largest source of development funds for developing countries. In fiscal year 1974 these two Specialized Agencies approved loans of about $4.3 billion to 77 countries. This meant that loan approvals had more than doubled over the previous five years, meeting the target of the energetic American President of the Bank, Robert McNamara. In September, 1980, at the annual meeting of the Bank, President McNamara said the bank had met a target of $7.6 billion for fiscal year 1980 loans, which easily made the International Bank the largest source of development funds in the world.

In its early days the International Bank made most of its loans for large projects such as dams and irrigation projects. For example, the first major loan to Thailand in 1949 was $17 million for a $50 million Chainat Dam project to help control the water of Thailand's central rice producing area. Since then the International Bank has helped finance additional dams that add to irrigation and flood control and provide most of Thailand's electric power. In recent years the Bank Group has emphasized loans for rural development, health, and population projects. These loans are made to local organizations with government participation that channel funds to farmers, schools, or health projects. For example, the first loan listed in the 1974 IDA Annual Report is to Burma for $17 million. "Some 330,000 farmers will benefit directly from this project which seeks to extend and rehabilitate irrigated paddy (rice) land, mostly in the Irrawaddy delta." The second loan listed is $11.6 million for livestock development for the Cameroon; it will help set up three 50,000 acre state ranches and develop livestock production in 150,000 private ranches and farms. "Almost

(over)

2 million acres of pastoral land will be cleared of the dreaded tsetse fly . . ." Altogether the International Bank Group has made loans like the above to over 112 countries and their institutions since it began operations.

The United States has subscribed about one-fourth of the IBRD's total capital and contributed about 40 percent of funds used for the operation of the IDA. The actual flow of funds from the United States to these institutions was less than U.S. commitments, however, since Bank disbursements lag behind loan approvals and the International Bank obtains most of its funds from borrowing and from repayments of loans.

An important service of the World Bank is to provide technical assistance. Its experts sit in the ministries of developing countries helping them to better use their own resources and attract other investments. With the financial leverage of the IBRD these international experts are able to obtain all kinds of economic data and exercise pressure on national policies that would not be accepted from experts of individual nations.

A major IBRD issue has been the demand of the developing countries for a greater voice in its decisions. The United States' and others' voting power in the IBRD is based on their share of the membership's GNP and trade, which gives the U.S. a dominant voice in the organization. The United States Treasury representatives have resisted diluting U.S. voting in the organization.

The International Monetary Fund. The International Monetary Fund (IMF), another Specialized Agency of the U.N. System, promotes financial cooperation and provides assistance to member countries with temporary balance of payment problems. The IMF in recent years has maintained a basic equilibrium in a period that saw fluctuations in the price of gold from $35 to over $600 an ounce, runs on international currencies, and extreme pressures put on the international monetary system by the transfer within a period of one year of an additional $85 billion to oil producing countries of the world.

The major function of the International Monetary Fund is to make loans to member countries having balance of payment problems. The rates of interest increase as borrowing increases, with the highest rates at approximately market rates of interest. Depending on the size of the borrowing the borrowing countries must make commitments to take specific steps to improve their financial position. Total quotas of the Fund are about $60 billion. Countries can borrow up to about six times their individual quotas, which depend on the size of their GNP and world trade. Other borrowing arrangements outside the quotas are available through a special fund financed by the oil producers and a trust fund financed from profits of sales of gold.[3]

In 1969 the IMF created a new world asset, the special drawing rights (SDRs) and in 1972 distributed over $9 billion of this paper gold to finance world monetary transactions. The distribution was based on the size of member quotas, and the United States with its large quota based on its GNP and trade received over $2 billion of this distribution. The IMF distributed another $8 billion in 1979 and 1980.

The IMF designed a world monetary reform based on the SDR through the Committee of Twenty which consisted of half of the representatives of developing countries. The reform included (1) increasing the quotas or lending authority of the IMF by over $10 billion from SDR 29 billion to SDR 39 billion; (2) abolition of an official price for gold and auctioning gold holdings of the Fund to benefit developing countries; (3) establishing a special fund to finance oil purchases mentioned below; (4) using the SDR as a basis for valuation of world currencies; (5) making the SDR the principal international reserve asset; and (6) legalizing a new system of exchange arrangements allowing "floating" or letting the market help determine exchange rates. This first major overhaul of the international monetary system since World War II was put into effect in May, 1978.

The International Monetary Fund also provides technical assistance to developing countries and has developed the most current and comprehensive international economic statistics in the world. Thus, the IMF has been in a key position to analyze and take action on the series of major financial problems that have arisen in the past decade.

It is noteworthy that Saudi Arabia on May 7, 1981,

signed a loan agreement bringing total Saudi loans to the
IMF to about $15 billion to help developing countries and
others to meet balance of payments problems on easier
terms than other IMF loans.[4]

The other U.N. Specialized Agencies which coordinate
international action on health, communications,
transportation, agriculture, labor standards, and other
international concerns are shown in Figure 12-1. These
organizations cooperate with each other under the
leadership of the U.N. organs. The UNDP, as indicated
above, coordinates their activities on technical assistance
matters and in emergencies.

Major Development Issues

The Third World countries use the U.N. General
Assembly, ECOSOC, UNCTAD, and other organs of the
U.N. System to voice their demands on development
issues. In Chapter 10 we noted how the OPEC countries
backed the claims of the Third World caucus for *higher
prices for their commodities,* luring them with the hope
the Third World, too, could attain some of the economic
advantages that OPEC obtained with its oil pricing
policies. In Chapter 11 we noted how the Third World
countries had successfully pressured the European
Community into granting them special trade concessions
in the European market, and how the United States had
reluctantly followed suit. These *preferential trade issues*
were at the top of the list of Third World demands. Further
down the list were demands for international agreements
to *limit the activities of multinational corporations.*
Chapter 11 noted how progress was also being made in the
U.N. in drafting a Code of Conduct for multinationals.

As the 1980s began, the problems of aid and investment
for development and for adjustment to the shock of
further increased energy prices came to the top of the
developing countries' agenda. In 1978 the world
economists had breathed a small sigh of relief that the
world economy had weathered almost a ten-fold increase
in oil prices from 1973 to 1978. However, by 1980 the
OPEC countries had doubled prices again. As the 1980s
began the United States experienced an alarming

Table 14-1 Changes in World Output and Balances on Current Account
1975-1980

	1975	1976	1977	1978	1979	1980
Real GNP (% Change)						
Industrial Countries*	-.8	5.3	3.8	4.0	3.4	1.0
Oil Exporting Countries	-.3	12.1	6.2	2.7	2.9	2.2
Non Oil Developing Countries	4.4	5.4	4.9	5.0	4.6	4.9
Balances on Current Account (Billion Dollars)						
Industrial Countries	16	-2	-5	31	-11	-51
Oil Exporting Countries	35	40	32	5	68	115
Non Oil Developing Countries	-46	-32	-28	-36	-55	-68

*Includes Canada, U.S., Japan, France, Germany, Italy, United Kingdom, Australia, Austria, Belgium, Denmark, Finland, Iceland, Ireland, Luxembourg, the Netherlands, New Zealand, Norway, Spain, Sweden, and Switzerland.
Source: *IMF Survey,* "World Economic Outlook Supplement," June 24, 1980.

inflation followed by a recession. This was accompanied by a slowdown in other industrial countries and an alarming rise in their deficit on current account (goods and services).

The growing interdependence of the world meant that the above developments would impact on the developing countries. They would face higher prices for their imported oil, a rise in interest rates in industrial countries trying to stabilize prices which would make it more expensive for developing countries to borrow from them, and a reduced demand by industrial countries for imports from developing countries. All this would make it harder for developing countries to buy the imports they needed for development. In 1980 their deficit in current account almost doubled in comparison with 1978. (See Table 14-1.)

The international financial community, therefore, was faced by a need for parts of the world system to borrow more than normally deemed prudent from other parts of the system that happened to hold the extra funds of the OPEC countries. The above developments posed a special challenge for the IMF to become more active in preventing a world financial disaster. There was also a need for more trade, which would be difficult to achieve in the face of nationalist and protectionist pressures.[5]

Following is the status of aid and investment as the above political and economic pressures came to focus on these policies.

Aid and Investment. The developing countries through the U.N. organs have continued to ask for an increased volume of aid with a target for all types of aid from developed countries equalling one percent of their GNP. Throughout the 1970s the Third World countries also demanded a "link" between issuance of IMF Special Drawing Rights and development needs, so that the bulk of this paper gold would not be issued to developed countries with the highest IMF quotas.

Most economic aid is provided bilaterally. The most authoritative figures on all types of aid transfers are compiled by the Development Assistance Committee (DAC) of the Organization for Economic Cooperation and Development (OECD) which is not part of the U.N. System. DAC estimated "total flows of resources" to developing countries in 1979 amounted to $82 billion. This included (1) "aid" — official government grants for economic development and government loans at low interest rates and (2) "other flows," which include grants from private agencies, and private loans and investments at commercial terms. The DAC figures excluded military grants and credits, loans for less than a year, and operations of the International Monetary Fund.

A total of about $82 billion "flows of resources" aid to developing countries in 1979 originated as follows:

About $30 billion of the above originated in government grants and credits. About $6.5 billion of this government assistance went through the U.N. System and other international organizations. Total assistance provided by Communist countries was very small. The Communist countries "cop out" of aid by asserting the ills of the developing countries were caused by colonial exploitation and therefore Communist countries have no responsibility for aid.

The United States was the main source of the flow of resources to developing countries, which is to be expected since its GNP is by far the largest in the world. However, in the 1970s it ranked about 13th out of 17 countries in

Table 14-2 Total Flow of Resources to Developing Countries, 1979

Source	Billion Dollars	Percent
DAC Countries	75.1	92
OPEC Countries	6.0	7
Communist Countries	.8	1
Total	81.9	100.0

*DAC countries are members of the Development Assistance Committee of the Paris-based Organization for Economic Co-operation and Development (OECD). They include Australia, Austria, Belgium, Canada, Denmark, Finland, France, Germany, Italy, Japan, Netherlands, New Zealand, Norway, Sweden, Switzerland, United Kingdom, and United States.
Source: *IMF Survey*, July 7, 1980, pp. 210, 210-211.

percent of GNP devoted to official and private flows of resources to developing countries.

Historically, countries important to U.S. security interests have received a major share of its aid. After the Marshall Plan for Europe ended in 1953, the U.S. emphasized aid to developing countries, but security interests continued to dominate the aid programs. In recent years the United States has provided a major share of its aid to Egypt and Israel to help calm the Middle East. However, the U.S. Congress also channeled more aid to the poorer nations. President Carter supported this trend by proposing that over 60 percent of U.S. bilateral aid go to countries with a per capita income of $300 or less and also proposed more aid through the World Bank and other multilateral institutions.[6]

The developed countries often stress the economic importance of private capital and private industry in development. Developing countries naturally prefer official government aid channeled through their own governments, since this gives their officials a chance to manage and direct the funds to projects they think are most needed. Private funds from the private sector of developed countries to private companies in the developing world are less attractive to many officials since they are subject only to indirect governmental controls. As indicated above, private financing provides well over half of the total flow of financial resources from developed countries.

The developed countries point out in U.N. debates that the private financing often involves the transfer of equipment, technical skills, management resources, and marketing skills that are highly productive in the development process. They add that development is primarily the responsibility of the developing countries, and that they should make every effort to attract this private capital. Such efforts fly in the face of the Communist-Marxist dogma which warns against neocolonialism and domination of the developing world through investments by capitalist circles. Nevertheless, many of the most rapidly growing economies in the developing world even with socialist philosophies have attracted large sums of private capital through special government incentives and promotion efforts. In Asia, for example, countries with marked success in development include Singapore, the Republic of China, the Republic of Korea, Thailand, Israel, Malaysia, and the British colony of Hong Kong. Their pragmatic policymakers encourage economic and commercial activities in the private sector, and their economies are oriented toward world trade and market forces.

A number of Asian countries with an opposite orientation — towards controls and government regulation and investments — have been less successful in attracting private loans and in their economic development record. These include India, Burma, Sri Lanka, and also Indonesia before 1965.

The value of government economic controls and investment, on the one hand, and private investment, on the other, is a controversial issue in development economics and in international debates on economic policies. The differing economic and ideological points of view on this basic issue underlie many of the policy problems between the developed and developing countries.

Science and Technology. Developing countries often strongly support resolutions for transferring scientific skills and technology to the developing world. This is not a controversial goal, and the United States has strongly supported new measures for expanding the capacity of international agricultural research centers, providing technical assistance to find new sources of energy, and research for improving the production of certain raw materials such as timber, jute, cotton, and natural rubber. A major demand of developing countries is for an international code of conduct on the "transfer of technology." At the Nairobi UNCTAD Conference of 1976 the United States agreed to set up a group to draft such a code. The group had not reached agreement on key issues at the end of 1980. Few developed countries' delegates privately have much confidence in these measures as a major solution to development problems, believing private firms are the most effective instruments for such transfer.

Industrialization. Most of the issues of industrialization are similar to those of the transfer of technology. Secretary Kissinger's 1975 speech at the U.N. pointed out that transnational enterprises have been the powerful instruments of modernization for transferring capital, management skills, and technology.

Food and Agriculture. Many resolutions and policy directives of the U.N. System have called for increasing food production and assistance to developing countries to meet critical world food needs. The World Food Conference of 1974 established a food aid target of 10 million tons of food grains for 1975-1976 and called for building world food grain reserves to cover major production shortfalls. The United States as the world's largest grain exporter has been the major country supplying food through the United Nations World Food Program. The U.S. also has supported proposals for an international system of grain reserves and for agricultural research.

Every year millions of refugees or poor farmers face starvation. In 1980 the U.N. and private relief agencies were helping refugees from the Ogaden war in Ethiopia, from the drought in the Sahel in north central Africa, from the war in Cambodia, from expulsion from North Vietnam, and from other less critical areas.[7] Usually the General Assembly or other elements of the U.N. System call for aid from the world community, and elements of the U.N. System help give assistance to those faced with disaster. A major challenge to the U.N. System is to devise arrangements that will stimulate food production in food surplus countries and provide emergency aid to those faced with starvation.

Other World Economic Problems

There are several other world problems which the developed countries consider of great importance for U.N. action, but the developing countries see as less important. Two of these problems are population and environment. The developed countries have been able to get the United Nations to support population and environment programs as a result of their strong influence in the organization. They have the largest missions to the United Nations and their delegates occupy important positions in its organizations. Following is a summary of the work of the United Nations System on these problems.

Population. In 1973 the UNDP took over U.N. population activities from other U.N. organs, which added about $42 million to its program. The United States had given major support to U.N. population programs and had provided over 40 percent of the funds. The UNDP operates in about 80 countries providing resources, as requested, in the population field. Experts from other parts of the U.N. System such as the World Health Organization, the International Labor Organization, and the U.N. Childrens Fund (UNICEF), assist these programs. Population has been a major emphasis of U.S. aid, and the U.S. exerts considerable influence on the U.N. Fund for Population Activities and the U.N. Population Commission in meetings and in informal discussions with their secretariats. Also, in recent years the World Bank under President McNamara has made substantial long range, low interest loans for population projects.

The U.N. sponsored World Population Conference was held in August, 1974, in Bucharest, Romania. Its major action was to adopt a "World Population Plan of Action" after much controversy. The Plan straddled the activist position that wants government action to control population growth, the conservative position that shys away from government intervention, and the natalist view that would encourage population growth. However, advocates of population control programs are able to cite from parts of the Plan in support of their goals of limiting population growth.

Environment. The U.N. Environment Program (UNEP) was set up by the U.N. Conference on the Human

Environment at Stockholm in 1972. This in large part reflected an initiative of the United States. The UNEP is part of the U.N. Secretariat and has used staff drawn largely from the other parts of the U.N. System. A major program of interest to the United States is the "Earth Watch" or "Global Environment Monitoring System" (GEMS), which is a program to monitor pollution and changes in the world's climate and environment. The UNEP also coordinates related activities in the U.N. System, including prohibiting of oil discharges in the oceans, which is being managed under the International Marine Consultative Organization (IMCO). The U.S. contribution to the Environment Program from 1973-1979 was about $50 million, which represented 32 percent of total contributions.

To sum up, there is a wide range of economic issues on which the developed world and the developing world have been working together constructively in the U.N. System including trade issues, international monetary reform, science and technology, agricultural research, emergency food aid, population problems, and environment issues. There is also a trend for the U.N. and multilateral organizations to take over more of the administration of aid. From 1965 to 1975 the volume of United Nations aid activities trebeled and net disbursements by the World Bank Group increased five-fold. In fiscal year 1980 the World Bank disbursed about $7.6 billion in aid, with increasing commitments for future years.

As might be expected, developing countries and developed countries in U.N. forums sometimes make criticisms and pass resolutions on economic issues that the U.S. and a few developed countries oppose. Nevertheless, looking at the broad range of U.N. activities there are wide areas of cooperation, and it is entirely unjustified to conclude that the constructive activities are being thwarted by a bloc of developing nations. Despite the serious oil crisis, the world food problems, and the deep ideological differences between nations, the international economic system with the cooperation and guidance of the United Nations System has survived serious shocks and strains and appears capable of dealing with these problems. However, this will require continued cooperation by the major world powers and an increasing

flow of resources to developing countries, which have been
hard hit by the oil and food crisis. In an interdependent
world international economics is not a zero sum game but
one in which all countries can gain if they work together.

Growing Responsibilities of International Institutions

The character of important international institutions
has been determined by the vision and drive of certain key
policymakers. The achievements of these institutions in
international affairs have been due in part to the strength
of their leadership and public support, but also in large
part to the increased challenges and tasks facing them.

It is interesting to note that the leaders who set the
course of the United Nations, the European Community,
the international financial institutions, and other
important international institutions were not prominent
world leaders. Secretary of State Cordell Hull, not
considered a strong Secretary of State, prevailed in his
concept of the United Nations as a worldwide
organization over the more limited concepts of some of the
most powerful world leaders of our era — President
Roosevelt, Prime Minister Churchill, and Marshall
Stalin. Hull's ideas of a strong world organization to keep
the peace were closer to the aspirations of leaders of other
countries and of the people. Jean Monnet, the father of the
European Community, was a second level official, but he
prevailed over the powerful French leader General de
Gaulle, perhaps because Monnet's supranational
European Community had a good start and widespread
public support before de Gaulle became president. John
Maynard Keynes from academia was a leading figure in
establishing the International Monetary Fund and World
Bank. President Robert McNamara of the World Bank
was a driving force in doubling its development lending in
a few years. In the above cases, the policymakers' courses
seemed to be successfully going with the tide of world
opinion.

The policymakers who were successful in using the
U.N. to settle major conflicts of the 1970s also worked with
the tide of world opinion as expressed in various U.N.

bodies. Secretary of State Kissinger received strong support for his Middle East peace initiatives from the U.N. Security Council, the General Assembly, and the U.N. Secretary-General. In 1973 Secretary General Waldheim mobilized a multinational peacekeeping force from U.N. units in Cyprus in less than 48 hours to perform the delicate mission of separating the Israeli and Egyptian fighting forces in the Sinai. Later he took a leading diplomatic role in keeping the lid on the Cyprus crisis.

Despite his personal efforts to get action from the countries involved, Secretary General U-Thant did not succeed in preventing the 1971 India-Pakistan War, but he helped mobilize the vast resources of the U.N. to help repatriate the 10 million refugees created by that war. The U.N. Security Council and General Assembly by overwhelming votes put pressure on Indira Gandhi to withdraw her forces promptly from East Pakistan. The leaders of sovereign states used bilateral diplomacy to help settle these crises, but they worked closely with and depended on the U.N. bodies for political and financial support.

Over the years the corps of ambassadors of many nations making up the Security Council and General Assembly have acquired an expertise in U.N. procedures and a habit of working together that provide the necessary backing for cease fire resolutions and mobilizing peacekeeping forces. These representatives of sovereign nations provide an internationalist and supranationalist type of support in a crisis. With the deadlines they face, many are not able to get detailed and informed instructions from their home offices on their votes and therefore are often influenced more by the atmosphere of the U.N. than they are by strictly national considerations.

In the U.N. arms limitation negotiations a corps of experts usually negotiates agreements separately from the regular representatives in the General Assembly. The General Assembly representatives, outside the Superpower System, however, manage by resolutions and similar political activities to support negotiations by keeping pressure on the big powers to carry out arms control measures.

In the SALT negotiation, which is a bilateral negotiation, military elements usually have a major voice, but they can be strongly influenced by a strong President and Secretary of State, who often are sensitive to U.S. public opinion and world opinion as expressed in U.N. bodies and the media. The United States has kept its NATO allies closely informed on the progress of negotiations. President Carter's style also was to keep the Senate and the media informed. The decisive role in SALT negotiations likely will be played by key senators.

Officials below the Secretary of State or Assistant Secretaries of State can play important roles in policymaking on U.N. economic development matters. U.N. policy guidelines are negotiated by diplomatic delegates assigned to New York. Many of them have worked together for years in their caucuses. Since they do not have the time or staff to research the many complicated issues, they tend to rely on experts or leaders from other countries. It is impossible for home offices of small countries to provide instructions on many of the complex issues, so in a sense the U.N. delegates operate independently from home offices and provide an element of supranationality to the process.

The United States as a large country with many agencies to call upon for expertise can get agency and even public input on important issues. For example, the strong U.S. Government support for U.N. population and environmental programs during the early 1970s was due in large part to the widespread support in principle for such programs by governmental agencies, the Congress, and the public. This was translated by State Department policymakers into funds and voting support for U.N. programs in these fields.

Not all diplomats and officials assigned to U.N. delegations are internationalists supporting U.N. programs. Some of them, particularly from the developed countries, resent the growing power of the U.N. agencies and the growing influence of the developing world in determining economic policies. There is much political activity within delegations between nationalists and internationalists, particularly on budget issues. (See box on page 403.)

Some of the international decisions may be removed

The U.N. Budget

Preparing instructions for the U.S. position on the U.N. budget is the primary responsibility of the administrative office of the Bureau of International Organization Affairs of the Department of State. The administrative types in that office traditionally complain about waste and extravagance in the U.N. They consult frequently with U.S. congressional staff, who are sympathetic to such charges and reinforce similar congressional charges during the many hearings on the budget. In 1972 a major U.S. initiative in the U.N. was to get the U.N. to put a ceiling of 25 percent as an assessment for one member. Assessments were based on the size of GNP, and the U.S. share under the formula was about 32 percent. Cables were sent out around the world to foreign offices to get support for the U.S. position, and the U.N. finally approved the resolution with the 25 percent ceiling, which lowered the assessment for one member — the United States.

The U.S. administrative types, however, continued to complain about the budget and in 1973 were on the verge of getting the Assistant Secretary to approve their instruction that would have had the U.S. vote against that U.N. budget. The policy types, who coordinated instruction on the many economic and political issues addressed by the U.N., rallied and pressured him for approval of the U.N. budget. As part of the effort I prepared a graph comparing the amount spent for the U.N. budget of about $75 million (to keep the peace), with the U.S. defense budget for war of about $90 billion, which was over 1,000 times larger. On the graph one could barely see the U.N. budget trend line at the bottom. The Assistant Secretary that year compromised and instructed the U.S. delegation to abstain on the budget vote. This, incidently, had no effect on the outcome since under the U.N. Charter the issue is decided by a 2/3 vote, and only a very small minority abstains or votes against the budget. (See Figure 14-1.)

from the national political processes because of the technical nature of the decisions. In the field of international finance experts arrange for tens of billions of dollars in credits and redesign the international monetary system with relatively little input from agencies other than the treasuries of the nations involved. Just as the national monetary and banking systems are insulated from the executive, legislative, and judicial branches, the international monetary system is insulated from the political authorities of the nation states. Moreover, at the working level many thousands of experts of the UNDP and the World Bank are carrying out aid programs in over 100 developing countries with little or no political direction from nation states. The technical point of view of such experts has little relation to power politics ideas of diplomats working in the Superpower System.

Officials of the United Nations System, the European Community, and other international organizations have acquired the habit of working together. Their expertise on issues has provided the institutions with an influence or supranationalism that has had a major impact on issues of war and peace. When security or economic crises arise, leaders of sovereign nations are forced to work with international institutions and encouraged to try to influence their actions. The national leaders lobby for support from representatives of nations assigned to these international bodies and try to get support from the media and public opinion. This tends to be a peaceful rather than a warlike process, and can help build a framework or atmosphere for the peaceful settlement of disputes.

The above political activities among policymakers for the international organizations and officials of the various nations involved have given a new dimension to international politics. International politics on security and economic issues no longer depend entirely on power moves of individual nations. Much of the international action on critical issues takes place within the framework of the U.N. System. Although the Superpowers still dominate many issues of peace and war, other countries through the U.N. institutions have helped settle wars, negotiate arms limitation agreements, and provide a forum where leaders can discuss and act on international economic and social problems.

There have been increasing challenges to the U.N. and increasing accomplishments to its credit. In many areas where international policymakers have been successful the United Nations has acquired an increased measure of supranational authority. Increasingly national leaders, the media, and the general public, even of the superpowers, are recognizing U.N. accomplishments and accepting this trend.

Summary

The United Nations Charter ranks economic and social development as one of its principle goals that is almost as important as maintaining peace. The General Assembly and subsidiary bodies including the Economic and Social Council and UNCTAD are major U.N. bodies for setting development guidelines. Determining these guidelines involves a political process throughout the U.N. System, and nations' representatives bargain and try to maintain consistency in their positions at many different levels of the System. The work of the System involves many meetings and debates which are not nearly as dramatic as the confrontations in the Security Council and General Assembly on security issues. Positive accomplishments of the U.N. in the field of development, therefore, tend to get overlooked in the news media and by the public.

The most effective organs for development aid are the World Bank for loans and the U.N. Development Program for technical assistance. They are the largest programs of this type in the world. There are also major U.N. programs for food relief, disaster relief, and economic and health services by the U.N. Specialized Agencies. The International Monetary Fund has a central role in maintaining international financial stability and aid for temporary balance of payments problems.

Delegates of developing countries in U.N. meetings focus on issues involving fair prices in world commodity trade, tariff preferences, aid and investment, food, industrialization, and multinational corporations. Developed countries generally press for strengthening environment and population programs. The strength and direction of these programs have been determined in large part by the vision and drive of certain key policymakers and public support for programs.

FOOTNOTES

1. *U.N. Chronicle,* July, 1979, pp. 44-53; *IMF Survey,* July 7, 1980, pp. 213-214; and Manolo B. Jara, "The Manila Session." *Development Forum,* June-July, 1960, p. 16.

2. This was disbanded after the 1971 war refugees were resettled.

3. *IMF Survey,* December 12, 1977, and January 26, 1981.

4. International Monetary Fund, *IMF Survey,* April 5, 1976, November 6, 1978, September 15, 1980, and May 18, 1981.

5. "Face the Worst," *The Economist* (London), July 12, 1980, pp. 14-15; *IMF Survey,* "World Economic Outlook Supplement," June 24, 1980.

6. "U.S. Foreign Assistance Programs" (U.S. Department of State, Bureau of Public Affairs: Washington, D.C., February 24, 1977). See also Chapter 4.

7. *Washington Post,* June 9, 1980.

PART SIX
The Final Decades of the Century

If we can understand international politics, this does not mean we can predict what will happen. Prediction, however, is an important process in learning that helps us refine our ability to evaluate international politics and to avoid repeating errors. The critical factors we can use in prediction are the strength and momentum of ideas, and the objective factors leaders can use to implement ideas. In the final chapter, we attempt to peer into the future and to indicate policies that could enable world leaders to build a foundation for peace.

15

Coexistence, Cooperation, or Conflict

Trends in the World System

Foreign policies consist of ideas of policymakers on international politics that have the backing of their governments. There is a legitimate question of whether it is possible to predict trends in international politics if they depend on such ephemeral factors as the ideas of officials. Also, governments and their leaders change frequently. If, as previously stated, policymakers can never be sure of what is going to happen tomorrow, how would it be possible to predict what will happen over the last part of this century?

When we take a policymaking approach to this problem of prediction, at least we know what to focus on — i.e., what ideas are likely to influence policymakers and obtain political support in future years, and what material resources are likely to be available to implement the ideas? This approach avoids a common error of those who attempt to predict the future on the basis of what they think would be rational foreign policies for various nations, or what they think would be in the "national interest" of powerful countries. If one could predict foreign affairs because they were determined by what is rational and in the interest of the peoples of nations and the world, we would be in the millenium with no wars and no violent disputes to disrupt international politics.

Groups as large as nations and international organizations share ideas and hold on to them, so that the ideas generate a policy momentum of their own. The ideas of U.S. and Russian leaders, the two major poles of the superpower system, have shown much less change since World War II than ideas in power centers of the other world systems. Looking into the future there are no signs of dramatic changes in the basic ideological frameworks and economic strength of these two superpowers. Russian Communist policymakers are not likely to change their allegiance to Communism and their desire to spread it.

A major change occurred during the 1970s in the Communist parties of Western Europe with the growth of Eurocommunism, which blurred the line between Communist ideas and those of social democracy. This ferment affected some of the Warsaw Pact satellites. In the fall of 1980 Polish trade unions led by those of Gdansk won a recognition of the right to strike and thereby to create a center of economic and even political power separate from the Communist Party. The implications for the heretofore monolithic systems of Eastern Europe and Russia were breathtaking. World leaders, particularly in Europe, remember how similar challenges triggered Soviet military suppression of dissent in Czechoslovakia in 1948 and 1968, East Germany in 1953, and Hungary in 1956.

Russian leaders in 1981 seemed set in their idea that a Soviet-dominated buffer of East European states was essential to Russian security. There were no signs the Russian leaders would permit these countries to follow Yugoslavia's example in withdrawing from the Warsaw Pact. However, while much of the world held its breath, the Soviet's initial willingness to tolerate the Polish union's actions without Russian military intervention indicated a loosening of Soviet controls within the Bloc.

Moreover, there has been a relaxation of internal

suppression of dissidents in the Soviet Union since the time of Stalin. There were still marked violations of human rights, but the pressure of a human rights campaign by Western leaders and by former Soviet citizens if maintained over a long period of years could further change the views of Soviet leaders. At times, they show themselves sensitive to world opinion. In recent years they have expatriated many of their dissidents instead of executing or imprisoning them as they did under Stalin.

Nationalism is the most powerful of ideologies and it has been particularly powerful when allied with Communism, as it was in Vietnam. However, another confrontation of ideas of nationalism and communism in Eastern Europe could cause the area to "go critical" and cause another explosion, possibly involving Western Europe and the U.S.

The arms race and competition between the military alliances of the two superpowers have been landmarks of international politics since World War II. Negotiations have been underway for years to reach agreement on the mutual reduction of armed forces in Europe with a withdrawal of Soviet and American forces from direct confrontation in Germany. Spokesmen of the alliances have indicated that progress in this direction depends on a favorable outcome of nuclear weapons negotiations. If such agreements are approved, a similar agreement on Mutual Balanced Force Reductions (MBFR) in Europe is a logical next step. This would markedly lessen tension in Europe and encourage closer cooperation between Eastern and Western Europe.

China also will achieve superpower status by the end of the century. The big question is whether it will maintain its hostility to the Soviet Union. Most Chinese experts expect this, but most experts also were surprised at the original split in the late 1950s. I would suggest that a reconciliation is possible. One strong Chinese leader emerging in the post-Mao period could bring this about. Such a development would not be as surprising as the 1972 detente between the United States and China, which was followed by normal diplomatic relations in 1979. If a Chinese-Russian reconciliation does come about, U.S. coexistence with both countries could channel the three-way relationship toward three-way cooperation rather than a two to one Communist confrontation with the United States. Such cooperation has been in the minds of U.S. policymakers looking far into the future, since they realize that arms control agreements and world peace efforts must include China to be effective.

The year 1979 began with a threatening conflict between Vietnam, a Russian ally, and Kampuchea, which was supported by China. The United States and its Southeast Asian allies watched the conflict uneasily. It was a difficult situation. There was little outside support for the Kampuchean regime, which was responsible, according to reliable reports, for at least hundreds of thousands of deaths of its own people. However, the non-Communist world did not want to encourage open aggression by Vietnam. In 1980 China "punished" Vietnam for the Kampuchean invasion by attacking Vietnam's northern border area and withdrawing. China also feared growing Soviet influence in Vietnam. Vietnam during the year responded by almost doubling the number of men under arms becoming one of the world's major military powers.

Meanwhile, the SEATO alliance had been weakened by North Vietnam's victory over South Vietnam and the United States, and the subsequent U.S. withdrawal from the area. Thailand and the Philippines succeeded in disbanding SEATO's military command while they tried to achieve reconciliation with victorious North Vietnam. Their underlying fear was that the two powerful Communist nations — North Vietnam and China — might give renewed support to the smoldering Communist insurgent movements in Thailand, Malaysia, Indonesia, the Philippines, and Burma. By 1981 China and Thailand reportedly were cooperating to support rebel forces opposing the Vietnamese troops occupying Kampuchea.

One of the keys to the future of East Asia is Taiwan. There were no prospects for a basic change in the views of its leadership toward the mainland. The Taiwanese have too much material prosperity at stake to want to come under the domination of the Communist regime on the mainland. Communist China stated it would be "patient" in regard to reuniting with Taiwan, but radical, aggressive leadership in Peking could easily create another crisis in the Taiwan Straits, which could fracture the Chinese-American detente.

There is a wide consensus among American leaders and in the American public that it is important to maintain a strong NATO alliance. The favorable public response to President Carter's call for increasing expenditures to meet the challenge of increased Soviet military spending indicated that the Cold War could be easily revived. The Soviet intervention in Afghanistan beginning in December, 1979, by over 100,000 troops — which was countered by President Carter's moves to obtain U.N. condemnation of this "invasion" — appeared to most observers to be the end of a decade of detente. He followed this by promoting a boycott of the 1980 Olympics in Moscow, limiting exports of grain, stopping shipments of high technology items to Russia, and supporting other measures to underline opposition to the invasion. These measures were reinforced by similar moves of other countries including the Western European countries. These moves halted progress in SALT negotiations. In 1981 President Reagan's acceleration of an arms buildup to meet a perceived Soviet military threat and his anti-Communist rhetoric intensified the Cold War. Future trends hinged on many factors including the war in Afghanistan, the Russian reaction to challenges of Polish trade unions, leadership changes in the Mideast, and Cuba's role in Central American revolutions.

In the early 1980s the world was still reeling from the shock of massive transfers of funds to the newly rich oil countries. Saudi Arabia through the blessings of Allah had a major problem of spending its new wealth. It was an important center of power in the multipolar system and it was spending billions of dollars to work toward its foreign policy aims of supporting anti-Communism and putting pressure on Israel to withdraw back to the 1967 borders. It was a conservative regime closely allied to the United States and other Western powers, and if King Khaled's princes continued to maintain control of the country, it would probably continue along the same path.

The effects of undreamed wealth on the old-fashioned political system could be explosive, however, and a new

Saudi leadership with radical ideas could put the Middle East into turmoil. If common sense and economic motives continue to guide the regime, it would continue along a conservative path supporting the present world economic and political system. This system has absorbed investments of the wealthy oil nations, and the investment income could guarantee the Saudis a life of ease as long as the system exists.

In 1973 and 1974 Saudi Arabia and other Arab nations gave strong support to Third World attempts to change the international economic order, but as the Saudi's oil wealth accumulated and was invested in the system, their support for the more radical policies of developing nations decreased. Nevertheless, the Western developed nations are committed through institutions and policies to reforming the international economic system, and moderate reforms continued.

The key to the course of future policies of Saudi Arabia may lie with its military officers who control billions of dollars worth of military equipment purchased with the new oil wealth. They may well continue to support the present regime. Even if they do not, the United States has been the major supplier of equipment and has close association with the military leadership, so they could be expected to continue along a similar foreign policy course. The overriding question that can determine the course of events is whether a Middle East settlement with Israel can be achieved. (Chapters 9 and 10.)

The European Community, the industrial center of power of the multipolar system, has transformed the international politics of Europe and made war between nations of Western Europe inconceivable. The question is not whether European economic integration will proceed, but how fast it will continue and whether political integration will continue. Faster or slower progress toward economic and political integration would not markedly change the international politics of the European Community and its relationships with the developing world and the United States. In other words, the European Community is probably one of the most stable elements of the multipolar systems of states and non-state power centers.

The future of Britain, a leader of the Community, with

its new oil wealth is bright although in 1981 it was troubled by inflation and other economic woes. With its tradition of international leadership it can be expected to continue to exercise a stabilizing influence in European and international politics. Germany, with its tradition of hard work and economic development and renunciation of both nuclear weapons and aspirations for superpower status, will also exercise a moderating influence in European affairs. France, after the turmoil of the late 1950s and the nationalist foreign policies of de Gaulle, also seemed to be veering toward a moderate center course of foreign policy. Barring a major international war or economic crisis, these three power centers will probably keep the European Community on its slow course toward a United States of Europe and have a moderating influence on the world scene.

An area of instability may come from the interaction of the European Community with Eastern Europe. There is resentment of Soviet domination, and an unexpressed yearning of many Eastern European leaders to open doors toward the West. This could be strongly resisted by the Soviet Union, and this is a major area of unpredictability. A nationalist explosion there could have a major effect on the superpower system and the multipolar system. (Chapter 8.)

Japan is another power center of conservatism in international politics primarily interested in commercial issues. Economically it is in a vulnerable position because of its almost complete dependence on OPEC oil and on foreign trade, particularly with the United States. Barring a major international economic crisis, however, it should exercise a conservative influence on international politics. It can continue to provide technology and act as an example to China and the developing countries of Asia, and in that way help them with problems of economic development. If it remains friendly with China and does not develop nuclear weapons, it can help maintain an equilibrium in Asia. (Chapter 10.)

Crises will undoubtedly appear outside the power centers of the multipolar system of states and non-state actors, but such crises are not likely to threaten the international political order unless they escalate into superpower confrontation. In 1978, the crises in Africa, particularly in Rhodesia, threatened to become areas of direct superpower confrontation. However, Prime Minister Thatcher of Britain and Lord Carrington, the Foreign Secretary, brought about a settlement of the Rhodesian issue in 1980. Settlement of that persisting problem promised to reduce the dangers of war in that part of Africa and give South Africa a chance to alleviate the condition of its Black minority before the situation exploded there. Russia continued to exert an unsettling influence through material help to radical regimes of Africa and indirect support to its Cuban comrades who assisted insurgent movements.

Major U.N. organs in the mid 1970s agreed that a code of conduct should be drafted to restrain undesirable activities of multinational corporations and also spell out their rights. Moreover, the media was primed to uncover examples of MNC's bribery and intervention. Thus, the days when the private oil cartel could coerce nations such as Iran, or ITT could intervene in key elections in Chile seemed to have passed. The MNCs seemed destined to tend to business rather than politics. They are unlikely to have a major effect on international policies in the latter part of this century, although they will probably continue to dominate economic activity outside the Communist Bloc and help maintain the present economic order. Their growing activities do not mean they will take functions away from nation states, which have the upper hand. Even a weak state like Saudi Arabia and a weak organization like OPEC proved they could take economic power and property away from the MNCs and make them like it.

In the 1970s the U.N. System was assuming more responsibility for settling conflicts, helping the developing world, and helping nations work together on trade, financial issues, and other development issues. The U.N. System, and particularly the International Monetary Fund, played a crucial role in the economic and political adjustments to the skyrocketing oil prices of the mid 1970s. The World Bank came to be the major source of long range development assistance. There appeared to be an irreversible trend for these institutions to increase their operations because they recycle repayments of their loans and continue to accumulate resources. Moreover, major aid donors tended to channel more of their aid through such international institutions. (Chapter 14.)

Peacemaking is the U.N.'s major function. In the 1970s the U.N. assisted in settling major crises arising from the India-Pakistan War, the Cyprus War, and the 1973 Mideast War. The U.N. also played a supporting role in working toward settling African disputes centering on Rhodesia, Namibia, and the Republic of South Africa. At the beginning of the 1980s it was engaged in the Iranian hostage crisis and Afghanistan crisis, and offering to help settle the Iran-Iraq war.

Although the major powers will probably prevent the U.N. from becoming a super authority able to enforce decisions for settling disputes, it has become much more than a convenient forum where sovereign states can meet to make decisions. There was a definite trend in the 1970s for the U.N. to take a more direct part in disputes by providing lightly armed peacekeeping forces and observer units. Secretary Waldheim also engaged in active diplomacy in the Cyprus and Mideast conflicts which continued to smoulder. (Chapter 12.)

In the arms limitation field a growing list of agreements sponsored by the U.N. is building a framework for peace. The SALT agreements, the non-proliferation treaty, and the test ban treaties are the most important. President Carter and President Brezhnev seemed anxious to conclude a new SALT agreement, but the ratification and negotiation process was brought to a halt by the Afghanistan crisis. Brezhnev and Carter, however, kept SALT ceilings in effect without the formal approval of the agreements, and the ball passed to President Reagan in January, 1981, who did not disown the ceilings.

There is no supranational authority to enforce the network of arms control agreements and there are no prescribed penalties for violations. The agreements depend on national leaders voluntarily abiding by them. This does not mean the system is weak, because monitoring devices can detect violations, and this fact helps to keep the participants honest. (Chapter 13.)

There has been a trend toward supranationalism that has paralled a tendency of most nations to comply with the peacemaking of the U.N. International Atomic Energy Inspectors have done an effective job in inspecting nuclear plants and controlling nuclear materials without interference of national authorities. The superpowers allow spy satellites to photograph their nuclear weapons installations. The U.N. Secretary General has supranational authority over certain areas where his peacekeeping troops patrol. These represent a minor erosion of nationalism, but more importantly they represent a desire of national leaders to cooperate in order to survive. (Chapter 13.)

It would be unscientific to attach too much significance to this trend. It is possible that the U.N. might, as it did in the late 1960s, assume more responsibilities on certain issues, yet be shut out of a major world crisis, which at that time was Vietnam.

Although it is risky to make specific predictions of foreign policies very far in the future because so many variables are involved, making predictions and setting goals are useful exercises for analysts and policymakers. Leaders who have the most impact are those who know what direction they want their countries' foreign policies to go and where to push and shove to get their ideas adopted. This helps them to be creative rather than just react to events or be frustrated by them.

For example, Foreign Minister, and later Chancellor, Willy Brandt for many years had an aim of bringing about his *Ostpolitik* to recognize the status quo in Central Europe and build bridges to the East. Growing public opinion in favor of such a policy enabled him to become Chancellor and implement his dream. Secretary of State Kissinger had an aim to achieve a strategic balance with the major Communist powers to lessen the chances of war. He grabbed at Mao's invitation for President Nixon to visit China and made arrangements with the top officials rather than pursuing it through a normal and difficult bureaucratic process, which would have involved answering embarrassing questions to the news media and Congress that could have undercut this initiative. His reputation is based on such initiatives and ambitious goals rather than mere reactions to events.

Professors, students, and foreign policy analysts should also make predictions and see how their evaluations turn out. This permits them to refine concepts and to make drastic revisions in ideas if facts and events do not bear out expectations.

We have not proceeded very far, however, toward

predicting how the world will look by the year 2000. Like many analysts who confine their predictions to extending trend lines, we end up expecting more of the same. However, politics is not that simple, and it is instructive to look at the major surprises of the past thirty years to help in making another attempt to peer into the future.

The Past Thirty Years

The past 30 years have been a sobering experience for those who would have tried to predict the events of that period. The Korean War, which inaugurated the 1950s, was a complete surprise to the Western world. Top policymakers appeared responsible for that cataclysm — Secretary of State Acheson had called attention to South Korea's lying outside the U.S. security system, and Stalin and Kim Il-sung of North Korea tried to take advantage of that opening. This demonstrates how policymaking is infinitely more serious than a game, since one mistake in foreign policy can bring disaster. During the war experts were surprised when hundreds of thousands of Chinese troops attacked and drove the United Nations forces back to the line near where the war started. That avalanche widened the rift between the Communist and "free world" nations, and it took 20 years after the end of the War for the United States and China to start a detente. The War stimulated the SEATO alliance and the U.S. bilateral security pacts of the Far East that still structure U.S. policies toward the area.

No prominent observers anticipated after the 1964 elections that President Johnson would deeply involve the United States in its longest war and that later he would, in effect, be forced to withdraw from running for President because of the violent political reaction the Vietnam War would cause in the United States.

The Middle East was an obvious trouble spot in 1950. The pessimists would have predicted wars in the Middle East. The area became a place of confrontation between the Soviet Union and the United States, which in 1973 resulted in the U.S. alerting its nuclear forces. Then the experts were confounded when Henry Kissinger brought about truce agreements based on U.N. peacekeeping forces in this area of historic hatreds.

None of the well known economists predicted that the Arab and other oil producers would get together to increase the price of petroleum by 10 times in the 1970s. This caused a great shock to the international economic system. Similarly, most economic observers did not then predict that the international economic system could adjust so quickly to the tremendous transfers of funds that this rise in prices entailed.

None of the well known observers of 1950 predicted in Europe the basic reconciliation between France and Germany that occurred after a few European visionaries proposed and then sold to the French government the plan for the European Coal and Steel Community. Similarly, the remarkable economic recovery and reconciliation of Germany and Japan with the West was a development that few, if any, foresaw. This was primarily a victory for the policymakers responsible for establishing liberal democracy and the market system in Germany and Japan during the occupation.

With the difficulty of predicting even a few years in advance, and with such surprising changes occurring in the past generation, it is probably best, in predicting, to present options on the most important issues and then indicate the probable direction policymakers will go. The most important issue in international relations is whether we are headed toward nuclear confrontation and disaster or toward detente among the superpowers and relative peace.

A Pessimistic Future

Confirmed pessimists would point out that war has always been a curse of civilizations. They would stress that the superpowers base their military strategies on the use of nuclear weapons, and that a future war involving the superpowers could easily result in the use of such weapons. The use of "tactical" nuclear weapons could virtually destroy a country, while the use of strategic weapons by the superpowers could destroy civilization as we now know it. Nuclear fallout could in the worst case estimate bring about an "On the Beach" situation in which fallout would spread, destroy the environment, and end human life. The less pessimistic would say that a large share of the world's population might survive in Asia, Latin America, Africa, Australia, and in a few other countries and island areas. Mao Tse-tung claimed such a war between the two superpowers is inevitable, and that in such an event hundreds of millions of Chinese would survive and build a civilization brighter than the one that exists today. This statement frightened not only the Western World but also Russia, China's former Communist ally.

A nuclear holocaust could begin in a number of ways. In Korea opposing military leaders face each other with chips on their shoulders. If South Korea were attacked, the United States might make good on a previous threat to use nuclear weapons, and the North Koreans might retaliate with weapons they would obtain secretly from the Soviet Union or China. This could escalate into a nuclear war.

Another possibility would be a surprise war in the explosive and unstable Middle East in which Israel might be overwhelmed by conventional forces of the Arab countries and as a last resort unleash nuclear weapons. The Arabs also might obtain nuclear weapons from a nuclear power and retaliate, or in a few years they might be able to make their own weapons like India did from materials diverted from a nuclear power plant. President Nixon and Secretary Kissinger confronted the Soviets with a threat of nuclear war in the Middle East in 1973, and with most of the world's energy resources located there the holocaust could start in that area.

There have been confrontations over Berlin. East Germany might decide to interfere with the routes to Berlin, which it could consider as exercising its sovereignty. The United States might consider such an act as aggression. Former Secretary of Defense Schlesinger has proposed in the event of a military crisis, such as an attack on Berlin, to fire a few nuclear weapons at military targets in the Soviet Union as a "warning." If the Soviets retaliated, a game of "nuclear chicken" could escalate out of control. A war might start by mistake. There were three false alarms of a nuclear attack in seven months after November, 1979.[1]

The above contingencies only begin to show the dangerous possibilities of nuclear confrontations if leaders direct foreign policy as if it were a game in power politics.

Another dismal possibility for the next 20 years is that some terrorist group would obtain control of a nuclear weapon. There will be thousands of pounds of plutonium and other nuclear materials circulating to peaceful power plants during the last part of the century. The countries of the world rely on the International Atomic Energy Agency to maintain controls, but some of the material still might be stolen. Another possibility is that a terrorist group might obtain control of a tactical nuclear weapon which it could use as blackmail against the United States or another major power. An average tactical nuclear weapon would destroy most of a medium sized city. There are 7,000 of these in Europe and several hundreds, at least, in the Far East. It might well be easier for terrorist groups to obtain one of these weapons than it would be to manufacture one out of smuggled plutonium. A nuclear explosion of such a weapon in a populated area could perhaps destroy a million people and represent the worst single disaster in the history of the world.

Another pessimistic possibility is a world economic crisis. The basis of payments for world trade and other international transactions is world reserve currencies, which are the dollar and the SDR (special drawing rights). If the leaders of the world monetary system and traders lose confidence in these currencies, which are not backed by gold or other assets, a full fledged crisis could develop. Many political systems could not stand the strain, and perhaps extremism and violence would occur. Such a crisis in the early 1930s prepared the way for World War II.

The above are pessimistic possibilities for the next 20 years. An optimistic assessment is also possible.

Options for Optimists

The optimists would point out that the serious crises of the last 35 years were worked out or alleviated without a nuclear war. As we enter the last 20 years of the century, they would add, there is no major international war. Although war threatened to break out in Lebanon, the

United States and other powers were working hard to contain the conflict of rival groups in Lebanon and to achieve an understanding between Israel and Syria. Egypt and Israel were still implementing their peace treaty. In 1981 the Iran-Iraq war of two outlaws had ground down to a stalemate. The world community had condemned Russian aggression in Afghanistan and it appeared to be contained. There was at least a temporary equilibrium in Southeast Asia between the Communist countries and their non-Communist neighbors after a long and tragic war in Vietnam. The non-Communist world was staying aloof from the war in Cambodia, which initially involved only the Communist countries, although it threatened to spill over into Thailand.

The optimist would point to the growing role of international institutions for negotiation of political and economic issues. A peacemaking process has been strengthened in the U.N. that involves other nations putting political pressure on warring nations to contain conflicts and use U.N. peacekeeping troops to monitor truces. In recent years this process of persuading members to "cool it" succeeded in the India-Pakistan War of 1971, the Cyprus War of 1974, and the Israel-Arab War of 1973.

The United Nations had deployed over 10,000 troops in the Middle East to keep Israel and the Arab nations apart. Similarly, such troops had been deployed in the Cyprus crisis, in other Middle East crises, and the India-Pakistan conflict. Such peacekeeping actions had become a recognized function of the U.N. These forces had a moral and political effect, even if they were not equipped to do serious fighting.

The European Community provided an encouraging example of how close economic arrangements could result in a political detente that made war between two former bitter enemies — France and Germany — extremely unlikely. Other countries were exploring the possibility of similar systems for their part of the world including ASEAN in Southeast Asia and the Latin American Common Market. Western Europe was reaching out to establish increased economic and political contacts with Eastern Europe, although it appeared unlikely that the Soviet Union would relax its grip on its Eastern European satellites for many years. Another 20 years, however, could see other Polands or Yugoslavias develop.

There was a good possibility of a more stable balance of power in Asia after the U.S. diplomatic recognition of China in 1979. China in June, 1980, offered to "resolutely support" Thailand if it were attacked by Vietnam.[2] The United States was trying after 1974 to strengthen deterrence in Asia by reaffirming alliance commitments to Japan, South Korea, Thailand, and the Philippines. Britain, Australia, and New Zealand still had a small military presence in Malaysia and Singapore and the obligation to consult there if the situation should become threatening.

The optimist would stress that the Soviet Union and the United States in 1980 were close to concluding a formal agreement putting a cap on the arms race in the numbers of strategic weapons, although the agreement would permit development of more powerful weapons. Although the Afghanistan invasion stopped the approval process, both powers during 1981 were still observing the SALT II limits.

Optimists would also point to how the international organizations and individual countries had adjusted to the shocks of world energy and food crises in the 1970s. They would have to admit, however, the developed countries, particularly Western Europe, would face a severe threat if another oil embargo were imposed, and such an embargo could come about if the Middle East conflicts escalated. Nevertheless, an optimist would add that Israel was further along the road toward peace than it had been since World War II.

Conclusions

Both optimists and pessimists can marshall reasoned arguments for their predictions. The practical task of political science, however, is not to make plans for utopias or to prepare for the worst, but to develop institutions to deter the violence and greed that occur when power is not restrained. The U.N. Security Council, the U.N. Specialized Agencies, and the European Economic Community are examples of institutions that reconcile economic or security interests. They can direct publicity against policies of violence and greed, and provide a world forum to embarrass leaders and policymakers who support harmful ideas.

The above review of constructive developments is helpful in determining politically possible goals for the rest of this century. Even pessimists should agree to work toward constructive goals that could at least temporarily avert war. An international agenda for peace, which optimists would say is possible and the pessimist would say is unrealistic, would include the following:

1. Reinforcement of the idea that war and intervention should not be used in international disputes.

2. Ending intervention by intelligence and paramilitary organizations in the affairs of other countries.

3. Increasing attention to human rights violations.

4. Conclusion of additional arms limitation agreements to put a cap on the arms race and to reduce the overkill capacity of the Superpowers.

5. Achievement of agreement on mutual troop reduction by NATO and Warsaw Pact countries through the MBFR negotiations already begun in Europe.

6. Strengthening the international peacemaking capability of the U.N. including making permanent arrangements for peacekeeping forces and giving more powers to the Secretary General to act in an emergency.

7. Provision by developed countries and oil producers of additional funds to help the poorest countries of the world meet their food and energy crises.

8. Formation by developing countries of Asia and elsewhere of common markets like Europe to help their countries develop and to establish a base for international cooperation on economic and political issues.

9. Increasing support for multilateral technical assistance and development efforts by U.N. organizations.

Policymakers of democracies to achieve the above aims for the next twenty years would need support by legislators and voters. Progress toward most of the above goals could take place even without a withdrawal of Russian troops from Afghanistan and a settlement of that crisis.

Over the long run such peacemaking efforts need the support by educators and the news media as well as by public officials. Many officials were inspired to enter the foreign affairs field by ideas they obtained in universities, and future leaders and future policies are being influenced by professors today. Ideas of cynicism can be self-fulfilling; ideas of naivety and weakness can invite aggression, while inspirational ideas can help policymakers work toward peaceful solutions of difficult world problems. Professors should not be Pollyannas, and they should teach about the real world. However, professors should look carefully at the facts, evaluate the implications of their teaching, and search their consciences before they assert or imply war is inherent in the international system, and before they assert the U.N. is not a useful instrument for settling conflicts.

News media should also examine their responsibilities. The news media are helpful to policymakers in publishing information they could not dig out for themselves. The media are essential to a free society to challenge powerful governments if their officials attempt to distort or conceal part of the truth. The news media of the free world by and large have done a good job in these areas. Nevertheless, free world news media feature confrontations and the dramatic developments of minor importance, but they often give little or no attention to the constructive efforts of international organizations and routine diplomacy. The media also are overly suspicious and assign cynical political motives to international initiatives, some of which may have legitimate and idealistic purposes. The media of the Communist and authoritarian countries, in particular, use violent language that reinforces images of confrontation.

Conflict, coexistence, or cooperation are major alternatives on many levels of policymaking. The past 35 years have seen confrontations and wars including the sacrifice of millions of youth and civilians in battle and the channeling of tremendous resources into military budgets. Support of peacemaking initiatives has been minuscule in comparison. If officials and the people who put them in power cannot make substantial commitments for international cooperation, the future is dark. If policymakers of powerful governments can cooperate, they might not solve all dangerous problems by the year 2000, but they could avoid nuclear war. They also could strengthen the international system for a permanent peace and a prosperous world economy in the 21st century.

Summary

A logical basis for prediction in international politics is to evaluate support for policy ideas and the material resources backing them. With this approach Western Europe seems to be an area of future stability with prospects of further integration. The Soviet Union seems confident in confronting the West, although it may have trouble in keeping Eastern Europe in line. It has a severe case of indigestion with its Afghanistan invasion, which has made the outlook ominous for detente with the West. Communist countries are fighting in Southeast Asia and the conflicts there could involve their neighbors. A major war could also break out of control in the Middle East, and in that strategic area a conflict could escalate into a world war. The United States and China seem intent on containing the above threats. The U.N. System also struggles to contain military conflicts and promote economic cooperation, and in recent years the U.N. has expanded its influence.

Predictions on the basis of past trends is risky, however, and the post World War II era has seen many surprises, such as the Korean War, the Vietnam War, and the petroleum crisis. With this in mind it is useful to consider pessimistic and optimistic options.

The pessimist would see many opportunities such as a Korean or Berlin crisis to trigger a war, including a nuclear war which could devastate civilization. The optimists would note we have avoided nuclear war for over 35 years and that there has been a growing trend for the United Nations to negotiate crises. Both optimists and pessimists can marshal reasoned arguments. The practical task of political science, however, is not to plan for utopias or to prepare for the worst. Rather it is to help establish institutions to contain aggressive drives, to promote welfare, and to prevent the unleashing of new weapons. With this in mind there is a long agenda of programs already begun for negotiating arms controls and promoting international economic and social development. Such programs are attainable, but they would need major and sustained support from educators, the news media, and the people as well as from public officials. If such support is not forthcoming, the future is dark.

FOOTNOTES

1. *Washington Post,* June 6, 1980, p. A-5, May 21, 1981, p. A-28.
2. *Washington Post,* June 26, 1980, p. 1.

Index